An Analysis of the Pali Canon

Edited by Russell Webb

A Reference Table of Pali Literature

Compiled by Bhikkhu Nyanatusita

Buddhist Publication Society Inc.
P.O. Box 61
54 Sangharaja Mawatha
Kandy, Sri Lanka
E-mail: bps@bps.lk
Web site: http://www.bps.lk
Tel: 0094 81 223 7283—Fax: 0094 81 222 3679

An Analysis of the Pali Canon

First BPS edition 1975
Second revised BPS edition 1991
Third revised BPS edition 2011

A Reference Table of Pali Literature

First edition: 2011

National Library and Documentation Service Board-
Cataloguing-In-Publication Data

Webb, Russel
An Analysis of Pali Canon: A Reference Table of Pali Literature/Russel Webb and Bhikkhu Nyanatusita.-Kandy: Buddhist Publication Society Inc., 2011
BP 607S.- 232p.; 22cm

ISBN 978-955-24-0376-7

i. 891.37 DDC 23 ii. Title
iii. Bhikkhu Nyanatusita, jt.au.

1. Pali Literature

ISBN 978-955–24–0376–7

Printed by
Ajith Printers (Pvt) Ltd.
342, Old Kesbewa Road, Rattanapitiya,
Boralesgamuwa, Sri Lanka.
Tel: +94 (0) 112517269

CONTENTS

An Analysis of the Pali Canon

A Reference Table of Pali Literature

An Analysis of the Pali Canon

Edited by Russell Webb

Abbreviations Used

AN	Aṅguttara Nikāya
AP	Abhidhamma Piṭaka
DN	Dīgha Nikāya
Dhp	Dhammapada
It	Itivuttaka
KN	Khuddaka Nikāya
Kha	Khandhaka
Khp	Khuddakapāṭha
Mil	*Milindapañhā*
MN	Majjhima Nikāya
Nidd	Niddesa
Paṭis	Paṭisambhidāmagga
SN	Saṃyutta Nikāya
Sn	Suttanipāta
SP	Sutta Piṭaka
SV	Suttavibhaṅga
Ud	Udāna
Vism	*Visuddhimagga*
VP	Vinaya Piṭaka

PREFACE

An Analysis of the Pali Canon was originally the work of A.C. March, the founder-editor of *Buddhism in England* (from 1943, *The Middle Way)*, the quarterly journal of The Buddhist Lodge (now The Buddhist Society, London). It appeared in the issues for Volume 3 and was later offprinted as a pamphlet. Finally, after extensive revision by I.B. Horner (the late President of the Pali Text Society) and Jack Austin, it appeared as an integral part of *A Buddhist Student's Manual*, published in 1956 by The Buddhist Society to commemorate the thirtieth anniversary of its founding. The basic analysis of the Tipiṭaka appeared in *The Maha Bodhi*, 37:19–42 (Calcutta 1929), and was reprinted in K.D.P. Wickremesinghe's *Biography of the Buddha* (Colombo 1972).

In the present edition, the basic analysis of the Canon has been left in its original state although some minor corrections had to be made. However, it has been found possible to fully explore the Saṃyutta and Aṅguttara Nikāyas together with three important texts from the Khuddaka Nikāya: Udāna, Itivuttaka, and Suttanipāta. It was deemed unnecessary to give similar treatment to the Dhammapada, as this popular anthology is much more readily accessible. The Paṭisambhidāmagga has also been analysed.

The index (except for minor amendments) was originally prepared by G.F. Allen and first appeared in his book *The Buddha's Philosophy*. In this edition it has been simplified by extensive substitution of Arabic for Roman numerals.

The Bibliography, a necessary adjunct in view of the reference nature of the whole work, has, however, been completely revised as a consequence of the vast output of books on the subject that have come on to the market over the past few decades. Indeed, it was originally intended to make this an exhaustive section of Pali works in the English language, past and present. A number of anthologies, however, include both *suttas* in their entirety and short extracts from the texts. In such cases the compiler has, where the works in question appear, only indicated the complete *suttas*, as it is hardly likely that brief passages in such (possibly out-of-print) books will be referred to by the student who can now so easily turn to complete texts. Moreover, to keep the Bibliography to a manageable size, it was also necessary to omit a number of anthologies which include selected translations available from other, more primary sources.

It is thus hoped that this short work will awaken in the reader a desire to study the original texts themselves, the most authoritative Buddhist documents extant. Space has precluded a detailed study of the Tipiṭaka from the standpoints of language and chronology, but the source books mentioned in the Bibliography will more than compensate for this omission.

Russell Webb
March 1991

P.S. In this third edition I have, in the Bibliography, included relevant doctoral dissertations, masters' theses, articles and online resource materials.

RW
October 2010

Note

An online edition of this booklet, containing hyperlinks to the works listed that have been digitalised and put online, is available on the BPS website's Online Library (www.bps.lk). Because websites frequently disappear and links often change, they are not included in this book.

BPS Editor

I. Textual Analysis

The Pāli Canon, also called the Tipiṭaka or "Three Baskets" (of doctrine), is divided into three major parts:

a) Vinaya Piṭaka: The Collection of Disciplinary Rules.
b) Sutta Piṭaka: The Collection of the Buddha's Discourses.
c) Abhidhamma Piṭaka: The Collection of Philosophical Treatises.

A. Vinaya Piṭaka—the Collection of Disciplinary Rules

Bhikkhu and Bhikkhunī Pātimokkha

The monastic code of the *bhikkhu* (Buddhist monk) contains 220 rules and 7 legal procedures, consisting of eight classes:

Four rules, if infringed, entail expulsion from the Order (*pārājika*).

These are sexual intercourse, theft, taking a human life or inciting another to commit suicide, and falsely boasting of supernormal attainments.

Thirteen rules entailing initial and subsequent meetings of the Sangha (*saṅghādisesa*). These include masturbation, lustful physical and verbal contact with a woman, creating a schism, etc.

Two rules are indefinite (*aniyata*). Whether the being alone with a woman is a *pārājika, saṅghādisesa* or *pācittiya* offence.

Thirty rules entail expiation with forfeiture (*nissaggiya pācittiya*). Rules dealing with improper possession of requisites such as robes.

Ninety-two rules entail expiation (*pācittiya*). Rules dealing with wrong conduct such as lying, damaging plants, possessing gold and silvers, etc.

Four rules require confession (*pāṭidesanīya*).

Seventy-five rules are concerned with etiquette and decorum (*sekhiya*).

Seven procedures are for the settlement of legal processes (*adhikaraṇasamatha*).

This section is followed by another called the *Bhikkhunīvibhaṅga,* providing similar guidance for nuns.

The monastic code of the *bhikkhunī* (Buddhist nun) contains 324 rules and 7 legal procedures, consisting of seven classes:

a) Eight rules, if infringed, entail expulsion from the Order (*pārājika*).
b) Seventeen rules entailing initial and subsequent meetings of the Sangha (*saṅghādisesa*).
c) Thirty rules entail expiation with forfeiture (*nissaggiya pācittiya*).
d) Hundred sixty-six rules entail expiation (*pācittiya*).
e) Eight rules require confession (*pāṭidesanīya*).
f) Seventy-five rules are concerned with etiquette and decorum (*sekhiya*).
g) Seven procedures are for the settlement of legal processes (*adhikaraṇasamatha*).

1. Suttavibhaṅga

The analysis of the Sutta or *Pātimokkha*. Each *Pātimokkha* rule is treated by way of an origin story (*nidāna*) leading up to the laying down of the rule, the rule, a word analysis (*padabhājanīya*) of the rule, and (usually) modifications of the rule and exceptions.

2. Khandhaka, sub-divided into Mahāvagga and Cūḷavagga

Rules, regulations and procedures which are not part of the Pātimokkha. The first chapter of the Mahāvagga contains a lengthy biography of the Buddha from his *sambodhi* up to the going forth of Sāriputta and Moggallāna. The last two chapters of the Cūḷavagga are accounts of the first and second councils.

(a) Mahāvagga:

1. Rules for admission to the Order.
2. The Uposatha meeting and recital of the *Pātimokkha* (code of rules).
3. Residence during the rainy season (*vassa*).
4. The ceremony concluding the retreat (*pavāraṇa*).
5. Rules for articles of dress and furniture.
6. Medicine and food.
7. The annual distribution of robes (*kaṭhina*).
8. Rules for sick Bhikkhus, sleeping, and robe-material.

9. The mode of executing proceedings by the Order.
10. Proceedings in cases of schism.

(b) Cūḷavagga (or Cullavagga):

1. Rules for dealing with offences that come before the Order.
2. Procedures for putting a Bhikkhu on probation.
3. Procedures for dealing with accumulation of offences by a Bhikkhu.
4. Rules for settling legal procedures in the Order.
5. Miscellaneous rules for bathing, dress, etc.
6. Rules for dwellings, furniture, lodging, etc.
7. Rules for schisms.
8. Classes of Bhikkhus, and duties of teachers and novices (*sāmaṇera*).
9. Rules for exclusion from the *Pātimokkha*.
10. Rules for the ordination and instruction of Bhikkhunīs.
11. Account of the First Council, at Rājagaha.
12. Account of the Second Council, at Vesālī.

3. Parivāra

Summaries and classification of the rules of the Vinaya arranged as a kind of catechism for instruction and examination purposes.

B. Sutta Piṭaka—the Collection of the Buddha's Discourses

The Sutta Piṭaka, the second main division of the Tipiṭaka, is divided into five sections or collections (*Nikāyas*) of discourses (*suttas*).

Dīgha Nikāya: the Collection of Long Discourses.
Majjhima Nikāya: The Collection of Middle Length Discourses.
Saṃyutta Nikāya: The Collection of Connected Discourses.
Aṅguttara Nikāya: The Collection of Numerical Discourses.
Khuddaka Nikāya: The Collection of Small Books.

1. Dīgha Nikāya

The Collection of Long Discourses is arranged in three *vaggas* or sections:

(a) Sīlakkhanda Vagga

1. Brahmajāla Sutta: "The Net of Brahmā" or the Perfect Net, in which are caught all the 62 heretical forms of speculation

concerning the world and the self taught by the Buddha's contemporaries.

2. Sāmaññaphala Sutta: "The Fruits of the Homeless Life." The Buddha explains to King Ajātasattu the advantages of joining the Buddhist Order and renouncing the life of the world.
3. Ambaṭṭha Sutta: Pride of birth and its fall. A dialogue with Ambaṭṭha on caste. Contains reference to the legend of King Okkāka, the traditional founder of the Sakya clan.
4. Soṇadaṇḍa Sutta: Dialogue with the, brahmin Soṇadaṇḍa on the characteristics of the true brahmin.
5. Kūṭadanta Sutta: Dialogue with the brahmin Kūṭadanta condemning animal sacrifice.
6. Mahāli Sutta: Dialogue with Mahāli on deva-like vision and hearing, and the attainment of full enlightenment.
7. Jāliya Sutta: On the nature of the life-principle as compared with the body.
8. Kassapasīhanāda Sutta: A dialogue with the naked ascetic Kassapa against self-mortification.
9. Poṭṭhapāda Sutta: A discussion with Poṭṭhapāda on the nature of the soul, in which the Buddha states the enquiry to be irrelevant and not conducive to enlightenment.
10. Subha Sutta: A discourse, attributed to Ānanda, on conduct, concentration, and wisdom.
11. Kevaḍḍha Sutta: The Buddha refuses to allow a Bhikkhu to perform a miracle. Story of the monk who visited the devas (deities) to question them.
12. Lohicca Sutta: Dialogue with the brahmin Lohicca on the ethics of teaching.
13. Tevijja Sutta: On the futility of a knowledge of the Vedas as means to attaining companionship with Brahmā.

(b) Mahā Vagga

14. Mahāpadāna Sutta: The Sublime Story of the Buddha Gotama and his six predecessors. Also, the Discourse on the Buddha Vipassi, describing his descent from the Tusita heaven to the commencement of his mission.
15. Mahānidāna Sutta: On the "chain of causation" and theories of the soul.
16. Mahāparinibbāna Sutta: The Great Discourse that records the passing of the Tathāgata into Parinibbāna.

17. Mahāsudassana Sutta: The Great King of Glory. The story of a previous existence of the Buddha, as King Sudassana, told by the Buddha on his death-bed.
18. Janāvāsabha Sutta: The Buddha relates the story of the yakkha (demon) Janāvāsabha to the people of Nādikā.
19. Mahāgovinda Sutta: The heavenly musician Pañcasikha relates the story of Mahāgovinda to the Buddha, who states that he himself was Mahāgovinda.
20. Mahāsamaya Sutta: The devas of the Pure Abode and their evolution.
21. Sakkapañha Sutta: Sakka, the lord of devas, visits the Buddha, and learns from him that everything that originates is also subject to dissolution.
22. Mahāsatipaṭṭhāna Sutta: Discourse on the Foundations of Mindfulness on the body, feelings, thoughts, and states of mind. With a commentary on the Four Noble Truths.
23. Payāsi Sutta: Kumārakassapa converts Payāsi from the heresy that there is no future life or reward of actions.

(c) Pāṭika Vagga

24. Pāṭika Sutta: Story of the disciple who follows other teachers because the Buddha does not work miracles or teach the origin of things.
25. Udumbarikasīhanāda Sutta: The Buddha discusses asceticism with the ascetic Nigrodha.
26. Cakkavattisīhanāda Sutta: Story of the universal king, the corruption of morals and their restoration, and the coming of the future Buddha Metteyya.
27. Aggañña Sutta: A discussion on caste, and an exposition on the origin of things (as in No.24) down to the origin of the four castes.
28. Sampasādanīya Sutta: A dialogue between the Buddha and Sāriputta, who describes the teaching of the Buddha and asserts his faith in him.
29. Pāsādika Sutta: The Delectable Discourse. Discourse of the Buddha on the perfect and the imperfect teacher.
30. Lakkhaṇa Sutta: The 32 marks of a Great Man.
31. Sigālovāda Sutta: The Sigāla homily on the duties of the householder to the six classes of persons.

32. Āṭānāṭiya Sutta: On the Four Great Kings and their spell for protection against evil.
33. Saṅgīti Sutta: Sāriputta outlines the principles of the teaching in ten numerical groups.
34. Dasuttara Sutta: Sāriputta outlines the doctrine in tenfold series.

2. Majjhima Nikāya

This division consists of 152 *suttas* of medium length arranged in 15 *vaggas,* roughly classified according to subject matter.

(a) Mūlapariyāya Vagga

1. Mūlapariyāya Sutta: How states of consciousness originate.
2. Sabbāsavā Sutta: On the elimination of the cankers.
3. Dhammadāyāda Sutta: Exhorting the Bhikkhus to realise the importance of the Dhamma and the unimportance of their physical wants.
4. Bhayabherava Sutta: On braving the fears and terrors of the forest. Also the Buddha's account of his enlightenment.
5. Anaṅgaṇa Sutta: A dialogue between Sāriputta and Moggallāna on the attainment of freedom from depravity.
6. Ākaṅkheyya Sutta: On those things for which a Bhikkhu may wish.
7. Vatthūpama Sutta: The parable of the soiled cloth and the defiled mind.
8. Sallekha Sutta: On the elimination of self and false views. How to efface defilements.
9. Sammādiṭṭhi Sutta: A discourse by Sāriputta on right views.
10. Satipaṭṭhāna Sutta: The same as DN 22, but without the detailed explanation of the Four Noble Truths.

(b) Sīhanāda Vagga

11. Cūḷasīhanāda Sutta: See No. 12 below.
12. Mahāsīhanāda Sutta: The short and the long "challenge" *suttas.* The futility of ascetic practices.
13. Mahādukkhakkhandha Sutta: See No. 14 below.
14. Cūḷadukkhakkhandha Sutta: The long and the short discourses on the suffering inherent in sensual pleasures.
15. Anumāna Sutta: By Moggallāna, on the value of introspection (There is no reference to the Buddha throughout).
16. Cetokhila Sutta: On the five mental bondages.

17. Vanapattha Sutta: On the advantages and disadvantages of the forest life.
18. Madhupiṇḍika Sutta: The Buddha gives a brief outline of his teaching, which Kaccāna amplifies.
19. Dvedhāvitakka Sutta: The parable of the lure of sensuality. Repetition of the Enlightenment as in No. 4.
20. Vitakkasaṇṭhāna Sutta: Methods of meditation to dispel undesirable thoughts.

(c) Tatiya Vagga

21. Kakacūpama Sutta: The simile of the saw. On the control of the feelings and the mind under the most severe provocation.
22. Alagaddūpama Sutta: Simile of the water-snake. Holding wrong views of the Dhamma is like seizing a snake by the tail.
23. Vammika Sutta: The simile of the smouldering ant-hill as the human body.
24. Rathavinīta Sutta: Puṇṇa explains the purpose of the holy life to Sāriputta.
25. Nivāpa Sutta: Parable of Māra as a sower or hunter laying baits for the deer.
26. Ariyapariyesana Sutta: The Noble Quest. The Buddha's account of his renunciation, search, and attainment of enlightenment.
27. Cūḷahatthipadopama Sutta: The short "elephant's footprint" simile, on the Bhikkhu's training.
28. Mahāhatthipadopama Sutta: The long "elephant's footprint" simile, on the Four Noble Truths.
29. Mahāsāropama Sutta: On the dangers of gain, honour and fame. Said to have been delivered when Devadatta left the Order.
30. Cūḷasāropama Sutta: Development of the preceding *sutta*. On attaining the essence of the Dhamma.

(d) Mahāyamaka Vagga

31. Cūḷagosiṅga Sutta: A conversation of the Buddha with three Bhikkhus, who speak on harmonious living and relate their attainments to him.
32. Mahāgosiṅga Sutta: A conversation between six Bhikkhus who discuss what kind of monk makes the forest beautiful.
33. Mahāgopālaka Sutta: On the eleven bad and good qualities of a herdsman and a monk.

34. Cūḷagopālaka Sutta: Simile of the foolish and wise herdsman crossing the river.
35. Cūḷasaccaka Sutta: A discussion between the Buddha and the debater Saccaka on the nature of the five aggregates and other topics.
36. Mahāsaccaka Sutta: The account of the Buddha's asceticism and enlightenment, with instructions on right meditation.
37. Cūḷataṇhāsaṅkhaya Sutta: Sakka asks the Buddha about freedom from craving and satisfactorily repeats his reply to Moggallāna.
38. Mahātaṇhāsaṅkhaya Sutta: Refutation of the wrong view of a Bhikkhu who thinks that it is consciousness that transmigrates.
39. Mahā-assapura Sutta: See No. 40 below.
40. Cūḷa-assapura Sutta: The great and the small discourses given at Assapura on the duties of an ascetic.

(e) Cūḷayamaka Vagga

41. Sāleyyaka Sutta: A discourse to the brahmins of Sālā. Why some beings go to heaven and some to hell.
42. Verañjaka Sutta: The same discourse repeated to the householders of Verañjā.
43. Mahāvedalla Sutta: A psychological discourse by Sāriputta to Mahākoṭṭhita.
44. Cūḷavedalla Sutta: A psychological discourse by the Bhikkhunī Dhammadinnā to the lay-devotee Visākha.
45. Cūḷadhammasamādāna Sutta: See No. 46 below.
46. Mahādhammasamādāna Sutta: The short and long discourses on the results of good and bad conduct.
47. Vīmaṃsaka Sutta: On the right methods of investigation of the Buddha.
48. Kosambiya Sutta: A discourse to the Bhikkhus of Kosambi on the evil of quarrelling.
49. Brahmanimantanika Sutta: The Buddha converts Baka the Brahmā from the heresy of permanency.
50. Māratajjanīya Sutta: Moggallāna admonishes Māra.

(f) Gahapati Vagga

51. Kandaraka Sutta: Discourse on the four kinds of personalities, and the steps to liberation.
52. Aṭṭhakanāgara Sutta: A discourse by Ananda on the ways of attainment of Nibbāna.

53. Sekha Sutta: The Buddha opens a new meeting hall at Kapilavatthu, and Ananda discourses on the training of the disciple.
54. Potaliya Sutta: The Buddha explains to Potaliya the real significance of the abandonment of worldliness.
55. Jīvaka Sutta: The Buddha explains the ethics of meat-eating.
56. Upāli Sutta: The conversion of Upāli the Jain.
57. Kukkuravatika Sutta: A dialogue on *kamma* between the Buddha and two ascetics.
58. Abhayarājakumāra Sutta: The Jain Nātaputta sends Prince Abhaya to question the Buddha on the condemnation of Devadatta.
59. Bahuvedanīya Sutta: On different classifications of feelings and the gradation of pleasure.
60. Apaṇṇaka Sutta: On the "Certain Doctrine," against various heresies.

(g) Bhikkhu Vagga

61. Ambalaṭṭhikarāhulovāda Sutta: The discourse on falsehood given by the Buddha to Rāhula.
62. Mahārāhulovāda Sutta: Advice to Rāhula on contemplation, stressing mindfulness of breathing.
63. Cūḷamāluṅkya Sutta: Why the Buddha does not answer certain types of speculative questions.
64. Mahāmāluṅkya Sutta: On the five lower fetters.
65. Bhaddāli Sutta: The confession of Bhaddāli, and the Buddha's counsel.
66. Laṭukikopama Sutta: Advice on renunciation of the world.
67. Cātuma Sutta: Advice to boisterous Bhikkhus at Cātuma.
68. Nālakapāna Sutta: The Buddha questions Anuruddha concerning certain points of the Dhamma.
69. Gulissāni Sutta: Rules for those who, like Gulissāni, live in the forest.
70. Kīṭāgiri Sutta: The conduct to be followed by various classes of Bhikkhus.

(h) Paribbājaka Vagga

71. Tevijjavacchagotta Sutta: The Buddha visits the ascetic Vacchagotta and claims that he is called *tevijja* (possessing the three-fold knowledge) because he has recollection of his

previous lives, supernormal vision, and knowledge of the way to the elimination of the taints (*āsava*).

72. Aggivacchagotta Sutta: The danger of theorising about the world, etc.
73. Mahāvacchagotta Sutta: Further explanation to Vacchagotta on the conduct of lay disciples and Bhikkhus.
74. Dīghanakha Sutta: The Buddha refutes the ascetic Dīghanakha. Sāriputta attains Arahatship.
75. Māgandiya Sutta: The Buddha relates his renunciation of the life of the senses, and speaks on the abandonment of sensual desires.
76. Sandaka Sutta: Ānanda refutes various wrong views in discussion with the ascetic Sandaka.
77. Māhasakuludāyi Sutta: On the five reasons why the Buddha is honoured.
78. Samaṇamaṇḍika Sutta: On the qualities of perfect virtue.
79. Cūḷasakuludāyi Sutta: The Jain leader Nātaputta, and the way to true happiness.
80. Vekhanassa Sutta: A repetition of part of the preceding *sutta*, with additional matter on the five senses.

(i) Rāja Vagga

81. Ghaṭīkāra Sutta: The Buddha tells Ānanda of his previous existence as Jotipāla.
82. Raṭṭhapāla Sutta: The story of Raṭṭhapāla, whose parents endeavoured in vain to dissuade him, from entering the Sangha.
83. Makhādeva Sutta: The story of the Buddha's previous life as King Makhādeva.
84. Madhurā Sutta: A discourse given after the Buddha's decease by Kaccāna to King Avantiputta on the real meaning of caste.
85. Bodhirājakumāra Sutta: The Buddha tells the story of his renunciation and enlightenment as in nos. 26 and 36 above.
86. Aṅgulimāla Sutta: Story of the conversion of Aṅgulimāla, the robber chief.
87. Piyajātikā Sutta: The Buddha's counsel to a man who has just lost a son, and the dispute between King Pasenadi and his wife thereon.
88. Bāhitika Sutta: Ānanda answers a question on conduct put by Pasenadi who presents him with his cloak.

89. Dhammacetiya Sutta: Pasenadi visits the Buddha and extols the holy life.
90. Kaṇṇakatthala Sutta: A conversation between the Buddha and Pasenadi on caste, the devas, and Brahmā.

(j) Brāhmaṇa Vagga

91. Brahmāyu Sutta: On the thirty-two marks of a Great Man, the Buddha's daily routine, and the conversion of the brahmin Brahmāyu.
92. Sela Sutta: The brahmin Sela sees the thirty-two marks of a Buddha and is converted (The same story is related in Suttanipāta 3:7).
93. Assalāyana Sutta: The brahmin Assalāyana discusses caste with the Buddha. An important presentation of the Buddha's teaching on this subject.
94. Ghoṭamukha Sutta: The brahmin Ghoṭamukha questions the monk Udena on the value of the life of renunciation, and builds an assembly hall for the Sangha.
95. Caṅkī Sutta: Discourse on brahmin doctrines, and the Buddha's way to realisation of ultimate truth.
96. Esukāri Sutta: Discourse on caste and its functions.
97. Dhānañjāni Sutta: Sāriputta tells the brahmin Dhānañjāni that family duties are no excuse for wrongdoing.
98. Vāseṭṭha Sutta: A discourse, mostly in verse, on the nature of the true brahmin (This recurs in Suttanipāta 3:9).
99. Subha Sutta: On whether a man should remain a householder or leave the world.
100. Saṅgārava Sutta: The brahmin woman who accepted the Dhamma, and a discourse on the holy life. Also repetition of parts of nos. 24 and 34 above.

(k) Devadaha Vagga

101. Devadaha Sutta: The Buddha discourses on the attainment of the goal by the living of a skilful life.
102. Pañcattaya Sutta: On five theories of the soul, and that the way of release (Nibbāna) does not depend on any of them.
103. Kinti Sutta: Rules for Bhikkhus who dispute about the Dhamma and who commit transgressions.
104. Samāgama Sutta: After the death of Nātaputta, the Buddha's discourse on dispute and harmony.

105. Sunakkhatta Sutta: The simile of extracting the arrow of craving.
106. Āneñjasappāya Sutta (or: Ānañjasappāya Sutta): Meditations on impassibility, the attainments, and true release.
107. Gaṇakamoggallāna Sutta: A discourse to Gaṇakamoggallāna on the training of disciples.
108. Gopakamoggalāna Sutta: After the decease of the Buddha, Ānanda explains to Vassakāra that the Dhamma is now the only guide.
109. Mahāpuṇṇama Sutta: The Buddha answers the questions of a Bhikkhu concerning the *khandhas.*
110. Cūḷapuṇṇama Sutta: A discourse on the untrue and true man.

(l) Anupada Vagga

111. Anupada Sutta: The Buddha praises Sāriputta and his analysis of mind.
112. Chabbisodhana Sutta: On the questions to ask a Bhikkhu who declares he has attained Arahantship.
113. Sappurisa Sutta: On the good and bad qualities of a Bhikkhu.
114. Sevitabbāsevitabba Sutta: Sāriputta expounds the right way to live the holy life.
115. Bahudhātuka Sutta: Lists of elements and principles in a dialogue between the Buddha and Ananda.
116. Isigili Sutta: The Buddha on Paccekabuddhas.
117. Mahācattārīsaka Sutta: Exposition of the Noble Eightfold Path.
118. Ānāpānasati Sutta: Mindfulness of breathing.
119. Kāyagatāsati Sutta: Meditation on the body.
120. Saṅkhārupapatti Sutta: On the development of the five qualities enabling a Bhikkhu to determine the conditions of his rebirth.

(m) Suññata Vagga

121. Cūḷasuññata Sutta: Meditation on emptiness.
122. Mahāsuññata Sutta: Instruction to Ānanda on the practice of meditation on emptiness.
123. Acchariyabbhūtadhamma Sutta: On the marvellous life of a Bodhisatta. A repetition of part of DN 14, but applied to the Buddha himself.
124. Bakkula Sutta: Bakkula converts his friend Acelakassapa.
125. Dantabhūmi Sutta: By the simile of elephant training, the

Buddha shows how one should instruct another in the Dhamma.

126. Bhūmija Sutta: Bhūmija answers the questions of Prince Jayasena.
127. Anuruddha Sutta: Anuruddha explains emancipation of mind to the householder Pañcakaṅga.
128. Upakkilesa Sutta: The Buddha appeases the quarrels of the Bhikkhus of Kosambi and discourses on right meditation.
129. Bālapaṇḍita Sutta: On rewards and punishments after death.
130. Devadūta Sutta: On the fate of those who neglect the messengers of death.

(n) Vibhaṅga Vagga

131. Bhaddekaratta Sutta: A poem of four verses, with a commentary on striving.
132. Ānandabhaddekaratta Sutta: Ānanda's exposition of the same poem.
133. Mahākaccanabhaddekaratta Sutta: Mahākaccāna expounds the same poem.
134. Lomasakaṅgiyabhaddekaratta Sutta: The Buddha expounds the same poem to Lomasakaṅgiya.
135. Cūḷakammavibhaṅga Sutta: The Buddha explains the various results of different kinds of *kamma*.
136. Mahākammavibhaṅga Sutta: The Buddha refutes those who deny the operation of *kamma*.
137. Saḷāyatanavibhaṅga Sutta: The analysis of the six senses.
138. Uddesavibhaṅga Sutta: Mahākaccāna speaks on an aspect of consciousness.
139. Araṇavibhaṅga Sutta: The middle path between two extremes, and the opposite courses that lead to conflicts and to their cessation.
140. Dhātuvibhaṅga Sutta: The story of Pukkusāti who recognises the Master by his teaching. The analysis of the elements.
141. Saccavibhaṅga Sutta: Statement of the Four Noble Truths. A commentary thereon by Sāriputta.
142. Dakkhiṇavibhaṅga Sutta: On gifts and givers.

(o) Saḷāyatana Vagga

143. Anāthapiṇḍikovāda Sutta: The death of Anāthapiṇḍika, his rebirth in the Tusita heaven, and his appearance to the Buddha.

144. Channovāda Sutta: Story of the Thera Channa who, when sick, was instructed by Sāriputta, but finally committed suicide.
145. Puṇṇovāda Sutta: The Buddha's instruction to Puṇṇa on bearing pleasure and pain.
146. Nandakovāda Sutta: Nandaka catechises Mahāpajāpatī and 500 Bhikkhunīs on impermanence.
147. Cūḷarāhulovāda Sutta: The Buddha takes Rāhula to the forest and questions him on impermanence. The devas come to listen to the discourse.
148. Chachakka Sutta: On the six sixes (of the senses).
149. Mahāsaḷāyatanika Sutta: On the right knowledge of the senses.
150. Nagaravindeyya Sutta: The Buddha's instruction on the kinds of ascetics and brahmins who are to be honoured.
151. Piṇḍapātapārisuddhi Sutta: Instruction to Sāriputta on the training of the disciple.
152. Indriyabhāvanā Sutta: The Buddha rejects the methods of the brahmin Pārāsariya for subduing the senses, and expounds his own method.

3. Saṃyutta Nikāya

This is the "grouped" or "connected" series of *suttas* which either deal with a specific doctrine or devolve on a particular personality. There are fifty-six *saṃyuttas* divided into five *vaggas* containing 2,889 *suttas*.

(a) Sagātha Vagga

1. *Devata Saṃyutta*: Questions of devas.
2. *Devaputta Saṃyutta*: Questions of the sons of devas.
3. *Kosala Saṃyutta*: Anecdotes of King Pasenadi of Kosala.
4. *Māra Saṃyutta*: Māra's hostile acts against the Buddha and disciples.
5. *Bhikkhunī Saṃyutta*: Māra's unsuccessful seduction of nuns and his arguments with them.
6. *Brahma Saṃyutta*: Brahmā Sahampati requests the Buddha to preach the Dhamma to the world.
7. *Brāhmaṇa Saṃyutta*: Bhāradvāja brahmin's encounter with the Buddha and his conversion.
8. *Vaṅgīsa Saṃyutta*: Vaṅgīsa, the foremost poet among the Bhikkhus, tells of his eradication of lust.

9. *Vana Saṃyutta*: Forest deities direct undeveloped Bhikkhus on the right path.
10. *Yakkha Saṃyutta*: Demons' encounters with the Buddha and with nuns.
11. *Sakka Saṃyutta*: The Buddha enumerates the qualities of Sakka, King of the Gods.

(b) Nidāna Vagga

12. *Nidāna Saṃyutta*: The explanation of Paṭiccasamuppāda (the doctrine of dependent origination).
13. *Abhisamaya Saṃyutta*: The encouragement to attain penetration of the Dhamma.
14. *Dhātu Saṃyutta*: The description of physical, mental, and abstract elements.
15. *Anamatagga Saṃyutta*: On the "incalculable beginning" (of *saṃsāra*).
16. *Kassapa Saṃyutta*: Exhortation of Kassapa.
17. *Lābhasakkāra Saṃyutta*: "Gains, favours and flattery."
18. *Rāhula Saṃyutta*: The instructing of Rāhula.
19. *Lakkhaṇa Saṃyutta*: Questions of Lakkhaṇa on *petas* (ghosts).
20. *Opamma Saṃyutta*: Various points of Dhamma illustrated by similes.
21. *Bhikkhu Saṃyutta*: Admonitions of the Buddha and Moggallāna to the Bhikkhus.

(c) Khandha Vagga

22. *Khandha Saṃyutta*: The aggregates, physical and mental, that constitute the "individual."
23. *Rādha Saṃyutta*: Questions of Rādha.
24. *Diṭṭhi Saṃyutta*: Delusive views arise from clinging to the aggregates.
25. *Okkantika Saṃyutta*: Entering the Path through confidence *(saddhā)* and through wisdom (*paññā*).
26. *Uppāda Saṃyutta*: Arising of the aggregates leads to *dukkha*.
27. *Kilesa Saṃyutta*: Defilements arise from the sixfold sense base and sense-consciousness.
28. *Sāriputta Saṃyutta*: Sāriputta answers Ānanda's question concerning the calming of the senses.
29. *Nāga Saṃyutta*: Enumeration of four kinds of *nāga* (serpents).

30. *Supaṇṇa Saṃyutta*: Enumeration of four kinds of *garuda* (magical birds).
31. *Gandhabbakāya Saṃyutta*: Description of the *gandhabbas* (celestial musicians).
32. *Valāhaka Saṃyutta*: Description of the cloud spirits.
33. *Vacchagotta Saṃyutta*: Vacchagotta's metaphysical questions.
34. *Samādhi Saṃyutta*: Enumeration of the four types of practisers of the *jhānas* (meditative absorptions).

(d) Saḷāyatana Vagga

35. *Saḷāyatana Saṃyutta*: The sixfold sense base and the correct attitude towards it.
36. *Vedanā Saṃyutta*: The three kinds of feeling and the correct attitude towards them.
37. *Mātugāma Saṃyutta*: The destinies of women according to their qualities.
38. *Jambukhādaka Saṃyutta*: Questions of the wanderer Jambukhādaka to Sāriputta.
39. *Sāmaṇḍaka Saṃyutta*: Questions of the wanderer Sāmaṇḍaka to Sāriputta.
40. *Moggallāna Saṃyutta*: Moggallāna explains the *jhānas* to the Bhikkhus.
41. *Citta Saṃyutta*: Senses and sense-objects are not intrinsically evil, only the unwholesome desires that arise through contact with them.
42. *Gāmaṇi Saṃyutta*: The definitions of "wrathful" and "kindly."
43. *Asaṅkhata Saṃyutta*: The Unconditioned (Nibbāna).
44. *Avyākata Saṃyutta*: Speculative questions put by King Pasenadi to Khema, Anuruddha, Sāriputta, and Moggallāna.

(e) Mahā Vagga

45. *Magga Saṃyutta*: The Noble Eightfold Path.
46. *Bojjhaṅga Saṃyutta*: The seven factors of enlightenment (mindfulness, investigation, energy, happiness, calm, concentration, and equanimity).
47. *Satipaṭṭhāna Saṃyutta*: The four foundations of mindfulness.
48. *Indriya Saṃyutta*: The five faculties (confidence, energy, mindfulness, concentration, and wisdom).
49. *Sammappadhāna Saṃyutta*: The four right efforts.
50. *Bala Saṃyutta*: The five powers (as for the faculties above).

51. *Iddhipāda Saṃyutta*: The four psychic powers (will, energy, thought, and investigation).
52. *Anuruddha Saṃyutta*: Supernormal powers attained by Anuruddha through mindfulness.
53. *Jhāna Saṃyutta*: The four *jhānas*.
54. *Ānāpāna Saṃyutta*: Mindfulness of breathing.
55. *Sotāpatti Saṃyutta*: Description of a "Stream-Enterer."
56. *Sacca Saṃyutta*: The Four Noble Truths.

4. Aṅguttara Nikāya

In the Aṅguttara Nikāya, the division is a purely numerical one. There are eleven classified groups (*nipātas*), the subject of the first being single items, followed by groups of two items, and so on, to the final group of eleven items. Each *nipāta* is divided into *vaggas*, each of which contains ten or more *suttas*, there being 2,308 *suttas* in all.

1. **Ekaka Nipāta**: The mind: Concentrated/unconcentrated, trained/untrained, cultivated/uncultivated; exertion; diligence; the Buddha, Sāriputta, Moggallāna, Mahākassapa; views: Right/wrong; concentration: Right/wrong.

2. **Duka Nipāta**: Two kinds of *kamma* (either producing results in this life or leading to rebirth); cause of origin of good and evil; hopes and desires; gain and *longevity*; two kinds of gifts (that of material things and that of Dhamma); two assemblies of Bhikkhus: Those who have realised/not realised the Four Noble Truths, and those who live/do not live in harmony.

3. **Tika Nipāta**: Three offences of body, speech, and mind; three praiseworthy acts: Generosity, renunciation, maintenance of parents; exertion of checking growth of unarisen evil states, developing unarisen good states, removing arisen evil states; heretical views, i.e., that pleasant and painful and neither-pleasant-nor-painful experiences are caused by previous actions, that these experiences are providential, that these experiences are causeless.

4. **Catukka Nipāta**: Undisciplined persons lack conduct, concentration, insight, emancipation; the ignorant increase demerit by praising the unworthy, blaming the worthy, rejoicing when one should not rejoice, not rejoicing when one should rejoice; four kinds of persons: Neither wise nor pious, not wise but pious, wise but impious, both wise and pious; Bhikkhus should remain content with their robes, alms, dwelling-places and medicines; four kinds

of happiness: Living in a suitable environment, association with a well-developed man, self-realisation, accumulated merit in the past; the four "divine abodes": Loving-kindness, compassion, sympathetic joy and equanimity; four qualities guarding a Bhikkhu against lapsing: Observation of *sīla*, control of the sense-doors, moderation in eating, constant mindfulness; four ways of self-concentration: For a happy condition in this life, for knowledge and insight, for mindfulness and self-possession, for destruction of the defilements; four persons fostering hatred, hypocrisy, gains and honours other than connected with the Dhamma; four mistaken views: Impermanence for permanence, pain for pleasure, non-self for self, impurity for purity; four faults of ascetics and brahmins: Drinking fermented liquor, addiction to sense pleasures, accepting money, earning their livelihood by unethical means; four fields of merit-bringing happiness: Rightly believing the Buddha as fully enlightened, the Dhamma as well expounded, the Sangha as well-established, the disciples as being free from impurities; four ways of living together: The vile with the vile, the vile with the good, the good with the vile, the good with the good; offering food gives the recipient: Long life, beauty, happiness, physical strength; four conditions for worldly prosperity: Persistent effort, protecting one's earnings, good friendship, balanced livelihood; four conditions for spiritual prosperity: Confidence, morality, charity, wisdom; four families of snakes to whom one should extend loving-kindness; four right efforts; four unthinkables: The sphere of a Buddha, the *jhānas*, *kamma* and result, speculating over the origin of the world; four pilgrimages: To the sites of the Buddha's birth, enlightenment, first sermon and decease; four kinds of beneficial/non-beneficial speech: Truthfulness/lying, non-backbiting/backbiting, gentle/harsh, thoughtful/frivolous; four essential qualities: Morality, concentration, wisdom and emancipation; four faculties: Confidence, energy, mindfulness, concentration; the four elements; four persons worthy of monuments: The Buddha, Paccekabuddhas, Arahants, "Wheel-turning" kings; Bhikkhus should not retire to the forest if given to: Lust, malice, envy, or lacking commonsense.

5. **Pañcaka Nipāta**: Five good characteristics of a disciple: Reverence, modesty, abstinence from unskilful acts, energy, wisdom; five mental hindrances: Sensual lust, ill will, sloth, restlessness and worry, sceptical doubt; five objects of meditation: The impure, non-self, death, disagreeableness of food, not finding

delight in the world; five evil qualities: Not free from passion, hatred, delusion, hypocrisy, malice; five good acts: Loving actions of body, speech and mind, observance of virtue, and holding to right views.

6. **Chakka Nipāta**: Sixfold duty of a Bhikkhu: Abstaining from distracting work, arguments, sleep and company; humility; association with the wise.

7. **Sattaka Nipāta**: Seven kinds of wealth: Reverence, good conduct, modesty, abstinence from unskilful acts, learning, renunciation, wisdom; seven kinds of attachment: Requesting favours, hatred, mistaken confidence, doubt, pride, worldly existence, ignorance.

8. **Aṭṭhaka Nipāta**: Eight causes of mindfulness/almsgiving/ earthquakes.

9. **Navaka Nipāta**: Nine contemplations: Impurity, death, disagreeableness of food, indifference to the world, impermanence, suffering resulting from impermanence, non-self, renunciation, equanimity; nine kinds of persons: Those who have trod the four paths to Nibbāna and experience the "fruits" together with the worldling, etc.

10. **Dasaka Nipāta**: Ten contemplations: Impermanence, non-self, death, disagreeableness of food, indifference to the world, bone, and four stages of a decomposing corpse: Worm-infested, black with decay, fissured through decay, bloated; ten kinds of purification through right knowledge, right liberation, and the eight steps of the Noble Eightfold Path.

11. **Ekadasaka Nipāta**: Eleven kinds of happiness/ways to Nibbāna/good and bad characteristics of a herdsman and a Bhikkhu.

5. Khuddaka Nikāya

This is the division of the shorter books of the Sutta Piṭaka, the "Division of Small Books," as Buddhaghosa called it. This Nikāya appears to have grown up generally after the older Nikāyas were closed and probably was incorporated into the Canon later. There are fifteen main divisions:

Khuddakapāṭha: The "Text of Small Passages" contains:

(1) *Saraṇattaya*: The thrice-repeated "Refuge Formula" for all Buddhists.

(2) *Dasasikkhāpada*: The Ten Precepts binding on Sāmaṇeras (novices).

(3) *Dvattiṃsakāra*: List of the 32 constituents of the body.

(4) *Kumārapañhā*: Catechism of ten questions for Sāmaṇeras.

(5) *Maṅgala Sutta*: A poem on the "greatest blessings" (*maṅgala*).

(6) *Ratana Sutta*: A poem on the Three Jewels: Buddha, Dhamma, and Sangha.

(7) *Tirokuḍḍa Sutta* (or: Tirokuṭṭa Sutta): A poem on the offerings to be made to the ghosts of departed relatives.

(8) *Nidhikaṇḍa Sutta*: A poem on the storing up of true treasure.

(9) *Metta Sutta*: A poem on loving-kindness.

Dhammapada: The Dhamma Path. It consists of 423 verses arranged in 26 *vaggas*.

Udāna: A collection, in eight *vaggas*, of eighty *udānas* or "inspired utterances" of the Buddha. They are mostly in verse and each is accompanied by a prose account of the circumstances which called it forth:

(1) *Bodhi Vagga*: Describes certain events following the Buddha's enlightenment, including the famous discourse to Bāhiya which stresses living in the present moment.

(2) *Mucalinda Vagga*: This *vagga* is named after the Nāga king who shielded the Buddha with his (cobra) hood.

(3) *Nanda Vagga*: The Buddha convinces his half-brother, Nanda, of the hollowness of worldly existence. Also contains admonitions to the Sangha.

(4) *Meghiya Vagga*: Ignoring the advice of the Buddha, Meghiya retires to a mango grove to practise meditation but his mind is soon assailed with unhealthy thoughts. On returning to the Buddha he is told that five factors should be cultivated by one with an undeveloped mind: good friendship, morality, profitable conversation, determination, and insight. Also contains the stories of Sundarī and the assault on Sāriputta by a yakkha.

(5) *Soṇathera Vagga*: Contains a visit of King Pasenadi to the Buddha, the discourse to the leper Suppabuddha, the elucidation of the eight characteristics of the Sāsana, and the first year of the Bhikkhu-life of Soṇa.

(6) *Jaccandha Vagga*: Contains the Buddha's hint at his passing away, Pasenadi's dialogue, and the story of the king who caused men, blind from birth, to each feel and describe an elephant (illustrative of partial realisation of truth).

(7) *Cūḷa Vagga*: Contains minor episodes, mainly concerning individual Bhikkhus.

(8) *Pāṭaligāma Vagga*: Contains the famous definition of Nibbāna as being unborn, unbecome, unmade, uncompounded; the Buddha's last meal and his admonition to Ānanda over Cunda; and the visit to Pāṭaligāma where the Buddha enunciated the five advantages of leading a pure life and the five disadvantages of not doing so.

Itivuttaka: A collection of 112 short *suttas* in four *nipātas*, each accompanied with verses. The collection takes its name from the words usually introducing each set of verses: *iti vuccati*, "thus it is said." The work comprises the ethical teachings of the Buddha:

(1) *Ekaka Nipāta*: Three *vaggas*. Lust, ill will, delusion, wrath, spite, pride, ignorance, craving, schism, lying, stinginess, are condemned; mindfulness, association with the wise, concord, mental peace, happiness, diligence, generosity and loving-kindness are praised.

(2) *Duka Nipāta*: Two *vaggas*. Elucidates guarding of the sense-doors and moderation in eating, skilful actions, healthy habits and correct views, serenity and seclusion, shame and dread, the two kinds of Nibbāna, and the virtues of leading an energetic ascetic life.

(3) *Tika Nipāta*: Five *vaggas*. Categorises factors which are threefold: evil roots, elements, feelings, thirsts, cankers, etc., and proclaims the ideal life of a Bhikkhu.

(4) *Catukka Nipāta*: Categorises factors which are fourfold: Bhikkhus' necessities, Noble Truths, etc., and emphasises purity of mind for a Bhikkhu.

Suttanipāta: "Collection of Suttas." This comprises five *vaggas* containing 70 *suttas* in all. The *suttas*, each containing from eight to fifty verses, are in verse with introductions in either verse or prose.

(a) Uragavagga:

1. Uraga Sutta: The Bhikkhu who discards all human passions (anger, hatred, craving, etc.) and is free from delusion and fear, is compared to a snake which has shed its skin.
2. Dhaniya Sutta: The complacent "security" of a worldling is contrasted with the genuine security of the Buddha.
3. Khaggavisāṇa Sutta: The wandering life of a Bhikkhu is praised. Family and social ties are to be avoided in view of

their *saṃsāric* attachments, excepting the "good friend" (*kalyāṇamitta*).

4. Kasībhāradvāja Sutta: Socially useful or mundane labour is contrasted with the no less important efforts of the Buddha striving for Nibbāna.
5. Cunda Sutta: The Buddha enumerates four kinds of *samaṇas*: A Buddha, an Arahant, a conscientious Bhikkhu, and a fraudulent Bhikkhu.
6. Parābhava Sutta: The "causes of personal downfall" in the moral and spiritual domains are enumerated.
7. Vasala or Aggika Bhāradvāja Sutta: In refutation of the charge "outcast," the Buddha explains that it is by actions, not lineage, that one becomes an outcast or a brahmin.
8. Metta Sutta: The constituents of the practice of loving-kindness towards all beings.
9. Hemavata Sutta: Two yakkhas have their doubts about the qualities of the Buddha resolved by him. The Buddha continues by describing the path of deliverance from death.
10. Āḷavaka Sutta: The Buddha answers the questions of the yakkha Āḷavaka concerning happiness, understanding, and the path to Nibbāna.
11. Vijaya Sutta: An analysis of the body into its (impure) constituent parts, and the mention of the Bhikkhu who attains Nibbāna through understanding the body's true nature.
12. Muni Sutta: The idealistic conception of a muni or sage who leads a solitary life freed from the passions.

(b) Cūḷavagga:

13. Ratana Sutta: A hymn to the Three Jewels: Buddha, Dhamma and Sangha.
14. Āmagandha Sutta: Kassapa Buddha refutes the Brahmanic view of defilement through eating meat and states that this can only come about through an evil mind and corresponding actions.
15. Hiri Sutta: A dissertation on the nature of true friendship.
16. Mahāmaṅgala Sutta: Thirty-eight blessings are enumerated in leading a pure life, starting with basic ethical injunctions and culminating in the realisation of Nibbāna.
17. Sūciloma Sutta: In reply to the threatening attitude of the yakkha Sūciloma, the Buddha states that passion, hatred, doubt, etc., originate with the body, desire and the concept of self.
18. Dhammacariya Sutta: A Bhikkhu should lead a just and pure life and avoid those of a quarrelsome nature and those who are slaves of desire.

19. Brāhmaṇadhammika Sutta: The Buddha explains to some old and wealthy brahmins the high moral standards of their ancestors and how they declined, following greed for the king's wealth. As a result they induced the king to offer animal sacrifice, etc., in order to acquire wealth and thus lost knowledge of the Dhamma.
20. Nava Sutta: Taking heed of the quality of the teacher, one should go to a learned and intelligent man in order to acquire a thorough knowledge of Dhamma.
21. Kiṃsīla Sutta: The path of a conscientious lay disciple, Dhamma being one's first and last concern.
22. Uṭṭhāna Sutta: An attack on idleness and laziness. Pierced by the arrow of suffering, one should not rest until all desire is eliminated.
23. Rāhula Sutta: The Buddha advises his son, the novice Rāhula, to respect the wise man, associate with him, and live up to the principles of a recluse.
24. Vaṅgīsa Sutta: The Buddha assures Vaṅgīsa that his late teacher, Nigrodhakappa, attained Nibbāna.
25. Sammāparibbājanīya Sutta: The path of a conscientious Bhikkhu disciple: Non-attachment, eradication of the passions, and understanding the nature of *saṃsāra*.
26. Dhammika Sutta: The Buddha explains to Dhammika the respective duties of a Bhikkhu and layman, the latter being expected to keep the five precepts and observe uposatha days.

(c) Mahāvagga:

27. Pabbajjā Sutta: King Bimbisāra of Magadha tempts the Buddha with his material resources and asks after his lineage. The Buddha states the fact of his birth amongst the Sakyans of Kosala and that he has seen through the illusive nature of sensual pleasures.
28. Padhāna Sutta: The graphic description of Māra's temptations immediately prior to the Buddha's Enlightenment.
29. Subhāsita Sutta: The language of Bhikkhus should be well-spoken, pleasing, correct, and true.
30. Sundarikabhāradvāja Sutta: The Buddha explains to the brahmin Sundarika, how one becomes worthy of the honour of receiving an offering.
31. Māgha Sutta: The Buddha explains the above to the layman Māgha, and elucidates the various kinds of blessings from offerings.

32. Sabhiya Sutta: Sabhiya, a wandering ascetic, could not obtain answers to his questions from the six famous teachers of the time. Hence he approaches the Buddha and becomes a disciple after obtaining satisfactory answers to his questions.
33. Sela Sutta: A brahmin, Sela, converses with the Buddha and is converted with his three hundred followers.
34. Salla Sutta: Life is short and all are subject to death, but the wise, who understand the nature of life, have no fears.
35. Vāseṭṭha Sutta: Two young men, Bhāradvāja and Vāseṭṭha, discuss a question regarding brahmins: The former states that one is a brahmin by birth, the latter that one becomes one only through actions. The Buddha subsequently confirms the latter view as being correct.
36. Kokāliya Sutta: Kokāliya falsely ascribes evil desires to Sāriputta and Moggallāna and subsequently comes to a painful end, through death and rebirth in one of the hells. The Buddha then enumerates the different hells and describes the punishment for slandering and back-biting.
37. Nālaka Sutta: The sage Asita's prophecy concerning the future Buddha Gotama. His sister's son, Nālaka, has the highest state of wisdom explained to him by the Buddha.
38. Dvayatānupassana Sutta: Suffering arises from substance, ignorance, the five aggregates, desire, attachment, effort, food, etc.

(d) Aṭṭhakavagga:

39. Kāma Sutta: To avoid the unpleasant effects, sensual pleasures should be avoided.
40. Gūhaṭṭhaka Sutta: In addition to the above, physical existence also should not be clung to if one is keen on attaining deliverance from *saṃsāra*.
41. Duṭṭhaṭṭhaka Sutta: One who praises his own virtue and is tied to dogmatic views (that differ from man to man and sect to sect) lives a restricted life. The sage, however, remains self-effacing and independent of philosophical systems.
42. Suddhaṭṭhaka Sutta: Knowledge of philosophical systems cannot purify one and there is the tendency to chop and change, never attaining inward peace. The wise, however, are not misled by passion and do not cling to anything in *saṃsāra*.
43. Paramaṭṭhaka Sutta: One should not engage in philosophical disputations. A true brahmin does not and thereby attains Nibbāna.
44. Jara Sutta: From selfishness come greed and regrets. The ideal Bhikkhu, a "homeless one," is independent and does not seek

purification through others.

45. Tissa Metteyya Sutta: The Buddha elucidates the kinds of undesirable effects that follow from sensual contacts.
46. Pasura Sutta: The folly of debates where both sides insult or deride each other. If defeated they become discontented. Therefore purification cannot result.
47. Māgandiya Sutta: Again, the Buddha emphasises to Māgandiya, a believer in purity through philosophy that purity can result only from inward peace.
48. Purābheda Sutta: The conduct and characteristics of a true sage: Freedom from craving, anger, desire, passion, and attachment; and he is always calm, thoughtful, and mentally equipoised.
49. Kalahavivāda Sutta: Arguments and disputes arise from deeply felt objects, etc.
50. Cūḷaviyūha Sutta: A description of the different schools of philosophy, all contradicting one another without realising that Truth is one.
51. Mahāviyūha Sutta: Philosophers only praise themselves and criticise others but a true brahmin remains indifferent to such dubious intellectual attainment and is thus calm and peaceful.
52. Tuvaṭaka Sutta: The Bhikkhu should sever the root of evil and cravings, learn the Dhamma, be calm and meditative, avoid talking, indolence, etc., and strictly follow his prescribed duties.
53. Attadaṇḍa Sutta: The sage should be truthful, undeceitful, sober, free from greed and slander, energetic, and without desire for name and fame.
54. Sāriputta Sutta: Again, this time in answer to Sāriputta's enquiry, the Buddha lays down the principles that should govern the life of a Bhikkhu.

(e) Pārāyanavagga:

This section consists of sixteen dialogues (*pucchā*) between the Buddha and sixteen brahmins. They all stress the necessity of eradicating desire, greed, attachment, philosophical views, sensual pleasures, indolence, and of remaining aloof, independent, calm, mindful, and firm in the Dhamma in order to attain Nibbāna:

55. Ajita.
56. Tissa Metteyya.
57. Puṇṇaka.
58. Mettagū.
59. Dhotaka.
60. Upasīva.

61. Nanda.
62. Hemaka.
63. Todeyya.
64. Kappa.
65. Jatukaṇṇī.
66. Bhadrāvudha.
67. Udaya.
68. Posāla.
69. Mogharāja.
70. Piṅgiya.

Vimānavatthu: The "Stories of Celestial Mansions," being 85 poems in seven *vaggas* on merit and rebirth in the heavenly worlds.

Petavatthu: This comprises 51 poems in four *vaggas* on rebirth as wandering ghosts (*petas*) through demeritorious actions.

Theragātha: "Verses of the Elders" (*theras*), containing 107 poems (1,279 *gāthas*).

Therīgāthā: "Verses of the Elder Nuns" (*therīs*), containing 75 poems (522 *gāthas*).

Jātaka: The Jātaka or Birth Stories is a collection of 547 stories purporting to be accounts of former lives of the Buddha Gotama. The Nidānakathā, or "Story of the Lineage," is an introductory commentary which details the life of the Buddha up to the opening of the Jetavana monastery at Sāvatthī, and also his former lives under preceding Buddhas.

Niddesa:

Mahāniddesa: A commentary/gloss on the *Aṭṭhakavagga* of the Suttanipāta; and

Cūḷaniddesa: A commentary/gloss on the *Pārāyanavagga* and the *Khaggavisāṇa Sutta*, also of the Suttanipāta.

The Niddesa is itself commented on in the *Saddhammapajjotikā* of Upasena and is there attributed to Sāriputta.

Paṭisambhidāmagga: A detailed analysis of concepts and practices already mentioned in the Vinaya Piṭaka and Dīgha, Saṃyutta and Aṅguttara Nikāyas. It is divided into three *vaggas*, each containing ten topics (*kathā*):

Mahā Vagga: Knowledge of impermanence and *dukkha* of compounded things, the Four Noble Truths, dependent origination, four planes of existence, false views, the five faculties, three aspects of Nibbāna, *kamma-vipāka*, the four paths to Nibbāna.

Yuganaddha Vagga: The seven factors of enlightenment, four foundations of mindfulness, four right efforts; four powers (will, energy, thought, investigation), the Noble Eightfold Path, four fruits of the monk's life (*patticariyā*) and Nibbāna; 68 potentialities.

Paññā Vagga: Eight kinds of conduct (*cariya*); postures (walking, sitting, standing, lying down), sense organs, mindfulness; concentration (the *jhānas*), the Four Noble Truths, the four paths to Nibbāna, the four fruits of a monk's life, and for the promotion of the world's welfare.

Apadāna: Tales in verse of the former lives of 550 Bhikkhus and 40 Bhikkhunīs.

Buddhavaṃsa: "The History of the Buddhas," in which the Buddha relates the account of his forming the resolve to become a Buddha and gives the history of the twenty-four Buddhas who preceded him.

Cariyāpiṭaka: Thirty-five tales from the Jātakas in verse illustrating seven out of the Ten Perfections (*pāramīs*): generosity, morality, renunciation, wisdom, energy, patience, truthfulness, determination, loving-kindness, and equanimity.

C. Abhidhamma Piṭaka—the Collection of Philosophical Treatises

The Abhidhamma Piṭaka is the third main division of the Pāli Canon. It consists of seven works which are systematic expositions of the doctrine from a strict philosophical point of view. They deal especially with the psychological analysis of phenomenal existence.

1. Dhammasaṅgaṇī: Enumeration of the *dhammas* or factors of existence. The work opens with a *mātikā*, a "matrix" or schedule of categories which classifies the totality of phenomena into a scheme of twenty-two triads (*tika*), sets of three terms, and a hundred dyads *(duka)*, sets of two terms. The *mātikā* also includes a Suttanta matrix, a schedule of forty-two dyads taken from the *suttas*. The *mātikā* serves as a framework for the entire Abhidhamma, introducing the diverse perspectives from which all phenomena are to be classified. The body of the Dhammasaṅgaṇī consists of four parts:

1. "States of Consciousness," which analyses all states of consciousness into their constituent factors, each of which is elaborately defined.
2. "Matter," which enumerates and classifies the various types of material phenomena.
3. "The Summary," offering concise explanations of all the terms in both the Abhidhamma and Suttanta matrixes.
4. "The Synopsis," offering more condensed explanations of the Abhidhamma matrix but not the Suttanta matrix.

2. Vibhaṅga: "Distinction or Determination." Continued analysis of the foregoing. The Vibhaṅga contains eighteen chapters, dealing in turn with the following: Aggregates, sense bases, elements, truths, faculties, dependent arising, foundations of mindfulness, supreme efforts, means to accomplishment, factors of enlightenment, the eightfold path, *jhānas*, illimitables (or *Brahma-vihāras*), training rules, analytical knowledges, kinds of knowledge, defilements, and "the heart of the doctrine" (a concise overview of the Buddhist universe).

3. Dhātukathā: "Discussion of Elements." This book discusses all phenomena with reference to the three schemes of aggregates, sense bases and elements. It attempts to determine whether, and to what extent, they are included or not included in them, and whether they are associated with them or dissociated from them.

4. Puggalapaññatti: The body of this work provides formal definitions of different types of individuals. It has ten chapters: The first deals with single types of individuals, the second with pairs, the third with groups of three, etc.

5. Kathāvatthu: Discussion of the points of controversy between the early "Hīnayāna" sects, and the defence of the Theravada viewpoint. Attributed to Moggaliputta Tissa, the president of the 3rd council, which was convened at Patna by the Emperor Asoka in the middle of the 3rd century BCE.

6. Yamaka: This book has the purpose of resolving ambiguities and defining the precise usage of technical terms. It is called the "Book of Pairs" because it employs throughout pairs of questions which approach the subject under investigation from converse points of view. For example, the first pair of questions runs thus: "Are all wholesome phenomena wholesome roots? And are all wholesome roots wholesome phenomena?" The book contains ten chapters: Roots, aggregates, sense bases, elements, truths, formations, latent dispositions, consciousness, phenomena, and faculties.

7. Paṭṭhāna: The "Book of Relations." Causation and the mutual relationship of phenomena are examined. The special contribution of the Paṭṭhāna is the elaboration of a scheme of twenty-four conditional relations (*paccaya*) for plotting the causal connections between different types of phenomena. The body of the work applies these conditional relations to all the phenomena included in the Abhidhamma matrix. The book has four great divisions: Origination according to the positive method, origination according to the negative method, origination according to the positive-negative method, and origination according to the negative-positive method. Each of these in turn has six subdivisions: Origination of triads, dyads, dyads and triads combined, triads and dyads combined, triads and triads combined, and dyads and dyads combined. In the Burmese-script Sixth Council edition of the Pali Canon, the Paṭṭhāna comprises five volumes totalling 2500 pages. Because of its great size as well as its philosophical importance, it is also known as the Mahāpakaraṇa, "the Great Treatise."

II. INDEX TO THE CANON

This index lists the principal sections and *suttas* of the Pāli Canon.

The number in the fourth column refers to the unit of analysis mentioned in the first column. Thus Khandha Saṃyutta SP SN 22 refers to the Sutta Piṭaka, Saṃyutta Nikāya, Saṃyutta No. 22, while Khandha Vagga SP SN 3 refers to the Sutta Piṭaka, Saṃyutta Nikāya, Vagga No. 3. When the number in the fourth column contains two parts separated by a colon, the first figure refers to the larger unit (*vagga* or *saṃyutta*), the second figure to the *sutta* within that unit.

Abhayarājakumāra Sutta	SP	MN	58
Abhidhamma Piṭaka	3rd of the 3 Piṭakas		
Abhisamaya Saṃyutta	SP	SN	13
Acchariya-abbhūtadhamma Sutta	SP	MN	123
Aggañña Sutta	SP	DN	27
Aggi(ka) Bhāradvāja Sutta	SP	KN	Sn 7
Aggivacchagotta Sutta	SP	MN	72
Ajitamāṇava Pucchā	SP	KN	Sn 55
Ākaṅkheyya Sutta	SP	MN	6
Alagaddūpama Sutta	SP	MN	22
Āḷavaka Sutta	SP	KN	Sn 10
Āmagandha Sutta	SP	KN	Sn 14
Ambalaṭṭhikarāhulovāda Sutta	SP	MN	61
Ambaṭṭha Sutta	SP	DN	3
Anupada Vagga	SP	MN	
Anamatagga Saṃyutta	SP	SN	15
Ānandabhaddekaratta Sutta	SP	MN	132
Anaṅgaṇa Sutta	SP	MN	5
Āneñjasappāya Sutta	SP	MN	106
Ānāpāna Saṃyutta	SP	SN	54
Ānāpānasati Sutta	SP	MN	118
Anāthapiṇḍikovāda Sutta	SP	MN	143
Anattalakkhaṇa Sutta	SP	SN	22:59
Aṅgulimāla Sutta	SP	MN	86
Aṅguttara Nikāya	SP	4th Nikāya	
Anumāna Sutta	SP	MN	15

Brāhmaṇa Vagga	SP	MN	
Brāhmaṇa Saṃyutta	SP	SN	7
Brāhmaṇa Vagga	SP	KN	Dhp 26
Brāhmaṇadhammika Sutta	SP	KN	Sn 19
Brahmanimantanika Sutta	SP	MN	49
Brahmāyu Sutta	SP	MN	91
Buddha Vagga	SP	KN	Dhp14
Buddhavaṃsa	SP	KN	
Cakkavattisīhanāda Sutta	SP	DN	26
Caṅkī Sutta	SP	MN	95
Cariyāpiṭaka	SP	KN	
Catukka Nipāta	SP	AN	4
Catukka Nipāta	SP	KN	It 4
Cātuma Sutta	SP	MN	67
Cetokhila Sutta	SP	MN	16
Chabbisodhana Sutta	SP	MN	112
Chachakka Sutta	SP	MN	148
Chakka Nipāta	SP	AN	6
Channovāda Sutta	SP	MN	144
Citta Saṃyutta	SP	SN	41
Citta Vagga	SP	KN	Dhp 3
Cūḷa-assapura Sutta	SP	MN	40
Cūḷadhammasamādāna Sutta	SP	MN	45
Cūḷadukkhakkhandha Sutta	SP	MN	14
Cūḷagopālaka Sutta	SP	MN	34
Cūḷagosiṅga Sutta	SP	MN	31
Cūḷahatthipadopama Sutta	SP	MN	27
Cūḷakammavibhaṅga Sutta	SP	MN	135
Cūḷamāluṅkya Sutta	SP	MN	63
Cūḷaniddesa	SP	KN	Nidd
Cūḷapuṇṇama Sutta	SP	MN	110
Cūḷarāhulovāda Sutta	SP	MN	147
Cūḷasaccaka Sutta	SP	MN	35
Cūḷasakuludāyi Sutta	SP	MN	79
Cūḷasāropama Sutta	SP	MN	30
Cūḷasīhanāda Sutta	SP	MN	11
Cūḷasuññata Sutta	SP	MN	121
Cūḷataṇhāsaṅkhaya Sutta	SP	MN	37
Cūḷavagga	VP	Kha	
Cūḷavagga	SP	KN	Ud 7
Cūḷavagga	SP	KN	Sn 2
Cūḷavedalla Sutta	SP	MN	44

Cūḷaviyūha Sutta	SP	KN	Sn 50
Cūḷayamaka Vagga	SP	MN	
Cunda Sutta	SP	KN	Sn 5
Dakkhiṇavibhaṅga Sutta	SP	MN	142
Daṇḍa Vagga	SP	KN	Dhp 10
Dantabhūmi Sutta	SP	MN	125
Dasaka Nipāta	SP	AN	10
Dasa Sikkhāpadā	SP	KN	Khp 2
Dasuttara Sutta	SP	DN	34
Devadaha Sutta	SP	MN	101
Devadaha Vagga	SP	MN	
Devadūta Sutta	SP	MN	130
Devaputta Saṃyutta	SP	SN	2
Devata Saṃyutta	SP	SN	1
Dhamma Sutta[1]	SP	KN	Sn 18
Dhammacakkappavattana Sutta	SP	SN	56:11
Dhammacariya Sutta	SP	KN	Sn 18
Dhammacetiya Sutta	SP	MN	89
Dhammadāyāda Sutta	SP	MN	3
Dhammapada	SP	KN	
Dhammasaṅgaṇi	AP	1st book of AP	
Dhammaṭṭha Vagga	SP	KN	Dhp 19
Dhammika Sutta	SP	KN	Sn 26
Dhanañjāni Sutta	SP	MN	97
Dhaniya Sutta	SP	KN	Sn 2
Dhātukathā	AP	3rd book of.AP	
Dhātu Saṃyutta	SP	SN	14
Dhātuvibhaṅga Sutta	SP	MN	140
Dhotakamāṇava Pucchā	SP	KN	Sn 59
Dīgha Nikāya	SP	1st Nikāya	
Dīghanakha Sutta	SP	MN	74
Diṭṭhi Saṃyutta	SP	SN	24
Duka Nipāta	SP	AN	2
Duka Nipāta	SP	KN	It 2
Duṭṭhaṭṭhaka Sutta	SP	KN	Sn 41
Dvattiṃsakāra	SP	KN	Khp 3
Dvayatānupassana Sutta	SP	KN	Sn 38
Dvedhavitakka Sutta	SP	MN	19
Ekaka Nipāta	SP	AN	1
Ekaka Nipāta	SP	KN	It 1

1. This is an alternate title for the Nava Sutta.

Ekadasaka Nipāta	SP	AN	11
Esukāri Sutta	SP	MN	96
Gahapati Vagga	SP	MN	
Gāmaṇi Saṃyutta	SP	SN	42
Gaṇakamoggallāna Sutta	SP	MN	107
Gandhabbakāya Saṃyutta	SP	SN	31
Ghaṭīkāra Sutta	SP	MN	81
Ghoṭamukha Sutta	SP	MN	94
Gopakamoggalāna Sutta	SP	MN	108
Gūhaṭṭhaka Sutta	SP	KN	Sn 40
Gulissāni Sutta	SP	MN	69
Hemakamāṇava Pucchā	SP	KN	Sn 62
Hemavata Sutta	SP	KN	Sn 9
Hiri Sutta	SP	KN	Sn 15
Iddhipāda Saṃyutta	SP	SN	51
Indriya Saṃyutta	SP	SN	48
Indriyabhāvanā Sutta	SP	MN	152
Isigili Sutta	SP	MN	116
Itivuttaka	SP	KN	
Jaccandha Vagga	SP	KN	Ud 6
Jāliya Sutta	SP	DN	7
Jambukhādaka Saṃyutta	SP	SN	38
Janāvāsabha Sutta	SP	DN	18
Jara Sutta	SP	KN	Sn 44
Jara Vagga	SP	KN	Dhp 11
Jātaka	SP	KN	
Jatukaṇṇimāṇava Pucchā	SP	KN	Sn 65
Jhāna Saṃyutta	SP	SN	53
Jīvaka Sutta	SP	MN	55
Kakacūpama Sutta	SP	MN	21
Kalahavivāda Sutta	SP	KN	Sn 49
Kāma Sutta	SP	KN	Sn 39
Kandaraka Sutta	SP	MN	51
Kaṇṇakatthala Sutta	SP	MN	90
Kapila Sutta	SP	KN	Sn 18
Kappamāṇava Pucchā	SP	KN	Sn 64
Kasībhāradvāja Sutta	SP	KN	Sn 4
Kassapa Saṃyutta	SP	SN	16
Kassapasīhanāda Sutta	SP	DN	8
Kathāvatthu	AP	5th book of AP	
Kāyagatāsati Sutta	SP	MN	119

Kāyavicchandanika Sutta[2]	SP	KN	Sn 11
Kevaḍḍha Sutta	SP	DN	11
Khaggavisāṇa Sutta	SP	KN	Sn 3
Khandha Saṃyutta	SP	SN	22
Khandha Vagga	SP	SN	
Khandhaka	VP		
Khuddaka Nikāya	SP	5th Nikāya	
Khuddakapāṭha	SP	KN	
Kilesa Saṃyutta	SP	SN	6
Kiṃsīla Sutta	SP	KN	Sn 21
Kinti Sutta	SP	MN	103
Kīṭāgiri Sutta	SP	MN	70
Kodha Vagga	SP	KN	Dhp 17
Kokāliya Sutta	SP	KN	Sn 36
Kosala Saṃyutta	SP	SN	3
Kosambiya Sutta	SP	MN	48
Kukkuravatika Sutta	SP	MN	57
Kumārapañhā	SP	KN	Khp 4
Kūṭadanta Sutta	SP	DN	5
Lābhasakkāra Saṃyutta	SP	SN	17
Lakkhaṇa Saṃyutta	SP	SN	19
Lakkhaṇa Sutta	SP	DN	30
Laṭukikopama Sutta	SP	MN	66
Lohicca Sutta	SP	DN	12
Loka Vagga	SP	KN	Dhp13
Lomasakaṅgiyabhaddekaratta Sutta	SP	MN	134
Madhupiṇḍika Sutta	SP	MN	18
Madhura Sutta	SP	MN	84
Māgandiya Sutta	SP	MN	75
Māgandiya Sutta	SP	KN	Sn 47
Magga Saṃyutta	SP	SN	45
Magga Vagga	SP	KN	Dhp 20
Māgha Sutta	SP	KN	Sn 31
Mahā-assapura Sutta	SP	MN	39
Mahācattārīsaka Sutta	SP	MN	117
Mahādhammasamādāna Sutta	SP	MN	46
Mahādukkhakkhandha Sutta	SP	MN	13
Mahāgopālaka Sutta	SP	MN	33
Mahāgosiṅga Sutta	SP	MN	32
Mahāgovinda Sutta	SP	DN	19

2. This is an alternate title for the Dhammacariya Sutta.

Mahāhatthipadopama Sutta	SP	MN	28
Mahākaccānabhaddekaratta Sutta	SP	MN	133
Mahākammavibhaṅga Sutta	SP	MN	136
Mahāli Sutta	SP	DN	6
Mahāmāluṅkya Sutta	SP	MN	64
Mahāmaṅgala Sutta	SP	KN	Khp
Mahānidāna Sutta	SP	DN	15
Mahāniddesa	SP	KN	Nidd
Mahāpadāna Sutta	SP	DN	14
Mahāparinibbāna Sutta	SP	DN	16
Mahāpuṇṇama Sutta	SP	MN	109
Mahārāhulovāda Sutta	SP	MN	62
Mahāsaccaka Sutta	SP	MN	36
Mahāsakuludāyi Sutta	SP	MN	77
Mahāsaḷāyatanika Sutta	SP	MN	149
Mahāsamaya Sutta	SP	DN	20
Mahāsamaya Sutta[3]	SP	KN	Sn 25
Mahāsāropama Sutta	SP	MN	29
Mahāsatipaṭṭhāna Sutta	SP	DN	22
Mahāsīhanāda Sutta	SP	MN	12
Mahāsudassana Sutta	SP	DN	17
Mahāsuññata Sutta	SP	MN	122
Mahātaṇhāsaṅkhaya Sutta	SP	MN	38
Mahāvacchagotta Sutta	SP	MN	73
Mahāvagga	VP	Kha	
Mahāvagga	SP	DN	
Mahāvagga	SP	SN	
Mahāvagga	SP	KN	Sn
Mahāvagga	SP	KN	Paṭis
Mahāvedalla Sutta	SP	MN	43
Mahāviyūha Sutta	SP	KN	Sn 51
Mahāyamaka Vagga	SP	MN	
Majjhima Nikāya	SP	2nd Nikāya	
Makhādeva Sutta	SP	MN	83
Mala Vagga	SP	KN	Dhp 18
Maṅgala Sutta[4]	SP	KN	Khp 5
Maṅgala Sutta[5]	SP	KN	Sn 16
Māra Saṃyutta	SP	SN	4

3. This is an alternate title for the Vijaya Sutta.
4. This is an alternate title for the Sammāparibbājanīya Sutta.
5. This is an alternate title for the Mahāmaṅgala Sutta.

Māratajjanīya Sutta	SP	MN	50
Mātugāma Saṃyutta	SP	SN	37
Meghiya Vagga	SP	KN	Ud 4
Metta Sutta	SP	KN	Khp 9
Metta Sutta	SP	KN	Sn 8
Mettagūmāṇava Pucchā	SP	KN	Sn 58
Moggallāna Saṃyutta	SP	SN	40
Mogharājamāṇava Pucchā	SP	KN	Sn 69
Moneyya Sutta[6]	SP	KN	Sn 37
Mucalinda Vagga	SP	KN	Ud 2
Mūlapariyāya Sutta	SP	MN	1
Mūlapariyāya Vagga	SP	MN	
Muni Sutta	SP	KN	Sn 12
Nagaravindeyya Sutta	SP	MN	150
Nāga Saṃyutta	SP	SN	29
Nāga Vagga	SP	KN	Dhp 23
Nālaka Sutta	SP	KN	Sn 37
Nālakapāna Sutta	SP	MN	68
Nanda Vagga	SP	KN	Ud 3
Nandakovāda Sutta	SP	MN	146
Nandamāṇava Pucchā	SP	KN	Sn 61
Nava Sutta	SP	KN	Sn 20
Navaka Nipāta	SP	AN	9
Nidāna Saṃyutta	SP	SN	12
Nidāna Vagga	SP	SN	
Niddesa	SP	KN	
Nidhikaṇḍa Sutta	SP	KN	Khp 8
Nigrodhakappa Sutta[7]	SP	KN	Sn 24
Niraya Vagga	SP	KN	Dhp 22
Nivāpa Sutta	SP	MN	25
Okkantika Saṃyutta	SP	SN	25
Opamma Saṃyutta	SP	SN	20
Opamma Vagga	SP	MN	3
Pabbajjā Sutta	SP	KN	Sn 27
Padhāna Sutta	SP	KN	Sn 28
Pakiṇṇaka Vagga	SP	KN	Dhp 21
Pañcaka Nipāta	SP	AN	5
Pañcattaya Sutta	SP	MN	102
Paññā Vagga	SP	KN	Paṭis

6. This is an alternate title for the Nālaka Sutta.
7. This is an alternate title for the Vaṅgīsa Sutta.

Paṇḍita Vagga	SP	KN	Dhp 6
Pāpa Vagga	SP	KN	Dhp 9
Paramaṭṭhaka Sutta	SP	KN	Sn 43
Parābhava Sutta	SP	KN	Sn 6
Pārāyanavagga	SP	KN	Sn
Paribbājaka Vagga	SP	MN	
Parivāra	VP		
Pāsādika Sutta	SP	DN	29
Pasūra Sutta	SP	KN	Sn 46
Pāṭaligāma Vagga	SP	KN	Ud 8
Pāṭika Sutta	SP	DN	24
Pāṭika Vagga	SP	DN	
Pāṭika Vagga	SP	M	
Paṭisambhidāmagga	SP	KN	
Paṭṭhāna	AP	7th book of AP	
Pāyāsi Sutta	SP	DN	23
Petavatthu	SP	KN	
Piṇḍapātapārisuddhi Sutta	SP	MN	151
Piṅgiyamāṇava Pucchā	SP	KN	Sn 70
Piya Vagga	SP	KN	Dhp 16
Piyajātika Sutta	SP	MN	87
Posālamāṇava Pucchā	SP	KN	Sn 68
Potaliya Sutta	SP	MN	54
Poṭṭhapāda Sutta	SP	DN	9
Puggalapaññatti	AP	4th book of AP	
Puṇṇakamāṇava Pucchā	SP	KN	Sn 57
Puṇṇovāda Sutta	SP	MN	145
Puppha Vagga	SP	KN	Dhp 4
Purābheda Sutta	SP	KN	Sn 4:10
Pūraḷāsa Sutta[8]	SP	KN	Sn 30
Rādha Saṃyutta	SP	SN	23
Rāhula Saṃyutta	SP	SN	18
Rāhula Sutta	SP	KN	Sn 23
Raja Vagga	SP	MN	
Ratana Sutta	SP	KN	Khp 6
Ratana Sutta	SP	KN	Sn 13
Rathavinīta Sutta	SP	MN	24
Raṭṭhapāla Sutta	SP	MN	82
Sabbāsava Sutta	SP	MN	2
Sabhiya Sutta	SP	KN	Sn 32

8. This is an alternate title for the Sundarikabhāradvāja Sutta.

Sacca Saṃyutta	SP	SN	56
Saccavibhaṅga Sutta	SP	MN	141
Sagātha Vagga	SP	SN	
Sahassa Vagga	SP	KN	Dhp 8
Sakkapañha Sutta	SP	DN	21
Sakka Saṃyutta	SP	SN	11
Saḷāyatana Saṃyutta	SP	SN	35
Saḷāyatana Vagga	SP	MN	
Saḷāyatana Vagga	SP	SN	
Saḷāyatana-vibhaṅga Sutta	SP	MN	137
Sāleyyaka Sutta	SP	MN	41
Salla Sutta	SP	KN	Sn 34
Sallekha Sutta	SP	MN	8
Samādhi Saṃyutta	SP	SN	34
Samāgama Sutta	SP	MN	104
Samaṇamaṇḍika Sutta	SP	MN	78
Sāmaṇḍaka Saṃyutta	SP	SN	39
Sāmaññaphala Sutta	SP	DN	2
Sammādiṭṭhi Sutta	SP	MN	9
Sammāparibbājanīya Sutta	SP	KN	Sn 25
Sammappadhāna Saṃyutta	SP	SN	49
Sampasādanīya Sutta	SP	DN	28
Saṃyutta Nikāya	SP	3rd Nikāya	
Sandaka Sutta	SP	MN	76
Saṅgārava Sutta	SP	MN	100
Saṅgīti Sutta	SP	DN	33
Saṅkhārupapatti Sutta	SP	MN	120
Sappurisa Sutta	SP	MN	113
Saraṇattaya	SP	KN	Khp 1
Sāriputta Saṃyutta	SP	SN	28
Sāriputta Sutta	SP	KN	Sn 54
Sātāgira Sutta[9]	SP	KN	Sn 9
Satipaṭṭhāna Saṃyutta	SP	SN	47
Satipaṭṭhāna Sutta	SP	MN	10
Sattaka Nipāta	SP	AN	7
Sekha Sutta	SP	MN	53
Sela Sutta	SP	MN	92
Sela Sutta	SP	KN	Sn 33
Sevitabbāsevitabba Sutta	SP	MN	114
Sigālovāda Sutta	SP	DN	31

9. This is an alternate title for the Hemavata Sutta.

Sīhanāda Vagga	SP	MN	
Sīlakkhandha Vagga	SP	DN	
Soṇadaṇḍa Sutta	SP	DN	4
Soṇathera Vagga	SP	KN	5
Sotāpatti Saṃyutta	SP	SN	55
Subha Sutta	SP	DN	10
Subha Sutta	SP	MN	99
Subhāsita Sutta	SP	KN	Sn 29
Sūciloma Sutta	SP	KN	Sn 17
Suddhaṭṭhaka Sutta	SP	KN	Sn 42
Sukha Vagga	SP	KN	Dhp 15
Sunakkhatta Sutta	SP	MN	105
Sundarikabhāradvāja Sutta	SP	KN	Sn 30
Suññata Vagga	SP	MN	
Supaṇṇa Saṃyutta	SP	SN	30
Suttanipāta	SP	KN	
Sutta Piṭaka	SP	2nd of the 3 Piṭakas	
Suttavibhaṅga	VP		
Taṇhā Vagga	SP	KN	Dhp 24
Tatiya Vagga	SP	M	
Tevijja Sutta	SP	DN	13
Tevijjāvacchagotta Sutta	SP	MN	71
Theragāthā	SP	KN	
Therapañha Sutta[10]	SP	KN	Sn 54
Therīgāthā	SP	KN	
Tika Nipāta	SP	AN	3
Tika Nipāta	SP	KN	3
Tirokuḍḍa Sutta	SP	KN	Khp 7
Tissametteyya Sutta	SP	KN	Sn 45
Tissametteyyamāṇava Pucchā	SP	KN	Sn 56
Todeyyamāṇava Pucchā	SP	KN	Sn 63
Tuvaṭaka Sutta	SP	KN	Sn 52
Udāna	SP	KN	
Udayamāṇava Pucchā	SP	KN	Sn 67
Uddesavibhaṅga Sutta	SP	MN	138
Udumbarikasīhanāda Sutta	SP	DN	25
Upakkilesa Sutta	SP	MN	128
Upāli Sutta	SP	MN	56
Upasīvamāṇava Pucchā	SP	KN	Sn 60
Uppāda Saṃyutta	SP	SN	26

10. This is an alternate title for the Sāriputta Sutta.

III. Bibliography

1. Translated Texts

The Pali Text Society (founded in 1881) has published English translations of the Pāli texts from 1909. To date (2011) only the Niddesa and Apadāna from the Khuddaka Nikāya and Yamaka from the Abhidhamma Piṭaka remain untranslated out of the entire Canon. Apart from their own series (PTS, and SBB—*Sacred Books of the Buddhists*), there are six others of note: *Sacred Books of the East* (SBE—reprinted from the 1960s by UNESCO via Motilal Banarsidass, Delhi); *The Wheel* and *Bodhi Leaf* series of the Buddhist Publication Society (BPS); The Maha Bodhi Society in either India or Sri Lanka (MBS); the (now defunct) Bauddha Sahitya Sabha (Buddhist Literature Society—BSS); Wisdom Publications of Boston; and the Buddhist Missionary Society (BMS) of Kuala Lumpur. In addition, a few individual texts have appeared from Sinhalese, Indian, Burmese, Thai, English, and American publishers.

(To avoid the tedium of indicating the years of reprints of those works that have run into several editions, only the years of the first and latest editions have been shown. In the case of BPS publications, however, because these are normally kept in print, only the year of initial publication is shown.)

A. Vinaya Piṭaka

I.B. Horner (tr.) *The Book of the Discipline.* PTS:

1. Suttavibhaṅga, 1938, 1992.
2. Suttavibhaṅga, 1940, 1993.
3. Suttavibhaṅga, 1942, 1993.
4. Mahāvagga, 1951, 1993.
5. Cullavagga, 1952, 1993.
6. Parivāra, 1966, 1993.

T.W. Rhys Davids and H. Oldenberg (tr.) *Vinaya Texts.* SBE:

1. Pātimokkha, Oxford 1881, Delhi 1975, 2003.
2. Mahāvagga, 1882, 1975, 2003.

3. Cullavagga, 1885, 1975, 2003.

P.V. Bapat & A. Hirakawa, *Shan-Chien-P'i-P'o-Sha, A Chinese Version by Saṅghabhadra of Samantapāsādika,* Poona 1970. (Despite the English subtitle, it is not identical with the *Samantapāsādikā,* but perhaps with one of its sources or a parallel version of another, non-Mahāvihāra Theravādin lineage; see Ananda W. Guruge, "*Shan-jian-lu-piposha* as an Authentic Source on the Early History of Buddhism and Asoka," in *Dhamma-Vinaya,* SLABS, Colombo 2005, pp. 91–110. According to Bapat the Chinese translator adapted the *Samantapāsādikā* to fit the Vinaya of the Dharmaguptaka tradition.)

Herbert Baynes, "A Collection of Kammavâcâs (monastic confessionals)," JRAS 1892, pp. 53–75).

J.F. Dickson (tr.), "The Upasampadā Kammavācā, being the Buddhist Manual of the Form and Manner of Ordering Priests and Deacons," Monastero di San Lazzaro degli Armeni, Venice 1875 and JRAS, N.S. VII, 1875, reprinted in Warren, *Buddhism in Translations,* Harvard 1896, and Piyadassi, *Ordination in Theravada Buddhism,* BPS 1963.

—"The Pātimokkha, being the Buddhist Office of the Confession of Priests," JRAS, N.S. VIII, 1876, reprinted *ibid.*

Ñāṇamoli (ed. and tr.), *The Pātimokkha.* Bangkok 1966, 1969.

Ñānatusita Bhikkhu, *A Translation and Analysis of the Pātimokkha,* text, translation and analysis of the Pātimokkha. Kandy 2011.

W. Pachow, "A Comparative Study of the Prātimokṣa on the basis of its Chinese, Tibetan, Sanskrit and Pali versions." *Sino-Indian Studies* 4 (1951), pp.18–46, 51–114, 115–93; 5 (1955), 1–45. Offprinted Delhi 2000.

William Pruitt (ed.) and K.R. Norman (tr.), *The Pātimokkha.* PTS 2001.

Thanissaro (tr.), *The Buddhist Monastic Code I.* Valley Center (CA) 1996, rev.ed., 2007; *II, ibid.*, 2002, rev.ed., 2007.

U Thumana (tr.), *Pārājika Pāḷi.* Yangon [Rangoon] 2001.

Mohan Wijayaratna, "Bhikkhunī-Pātimokkha" (translation and text), Appendix 1/2, in *Buddhist Nuns: The Birth and Development of a Women's Monastic Order.* Colombo 2001, Kandy 2010.

B. Sutta Pitaka

Dīgha Nikāya

T.W. and C.A.F. Rhys Davids (tr.), *Dialogues of the Buddha.* SBB:

1. Suttas 1–13, 1899, 1995.
2. Suttas 14–23, 1910, 1995.

3. Suttas 24–34, 1921, 1995.

Maurice Walshe (tr.), *Thus Have I Heard: The Long Discourses of the Buddha.* London 1987.

Partial translations

P. Anatriello, *The Long Discourses of the Buddha.* Bognor Regis 1986. Comprises a selection with narrative themes.

A.A.G. Bennett (tr. 1–16), *Long Discourses of the Buddha.* Bombay 1964.

Bhikkhu Bodhi (tr.), *Discourse on the All-Embracing Net* of *Views: The Brahmajāla Sutta and its Commentarial Exegesis.* BPS 1978, rev.ed. 2007. Partial offprint: *A Treatise on the Pāramīs.* BPS 1996.

—*The Great Discourse on Causation: The Mahānidāna Sutta and its Commentaries.* BPS 1984, rev.ed., 2000, 2010.

—*The Discourse on the Fruits of Recluseship: The Sāmaññaphala Sutta and its Commentaries.* BPS 1989, rev. ed., 2008.

Acharya Buddharakkhita, *Satipaṭṭhāna System of Meditations.* Bangalore 1980. Pali text and tr. of Mahāsatipaṭṭhāna Sutta (DN 22).

—*The Buddha, the Arahats and the Gods.* Bangalore 1989. Pali text and translation of Mahāsamaya Sutta (DN 20).

—*Invisible Protection.* Bangalore 1990. Pali text and tr. of Āṭānāṭiya Sutta (DN 32).

Burma Piṭaka Association (tr.), *Ten Suttas from Dīgha Nikāya* (DN 1, 2, 9, 15, 16, 22, 26, 28, 29, 31). Rangoon 1984, Sarnath 1987, Delhi 1999.

Steven Collins, "The Discourse on What is Primary (Aggañña-Sutta). An Annotated Translation." *Journal of Indian Philosophy* 21.4 (Dordrecht 1993), pp. 301–93. Offprinted, New Delhi 2001.

Albert J. Edmunds (tr. DN 4), *A dialogue on former existence and on the marvellous birth and career of the Buddhas, between Gotamo and his monks.* Philadelphia 1899.

S.N. Goenka *et al.* (ed.), *Mahā Satipaṭṭhāna Sutta.* Igatpuri 1985. Repr. as *Mahāsatipaṭṭhāna Sutta. Great Discourse on the Establishing of Awareness.* Seattle 1996, Onalaska (WA) 2005.

—and Patrick Given-Wilson, *Satipaṭṭhāna Sutta Discourses.* Igatpuri and Seattle 1998. Talks from a course in Mahāsatipaṭṭhāna Sutta.

Trevor Ling, *The Buddha's Philosophy of Man.* London 1981. Revised versions of Rhys Davids' translations of DN 2, 4, 5, 9, 12, 16, 22, 26, 27, 31.

Usha McNab et al (tr. 32), *The Suttanta on the Marks.* Samatha Trust (Powys, Wales) 1996.

Mahāsi Sayādaw, *Discourse on Sakkapañha Sutta.* Rangoon 1980.

T.W. Rhys Davids (tr.), *Tevijja Sutta.* London 1891. BPS 1963.
—*Kūṭadanta Sutta*, BPS 1968.
—*Sigālovāda Sutta.* Colombo 1972.
—(tr.15 and 22), *Two Dialogues from Dialogues of the Buddha.* New York 1972.
Sīlācāra (tr. 2), *The Fruit of the Homeless Life.* London 1917.
U Sīlānanda (tr. 22), *Four Foundations of Mindfulness.* Boston 1990.
S. Sumaṅgala (tr.), *Saṅgīti Sutta.* MBS, Colombo 1904. Repr.in *The Mahā Bodhi*, 12–13, 2 parts, Calcutta 1905.
Ṭhānissaro Bhikkhu (tr.), *Handful of Leaves. Volume One: An Anthology from the Dīgha and Majjhima Nikāyas.* Santa Cruz (CA) 2002, rev.ed, 2004. Includes DN 2, 11, 12, 15, 16 (5 and 6), 21 (excerpt), 22.
—*Volume Five: An Anthology from the Five Nikāyas.* 2007. Includes DN 9.
Union Buddha Sasana Council (tr.), *Brahmajāla Sutta.* Rangoon 1958.
—*Sāmaññaphala Sutta.* Rangoon 1958.
Sister Vajirā (tr. 21), *Sakka's Quest.* BPS 1959.
Sister Vajirā and Francis Story (tr. 16), *Last Days of the Buddha.* BPS 1964, rev. ed. 1988, 2007.

Majjhima Nikāya

Lord Chalmers (tr.), *Further Dialogues of the Buddha.* SBB:

1. Suttas 1–76, 1926, Delhi 1988.
2. Suttas 77–152, 1927, Delhi 1988.

I.B. Horner (tr.), *The Middle Length Sayings.* PTS:

1. Suttas 1–50, 1954, 1995.
2. Suttas 51–100, 1957, 1994.
3. Suttas 101–152, 1959, 1993.

Bhikkhu Ñāṇamoli and Bhikkhu Bodhi (tr.), *The Middle Length Discourses of the Buddha.* Boston 1995, 2005.

Partial translations

Egerton C. Baptist, *The Conversion of Saccaka.* Galle, no date. Narrative versions of MN 35 and 36.
Bhikkhu Bodhi (tr.), *The Discourse on the Root of Existence: The Mūlapariyāya Sutta and its Commentarial Exegesis.* BPS 1980, rev.ed., 2006.
Acharya Buddharakkhita (tr. 2), *Mind Overcoming its Cankers.* Bangalore 1978, BPS 2005.
Burma (Myanmar) Piṭaka Association (tr.), *Twenty-Five Suttas from Mūlapaṇṇāsa.* (repr.) Delhi 1990.

—*Twenty-Five Suttas from Majjhimapaṇṇāsa*. *Ibid*. 1991.
—*Twenty-Five Suttas from Uparipaṇṇāsa*. *Ibid*.[11]
David Evans (tr.), *The Discourses of Gotama the Buddha, Middle Collection*. London 1992.
K. Sri Dhammānanda (ed. and tr. 10), *Satipaṭṭhāna Sutta: The Foundations of Mindfulness*. BMS 1982.
Jotiya Dhirasekera (tr. 22), "Parable of the Snake." *Encyclopaedia of Buddhism*, Research Studies Series 1. Colombo 1983.
I.B. Horner (tr. 107 & 125), *Taming the Mind*. BPS 1963.
—(tr. 26), *The Noble Quest*. BPS 1974.
Mahāsi Sayādaw, *A Discourse on the Sallekha Sutta*. Rangoon 1981.
—*Cullavedalla Sutta or Discourse on Various Aspects of the Buddha's Dhamma*. Rangoon 1981.
—*Vammika Sutta*. Rangoon 1982, Selangor 1994.
Ñāṇamoli (tr. 90 *suttas*, ed. Khantipālo), *A Treasury of the Buddha's Discourses*. 3 vols, Bangkok 1980.
—(tr. 122), *The Greater Discourse on Voidness*. BPS 1965.
—(tr. 82), *Raṭṭhapāla Sutta*. BPS 1967.
—(tr. 41, 57, 135, 136), *The Buddha's Words on Kamma*. BPS 1977.
—(tr. 139), *The Exposition of Non-Conflict*. BPS 1979.
—(tr. 9 and commentary), *The Discourse on Right View*. BPS 1991.
Ñāṇananda (tr. 131), *Ideal Solitude*. BPS 1973.
Nārada and Mahinda (tr. 51, 54), *Kandaraka and Potaliya Suttas*. BPS 1965.
—(tr. 60, 63, 56), *Apaṇṇaka, Cūla Māluṅkya and Upāli Suttas*. BPS 1966.
Thich Nhat Hanh (tr. 10), *Transformation and Healing. Sutra on the Four Establishments of Mindfulness*. Berkeley 1990. Includes essay and translations from Chinese Tripiṭaka versions of *sutta* as well.
—(tr. 118), *Breathe! You are Alive: Sutra on the Full Awareness of Breathing*.Berkeley 1990.

---

11. N.B. The Association was founded in Rangoon 1980 and the Foreword to the first translation (by U Htin Fatt, above) was dated 16.11.86. However, the first reprint in 2003 appeared under the authority of the Department for the Promotion and Propagation of the Sāsana (Ministry of Religious Affairs) and distributed by the Department of Research & Compilation, Sītagū International Buddhist Academy, Sagaing Hills, Sagaing (Myanmar). A further reprint was printed in Kuala Lumpur and published by Selangor Buddhist Vipassanā Meditation Society in 2004.

—(tr. 131), *Our Appointment with Life*. Berkeley 1990. Includes essay based on Bhaddekaratta Sutta.
—(tr. Chinese equivalent of 22), *Thundering Silence. Sutra on Knowing the Better Way to Catch a Snake*. Berkeley 1993
Nyanaponika (tr. 61, 62, 147), *Advice to Rāhula*. BPS 1961.
—(tr. 22), *The Discourse on the Snake Simile*. BPS 1962.
—(tr. 7, 8), *The Simile of the Cloth and the Discourse on Effacement*. BPS 1964.
—(tr. 28), *The Greater Discourse on the Elephant footprint Simile*. BPS 1966.
Nyanasatta (tr. 10), *The Foundations of Mindfulness*. BPS 1960.
Sīlācāra (tr.), *The First Fifty Discourses*. Breslau-London 1912, Munich 1924, Delhi 2005.
Soma (tr. 10 and commentary), *The Way of Mindfulness*. Kandy 1941, Colombo 1949, BPS 1967, 2003.
—(tr. 9 and commentary), *Right Understanding*. BSS 1946.
—(tr. 10), *Foundations of Mindfulness*. Colombo 1956, Dehiwela 1962.
—(tr. 20), *The Removal of Distracting Thoughts*. BPS 1960.
—(tr. 27), *The Lesser Discourse on the Elephant-footprint Simile*. BPS 1960.
—(tr. 35), *An Old Debate on Self*. BPS 1962.
S. Sumaṅgala (tr.), *Mūlapariyāya Sutta*. MBS, Colombo 1908.
Ṭhānissaro Bhikkhu (tr.), *Handful of Leaves. Volume One: An Anthology from the Dīgha and Majjhima Nikāyas*. Santa Cruz (CA) 2002, rev.ed.,2004. Includes MN 1, 2, 4, 18–20, 21 (excerpt), 24, 36 (excerpt), 44, 45, 58, 61, 63, 72, 75 (excerpt), 82 (excerpt), 87, 95 (excerpt), 105, 106, 108, 109, 110, 117–119, 121, 126, 131, 135, 138, 140, 146, 148, 149, 152.
—*Volume Five: An Anthology from the Five Nikāyas*. 2007. Includes MN 9, 13, 14, 22, 26–28, 53, 54 (excerpt), 66, 70, 78, 82 (excerpt), 86, 90, 101, 122, 137, 143.

Saṃyutta Nikāya

The Book of the Kindred Sayings. PTS, reprinted Delhi 2005:

1. Saṃyuttas 1–11, tr. C.A.F. Rhys Davids, 1917, 1993.
2. Saṃyuttas 12–21, tr. C.A.F. Rhys Davids and F.L. Woodward, 1922, 1990.
3. Saṃyuttas 22–34, tr. F.L. Woodward, 1927, 1995.
4. Saṃyuttas 35–44, 1927, 1993.
5. Saṃyuttas 45–56, 1930, 1994.

Partial translations

Bhikkhu Bodhi (tr.), *The Connected Discourses of the Buddha*. 2 vols, Boston 2000.
—(tr. 12:23), *Transcendental Dependent Arising*. BPS 1980. A translation and exposition of the Upanisa Sutta, from the Nidānasaṃyutta.
Buddharakkhita (tr. 56:11), *Setting in Motion the Wheel of Truth*. Bangalore 1990.
Burma (Myanmar) Piṭaka Association (tr.), *Nidāna Saṃyutta*. Delhi 1993.
—*Khandha Saṃyutta*. Delhi 1996.
U Hla Maung (tr.), *Saḷātanavagga Saṃyutta: Division of Discourses with Verses*. Yangon 1998.
John D. Ireland (tr.), *Saṃyutta Nikāya: An Anthology I*. BPS 1967.
U Ko Lay (tr.), *Mahāvagga Saṃyutta: Division of Discourses with Verses*. Yangon 1998.
Mahāsi Sayādaw (tr. 22:22), *Bhāra Sutta or Discourse on the Burden of Khandha*. Rangoon 1980.
—(tr. 56:11), *Discourse on the Wheel of Dhamma*. Rangoon 1981.
—(tr.22:122), *Discourse on Silavanta Sutta*. Rangoon 1982.
—(tr. SN 35:95), *Mālukyaputta Sutta*. Rangoon 1981, Selangor 1992.
—(tr. 22:59), *Anattalakkhaṇa Sutta or Great Discourse on Not Self*. Rangoon 1983, Bangkok 1996.
N.K.G. Mendis (ed. and tr. 22:59), *On the No-Self Characteristic*. BPS 1979.
Ñāṇamoli (tr. 22:59, 35:28, 56:11), *Three Cardinal Discourses of the Buddha*. BPS 1960.
—(tr. 10:60), *The Girimānanda Sutta: Ten Contemplations*. BPS 1972.
Ñāṇananda (tr.), *Saṃyutta Nikāya: An Anthology II*. BPS 1972.
Nārada (tr.), *The First Discourse of the Buddha*. Colombo 1972.
Nyanaponika (tr. Vedanā-Saṃyutta), *Contemplation of Feeling*. BPS 1983, 2008.
Nyanasatta (tr. 35:197, 200—abridged), *Two Buddhist Parables*. BPS 1958.
Soma (ed. and tr.), *Dhammacakkappavattana Sutta*. BPS 1960, 2011.
Ṭhānissaro Bhikkhu (tr.), *Handful of Leaves. Volume Two: An Anthology from the Saṃyutta Nikāya*. Santa Cruz (CA) 2003, rev.ed., 2006. Comprises 189 suttas.
—*Volume Five: An Anthology from the Five Nikāyas*. 2007. Includes 74 suttas.
U Tin U (tr.), *Sagāthavagga Saṃyutta: Division of Discourses with Verses*. Yangon 1998, Delhi 2004.

Sister Vajirā (tr.), *Dhammacakkapavattana Sutta*. MBS, Sarnath 1944, 1952.

M.O'C. Walshe (tr.), *Saṃyutta Nikāya: An Anthology III*. BPS 1985.

Aṅguttara Nikāya

The Book of the Gradual Sayings. PTS, reprinted Delhi 2006:

1. Nipātas 1–3, tr. F.L. Woodward, 1932, 1993.
2. Nipāta 4, 1933, 1990.
3. Nipātas 5–6., tr. E. M. Hare, 1934, 1995.
4. Nipātas 7–9, 1935, 1993.
5. Nipātas 10–11, tr. F.L. Woodward, 1936, 1994.

Partial translations

Bhikkhu Bodhi (tr.), *Numerical Discourses of the Buddha. An Anthology of Suttas from the Aṅguttara Nikāya*. Walnut Creek (CA) 1999.

E.R.J. Gooneratne (tr. 1–3), *Aṅguttara Nikāya*. Galle 1913.

E. Hardy (ed.), *Aṅguttara-Nikāya V*. PTS 1900, 1958. Appendix I. Analytical Table of the eleven Nipātas.

A.D. Jayasundera (tr. IV), *The Book of the Numerical Sayings*. Adyar 1925.

Susan Elbaum Jootla (tr. 9:20), *The Scale of Good Deeds: The Message of the Velāma Sutta*. BPS 1990.

Mahāsi Sayādaw, *Discourse on Ariyāvāsa Sutta* (4:28). Rangoon 1980.

Ñāṇananda, *The Magic of the Mind*. BPS 1974. An exposition of the Kālakārāma Sutta (4:24).

Nyanaponika (tr.), *Aṅguttara Nikāya: An Anthology II*. BPS 1972, rev.ed. by Bhikkhu Bodhi, 2007.

Soma (tr. 3:56), *Kālāma Sutta: The Buddha's Charter of Free Enquiry*. BPS 1959. Repr.in Nyanaponika (ed.) *The Road to Inner Freedom*. BPS 1982.

Ṭhānissaro Bhikkhu (tr.), *Handful of Leaves. Volume Three: An Anthology from the Aṅguttara Nikāya*. Santa Cruz (CA) 2003. Comprises 194 suttas.

—*Volume Five: An Anthology from the Five Nikāyas*. 2007. Includes 67 suttas.

U Thein Maung (tr.), *Ekaka & Duka Nipāta Pāḷi*. Yangon 2001.

—*Tika Nipāta Pāḷi*. *Ibid*.

Saber Uddiyan (tr. & commentary), *Kalama Sutta: The Buddha's Charter of Free Enquiry*. Kathmandu 2010.

Khuddaka Nikāya

Khuddakapāṭha

Bhadragaka, *Khuddaka-Pāṭha or Short Buddhist Recitations.* Bangkok 1953

N.K. Bhagwat (tr.). Bombay 1931.

Acharya Buddharakkhita, *Khuddaka Pāṭha.* Bangalore 1980.

Robert Caesar Childers, "*Khuddaka Pāṭha,*" JRAS, N.S IV (1870), pp. 309–39.

Ñāṇamoli, *Minor Readings.* PTS 1960, 1991.

Pe Maung Tin (tr.). Rangoon 1913.

C.A.F. Rhys Davids, *The Text of the Minor Sayings.* SBB 1931, 1997.

Sangharakshita (v–ix) serialised in *The Mahā Bodhi* 58, Calcutta 1950, reprinted in *The Enchanted Garden.* FWBO, London 1978, 1980.

Ṭhānissaro Bhikkhu (tr.), *Handful of Leaves. Volume Four: An Anthology from the Khuddaka Nikāya.* Santa Cruz (CA) 2003, rev.ed., 2006..

F.L. Woodward in *Some Sayings of the Buddha.* London 1925, 1960, New York 1973.

Dhammapada

Translated under the following titles if different from Dhammapada:

E.W. Adikaram (tr.). Colombo 1954.

Bhikkhu Ānandajoti (ed.), *A Comparative Edition of the Dhammapada.* Battaramulla 2007. Pali text with parallels from Sanskritised Prakrit, edited together with a study of the Dhammapada collection.

B. Ānanda Maitreya (tr.), serialised in *Pali Buddhist Review* 1 and 2, London 1976–77, and off printed as *Law Verses.* Colombo 1978, rev. ed., New York 1988.

Anon, comp. or tr. for The Cunningham Press, Alhambra (CA) 1955. Repr. by The Theosophical Society, Bombay 1957, 1965.

J. Austin (comp.). The Buddhist Society, London 1945, 1978.

Irving Babbitt (tr.). New York 1936, 2009.

Anne Bancroft (comp.). Rockport (MA), Shaftesbury and Brisbane 1997.

N.V. Banerjee (ed. and tr.). New Delhi 1989, 2000.

Bhadragaka (comp.), *Collection of Verses on the Doctrine of the Buddha.* Bangkok 1952 (printed 1965!).

N.K. Bhagwat (tr.). Bombay 1931, Hong Kong 1968.

Srikrishna Datta Bhatta (tr.), *nava saṃhita.* Varanasi 1972. Text 'rearranged' by Vinoba.

S. Brahmachari (ed. Devanagari text & tr.). Bodhgaya 1980.
A.P. Buddhadatta (ed. and tr.). Colombo 1954, Bangkok 1971.
Acharya Buddharakkhita (tr.). MBS, Bangalore 1966, Buddhayoga Meditation Society, Fawnskin (CA), Syarikat Dharma, Kuala Lumpur 1984, BPS 1985, 2007.
E.W. Burlingame (tr. incl. commentary). *Buddhist Legends.* 3 vols, Harvard 1921, PTS 1979. Selected and rev. by Khantipālo for *Buddhist Stories.* 4 vols, BPS 1982–88.
Thomas Byrom (comp.). London 1976.
John Ross Carter and Mahinda Palihawadana (ed. and tr.). New York and Oxford 1987, 1998; without the commentary, 2000.
Thomas Cleary (tr.). New York and London 1995.
J.P. Cooke and O.G. Pettis (tr.). Boston 1898.
Department of Pali, University of Rangoon, *Dhammapada Commentary.* Rangoon 1966.
U. Dhammajoti (tr.). MBS, Benares 1944.
Eknath Easwaran (tr.). Blue Mountain Center, Berkeley 1986, London 1987.
Albert J. Edmunds (tr.), *Hymns of the Faith.* La Salle (IL) 1902.
Anthony Elenjimittam, *Buddha's Teachings.* Allahabad 1975.
David Evans (tr.), *The Dhamma Way.* Leeds 1988.
Gil Fronsdal (tr.). Boston 2005.
D.J. Gogerly (tr. vaggas 1–18) in *The Friend IV,* Colombo 1840. Repr. in *Ceylon Friend,* Colombo 1881 and in his collected works, *Ceylon Buddhism II,* London 1908.
James Gray (tr.). Rangoon 1881, Calcutta 1887.
K. Gunaratana (tr.). Penang 1937.
Norton T.W. Hazeldine (tr.), *The Dhammapada, or the Path of Righteousness.* Denver 1902.
Amara Hewamadduma (ed.), *Dhammapada, Pali-Sinhala-Tamil-English Version.* Colombo 1994.
Raghavan Iyer (ed. and tr.). Santa Barbara 1986.
U.D. Jayasekera (ed. and tr.). Dehiwela 1992.
David J. Kalupahana (ed. and tr.), *A Path of Righteousness.* Lanham 1986.
Suzanne Karpeles (? tr.), serialised in *Advent.* Pondicherry 1960–65. Repr. in *Questions and Answers, Collected Works of the Mother 3.* Pondicherry 1977.
Harischandra Kaviratna (ed. and tr.), *Wisdom of the Buddha.* Theosophical University Press, Pasadena 1980.
Khantipālo (tr.), *Growing the Bodhi Tree.* Bangkok 1966; *The Path of Truth.* Bangkok 1977. Repr. as *Verses of the Buddha's Teaching.*

Kaohsiung 1989.
Ravindra Kumar (tr. into Hindi and English), *Gautama Buddha and the Dhammapada*. New Delhi 2007.
C. Kunhan Raja (ed. Devanāgarī text & tr.), *Dhammapada, holy text of the Buddhists.* Adyar 1956, Madras 1984.
P. Lal (tr.). New York 1967.
Geri Larkin, *The Still Point Dhammapada: living the Buddha's essential teachings.* New York and San Francisco 2003.
T. Latter (tr.). Moulmein 1850.
Wesley La Violette (free rendering and interpretation). Los Angeles 1956.
Jack Maguire, Woodstock (VT) 2005.
G.P. Malalasekera (tr. unpublished by PTS). Colombo 1969.
Juan Mascaro (tr.). Harmondsworth 1973.
F. Max Müller (tr.). London 1870, SBE—Oxford 1881, New York 1887, Delhi 2004, St.Petersburg (FL) 2008). Included in John B. Alphonso-Karkala, *An Anthology of Indian Literature* (Harmondsworth 1971 - selection only), Lewis Browne, *The World's Greatest Scriptures* New York 1945, 1961 - selection only), E.A. Burtt, *The Teachings of the Compassionate Buddha* (New York 1955, 1963), Allie M. Frazier, *Readings in Eastern Religious Thought* II (Philadelphia 1969 - selection only), C.H. Hamilton, *Buddhism, a Religion of Infinite Compassion* (New York 1952), Charles F. Horne, *The Sacred Books and Early Literature of the East* X (New York 1917, Delhi 1987), Raymond van Over, *Eastern Mysticism* I (New York 1977 - selection only), Lin Yutang, *The Wisdom of China and India* (New York 1942) and *The Wisdom of India* (London 1944, Bombay 1966).
Mya Tin (tr.). Rangoon 1986, Yangon 1990 (verses, stories, verses), Delhi 1990, Yangon 1993 (verses only), Sagaing 2003, Selangor 2004.
Nārada (ed. and tr.). Kandy 1940, London 1954, 1972, Saigon 1963, Calcutta 1970, Colombo and New Delhi 1972, BMS 1978, Taipei 1993, Dehiwela 2000, and, with summary of commentary to each verse by K. Sri Dhammānanda, BMS 1988; tr. incl. in *The Path of Buddhism*, Colombo 1956.
K.R. Norman (tr.), *The Word of the Doctrine*. PTS 1997, 2000.
Piyadassi (tr.), *Selections from the Dhammapada*. Colombo 1974.
Piyadassi (tr. incl. Commentary), *Stories of Buddhist India*. 2 vols, Moratuwa 1949, 1953.
Swami Premananda (tr.), *The Path of the Eternal Law.* Self-Realisation Fellowship, Washington (DC) 1942.

S. Radhakrishnan (ed. and tr.). Oxford 1950, 1991, Madras 1968, 1997, Delhi 1980; incl. in S. Radhakrishnan and Charles A. Moore (ed.), *A Source Book in Indian Philosophy*. Princeton and Oxford 1957, and *The Buddhism Omnibus*. New Delhi and New York 2004.

P. Sri Ramachandrudu (ed. Devanagari text & tr.), Hyderabad 1976.

C.A.F. Rhys Davids (ed. and tr.),. *Verses on Dhamma*. PTS 1931, 1997.

Valerie J. Roebuck (tr.), London 2010.

Sangharakshita (tr. vaggas 1–12) serialised in *FWBO Newsletter*, London 1969 ff.

W. Sarada (Mahāthera), *Treasury of Truth: Illustrated Dhammapada*. Singapore 1994. Pali text, explanatory translation of the verses with commentary.

K.T.S. Sarao (ed. & tr.), *The Dhammapada. A Translator's Guide*. New Delhi 2009.

S.E.A. Scherb (tr.), "The golden verses of the Buddha." A selection for the *Christian Register*, Boston 1861.

Karma Yonten Senge (Lawrence R. Ellyard), *Everyday Buddha. A Contemporary Rendering of the Buddhist Classic, The Dhammapada*. New Alresford (Hampshire) 2005.

Mahesh Kumar Sharan (ed. and tr.). New Delhi 2006.

Sīlācāra (tr.), *The Way of Truth*. The Buddhist Society of Great Britain and Ireland, London 1915.

Sīlānanda (ed. and tr.), *The Eternal Message of Lord Buddha*. Calcutta 1982.

B. Siri Sivali (tr.). Colombo 1954, 1961.

W. Somalokatissa (tr.). Colombo 1953, 1969

Ṭhānissaro Bhikkhu (Geoffrey DeGraff, tr.). Barre (MA) 1998.

Roger Tite (comp.—unpublished). Southampton 1974.

P.L. Vaidya (tr.). Poona 1923, 1934.

W.D.C. Wagiswara and K.J. Saunders (tr.), *The Buddha's Way of Virtue*. London 1912, 1927.

Glenn Wallis (tr.), *Verses on the Way*. New York 2004.

Sathienpong Wannapok (tr.), *The Buddha's Words*. Bangkok 1979, 1988

S.W. Wijayatilake (tr.), *The Way of Truth*. Madras 1934.

F.L. Woodward (tr.), *The Buddha's Path of Virtue*. Adyar 1921, 1949.

Udāna

Bhadragaka (tr.), *80 Inspiring Words of the Buddha*. Bangkok 1954.

John D. Ireland (tr.), *The Udāna: Inspired Utterances of the Buddha*. BPS 1990. Reprinted as *The Udāna and Itivuttaka*. BPS 2007.

Peter Masefield (tr.), *The Udāna*. PTS 1994.

D.M. Strong (tr.), *The Solemn Utterances of the Buddha*. London 1902.

Ṭhānissaro Bhikkhu, *Handful of Leaves. Volume Four* (*op.cit.*). Excluding I.4, 5, 7–9; II.8; III.6, 9; IV.2, 5, 8; V.8; VI.1, 10; VII.5, 7, 8; VIII.5–7.

F.L. Woodward (tr.), *Verses of Uplift*. SBB 1935, 1948.

Itivuttaka

John D. Ireland (tr.), *The Itivuttaka: The Buddha's Sayings*. BPS 1991. Repr. as *The Udāna and Itivuttaka*. BPS 2007.

J.H. Moore (tr.), *Sayings of the Buddha*. New York 1908,1965, New Delhi 1981.

Peter Masefield (tr.), *The Itivuttaka*. PTS 2000.

Ṭhānissaro Bhikkhu (tr.), *This Was Said by the Buddha*. Barre (MA) 2001. Also in *Handful of Leaves. Volume Four* (*op.cit.*).

F.L. Woodward (tr.), *As it was Said*. SBB 1935, 1948.

Sutta-Nipāta

G.F. Allen (tr. 4), *Aṭṭhaka*. Bambalapitiya 1958. Repr. in G.F. Allen *The Buddha's Philosophy*. London 1959.

Lord Chalmers (ed. and tr.), *Buddha's Teachings*. Cambridge (MA) 1932,1999, Delhi 2000.

Sir Muthu Coomaraswamy (tr. 1, 2, 3:7–9, 4:1), *Dialogues and Discourses of Gotama Buddha*. London 1874.

V. Fausböll (tr.), *A Collection of Discourses*. SBE, Oxford 1880, Delhi 1988.

E.M. Hare (tr.), *Woven Cadences of Early Buddhists*. SBB 1945, 1947.

John D. Ireland (tr. selection), *The Discourse Collection*. BPS 1965.

N.A. Jayawickrama, *Suttanipāta: Text and Translation*. Post-Graduate Institute of Pali and Buddhist Studies, Colombo. 2001.

(Mom Chao) Upalisan Jumbala (tr. 5), *The Solasapañha*. Bangkok 1956

Mahāsi Sayādaw, *A Discourse on Hemavata Sutta*. Rangoon 1980.

—*Sammā Paribbājaniya Sutta*. Rangoon 1981.

—*Tuvataka Sutta*. Rangoon 1982.

—*Purābheda Sutta or The Dhamma One Should Accomplish Before Death*. Rangoon 1983.

K.R. Norman (tr.) with alternative translations by I.B. Horner and Walpola Rāhula, *Group of Discourses* I. PTS 1984; repr. as *The Rhinoceros Horn and other Early Buddhist Poems*. PTS 1985; rev. tr. with introduction and notes by K.R. Norman, PTS 1992, repr. with corrections, PTS 2006.

Nyanaponika (ed. and tr. 1:1), *The Worn-Out Skin*. BPS 1977.

Piyasīlo (tr.), *Book of Discourses I*. Petaling Jaya 1989.
H. Saddhātissa (tr.), *The Sutta-Nipāta*. London 1985.
Ṭhānissaro Bhikkhu (tr.) *Handful of Leaves. Volume Four* (*op.cit.*). Excluding I.6, 7, 9; II.2, 5–7, 11–14; III.4–7, 9, 10; IV.5.
U Tin Oo (tr.), Sagaing and Selangor 2002.
Sister [UK] Vajirā (and SL Dhammajoti)
I. Uragavagga. MBS, Sarnath 1941; II. Cūlavagga. *Ibid.* 1942.

Vimānavatthu and Petavatthu

Henry S. Gehman (tr.), *Stories of the Departed*. SBB 1942, 1993.
I.B. Horner (tr.), *Stories of the Mansions*. SBB 1993.
U Htin Fatt (tr. Vimānavatthu), Sagaing and Selangor 2002; (tr. Petavatthu), Sagaing 2003, Selangor 2004.
Jean Kennedy (tr.), *Stories of the Mansions*. SBB 1942.
B.C. Law (summaries), *The Buddhist Conception of Spirits*. Calcutta 1923, Varanasi 1974, Delhi 1997, New Delhi 2005.
—*Heaven and Hell in Buddhist Perspective*. Calcutta 1925, Varanasi 1973, Delhi 2005.
P. Masefield (tr.), *Vimāna Stories*. PTS 1990.

Thera-Therīgāthā

V.F. Gunaratana (tr. selection), *The Message of the Saints*. BPS 1969.
Edmund Jayasuriya, *Thera-Therigatha. Inspired Utterances of Buddhist Monks and Nuns* (based on the translations by C.A.F. Rhys Davids and K.R. Norman). Dehiwela 1999.
Khantipālo (tr. verses of Tālapuṭa Thera, with commentary), *Forest Meditations*. BPS 1977.
Susan Murcott, *The First Buddhist Women*. Berkeley 1991. Translation and commentary of Therīgāthā.
K.R. Norman (tr.), *The Elders' Verses*. 2 vols, PTS 1969/71, 2007; I. *Poems of Early Buddhist Monks*, 1997; II. *Poems of Early Buddhist Nuns*, 1997.
Damayanthi Ratwatte (tr.), *Selected Translations of the Theri Gatha: Songs of Buddhist Nuns*. Kandy 1983.
C.A.F. Rhys Davids (tr.), *Psalms of the Brethren*. PTS 1913, 1994.
—*Psalms of the Sisters*. PTS 1909; repr. with Norman II as *Poems of Early Buddhist Nuns*. PTS 1997.
Both Rhys Davids vols repr. as *Psalms of the Early Buddhists*, PTS 1980, and *Sacred Writings of the Buddhists*, 3 vols, New Delhi 1986.
C.A.F. Rhys Davids (tr. selection), *Poems of Cloister and Jungle*. London 1941.
Andrew Schelling and Anne Waldman (tr. selection), *Songs of the Sons and Daughters of Buddha*. Boston 1996.

Soma (tr. verses of Tālapuṭa Thera), *His Last Performance,* Kandy 1943.

Ṭhānissaro Bhikkhu (tr.), *Handful of Leaves. Volumes Four* and *Five* (*op.cit.*). Includes selections from Thag-Thīg.

Jātaka

Ellen C. Babbit, *Jataka Tales.* New York 1912. Retellings.

Ethel Beswick, *Jātaka Tales.* London 1956. 35 tales based on Cowell's tr.

W.B. Bollée (ed. and tr.), *Kuṇāla Jātaka.* SBB 1970.

E.B. Cowell (tr.), *Jātaka Stories.* 6 vols, Cambridge 1895–1905; repr. in 3 vols, PTS 1972, 1981, Delhi 1990, 2008. The only complete translation of the Jātakas.

L.H. Elwell (tr.), *Nine Jātakas.* Boston 1886.

Fausböll (tr.), *Five Jātakas.* Copenhagen and London 1861.

—*The Dasaratha-jātaka, being the Buddhist story of King Rāma. Ibid.* 1871.

—*Ten Jātakas. Ibid.* 1872, Whitefish (MT) 2007.

—*Two Jātakas* (33 and 20). JRAS N.S. V (1871).

H.T. Francis (tr.), *The Vedabbha Jātaka.* Cambridge 1884.

H.T. Francis and E.J. Thomas (tr.), *Jātaka Tales.* Cambridge 1916, Bombay 1970. Comprises 114 tales.

Richard Gombrich and Margaret Cone (tr. Vessantara Jātaka), *The Perfect Generosity of Prince Vessantara.* Oxford 1977.

I.B. Horner (ed. and tr.), *Ten Jātaka Stories.* London 1957, Bangkok 1974. Designed to illustrate each of the Ten Perfections.

N.A. Jayawickrama, *The Story of Gotama Buddha.* PTS 1990, 2002. Translation of *Jātaka-nidāna.*

C.S. Josson, *Stories of Buddha's Births: A Jātaka Reader.* New York 1976.

Ken and Visakha Kawasaki, *Jātaka Tales of the Buddha: An Anthology.* Three volumes. BPS 2010. A retelling besed on Cowell (*op. cit.*).

Rafe Martin, *The Hungry Tigress: Buddhist Legends and Jātaka Tales.* Berkeley 1990. A free retelling of selected Jātakas and other Buddhist stories.

R. Morris (tr.), "Jātaka Tales from the Pali." *Folklore Journal* II–IV, London 1887.

Piyasīlo, *Jātaka Stories.* Petaling Jaya, Selangor 1983. A free adaptation of the last ten Jātakas.

C.A.F. Rhys Davids (tr.), *Stories of the Buddha.* London 1929, New York 1989. Comprises 47 tales.

T.W. Rhys Davids (tr.), *Buddhist Birth Stories.* London 1880; rev. ed. by C.A.F. Rhys Davids, 1925, and Leiden and Delhi 1973, 2004.

Comprises the *Nidāna-Kathā* and the first 40 Jātakas.
Sarah Shaw (tr.), *The Jātakas: Birth Stories of the Bodhisatta*. Delhi and New York 2006. Comprises 26 tales.
E. Wray, C. Rosenfield and D. Bailey, *Ten Lives of the Buddha. Thai temple paintings and Jātaka tales.* New York 1972.

Paṭisambhidāmagga

Ñāṇamoli (tr.), *The Path of Discrimination*. PTS 1982, 1997.

Apadāna

Jonathan S. Walters (tr.), "Gotami's Story." *Buddhism in Practice,* ed. Donald S.Lopez. Princeton 1995, pp. 113–38.

Buddhavaṃsa

I.B. Horner (tr.), *Chronicle of Buddhas.* SBB 1975.
B.C. Law (tr.), *The Lineage of the Buddhas.* SBB 1938.
Meena Talin (tr.), *The Genealogy of the Buddhas.* Bombay 1969.
Vicittasārābhivaṃsa (Mingun Sayādaw), *The Great Chronicle of Buddhas.* Rangoon 1994, Selangor 1997. Translation of the Burmese edition of the Buddhavaṃsa in 6 vols and 8 books. Including copious explanations by the Mingun Sayādaw.

Cariyāpiṭaka

I.B. Horner (tr.), *Basket of Conduct*. SBB 1975.
B.C. Law (tr.), *Collection of Ways of Conduct*. SBB 1938.

C. Abhidhamma Pitaka

Dhammasaṅgaṇī: tr. U Kyaw Khine, *The Dhammasangini: Enumeration of Ultimate Realities.* Yangon 1996; 2 vols., Delhi 1999.
—tr. C.A.F. Rhys Davids, *A Buddhist Manual of Psychological Ethics.* RAS, London 1900, Delhi 1975, 1996. PTS reprint 1974, 1993.
Vibhaṅga: tr. U Thittila, *The Book of Analysis.* PTS 1969,1988.
Dhātukathā: tr. U Nārada, *Discourse on Elements.* PTS 1962, 1995.
Puggalapaññatti: tr. B.C. Law, *A Designation of Human Types.* PTS 1922, 1992.
Kathāvatthu: tr. S.Z. Aung and C.A.F. Rhys Davids, *Points of Controversy.* PTS 1915, 1993.
Yamaka I (I–V): tr. U Nārada and U Kumārābhivaṃsa, *The Book on Pairs.* Penang 1998.
Paṭṭhāna (part of the Tikapaṭṭhāna): tr. U Nārada, *Conditional Relations.* PTS I. 1969, 1992, II. 1981, 1993.

2. Anthologies

G.F. Allen, *Buddha's Words of Wisdom*. London 1959, Dehiwela 2002. Sayings for each day of the year compiled from SP, mainly Sn.

Herbert Baynes (tr.), *The Way of the Buddha*. London 1906, New York 1913. Including Dhp XX—The Way.

Stephan Beyer (tr.), *The Buddhist Experience: Sources and Interpretations*. Belmont 1974.

Bhikkhu Bodhi (ed.), *In the Buddha's Words. An Anthology of Discourses from the Pāli Canon*. Boston 2005. Large collection organised on the scheme of the three benefits of practice of the Dhamma.

E.M. Bowden, *The Imitation of Buddha*. London 1891, Delhi 1989. Quotations from mainly Pāli texts for each day of the year.

E.H. Brewster, *The Life of Gotama the Buddha*. London 1926, Varanasi 1975. Compiled exclusively from the Pāli Canon as tr. by the Rhys Davids.

Kerry Brown and Joanne O'Brien (eds.), *The Essential Teachings of Buddhism*. London 1989. Includes I. Theravada: 1. Thailand—daily readings from SP compiled by Ajahn Tīradhammo; 2. Sri Lanka—same, by W. G. Weeraratna and Dhanapala Samarasekara.

Buddhist Lodge, The, *Selected Buddhist Scriptures from the Pāli Canon of the Theravāda School*. London 1930.

E.W. Burlingame (tr.), *Buddhist Parables*. New Haven 1922, Delhi 2004. Comprises over 200 allegories, anecdotes, fables and parables from VP, SP, AN, Dhp Commentaries, and Mil.

—*The Grateful Elephant and Other Stories*. New Haven 1923. 26 stories extracted from *Buddhist Parables*.

E.A. Burtt (ed.), *The Teachings of the Compassionate Buddha*. New York 1955, 1963. Includes selections from Mahāvagga and Thera-Therīgāthā (Rhys Davids), Dhp (Max Müller), Sn (Chalmers), etc.

Paul Carus, *The Gospel of Buddha*. LaSalle (IL) 1894, London 1943, 1974, Tucson (AZ) 1972, New Delhi 1981, Varanasi 2006. Selection offprinted as *Sayings of Buddha*. New York 1957.

Edward Conze, (ed.) *Buddhist Texts through the Ages*. Oxford 1954, New York 1964, New Delhi 2008. Includes I.B. Horner (tr.) selection mainly from VP and SP.

—(tr.) *Buddhist Scriptures*. Harmondsworth 1959, 1971.

—*The Way of Wisdom: The Five Faculties*. BPS 1964. Illustrated from MN, SN, Mil and Vism.

A.K. Coomaraswamy and I.B. Horner (tr.), *The Living Thoughts of Gotama the Buddha*. London 1948, Bombay 1956, New Delhi 1982, Delhi 1999, Louisville (KY) 2001. Includes extracts from VP and SP (and Commentaries), Mil and Vism.

S. Dhammika (ed. & tr.) *Gemstones of the Good Dhamma*. BPS 1987. A short selection of verses from SP and Mil, Pāli and English on facing pages.

—(comp.), *Buddha Vacana, Daily Readings from Sacred Literature of Buddhism*. Singapore 1989.

Sudhakar Dikshit, *Sermons and Sayings of the Buddha*. Bombay 1958, 1977. A selection from VP and SP.

Albert J. Edmunds, "Gospel Parallels from Pali Texts." *The Open Court* XIV-XVI, 1900–1902. A collection of excerpts from the Pāli canon, presented to show their thematic relation to Christian scriptures.

David Evans, *The Buddha Digest: Modern verses based on ancient texts*. (published privately) Leeds 2000.

—*The Buddha Digest: Modern transcriptions of Pali texts. Ibid.* 2004.

The Five Nikāyas: Discourses of the Buddha I. Rangoon 1978. Offprints from *The Light of the Dhamma*, including the Pātimokkha, DN 1–3, MN 21, 26, 33, 44, 55, 67, 118, 129, 135, SN 12:1, 62, 70; 22:56, 57, 59, 86; 35:132, 197, 241; 55:7; 56:11; AN 1:1–50; 3:55, 61; 4:53; 5:33, 145, 171, 174, 180; 6:63; 8:30, 34, 41; Khp 7, Sn II:2 and *suttas* selections from the Vibhaṅga and Dhp Commentary.

N. Gangulee, *The Buddha and His Message*. Bombay 1957.

Rupert Gethin (tr.), *Sayings of the Buddha*. Oxford 2008. Includes DN 2, 16, 17, 27, 31; MN 10, 20, 22, 63, 85, 136; and selections from SN and AN.

Dwight Goddard (ed.), *A Buddhist Bible*. New York 1932, Boston 1970. Includes DN 13, MN 118, all of Nyanatiloka's *Word of the Buddha*.

C.H. Hamilton, *Buddhism, a Religion of Infinite Compassion*. New York 1952. Includes selections from SP in standard early translations.

John J. Holder (tr.), *Early Buddhist Discourses*. Indianapolis 2006. Comprises new translations of DN 9, 13, 15, 22, 26, 31, MN 18, 22, 26, 38, 58, 63, 72, 93, Kālāma Sutta and extracts from SN.

I.B. Horner (tr.from SP), *Early Buddhist Poetry*. Colombo 1963.

Christmas Humphreys, *Thus Have I Heard*. The Buddhist Society, London 1948. A reprint of *Selected Buddhist Scriptures ...*, *op.cit.*

Khantipālo, *The Splendour of Enlightenment*. 2 vols, Bangkok 1976. A life of the Buddha extracted from Pāli (PTS Translation Series) and early Buddhist Sanskrit texts

—*Buddha, My Refuge: Contemplation of the Buddha based on the Pali Suttas*. BPS 1990. Texts on the Buddha from SP, arranged by way of the nine Buddha-virtues (*Buddhaguṇa*).

David Maurice (tr.), *The Lion's Roar*. London 1962, New York 1967. Anthology mostly from SP, includes Pātimokkha.

Ñāṇamoli, *The Practice of Loving kindness*. BPS 1959. Comprises the Karaṇīyametta Sutta and short extracts from texts on this subject.

—*Mindfulness of Breathing*. BPS 1964. Includes MN 118 and related passages.

—(tr.) *The Life of the Buddha*. BPS 1972, 2006 (Seattle 2001). Compiled from VP and SP. Partial offprint as *The Buddha's Teaching in His Own Words*. BPS 1998.

Nārada, (tr), *The Life of Buddha (in his own words)*. Adyar 1931.

—(tr.), *Everyman's Ethics*. BPS 1959. Comprises DN 31, AN 8:54, Sn 1:6, 2:4. Republished in *A Constitution for Living*. BPS 2007.

Nyanaponika (tr.), *The Five Mental Hindrances*. BSS 1947, BPS 1961. Selected passages from the Canon and Commentaries.

—*The Four Nutriments of Life*. BPS 1967. A selection mainly from SN and its Commentary.

—*The Roots of Good and Evil*. BPS 1978. Extracts mainly from AN.

Nyanatiloka (tr.), *Word of the Buddha*. Rangoon 1907, London 1950, Santa Barbara (CA) 1950, 18th English ed., BPS 2001. The first really systematic exposition of the entire teachings of the Buddha presented in the Master's own words as found in the Sutta Piṭaka in the form of the Four Noble Truths.

—(tr.) *The Buddha's Path to Deliverance,* in its Threefold Division and Seven Stages of Purity. BSS 1952, BPS 1982. Compiled from SP.

Geoffrey Parrinder, *The Wisdom of the Early Buddhists*. London 1977. 108 extracts mainly from DN (Rhys Davids) and MN (Horner), reprinted as *The Sayings of the Buddha*. London 1991.

S. Radhakrishnan and Charles A. Moore (ed.), *A Source Book in Indian Philosophy*. Princeton-Oxford 1957. Includes MN 141 (Chalmers), Dhp (Radhakrishnan), extracts from the Udāna and Itivuttaka (Woodward), etc.

T.W. Rhys Davids (tr.), *Buddhist Suttas*. SBE 1881, New York 1969, London 2001, Delhi 2003. Comprises DN 13, 16, 17; MN 2, 6, 16; SN 56:11.

Stanley Rice, *The Buddha Speaks Here and Now, Fundamental Buddhist Scriptures interpreted in Contemporary Idiom*. BPS 1981. Reformulations of DN 2, MN 10, 20, 22, 43, 131; several other suttas from SN, AN, and Sn.

K.J. Saunders, *The Heart of Buddhism. An Anthology of Buddhist Verse*. Oxford 1915, Varanasi 1998.

Sayings of the Buddha. Singapore 1993. (Author unknown)

Peter Skilling (ed.), *Beyond Worldly Conditions*. Bangkok 1999. Translations and commentaries on the Lokadhamma Sutta and related texts.

Lucien Stryk (ed.) *World of the Buddha*, New York 1968, 1982. Includes extracts from SP, Mil and Vism (Warren).

J. Subasinha, *Buddhist Rules for the Laity*. Madras 1908, Delhi 1997. Comprises DN 31 and AN 8:54.

Sugatananda (Francis Story), *Saṅgīti*. Rangoon 1954. Includes synopses of DN 1, 13, 27, MN 98, Sn I-7,8, III-3, IV-1,7.

—*Taming the Mind*. BPS 1963. Short passages from SP.

Luang Suriyabongs (comp.), *A Buddhist Anthology*. Bangkok 1956. Extracts from VP and SP on the subjects of the Buddha, Dhamma, Sangha and Lay Disciple.

Ṭhānissaro Bhikkhu (tr.) *Handful of Leaves, Volume Five: An Anthology from the Five Nikāyas*. Redwood City (CA) 2004.

—*That the True Dhamma Might Last a Long Time: Readings Selected by King Asoka. Ibid.* 1996. Suttas which King Asoka selected as representative of the essence of the Dhamma.

J. Thomas (tr.), *Buddhist Scriptures*. London 1913.

—*Early Buddhist Scriptures*. London 1935, New York 1974, New Delhi 1996. Contains a wide selection from SP.

—*The Road to Nirvana*. London 1950, Rutland (VT) 1992. Selected texts.

Vajirañāṇavarorasa *Dhammavibhāga: Numerical Sayings of Dhamma*. 2 vols, Bangkok 1968–70.

Glenn Wallis (tr.), *Basic Teachings of the Buddha. A New Translation and Compilation, with a Guide to Reading the Texts*. New York 2007. 16 suttas including DN 13, 22, MN 63, 118.

E. Ward, *Light from the East, being Selections from the Teachings of the Buddha*. London 1905.

Henry Clarke Warren (tr.), *Buddhism in Translations*. Harvard 1896, New York 1972, 2005, Delhi 2007. Also reprinted as *Buddhist Discourses* (Delhi 1980) and *A Buddhist Reader. Selections from the Sacred Books* (New York 2004). Comprises selections from VP, SP, Jātakas, DN Commentary, Mil and Vism.

—See also *Buddhism: Pali Text with English Translation*, ed. N.C. Panda, rev. & enl. ed., 2 vols, Delhi 2008.
—*The Life of the Buddha*. Harvard 1923, New Delhi 2003, Delhi 2005. Compiled from relevant sections of the above work. Rev. ed., *Everyman's Life of the Buddha*. Conesville 1968. A further selection appeared as *The Wisdom of Buddha*. New York 1968.
F.L. Woodward (tr.), *Some Sayings of the Buddha*. London 1925, 1974, New York 1973, New Delhi 2002. Short passages from VP and SP. Repr. as *The Wisdom of Buddha*. Gurgaon 2005.

3. Devotional Manuals (*romanised Pāli texts and translations*)

Ānandajoti Bhikkhu, *Safeguard Recitals*. Kandy, 2004. An edition and translation of the *Catubhāṇavārapāḷi* or *Mahāparitta*.
Herbert Baynes (ed. & tr.), "The Mirror of Truth, or Bauddha Confession of Faith." *Wiener Zeitschrift für die Kunde des Morgenländes* X, 1896, pp. 242–51.
Acharya Buddharakkhita, *Buddhist Manual for Everyday Practice*. Bangalore 1986.
K. Sri Dhammananda, *Handbook of Buddhists*. BMS 1965—*Daily Buddhist Devotions*. BMS 1991, 1993.
B. Dhammaratana, *Aura of the Dhamma*. Singapore 1979.
S.N. Goenka, *The Gem Set in Gold*. Onalaska (WA) 2006. Dhamma chanting with Pāli and Hindi texts.
Khantipālo, *Buddhist Texts for Recitation*. BPS 1974.
—*Namo: Chanting Book*. Wisemans Ferry, NSW (Australia) 1988.
Khantipālo and Jotimano, *Book of Chants (a compilation, being the romanised edition of the Royal Thai Chanting Book)*. Bangkok 1975.
Mahamakuta Educational Council, *Excerpts from the Book of Recitations*. Bangkok 1957.
Rāngphim Mahāmakutrātchamitthayālai (comp.), *Pali Chanting, with Translations*. Bangkok 1974, 1983.
Nārada and Kassapa, *The Mirror of the Dhamma. Colombo,* 1926, BPS 1963, Dehiwela 2005.
Pe Maung Tin, *Buddhist Devotion and Meditation*. SPCK, London 1964.
B. Pemaratana, *Way to the Buddha*. Penang 1964, 1970.
D.G. Ariyapala Perera, *Buddhist Paritta Chanting Ritual*. Dehiwela 2000.
Piyadassi, *The Book of Protection*. BPS 1975. Translation of the *paritta* book.

Piyasīlo, *The Puja Book: Paritta, Plainchant, and Rites of Passage*. 4 vols, Petaling Jaya 1990–92.
Rewata Dhamma, *Mahā Paritta. The Great Protection*. Birmingham Buddhist Vihara 1996.
H. Saddhātissa, *Handbook of Buddhists*. MBS, Sarnath 1956, 1973.
—and Russell Webb, *A Buddhist's Manual*. MBS, London 1976.
—and Ven. Pesala, *ibid*. 2nd rev. ed., 1990.
H.L. St. Barbe (tr.), "The Namakkāra (stanzas of praise/worship)." JRAS N.S. XV, 1883, pp. 213–20.
U Sīlāndābhivaṃsa (tr. 11 protective *suttas*), *Paritta Pāli and Protective Verses*. Rangoon 2000.
Sao Htun Hmat Win, *Eleven Holy Discourses of Protection*. Mahā Paritta Pāli, including the apocryphal *Pubbaṇha Sutta*. Rangoon 1981.
—*Basic Principles of Burmese Buddhism*. Rangoon 1985.
Somboon Siddhinyano, *Romanization of the Pāli Chanting Book*. Bangkok 1985, Wolverhampton Buddha Vihara 1987.
Jandamit Vorasak (comp.), *Pali Recitations, with English Versions*. Bangkok 1989.
K. Wimalajothi, *Buddhist Chanting*. Dehiwela 2003.

4. Post-Canonical and Commentarial Literature

A. The Commentaries (in English translation)

U Ba Kyaw and P. Masefield, *Peta-Stories*. (*Paramatthadīpanī*, Dhammapāla's commentary on the Petavatthu.) SBB 1980.
Mabel Bode, "Women Leaders of the Buddhist Reformation." [From the *Manorathapurāṇī*, Buddhaghosa's commentary on the Aṅguttara Nikāya.] JRAS 1893, pp. 517–66, 763–98.
Acharya Buddharakkhita, *An Unforgettable Inheritance*. [Commentary on Dhp I and II.] 4 volumes. MBS, Bangalore 1973–89.
E.W. Burlingame, *Buddhist Legends*. [Buddhaghosa's *Dhammapadaṭṭhakathā*.] 3 volumes, Harvard 1921, PTS 1995, Delhi 2005.
P. Godahewa, *Samanta-pāsādikā (Bāhira Nidāna Vaṇṇanā)*. [Introduction to the *Samantapāsādika*, Buddhaghosa's commentary on the Vinaya Piṭaka.] Ambalangoda 1954.
I.B. Horner, *Clarifier of the Sweet Meaning*. [*Madhuratthavilāsinī*, Buddhadatta's commentary on the Buddhavaṃsa.] SBB 1978.
N.A. Jayawickrama, *The Inception of Discipline and the Vinaya Nidāna*. [As for Godahewa.] SBB 1962.
—*Story of Gotama Buddha*. [*Nidānakathā* of the *Jātakaṭṭhakathā*.] PTS 1990.

—"The Exegesis of the Sabbāsavasutta" [tr. M2 from the *Papañcasūdanī*] in *Buddhist and Pali Studies in Honour of The Venerable Professor Kakkapalliye Anuruddha*, ed. K.L. Dhammajoti and Y. Karunadasa. Hong Kong 2009, pp.1–41.

Khantipālo, *Buddhist Stories.* [Selected and revised from Burlingame, *op. cit.*] 4 parts, BPS 1982–88.

B.C. Law, *The Debates Commentary.* [Buddhaghosa's *Kathāvatthu-ppakaraṇaṭṭhakathā*, part of the *Pañcappakaraṇa-ṭṭhakathā*.] PTS 1940, 1988.

Peter Masefield, *Elucidation of the Intrinsic Meaning so Named.* [Dhammapāla's commentary on the Vimānavatthu.] SBB 1989.

—*Itivuttaka Commentary.* 2 vols, PTS 2008–9.

—*Udāna Commentary.* 2 vols, PTS 1994–95.

Ñāṇamoli, *Illustrator* (from *Minor Readings and Illustrator).* [*Paramatthajotikā*, Buddhaghosa's commentary on the Khuddakapāṭha.] PTS 1960, 1991.

—*The Dispeller of Delusion.* [*Sammohavinodanī*, Buddhaghosa's commentary on the Vibhaṅga.] SBB I, 1987, II, 1991.

Nyanaponika (ed.), *Stories of Old*. BPS 1963. An anthology from the Commentaries.

Andrew Olendzki, "Guhatthaka-suttaniddeso. Upon the Tip of a Needle" [excerpt from the *Mahāniddesa*]. Retrieved from www.accesstoinsight.org/tipitaka/kn/nm/nm.2.04.olen.html

Pe Maung Tin, *The Expositor.* [*Atthasālinī*, Buddhaghosa's commentary on the Dhammasaṅgaṇī.] 2 vols, PTS 1920–21, 1976.

William Pruitt, *The Commentary on the Verses of the Theris.* PTS 1998.

Junjirō Takakusu, "Pāli Elements in Chinese Buddhism. A Translation of Buddhaghosa's Samantapāsādika, a Commentary on the Vinaya, found in the Chinese Tripiṭaka." *Journal of the Royal Asiatic Society* NS 28, 1898, pp.415–39.

Yang-Gyu An, *The Buddha's Last Days. Buddhaghosa's Commentary on the Mahāparinibbāna Sutta*. PTS 2003.

B. Pāli Exegeses (in English translation)

Abhidhammatthasaṅgaha

S.Z. Aung and C.A.F. Rhys Davids, *Compendium of Philosophy.* PTS 1910, 1995, Whitefish (MT) 2003.

Egerton C. Baptist, *Abhidhamma for the Beginner.* Colombo 1959, Dehiwela 2004.

Bhikkhu Bodhi (ed. and tr.), *A Comprehensive Manual of Abhidhamma*. BPS 1993, 2006.

C.L.A. de Silva, *A Treatise on Buddhist Philosophy or Abhidhamma.* Colombo 1937, Delhi 1997.

Huyen-Vi, *The Four Abhidhammic Reals.* Linh-Son, Joinville-le-Pont (Paris) 1982.

Jagdish Kashyap, *The Abhidhamma Philosophy I.* Benares 1942, Patna 1954, Delhi 1982.

Nārada, *A Manual of Abhidhamma.* Colombo 1956, BPS 1968, Rangoon 1970; rev. ed. BPS 1975.

R.P. Wijeratne and Rupert Gethin (tr., and *Abhidhammavibhāvini*), *Summary of the Topics* and *Exposition of the Topics of Abhidhamma.* PTS 2002.

Milindapañhā

R. Basu, *A Critical Study of the Milindapañha.* Calcutta 1978.

I.B. Horner, *Milinda's Questions.* 2 vols, SBB 1963–64, 1990–91.

N.K.G. Mendis (ed.), *The Questions of King Milinda—An Abridgement of the Milindapañhā.* BPS 1993, 2007. Introduction by Bhikkhu Bodhi.

Minh Chau, *Milindapañha and Nāgasenabhikshusūtra.* Calcutta 1964. A comparative study.

Bhikkhu Pesala, *The Debate of King Milinda* [abridged]. Delhi 1991.

C.A.F. Rhys Davids, *The Milinda-Questions.* London 1930, Delhi 1997, Richmond (Surrey) 2000. *An inquiry into its place in the history of Buddhism with a theory as to its author.*

T.W. Rhys Davids, *The Questions of King Milinda.* 2 vols, SBE 1890–94, New York 1969, Delhi 2005.

V. Trenckner, *Pali Miscellany.* London 1879. Edition and translation of a "specimen of Milindapañho."

Nettippakaraṇa

Ñāṇamoli, *The Guide.* PTS 1962, 1977.

George D. Bond, "*The Netti-Pakaraṇa*: A Theravādin Method of Interpretation." *Buddhist Studies in honour of Walpola Rahula,* ed. S. Balasooriya *et al.*, London 1980, pp.16–28.

Peṭakopadesa

Ñāṇamoli, *Piṭaka-Disclosure.* PTS 1964, 1979.

Rūpārūpavibhāga

B.N. Chaudhury, *Abhidhamma Terminology in the Rūpārūpavibhāga.* Calcutta 1983.

Robert Exell, "The Classification of Forms and Formless Things." *Visākha Puja,* Bangkok 1964, JPTS XVII, 1992, pp. 1–12.

D.K. Barua (ed. & tr.), *Rūpārūpa-vibhāga of Ācariya Buddhadatta Thera*. Calcutta 1995.

Vimuttimagga

Anālayo, "The Treatise on the Path to Liberation and the *Visuddhimagga*." *Fuyan Buddhist Studies* 2009.4, pp.1–15.
N.R.M. Ehara, Soma and Kheminda, *The Path of Freedom*. Colombo 1961, BPS 1977, 1995.
T. Hayashi, "The *Vimuttimagga* and Early Post-Canonical Literature." 3 parts, *Bukkyō Kenkyū* 31, 2003, pp.91–122; 32, 2004, pp.59–82; 34, 2006, pp.5–33.
Lalen Kumar Jha, *The Vimuttimagga, a critical study*. Delhi 2008.
Makoto Nagai, "The *Vimutti-Magga*, the 'Way to Deliverance'. The Chinese Counterpart of the Pāli *Visuddhi-magga*." JPTS, 1919, pp.69–80.

Visuddhimagga

Jion Abe, *Saṅkhepatthajotani Visuddhimaggacullaṭīkā Sīla-Dhutaṅga: A study of the first and second chapters of the Visuddhimagga and its Commentaries*. Poona 1981.
P.V. Bapat, *Vimuttimagga and Visuddhimagga: A Comparative Study*. Poona 1937, BPS 2010.
Edward Conze, *Buddhist Meditation*. London 1956, Abingdon 2008. Includes extensive passages from Vism.
U Dhammaratana, *Guide through Visuddhimagga*. MBS, Varanasi 1964, Colombo 1980.
Damien Keown, "Morality in the *Visuddhimagga*." *Journal of the International Association of Buddhist Studies* 6, 1983, pp.61–75.
Baidyanath Labh, *Paññā in Early Buddhism, with special reference to Visuddhimagga*. Delhi 1991.
Robert Mann and Rose Youd, *Buddhist Character Analysis* (based on Vism). Bradford-on-Avon 1992.
Ñāṇamoli, *The Path of Purification*. Colombo 1956, BPS 1975, 1999, 2010; 2 vols, Berkeley 1976, Singapore and Taipei 2003.
Pe Maung Tin, *The Path of Purity*. PTS, 3 vols, 1922–1931; 1 vol, 1975.
Vyañjana, *Theravāda Buddhist Ethics with special reference to Visuddhimagga*. Calcutta 1992.

C. Non-Indian Pāli Literature

Burma (Myanmar from 1989)

Chester Bennett (tr. *Mālālaṅkāravatthu*), "Life of Gaudama." *Journal of the American Oriental Society* III, New York 1853. Revised by Michael Edwardes as *A Life of the Buddha*. London 1959.

Paul Bigandet (tr. *Tathāgata-udāna*), *The Life or Legend of Gaudama*. 2 vols, Rangoon 1858, London 1911–12

Mabel H. Bode, *The Pali Literature of Burma*. London 1909, 1966.

Asha Das, *The Glimpses of Buddhist Literature*. Calcutta 2000. A critical study and translation of the Gandhavaṃsa.

Dorothy H. Fickle, "An Historical and Structural Study of the Paññāsa Jātaka." Ph.D. diss., Pennsylvania 1978.

Emil Forchhammer, *Report on the Pali Literature of Burma*. Calcutta 1879.

James Gray (ed. and tr.), *Buddhaghosuppatti or Historical Romance of the Rise and Career of Buddhaghosa*. London 1892, 2001; New Delhi 1999.

Ann Appleby Hazelwood (tr.), "*Pañcagatidīpanī*." JPTS XI, 1987, pp. 133–59.

Mahāsi Sayadaw, *The Progress of Insight*. BPS 1965. A contemporary Pali treatise on *satipatthāna* meditation, with translation by Nyanaponika.

Sri Lanka (Ceylon)

Achariya Buddharakkhita, *Halo'd Triumphs*. Bangalore 2001. Pāli text, translation and explanation of the Jayamaṅgala Gāthā.

James D'Alwis, *A Descriptive Catalogue of Sanskrit, Pali and Sinhalese Literary Works of Ceylon*. 3 vols, Colombo 1870.

C. Duroiselle (tr.), *Jinacarita or "The Career of the Conqueror."* London 1906, Delhi 1982, Whitefish (MT) 2007.

D.J. Gogerly, "Buddhism." *The Orientalist* I, 1884, pp. 204–5. A detailed summary of the *Rasavāhinī*

R.F. Gombrich (ed. and tr.), "*Kosalabimbavaṇṇanā*." In *Buddhism in Ceylon and Studies in Religious Syncretism in Buddhist Countries*, ed. Heinz Bechert, Göttingen 1978.

James Gray (tr.), *Jinālaṅkāra or "Embellishments of Buddha."* London 1894, SBB 1981

Charles Hallisey, "Devotion in the Buddhist Literature of Medieval Sri Lanka." Ph.D. diss., Chicago 1988.

—(ed.), "*Tuṇḍilovāda*: an Allegedly Non-Canonical Sutta." JPTS XV, 1990, pp. 155–95.

—(tr.), "The Advice to Layman Tuṇḍila." *Buddhism in Practice*, ed. Donald S. Lopez. Princeton 1995, pp. 302–13.

N.A. Jayawickrama, "Literary Activity in Pali." *Pali Buddhist Review* 5, 1980, pp.76–88. Repr. from *Education in Ceylon* I, ch.7, Min. of Education and Cultural Affairs, Colombo 1969.

Ann Appleby Hazelwood (tr.), *Saddhammopāyana*. JPTS XII, 1988, pp. 65–168.

B.C. Law (tr. *Telakaṭāhagāthā*), "Verses on Oil-Pot." *Indian Culture* V. Calcutta 1938–39.

—(tr. *Saddhammasaṅgaha*), *A Manual of Buddhist Historical Records.* Calcutta 1963, Delhi 1999

G.P. Malalasekera, *The Pali Literature of Ceylon.* London 1928, Colombo 1958, BPS 1994.

Junko Matsumura, *The Rasavāhinī of Vedeha Thera Vaggas V and VI: Migapotaka-Vagga and Uttaroḷiya-Vagga.* Osaka 1992.

—"Remarks on the Rasavāhinī and the Related Literature." JPTS XXV, 1999, pp. 155–72.

"Materials for the Rasavāhinī: a reconsideration of the Sahassavatthaṭṭhakathā and its relationship to the Rasa-vāhinī." *Indogaku Bukkyōgaku Kenkyū* 52.1, 2003, pp.455–58.

Maung Tin (tr.), "Abhisambodhi Alaṅkāra: The Embellishments of Perfect Knowledge." *Journal of the Burma Research Society* I–III, Rangoon 1912–13.

Primoz Pecenko, "Sāriputta and his works." JPTS XXIII, 1997, pp. 159–79.

—"*Līnatthapakāsinī* and *Sāratthamañjūsā*: The *Purānaṭīkās* and the *Ṭīkās* on the Four Nikāyas." JPTS XXVII, 2002, pp. 61–113.

—"The Ṭīkās on the Four Nikāyas: Līnatthapakāsinī and Sāratthamañjūsā." *Indologica Taurinensia* XXX, 2004, pp.201-27.

Widurupola Piyatissa (ed. and tr.), *Kāmalañjali: With Folded Hands.* Colombo 1952; repr. in P. Sugatānanda, *Sangīti.* Rangoon 1954. A modern devotional poem.

William Pruitt (tr.), "*Anāgatavaṃsa,* The Chronicle of the Future Buddha" in Sayagyi U Chit Tin, *The Coming Buddha, Ariya Metteyya.* BPS 1992, pp. 49–61; rev.tr. by K.R. Norman, "The Chronicle of the Future [Buddha]." JPTS XXVIII, 2006, pp.19–32; *Collected Papers VIII.* PTS 2007, pp.224–60.

Telwatte Rāhula (ed. and tr.), "*Rasavāhinī: Jambudīpuppattivatthu.*" Ph.D. diss., ANU (Canberra) 1981.

—"The *Rasavāhinī* and the *Sahassavatthu*: A comparison." *Journal of the International Association of Buddhist Studies* 7, 1984, pp.169–84.

S.K. Rāmachandra Rao (ed. and tr. *Telakatāhagāthā*), "Song in the Cauldron of Oil." *Quarterly Journal of the Mythic Society* XLVII, Bangalore 1957.

W.H.D. Rouse (tr.), "Jinacarita." JPTS 1905, pp.1–65, repr. Oxford 1978, New Delhi 1985.

H. Saddhātissa (ed.), *Upāsakajanālankāra* (with English synopsis of the "Adornment of the Buddhist Laity.") PTS 1965.

—(tr. and ed.), *The Birth Stories of the Ten Bodhisattas and the*

Dasabodhisattuppattikathā. SBB 1976.

—(tr. Khema's *Nāmarūpasamāso*), "The Summary of Mind and Matter." JPTS XI ,1987, pp.5–31.

C. Sameresingha (tr. *Telakaṭāhagāthā*), "The Dying Rahat's Sermon." *The Buddhist Ray*, Santa Cruz (CA) 1889–90; repr. in *Pali Buddhist Review* 2, London 1977.

Laksmana Sāstri (tr. from the *Rasavāhinī*), "Buddhist Legends of Asoka and his Times." *Journal of the Asiatic Society of Bengal*. N.S. 6, 1910, pp. 52–72

H.C. Warren (partial tr. of the *Anāgatavaṃsa*), "The Buddhist Apocalypse" (describing the disappearance of the Buddha's Teaching). *Buddhism in Translations* (*op.cit.*), pp.481–87.

Thailand (Siam)

Steven Collins, "The Story of the Elder Māleyyadeva." JPTS XVIII, 1993, pp. 65–96.

Kate Crosby, "A Theravāda Code of Conduct for Good Buddhists: The *Upāsakamanussavinaya*." *Journal of the American Oriental Society* 126 (2006), pp.177–87.

Oscar von Hinüber, "Pāli Manuscripts of Canonical Texts from North Thailand. A Preliminary Study." *Journal of the Siam Society* 71, 1983, pp.75–88.

—"On Some Colophons of Old Lānnā Pāli Manuscripts." *Proceedings of the 4th International Conference on Thai Studies* IV, Kunming 1990, pp.56–77.

—"Chips from Buddhist Workshops. Scribes and Manuscripts from Northern Thailand." JPTS XXII, 1996, pp. 35–57.

—"Lān^2 Nā as a Centre of Pāli Literature During the Late 15th Century." JPTS XXVI, 2000, pp.119–37.

Padmanabh S. Jaini, "*Akāravattārasutta*: An 'Apocryphal' Sutta from Thailand." *Indo-Iranian Journal 35*, 1992, pp. 192–223.

(Bh.) P.L. Likhitananta, "History of Buddhism in Thailand." Ph.D. diss., Magadh Univ., Patna 1970. Part I:4. Introduction of Theravāda and Pāli Literature; Part II (pp.208–344): 1.The Golden Age of Pāli Scholarship in Northern Thailand, 2.The Pāli Literature in Fifteenth and Sixteenth Century, 3.The Pāli Literature in Seventeenth, Eighteenth and Nineteenth Century, 4.Literary Contributions of Thai Scholars.

Bunyen Limsawaddi (tr.), "Stanzas on the Ten Perfections" in *The Wisdom Gone Beyond*. Bangkok 1966.

Hans Penth, "Buddhist Literature of Lān Nā on the History of Lān Nā's Buddhism." JPTS XXIII, 1997, pp. 43–81.

H. Saddhātissa, "Pāli Literature of Thailand." *Buddhist Studies in Honour of I.B. Horner*, ed. L.S. Cousins *et al.*, Dordrecht 1974, pp.211–25.

—"A Survey of the Pāli Literature of Thailand." *Amalā Prajñā (Professor P.V. Bapat Felicitation Volume)*, ed. N.H. Samtani and H.S. Prasad, Delhi 1989, pp.41–46.

—Both articles repr. in *Pāli Literature of South-East Asia*. Singapore 1992, Dehiwela 2004, pp.11–31, 61–68.

Peter Skilling, "The Sambuddha verses and later Theravādin Buddhology." JPTS XXII, 1996, pp. 151–83.

Daniel M. Veidlinger, *Spreading the Dhamma: Writing, Orality, and Textual Transmission in Buddhist Northern Thailand*. Honolulu 2006.

Kenneth E. Wells, *Thai Buddhism: Its Rites and Activities*. Bangkok 1940, 1975. A comprehensive survey which includes (in translation) all the Pāli stanzas recited on all religious, social and state occasions.

Cambodia and Laos

Jacqueline Filliozat and Peter Masefield, "Two Indo-Chinese Pali Versions of the Petavatthu." *Mahachulalongkorn Journal of Buddhist Studies* 1, 2008, pp.11–18.

Charles Hallisey, "The Sutta on Nibbāna as a Great City." *Buddhist Essays. A Miscellany*, ed. P. Sorata Thera et al. London 1992, pp. 38–67. Repr. as "*Nibbānasutta*: an allegedly non-canonical sutta on *Nibbāna* as a Great City." JPTS XVIIII, 1993, pp.97–130.

Peter Masefield, "Indo-Chinese Pali." *Mahachulalongkorn Journal of Buddhist Studies* 1, 2008, pp.1–9.

—"Petavatthu Translation." *Ibid.*, pp.19–25.

H. Saddhātissa, "Pāli Studies in Cambodia." *Buddhist Studies in honour of Walpola Rāhula*, ed. S. Balasooriya et al, London 1980, pp.242–50.

—"Pāli Literature in Cambodia." JPTS IX, 1981, pp.178–97.

—"Pāli Literature from Laos." *Studies in Pali and Buddhism. A Memorial Volume in Honor of Bhikkhu Jagdish Kashyap*, ed. A.K. Narain, Delhi 1979, pp.327–40.

—All three articles repr. in *Pāli Literature of South-East Asia*. Singapore 1992, Dehiwela 2004, pp.69–126.

5. Studies from Pāli and Related Sources

A. General Studies

Oliver Abeynayake, "Sri Lanka's Contribution to the Development of the Pali Canon." *Buddhism for the New Millenium*, London 2000, pp.163–83.

E. W. Adikaram, *The Early History of Buddhism in Ceylon*. Colombo 1946.

G.F. Allen, *The Buddha's Philosophy*. London 1959, 2008.

Mark Allon, "The Oral Composition and Transmission of Early Buddhist Texts." *Indian Insights: Buddhism, Brahmanism and Bhakti*, ed. P. Connoly, London 1997, pp.39–61.

Roy C. Amore, "The Concept and Practice of Doing Merit in Early Theravāda Buddhism." Ph.D. diss., Columbia (NY) 1970.

Carol S. Anderson, *Pain and its Ending. The Four Noble Truths in the Theravāda Buddhist Canon*. Richmond (Surrey) 1999, Delhi 2001.

Anālayo, "The Vicissitudes of Memory and Early Buddhist Oral Transmission." *Canadian Journal of Buddhist Studies* 5, 2009, pp.5–19.

—"The Influence of Commentarial Exegesis on the Transmission of Āgama Literature in Translating Buddhist Chinese." *Problems and Prospects*, ed. K. Meisig, Wiesbaden 2010, pp.1–20.

—*The Genesis of the Bodhisattva Ideal*, Hamburg, 2010.

K. Anuruddha, "Studies in Buddhist social thought as documented in the Pali tradition." Ph.D. diss., Lancaster 1972.

Harvey B. Aronson, *Love and Sympathy in Theravada Buddhism*. Delhi 1980, 1986. A survey based on the four main Nikāyas, their Commentaries and Vism.

Arnold Aronroff, "Contrasting Modes of Textual Classification: The Jātaka Commentary and its Relationship to the Pali Canon." Ph.D. diss., Chicago 1982.

A.J. Bahm, *Philosophy of the Buddha*. London 1958, New York 1969. A basic introduction extracted from the texts.

Biswanath Banerjee and Sukomal Chaudhuri (ed.), *Buddha and Buddhism*. Kolkata (Calcutta) 2005.

S.C. Banerji, *An Introduction to Pali Literature*. Calcutta 1964.

P.V. Bapat (ed.), *2500 Years of Buddhism*. Delhi 1956, 1987. Includes a survey of VP, SP and Dhp.

Egerton C. Baptist, *In the Footsteps of the Sākyamuni* (Ānupubbi-Kathā). Colombo 1962. The Buddha's gradual method of teaching.

A. Barua, "The editing of the *Peṭakopadesa*, with critical apparatus and commentary." Ph.D. diss., London 1933.

Heinz Bechert, "The Writing Down of the Tripiṭaka in Pāli." *Wiener Zeitschrift für die Kunde Südasiens* 36, pp.45–53.

V. Bhattacharya, *Buddhist Texts as recommended by Asoka*. Calcutta 1948.

Anne M. Blackburn, *Buddhist Learning and Textual Practice in the Eighteenth-Century Lankan Monastic Culture*. Princeton 2001. Based on her doctoral dissertation (Chicago 1996), "The Play of the Teaching in the Life of the Sāsana."

Kathryn R. Blackstone, *Women in the Footsteps of the Buddha. Struggle for Liberation in the Therigatha*. London 1998.

Mabel H. Bode, "The legend of Raṭṭhapāla in the Pali Apadāna and Buddhaghosa's Commentary." *Mélanges d'Indianisme* [Sylvain Lévi felicitation volume], Paris 1911, pp.183–92

S. Bodhesako, *Beginnings, Collected Essays*. BPS 2008. The 1st essay, "Beginnings: The Pali Suttas," on the authenticity of the Pāli Canon, was published by the BPS in 1987; the 2nd essay, "Change: An Examination of Impermanence in Experience" was originally published as *Change*, Colombo 1988.

Bhikkhu Bodhi, *The Noble Eightfold Eightfold Path*. BPS 1984.

Mathieu Boisvert, *The Five Aggregates: Understanding Theravāda Psychology and Soteriology*. Waterloo (Ontario) 1995, Delhi 1997.

George D. Bond, *The Word of the Buddha*. Colombo 1982. On the Tipiṭaka and its interpretation in Theravāda Buddhism.

Acharya Buddharakkhita, *Mettā: The Philosophy & Practice of Universal Love*. BPS 1989.

John B. Buescher, "The Buddhist Doctrine of Two Truths in the Vaibhāṣika and Theravāda Schools." Ph.D. diss., Virginia, Charlottesville 1983.

John Bullitt, *Beyond the Tipitaka. A Field-Guide to Post-canonical Pali literature* (2002). Retrieved from www.accesstoinsight.org/lib/index.html

Siddhi Butr-Indr, *The Social Philosophy of Buddhism*. Bangkok 1973.

Marie B. Byles, *Footprints of Gautama the Buddha*. London 1957, Wheaton (IL) 1967. The biography of the Buddha related by Yasa, based on texts from VP and SP.

Dennis Candy, *Peace in the Buddha's Discourses, A Compilation and Discussion*. BPS 2008.

John Ross Carter (ed.), *The Threefold Refuge in the Theravāda Buddhist Tradition*. Chambersburg (PA) 1982.

W.D. Chandima-Wijebandara, "A study of early Buddhism as a critique of its contemporary religio-philosophic milieu." Ph.D. diss., Lancaster 1974.

Pratap Chandra, *Metaphysics of Perpetual Change. The Concept of Self in Early Buddhism.* Bombay 1978.

Heramba Nath Chatterji, *Comparative Studies in Pāli and Sanskrit Alaṅkāras.* Calcutta 1960.

P. Cholvarn, "Nibbāna as Self or Not Self: Some Contemporary Thai Discussions." M.Phil. diss., Bristol 2007.

Angraj Choudhary, *Essays in Buddhism and Pali Literature.* Delhi 1994.

Steven Collins, *Selfless Persons: Imagery and thought in Theravāda Buddhism.* Cambridge 1982, 1994. Based on his doctoral dissertation (Oxford 1982), "Personal Continuity in Theravāda Buddhism."

—"On the very idea of the Pali Canon." JPTS XV, 1990, pp. 89–126. Repr. in *Buddhism. Critical Concepts in Religious Studies* I, ed. Paul Williams, Abingdon 2005, pp.72–95.

—"Notes on Some Oral Aspects of Pāli literature." *Indo-Iranian Journal* 35, 1992, pp.121–35.

H.S. Cooray, "The Origin and Development of Navaṅga in Buddhist Literature." M.A. thesis, Univ. of Ceylon, 1964.

L.S. Cousins, "Pali Oral Literature." *Buddhist Studies. Ancient and Modern,* ed. Philip Denwood and Alexander Piatigorsky. London 1983, pp.1–11. Repr. in *Buddhism. Critical Concepts in Religious Studies* I, ed. Paul Williams, Abingdon 2005, pp.96–104.

Mary Cummings, *The Lives of the Buddha in the Art and Literature of Asia.* University of Michigan, Ann Arbor 1982. Includes a selection from the Jātakas.

Sally Cutler [Mellick], "A Critical Edition, with translation, of selected portions of the Pāli Apadāna." Ph.D. diss., Oxford 1993.

James D'Alwis, *Buddhism: its Origins, History and Doctrines, its Scriptures and their Language, Pali.* Colombo 1862, JPTS 1883, repr. 1978.

Asha Das, *A Literary Appraisal of Pali Poetical Works.* Calcutta 1994.

Subas Chandra Dash, *Bibliography of Pali and Buddhism.* Poona 1994.

G.V. Davane, *Pali Language and Literature: A Systematic Survey and Historical Study.* New Delhi 1994.

—*Language: History and Structure; Literature: Canonical Pali Texts.* New Delhi 1998.

—*Literature: Non-canonical Pali Texts. Ib.*

C. de Saram, *The Pen Portraits of Ninety-Three Eminent Disciples of the Buddha*. Colombo 1971.
Nalini Devdas, *Cetanā and the Dynamics of Volition in Theravāda Buddhism*. Delhi 2008.
M.G. Dhadhale, *Some Aspects of Buddhist Literary Criticism, as gleaned from Pali sources*. Bombay 1975.
—*Synonymic Collocations in the Tipiṭaka: A Study*. Poona 1980.
Mark Wesley Earl, "The idea of salvation in the Vinaya and Sutta Piṭakas." MA thesis, Birmingham 1959.
James Egge, *Religious Giving and the Invention of Karma in Theravāda Buddhism*. Richmond (Surrey) 2002.
Toshiichi Endo, *Dāna: The Development of Its Concept and Practice*. Colombo 1987.
—"The Aṭṭhakathā as Source-material of the Pāli Commentaries." *Dhamma-Vinaya: Essays in Honour of Venerable Professor Dhammavihari (Jotika Dhirasekera)*, ed. Asanga Tilakaratne, *et al*. Peradeniya 2005.
—"The *Mahā-aṭṭhakathā-s*: Some Observations on the Date of of Their Compilation." *Buddhist and Pali Studies in Honour of The Venerable Professor Kakkapalliye Anuruddha*, ed. K.L. Dhammajoti and Y. Karunadasa. Hong Kong 2009, pp.169–81.
Jan T. Ergardt, *Faith and Knowledge in Early Buddhism*. Leiden 1977. An analysis of the contextual structures of an Arahant-formula in the Majjhima Nikāya.
J. Evola, *The Doctrine of Awakening. A study on the Buddhist Ascesis*. London 1951, Rochester (Vermont) 1995. Illustrated from the four main Nikāyas, Dhp and Sn, this work remains the most radical interpretation of the subject.
P.L. Farkas, "The fourth noble truth: a study in Buddhist ethics." Ph.D. diss., Aberdeen 1931.
Rein Fernhout, *Canonical Text Bearers of Absolute Authority. Bible, Koran, Veda, Tipiṭaka: A Phenomenological Study*. Amsterdam 1994.
Ellison Banks Findly, *Dana: giving and getting in Pali Buddhism*. Delhi 2003.
Ralph Flores, *Buddhist Scriptures as Literature: Sacred Rhetoric and the Uses of Theory*. New York 2008.
Michael Freedman, "The Characterization of Ānanda in the Pali Canon of the Theravāda: A Hagiographic Study." Ph.D. diss., McMaster (Ontario) 1977.
Oliver Freiberger, "The Buddhist Canon and the Canon of Buddhist Studies." *Journal of the International Association of Buddhist Studies* 27, 2004, pp.261–83.

(Lt.Col.) G.E. Fryer, *Note on the Pali Grammarian Kaccāyana*. Calcutta 1882.

Paul Fuller, *The Notion of Diṭṭhi in Theravāda Buddhism*. Richmond (Surrey) 2004.

Aruna K. Gamage, "Some Observations on the Exegetical Elaborations on the Pāli Canon in the Aṭṭhakathā-s." *Buddhist and Pali Studies ... Anuruddha, op.cit.*, pp.603–16.

Wilhelm Geiger, *Pali Literature and Language*. Calcutta 1943, Delhi 1968, New Delhi 1996. Rev. by K.R. Norman as *Pāli Grammar*. PTS 1994.

Rupert Gethin, "The Five Aggregates in the Nikāyas and Early Abhidhamma." M.A. thesis, Manchester 1982.

—*The Buddhist Path to Awakening. A Study of the Bodhi-Pakkhiyā Dhammā*. Leiden 1992. Based on his doctoral dissertation, Manchester 1987.

—*The Foundations of Buddhism*. Oxford 1998.

—"Mythology as Meditation: from the Mahāsudassana Sutta to the Sukhāvatīvyūha Sūtra." JPTS XXVIII, 2006, pp.63–112.

A.R. Giles, "Dukkha in Theravāda and Early Mahāyāna Buddhism." M.Th. thesis, King's College, London 1976.

Helmuth von Glasenapp, *Vedanta and Buddhism*. BPS 1958.

—*Buddhism and Christianity*. BPS 1959.

—*Buddhism, a Non-Theistic Religion*. New York 1966, London 1970. Includes extensive references to *devas* in the Pāli Canon.

Richard Gombrich, *How Buddhism Began: The Conditioned Genesis of the Early Teachings*. London and Atlantic Highlands (NJ) 1996, Richmond (Surrey) 2000.

—*What the Buddha Thought*. London and Oakville (CT) 2009.

L.R. Goonesekere, *Buddhist Commentarial Literature*. BPS 1967.

L. Grey, *Concordance of Buddhist Birth Stories*. PTS 1990, 2000.

Georg Grimm, *The Doctrine of the Buddha: The Religion of Reason and Meditation*. Leipzig 1926, East Berlin 1958, Delhi 1973. Despite the controversial nature of this classic tome, the author claimed that "he has built up his work exclusively on the Sutta Piṭaka."

G. Grönbold *Die Worte des Buddha in den Sprachen der Welt/The Words of the Buddha in the Languages of the World. Tipiṭaka-Tripiṭaka-Dazangjing-Kanjur*. Munich 2005.

Henepola Gunaratana, *The Path of Serenity and Insight: Explanation of the Buddhist Jhanas*. Delhi 1985, New Delhi 1995. (The American Univ., WA-DC 1980.) Based on his doctoral dissertation "A Critical Analysis of the Jhānas in Theravāda Buddhist Meditation."

Mirisse Gunasiri, *The Buddha and His Ethics*. Colombo 1962, 1965. Includes some popular *suttas* in condensed form.

R.A.L.H. Gunawardana, *Robe and Plough, Monasticism and Economic Interest in Early Medieval Sri Lanka*. Tucson 1979. Discusses the transmission and origin, etc, of several Pāli texts.

Ānanda W.P. Guruge, *Buddhism: The Religion and Its Culture*. Madras 1975, rev. ed., Colombo 1984. Includes a concise analysis of Buddhist Literature (Ch. V) together with an anthology from SP (Ch. VI).

Edith (Ludowyk-) Gyömröi, "The Role of the Miracle in Early Pali Literature." University of Ceylon doctoral dissertation, 1944.

J.R. Halder, *Early Buddhist Mythology*. New Delhi 1977. A comprehensive study based mainly on the Vimānavatthu, Petavatthu and Buddhavaṃsa.

Sue Hamilton, *Identity and Experience: The Constitution of the Human Being According to Early Buddhism*. London 1996. Based on her doctoral dissertation, Oxford 1992.

—*Early Buddhism: A New Approach*. London 2000.

Peter Harvey, "The concept of the person in Pāli Buddhist literature." Ph.D. diss., Lancaster 1982.

—*An Introduction to Buddhism: Teachings, History and Practices*. Cambridge 1990, Delhi 199?

—*The Selfless Mind: Personality and Consciousness, and Nirvana in Early Buddhism*. Richmond (Surrey) 1995.

—*An Introduction to Buddhist Ethics*. Cambridge 2000.

K.L. Hazra, *History of Theravāda Buddhism in South-East Asia*. New Delhi 1982.

—*Studies on Pali Commentaries*. New Delhi 1991.

—*Pāli Language and Literature*. 2 vols, New Delhi 1994.

—*Rise and Decline of Buddhism in India*. New Delhi 1998.

—*Buddhist Annals and Chronicles of South-East Asia*. New Delhi 2002.

Hellmuth Hecker, *Lives of the Disciples I*. BPS 1967. Contains "The Upāsaka Citta," "The Bhikkhu Citta," and "Father and Mother Nakula."

—*Life of Mahā Moggallāna*. BPS 1979.

—*Ānanda: The Guardian of the Dhamma*. BPS 1980.

—*Life of Aṅgulimāla*. BPS 1984.

—*Anāthapiṇḍika: The Great Benefactor*. BPS 1986.

—*Mahā Kassapa: Father of the Sangha*. BPS 1987.

—*Anuruddha: Master of the Divine Eye*. BPS 1989.

Oscar von Hinüber, *Selected Papers*. PTS 1995.

—*A Handbook of Pāli Literature*. Berlin, New York, New Delhi 1996.

Frank J. Hoffman, *Rationality and Mind in Early Buddhism*. Delhi 1987.

—and Deegalle Mahinda (ed.), *Pāli Buddhism*. Richmond (Surrey) 1996.

I.B. Horner, *Women under Primitive Buddhism*. London 1930, Delhi 1973, Amsterdam 1975.

—*The Early Buddhist Theory of Man Perfected. A Study of the Arahant*. London 1936, Amsterdam 1975, New Delhi 1979.

—*The Basic Position of Sīla*. BSS 1950.

—*Women in Early Buddhist Literature*. BPS 1961.

—*Early Buddhism and the Taking of Life*. BPS 1967.

Huyen-Vi, *A Critical Study of the Life and Works of Sāriputta Thera*. Saigon 1972, Linh-So'n Buddhist Association, Paris 1989.

Soon-Il Hwang, *Metaphor and Literalism in Buddhism. The Doctrinal History of Nirvāṇa*. Abingdon 2006.

John D. Ireland, *Comments on the Buddha Word*. BPS 1963.

—*The Buddha's Practical Teaching*. BPS 1965.

Louise Ireland-Frey, *The Blossom of Buddha. A novel on the life of Gautama based on the Pali Canon and other Buddhist scriptures*. Nevada City 2008.

K.N. Jayatilleke, *Early Buddhist Theory of Knowledge*. London 1963, Delhi 2004, Abingdon 2008. Based on his doctoral dissertation (London 1961), "The epistemological basis of thought of the Pali Canon, with special reference to the Nikāyas."

—"The Principles of International Law in Buddhist Doctrine." *Recueil des Cours*, Vol.120, The Hague 1967, pp. 441–567. Offpr. as *Dhamma, Man and Law*. Singapore 1988. Included in *Facets of Buddhist Thought, Collected Essays*, BPS 2010.

—*The Message of the Buddha* (ed. and intro. by Ninian Smart). London 1975, BPS 2000. Included in *Facets of Buddhist Thought, Collected Essays*, BPS 2010.

S. Jayawardhana, *Handbook of Pali Literature*. Colombo 1994.

N.A. Jayawickrama, "*Papañcasūdanī*: The Commentary to the *Majjhimanikāya*." *Journal of Buddhist Studies* (Sri Lanka) 1, 2003, pp.73–119; 2, 2004, pp.1–57.

Rune E.A. Johansson, *The Psychology of Nirvana*. London 1969, New York 1970. The goal of Buddhism clarified by means of SP.

—*The Dynamic Psychology of Buddhism*. London 1983. A study of *paṭiccasamuppāda* from SP.

Susan Elbaum Jootla, *Inspiration from Enlightened Nuns*. BPS 1988. An essay based on the Therīgāthā and Bhikkhunī Saṃyutta.

T. Kariyawasam, "The development of Buddhology in the early

Mahāyāna and its relation to the Pali Nikāyas." Ph.D. diss., Lancaster 1974.
W.S. Karunaratne, *The Theory of Causality.* Nugegoda 1988. Based on his doctoral dissertation (London 1956), "The development of the theory of causality in early Theravāda Buddhism."
S.M. Katre, "Early Buddhist Ballads and their relation to the older Upanishadic Literature." Ph.D. diss., London 1931.
Damien Keown, *The Nature of Buddhist Ethics.* Basingstoke 1996, 2001.
Khantipālo, *Pointing to Dhamma.* Bangkok 1973. Thirty discourses based on Pāli texts.
—*Banner of the Arahants.* BPS 1979, 2008. A detailed history and account of the Bhikkhu- and Bhikkhunī-Saṅgha.
Hegoda Khemananda, *Logic and Epistemology in Theravāda.* Colombo 1993.
Kheminda, *Path Fruit and Nibbāna.* Colombo 1965. The path to Nibbāna illustrated from Pāli sources.
—*The Way of Buddhist Meditation (Serenity and Insight according to the Pali Canon).* Colombo 1982.
Winston L. King, *In the Hope of Nibbana: The Ethics of Theravada Buddhism.* LaSalle (IL) 1964, Seattle 2001. Based on VP and SP.
Ria Kloppenborg, *The Paccekabuddha.* Leiden 1974, abridged ed. BPS 1983. A study of asceticism from canonical and commentarial literature, including a translation of Sn 1:3.
Ko Lay, *Guide to Tipiṭaka.* Rangoon 1986, Delhi 1990, Bangkok 1993, Dehiwela 1998.
Tse-fu Kuan, *Mindfulness in Early Buddhism. New Approaches through Psychology and Textual Analysis of Pāli, Chinese and Sanskrit Sources.* Abingdon 2007.
Baidyanath Labh, *Paññā in Early Buddhism.* Delhi 1991. A philosophical analysis with special reference to Vism.
Étienne Lamotte, "The Assessment of Textual Authenticity in Buddhism." *Buddhist Studies Review* 1, 1984, pp.4–15.
—"The Assessment of Textual Interpretation in Buddhism." *Ibid.* 2, 1985, pp.4–24.
—Both articles repr. in *Buddhism. Critical Concepts in Religious Studies* I, ed. Paul Williams, Abingdon 2005, pp.188–213.
Bimala Churn Law, *The Life and Work of Buddhaghosa.* Calcutta 1923, Bombay 1946, Delhi 2005.
—"Non-Canonical Pali Literature." *Annals of the Bhandarkar Oriental Research Institute* (Poona) XIII, Part II (1930–31), pp.97–143.

—*A History of Pali Literature*. 2 vols, London 1933, Varanasi 2002. Vol. I comprises a detailed analysis of SP.

Ledi Sayadaw:[12]

1. *Bodhipakkhiya Dīpanī: The Requisites of Enlightenment*. BPS 1971, 2007.
2. "Catusacca Dīpanī: Manual of the Four Truths."
3. *Maggaṅga Dīpanī: Manual of the Constituents of the Noble Path*. Rangoon 1961, Abingdon 1984. Rev. ed., *The Noble Eightfold Path and its Factors Explained*. BPS 1977, 1998.
4. "Sammādiṭṭhi Dīpanī: Manual of Right Understanding." *The Light of the Dhamma* N.S. II, 1982.
5. *Vipassanā Dīpanī: Manual of Insight*. Mandalay 1915, BPS 1961.
6. *Paṭṭhānuddesa Dīpanī: Buddhist Philosophy of Relations*. BPS 1986.
7. *Niyama Dīpanī: Manual of Cosmic Order*. Mandalay 1921.
8. *Alin-Kyan and Vijjāmagga Dīpanī: The Manual of Light and The Manual of the Path to Higher Knowledge*. BPS 2007.
9. *Ānāpānasati Dīpanī: Manual of Mindfulness of Breathing*. BPS 1999.
10. *Uttamapurisa Dīpanī: A Manual of the Excellent Man*. BPS 2000.

T.O. Ling, *Buddhism and the Mythology of Evil*. London 1962. A comprehensive survey of all references to Māra in the Pāli Canon.

Friedgard Lottermoser, "Quoted Verse Passages in the Works of Buddhaghosa. Materials towards the study of the Sīhaḷāṭṭhakathā." Ph.D. diss., Göttingen 1979.

James P. McDermott, *Development in the Early Buddhist Concept of Kamma/Karma*. New Delhi 1984

Joseph G. McKeon, "Faith in Early Buddhist Teachings." Ph.D. diss., Fordham (NY) 1978.

Bandu W. Madanayake, "The Concept of Saññā in Theravāda Buddhism." M.A. thesis, Toronto 1978.

---

12. N.B. Manuals 1 to 7 and part of 8 (*Alin-Kyan*, partially) also appeared in the first series of *The Light of the Dhamma* (Rangoon 1950s-60s) and were offprinted, minus manual 7, in one volume entitled *The Manuals of Buddhism*. Rangoon 1965, Bangkok 1978, Delhi 1997; Manuals of Dhamma, Igatpuri 1999.

—"The Study of Saṅkhāras in Early Buddhism." Ph.D. diss., Toronto 1987.

T. Magness, *Sammā Diṭṭhi. A Treatise on Right Understanding.* Bangkok circa 1960.

Mahāsi Sayadaw, *On the Nature of Nibbāna*. Rangoon 1981, Subang Jaya 1992.

—*Brahmavihāra Dhamma*. Rangoon, 1985. On the 4 Divine Abidings.

—*A Discourse on Dependent Origination*. Bangkok 1999.

Peter Masefield, *Divine Revelation in Pali Buddhism*. Colombo 1986, Abingdon 2008. Based on his doctoral dissertation (Lancaster 1980), "Thus They Once Heard: Oral Initiation in the Pali Nikāyas."

Bruce Matthews, *Craving and Salvation: A Study in Buddhist Soteriology.* Waterloo (Ontario) 1983. Based on his doctoral dissertation (McMaster 1974), "The Concept of Craving in Early Buddhism."

Junko Matsumura, "The Sumedhakathā in Pāli Literature: Summation of Theravāda-tradition versions and proof of linkage to the Northern textual Tradition." *Indogaku bukkyōggaku kenkyū* 56, 2008, pp.1086–94. Enlarged ed., "The *Sumedhakathā* in Pāli Literature and Its Relation to the Northern Buddhist Textual Tradition," *Journal of the International College for Postgraduate Buddhist Studies* XIV, 2010, pp.101–33.

Veerachart Nimanong, "*Theravāda* Methods of Interpretation on Buddhist Scriptures." *International Journal of Buddhist Thought & Culture* 6, Seoul 2006, pp.77–120.

Sodo Mori, *Studies of the Pali Commentaries.* Niza 1989.

—"The Origin and History of the Bhānaka Tradition." *Ananda A.W. Guruge Felicitation Volume,* ed. Y. Karunadasa, Colombo 1990, pp.123–29.

Supaphan Na Bangchang, "A Critical Edition of the Mūlapariyāyavagga of Majjhimanikāya-aṭṭhakathāṭīkā." Ph.D. diss., Peradeniya 1981.

Sunthorn Na Rangsi, *The Buddhist Concepts of Karma and Rebirth.* Bangkok 1976. With special reference to the Pāli Canon. Chapter IV on rebirth and the planes of existence has been reprinted as *The Four Planes of Existence in Theravāda Buddhism.* BPS 2006

Muni Shri Nāgarajji, *Āgama and Tripiṭaka: A Comparative Study I, Historical Background.* New Delhi 1986

Hajime Nakamura, *Gotama Buddha.* Los Angeles-Tokyo 1977.

Ñāṇananda, *Concept and Reality in Early Buddhist Thought*. BPS 1971. An essay on *papañca* and *papañca-saññā-saṅkha*.

H. Ñāṇavāsa, "The development of the concept of Buddha in Pali Literature." Ph.D. diss., Univ. of Ceylon, 1964.

Ñāṇavīra Thera, *Notes on Dhamma*, 1st edition, Colombo 1963. 2nd edition, Nieuwerkerk a/d IJssel 2011. Repr. together with collected letters as *Clearing the Path,* Colombo 1987, Nieuwerkerk a/d IJssel 2011. Republished in two parts, Colombo 2001–02. Notes and essays, often polemical, arguing for a "one life" interpretation of *paṭicca-samuppāda*, etc.

—*Seeking the Path: Early Writings of Ñāṇavīra Thera (1954-1960)*, Nieuwerkerk a/d IJssel 2011.

Ñāṇatusita Bhikkhu, *Reference Table of Pali Literature*. Kandy 2011. A comprehensive table listing all known Pāli texts with references.

Nārada, *The Life of Venerable Sāriputta*. Ratnapura 1929.

—*The Bodhisatta Ideal*. Colombo 1963. The Ten Perfections illustrated from the Jātakas.

—*The Buddha and His Teachings*. Saigon 1964, Colombo 1973, BMS 1977, BPS 1980.

K.R. Norman, *Pali Literature*. Wiesbaden 1983.

—"On Translating from Pāli." *One Vehicle*. Singapore 1984, pp.77–87; *Buddhist Essays. A Miscellany. A Memorial Volume in Honour of Venerable Hammalawa Saddhātissa*, ed. P. Sorata Thera, *et al.* London 1992, pp.1–25; *Collected Papers III*. PTS 1992, pp.60–81.

—"The Pāli Language and Scriptures." *The Buddhist Heritage*, ed. Tadeusz Skorupski. Tring 1989, pp.29–53; *Collected Papers IV.* PTS 1993, pp.92–123.

—*A Philological Approach to Buddhism*. SOAS, London 1997, PTS 2006.

—"On Translating Literally." JPTS XXX, 2009, pp.81–97.

Nyanaponika, *The Heart of Buddhist Meditation*. Colombo 1954, London 1962, 1983, New York 1969, BPS 1992, 2005, York Beach (ME) 1996. Includes MN 10 and related texts.

—*Anatta and Nibbāna*. BPS 1959, repr. in *Pathways of Buddhist Thought*. London 1971.

—*Buddhism and the God-Idea*. BPS 1962.

—*The Life of Sāriputta*. BPS 1966.

—*Contemplation of Feelings*. BPS 1993, 2008. Including a translation of the Vedanā Saṃyutta.

—*The Vision of Dhamma: Buddhist Writings of Nyanaponika Thera*. London 1986, BPS 2007.

—*The Vision of Dhamma: Buddhist Writings of Nyanaponika Thera.* London 1986, BPS 2007.
Nyanaponika and H. Hecker, *Great Disciples of the Buddha.* Boston 1997, BPS 2007.
(Somdet Phra) Nyanasamvara (formerly Phra Sasana Sobhana). *Contemplation of the Body.* Bangkok 1974. The transcription of 19 talks on mindfulness of the body.
C. Nyanasatta, *Basic Tenets of Buddhism*. Colombo 1965.
Hermann Oldenberg, *Buddha: His Life, His Doctrine, His Order.* London 1882, Delhi 1971. The first major exposition of Buddhism in the West based entirely on the Pāli Canon.
A.R. Olendzki, "Interdependent origination and cessation: the paticca-samuppāda as an early Buddhist model of liberation." Ph.D. diss., Lancaster 1987.
G.C. Pande, *Studies in the Origins of Buddhism.* Allahabad University 1957, Delhi 1974, 2006. Includes a comprehensive analysis of the four main Nikāyas.
Lakshuman Pandey, "Buddhist Conception of Omniscience." Ph.D. diss., McMaster (Ontario) 1972.
P.A. Payutto, *A Constitution for Living*. Bangkok 1979, rev.ed., BPS 2007. A code of lay ethics based on the Sigālovāda Sutta and other suttas.
—*Good, Evil and Beyond*. Bangkok 1993. On kamma in the Buddha's Teaching.
—*Dependent Origination*. Bangkok 1994.
—*The Pali Canon. What a Buddhist Must Know.* Bangkok 2003.
Primoz Pecenko, "The History of the Nikāya Subcommentaries (*ṭīkās*) in Pāli Bibliographic Sources." JPTS XXX, 2009, pp. 5–32.
Hans H. Penner, *Rediscovering the Buddha. The Legends and Their Interpretations.* New York 2009. In Part One, classic stories of the Buddha are "drawn from various texts of Theravāda Buddhism."
T.H. Perera, *The Four Cankers.* BPS 1967. Illustrated from SP.
Joaquin Perez-Remon, *Self and Non-Self in Early Buddhism*. The Hague 1980.
Ole Holten Pind, "Buddhaghosa—His Works and Scholarly Background." *Bukkyō Kenkyū* 21, 1992, pp.135–56.
Piyadassi, *The Buddha. His Life and Teaching*. BPS 1961. Illustrated from VP and SP.
—*The Buddha's Ancient Path*. London 1964, BPS 1974. A detailed analysis of the Four Noble Truths and Noble Eightfold Path.
Ilkka Pyysäinen, *Beyond Language and Reason. Mysticism in Indian Buddhism*. Helsinki 1993.

Walpola Rāhula, *What the Buddha Taught*. Bedford 1959, New York 1962, Dehiwela 2006. Includes a short anthology from SP.

R. Rajapaksa, "A philosophical investigation of the ethical hedonism and the theory of self implicit in the Pali Nikāyas." Ph.D. diss., London 1975.

Rajesh Rañjan, *Exegetical Literature in Pali: Origin and Development*. Delhi 2005.

Niharranjan Ray, *Theravāda Buddhism in Burma*. Calcutta, 1946, Chieng Mai 2002.

Noble Ross Reat, "The origins of Buddhist psychology." Ph.D. diss., Lancaster 1980.

C.A.F. Rhys Davids, *Buddhist Psychology*. London 1914, New Delhi 2002. An inquiry into the analysis of mind in Pāli literature. Rewritten as *The Birth of Indian Psychology and its Development in Buddhism*. London 1936.

T.W. Rhys Davids, *Buddhism: Its History and Literature*. New York 1896, Calcutta 1962, Varanasi 1975—Lecture II from *The Hibbert Lectures 1881*. London 1891. Includes probably the earliest accurate analysis of the Pāli Canon.

—*Buddhist India*. New York 1903, Calcutta 1957.

Alec Robertson, *The Triple Gem and the Uposatha*. Colombo 1971. "An analysis of the cardinal doctrinal teachings and observances associated with the Full-Moons," extensively illustrated from canonical and post-canonical sources.

R. H. Robinson & W. L. Johnson, *The Buddhist Religion: A Historical Introduction*. Belmont 1996.

H. Saddhātissa, *Buddhist Ethics: Essence of Buddhism*. London 1970, 1987.

—*The Buddha's Way*. London 1971. Includes selected suttas.

—*The Life of the Buddha*. London 1976. Includes the salient features of the Buddha's teaching mission based on VP and SP.

Pragati Sahni, *Environmental Ethics in Buddhism*. Abingdon 2007.

E.R. Saratchandra, *Buddhist Psychology of Perception*. Colombo 1958, Dehiwela 1994.

K.J. Saunders, *Gotama Buddha*. New York 1922. A biography based on the canonical account.

Juliane Schober (ed.), *Sacred Biography in the Buddhist Traditions of South and Southeast Asia*. Honolulu 1997.

Martin Seeger, "Thai Buddhist Studies and the Authority of the Pali Canon." *Contemporary Buddhism* 8, 2007, pp.1–18.

—"Phra Payutto and Debates 'On the Very Idea of the Pali Canon' in Thai Buddhism." *Buddhist Studies Review* 26, 2009, pp.1–31.

Ved Seth, *Study of Biographies of the Buddha based on Pali and Sanskrit sources*. New Delhi 1992.
Sarah Shaw, *Buddhist Meditation*. Richmond (Surrey) 2006, Abingdon 2008. Includes DN 2 and MN 10.
Sīlācāra, *Lotus Blossoms*. Adyar 1914, 1968. Essays on the Four Noble Truths illustrated from SP.
Sheo Kumar Singh, *History and Philosophy of Buddhism*. Patna 1982. Based mainly on Pāli canonical and exegetical literature.
K.P. Sinha, *Nairatmya-Vada: The Buddhist Theory of Not- Self*. Calcutta 1985.
L. Siridhamma, "The Theory of Kamma in Early Theravāda Buddhism." D.Phil. diss., Oxford 1976.
Peter Skilling and Santi Pakdeekham, *Pali Literature Transmitted in Central Siam*. 2 vols, PTS 2002 & 2004.
Harcharan Singh Sobti, *Nibbāna in Early Buddhism*. Delhi 1985. Based on Pāli sources from 6th BCE to 5th CE.
K.D. Somadasa, *Catalogue of the Nevill Collection of Sinhalese Manuscripts in The British Library*. 5 vols, PTS 1987–1995. Nevill's notes, etc, provide information about numerous Pāli texts.
G.A. Somaratne, "Intermediate Existence and the Higher Fetters in the Pāli Nikāyas." JPTS XXV, 1999, pp. 121–54.
R.L. Soni, *The Only Way to Deliverance*. Boulder 1980. Includes DN 22.
Susan C. Stalker, "A Study of Dependent Origination: Vasubandhu, Buddhaghosa, and the Interpretation of Pratītya-samutpāda." Ph.D. diss., Pennsylvania 1987.
John S. Strong, *The Experience of Buddhism: Sources and Interpretations*. Belmont 1995.
Bhikkhu Sujāto, *A Swift Pair of Messengers: Calm with Insight from the Buddha's Lips*. Penang 2001.
—*A History of Mindfulness: How Insight worsted Tranquility in the Satipaṭṭhāna Sutta*. Taipei 2005.
M. Sumanatissa, "Kamma and Kamma-Vipāka in the Nikāyas." M.A. thesis, Manchester 1974.
Donald K. Swearer, *A Guide to the Perplexed: The Satipaṭṭhāna Sutta*. BPS 1973.
A. Syrkin, "Notes on Pāli Canonic Style." *Pali Buddhist Review* 6, 1981–82, pp.69–87.
S. Tachibana, *The Ethics of Buddhism*. Oxford 1926, BSS 1961, London and Totowa (NJ) 1981, Richmond (Surrey) 1995. A study from the SP.

Meena Talin, *Women in Early Buddhist Literature.* Bombay University 1972. Includes *Bhikkhunī Pātimokkha.*
Serena Tennekoon, *An Introduction to Three Sociologically Significant Buddhist Concepts; Kamma, Dāna, Dhamma.* Colombo 1981.
N. Tetley, "The Doctrine of Rebirth in Theravāda Buddhism." D.Phil. diss., Bristol 1990.
Vijay Kumar Thakur, *Social Dimensions of Buddhism.* Varanasi 2001.
Ṭhānissaro Bhikkhu (tr.) *The Mind Like Fire Unbound: An Image in Early Buddhist Discourses.* Barre (MA) 1993, rev. ed., 1999. On the use of fire imagery in early Buddhism to describe Nibbāna.
—*The Wings to Awakening.* Barre 1996. On the *bodhipakkhiyā dhammā.*
—*Noble Strategy: Essays on the Buddhist Path.* Valley Center (CA) 1999.
—*Refuge: an introduction to the Buddha, Dhamma Sangha. Ibid.* 2001.
—*Purity of Heart: Essays on the Buddhist Path. Ibid.* 2006.
—"Computerization of the Buddhist Scriptures for the Twenty-First Century." *Buddhism for the New Millenium,* London 2000, pp.217–30.
E.J. Thomas, *The Life of Buddha as Legend and History.* London 1927, 1975, Delhi 2003.
—*The History of Buddhist Thought.* London 1933, Richmond (Surrey) 1997. Includes a short analysis of the Pāli Canon (pp.266–76).
Asanga Tilakaratne, *Nirvana and Ineffability.* Postgraduate Institute of Pali and Buddhist Studies, Colombo 1993.
H.H. Tilbe, *Pali Buddhism.* Rangoon 1900, New Delhi 1979.
Mahesh Tiwary, *Sīla, Samādhi and Prajñā: The Buddha's Path of Purification.* Patna 1987.
Entai Tomomatsu, *Lectures on the Dhammapada.* Tokyo 1956–59.
—*Lectures on the Saṃyutta Ratha.* Tokyo 1960.
Tran Hoan Tru'o'ng, "A Study in the Ethics of Theravāda Buddhism." Ph.D. diss., Magadh Univ., Patna 1972.
H. Vinita Tseng, "The *Nidānavagga* of *Sāratthappakāsinī.*" D.Phil. diss., Oxford 2001.
Paravahera Vajirañāṇa, *Buddhist Meditation in Theory and Practice.* Colombo 1962, BMS 1975. 'A General Exposition according to the Pali Canon of the Theravada School'.
Nina van Gorkom, *Buddhism in Daily Life.* Bangkok 1977. Illustrated by relevant passages from SP.
Tilmann Vetter, *The Ideas and Meditative Practices of Early Buddhism.* Leiden 1988. Includes conference paper, "Mysticism in the Aṭṭhakavagga."

—*The 'Khandha Passages' in the Vinayapiṭaka and the four main Nikāyas*. Vienna 2000.

A.K. Warder, *Indian Buddhism*. Delhi 1970, rev. ed. 1980.

K.S. Warnasuriya, "Social philosophy of Buddhism." Ph.D. diss., Lancaster 1975.

David Webster, *Philosophy of Desire in the Buddhist Pali Canon*. London 2005, Abingdon 2010.

W.G. Weeraratne, "The role of the individual in Buddhism according to Buddhist teachings." Ph.D. diss., Lancaster 1975. Published privately, Colombo 19--.

R.G. de S. Wettimuny, *The Buddha's Teaching: It's Essential Meaning*. Colombo 1969. Based on Ñāṇavira's radical interpretation of the earliest Nikāya material.

—*The Buddha's Teaching and the Ambiguity of Existence*, Colombo 1978.

K.D.P. Wickremesinghe, *The Biography of the Buddha*. Colombo 1972. A detailed narrative interspersed with extracts from VP and SP.

Chandima Wijebandara, *Early Buddhism, its religious and intellectual milieu*. Postgraduate Institute of Pali and Buddhist Studies, Colombo 1993.

O.H. de A. Wijesekera, *The Three Signata*. BPS 1960. Essay on *anicca, dukkha* and *anattā* illustrated from SP.

D.M. Williams, "The nature and function of the Paṭiccasamuppāda within the Theravāda canon." Ph.D. diss., Manchester 1971.

Martin Wiltshire, *Ascetic Figures before and in Early Buddhism*. Berlin 1990. Based on his doctoral dissertation (Lancaster 1980), "The Origins of the Paccekabuddha Concept."

B. Wimalaratana, "The Concept of the Mahāpurisa in Buddhist Literature and Iconography." Ph.D. diss., Lancaster 1980

M. Winternitz, *History of Indian Literature II*. Calcutta 1933, New York 1971, New Delhi 1972.

Alexander Wynne, "The Oral Transmission of Early Buddhist Literature." *Journal of the International Association of Buddhist Studies* 27, 2004, pp.97–127.

—"The Historical Authenticity of Early Buddhist Literature: A Critical Evaluation." *Wiener Zeitschrift für die Kunde Südasiens* XLIX, 2005, pp.35–70.

Yashpal, *A Cultural Study of Early Pali Tipiṭakas* . 2 vols, Delhi 1998.

Ryudo Yasui, *Theory of Soul in Theravāda Buddhism*. Calcutta 1994.

Paul Younger, *The Indian Religious Tradition*. Varanasi 1970. "Studies in the concept of *duḥkha* or suffering."

Stefano Zacchetti, "Some Remarks on the '*Peṭaka* Passages' in the *Da zhidu lun* and their Relation to the Pāli *Peṭakopadesa.*" *Annual Report of the International Research Institute for Advanced Buddhology at Soka Universityfor the Academic Year 2006,* Tokyo 2007, pp.67–85.

—"An early Chinese translation corresponding to Chapter 6 of the *Peṭakopadesa.* An Shigao's *Yin chi ru jing* T 603 and its Indian original: a preliminary survey." *Bulletin of the School of Oriental and African Studies* 65, 2002, pp.74–98.

B. Vinaya Studies

Bhikkhu Ariyesako, *The Bhikkhus' Rules: A Guide for Laypeople.* Kallista (Victoria, Australia) 1998. The Theravādin Buddhist Monk's Rules compiled and explained.

Subhra Barua, *Monastic Life of the Early Buddhist Nuns.* Calcutta 1997.

D.N. Bhagavat, *Early Buddhist Jurisprudence.* Poona 1939. A study of the Vinaya.

Anne M. Blackburn, "Looking for the *Vinaya*: Monastic Discipline in the Practical Canons of the Theravāda." *Journal of the International Association of Buddhist Studies* 22, 1999, pp.281–309.

William M. Bodiford, *Going Forth. Visions of Buddhist Vinaya.* Honolulu 2005.

Torkel Brekke, "The Skandhaka of the Vinayapiṭaka and its Historical Value." *Wiener Zeitschrift für die Kunde Südasiens* XLII, 1998, pp.23–40.

Jotiya Dhirasekera, *Buddhist Monastic Discipline.* Colombo 1982. Based on his doctoral dissertation (Univ. of Ceylon, 1964), "Buddhist Monastic Discipline: a study of its origin and development in relation to the Sutta and Vinaya Piṭakas."

Antony Fernando, "Buddhist Monastic Life according to the Vinaya Piṭaka and the Commentaries." Ph.D. diss., Gregorian Univ., Rome 1961.

—"Buddhist Monastic Attire." Ph.D. diss., Vidyalankara 1978.

Erich Frauwallner, *The Earliest Vinaya and the Beginnings of Buddhist Literature.* Rome 1956.

Charles Hallisey, "Apropos the Pāli Vinaya as a Historical Document." JPTS XV, 1990, pp.197–208.

R. Spence Hardy, *Eastern Monachism,* 'An account of the origins, laws, discipline, sacred writings, religious ceremonies and present circumstances of the order of mendicants founded by Gotama Buddha.' Compiled from Sinhalese Pali manuscripts, etc. London 1850, Delhi 1989.

O.v. Hinüber, *The Oldest Pāli Manuscript. Four Folios of the Vinaya-Piṭaka from the National Archives, Kathmandu.*Untersuchungen zur Sprachgeschichte und Handschriftenkunde des Pāli II, Akademie der Wissenschaften und der Literature, Mainz. Stuttgart 1991.

—"Buddhist Law According to the Theravāda-Vinaya." *Journal of the International Association of Buddhist Studies* 18.1, 1995, pp.7–45.

—*Ib.* "II: Some Additions and Corrections." *Ib.* 20.2, 1997, pp.87–92.

—"Structure and Origin of the Pātimokkhasutta of the Theravādins." *Acta Orientalia Hungaricae* 51, 1998, pp.257–65.

John C. Holt, *Discipline: The Canonical Buddhism of the Vinayapiṭaka.* Delhi 1981. Based on his doctoral dissertation, Chicago 1977.

Ute Husken, "The Legend of the Establishment of the Buddhist Order of Nuns in the Theravāda Vinaya-Piṭaka." JPTS XXVI, 2000, pp. 43–69.

Jinananda, "A study of the Pali Vinaya Mahāvagga in comparison with the corresponding sections of the Gilgit manuscripts." Ph.D. diss., London 1953.

Prince Jinavarasirivaḍḍhana, *Sāmaṇerasikkha—the Novice's Training*. Bangkok 1967.

Chatsumarn Kabilsingh, *A Comparative Study of Bhikkhunī Pātimokkha*, Varanasi 1984.

—*The Bhikkhunī Pātimokkha of the Six Schools.* Bangkok 1991.

Edith Nolot, "Studies in Vinaya Technical Terms I–III." JPTS XXII, 1996, pp. 73–150; *IV-X*. JPTS XXV, 1999, pp. 1–111.

Patrick Olivelle, *The Origin and Early Development of Buddhist Monachism.* Colombo 1974.

Maulichand Prasad, *A Comparative Study of Abhisamācārikā: Abhisamācārikā-Dharma-Vinaya of the Arya Mahāsghika-Lokottaravādins and Pali Vinaya of the Theravādins.* Patna 1984.

Charles S. Prebish, *A Survey of Vinaya Literature.* Taipei 1994, London 1996.

Ṭhānissaro Bhikkhu (Geoffrey de Graff), *The Buddhist Monastic Code I and II.* Valley Center (CA) (rev. ed.) 2007. Extensive explanation of the *Pātimokkha and Suttavibhaṅga* rules (Part I) and the *Khandhaka* regulations and rules (Part II).

Chandrika Singh Upasak, *Dictionary of Early Buddhist Monastic Terms.* Varanasi 1975, Patna 2001.

Vajirañāṇavarorasa, *Ordination Procedure.* Bangkok 1963, rev. 1990. Includes chapters explaining the basis of Vinaya.

—(tr. *Vinayamukha*), *The Entrance to the Vinaya.* 3 volumes, Bangkok 1970–83. An introduction to the Vinaya including an

explanation of the *pātimokkha* rules.
—*Navakovāda. Instructions for Newly Ordained Bhikkhus and Sāmaṇeras.* Bangkok 1971. Explains basic rules to be observed.
Malcolm B. Voyce, "Aspects of the Nature of the Responsa." (An introduction to the Vinaya.) M.A. thesis, London 1977.
—"The Legal Aspects of Early Buddhist Vinaya." Ph.D. diss., London 1982.
Mohan Wijayaratna, *Buddhist Monastic Life According to the Texts of the Theravāda Tradition.* Cambridge 1990.
—*Buddhist Nuns. The Birth and Development of a Women's Monastic Order.* Colombo 2001, BPS 2010.

C. Sutta Studies

Oliver Abeynayake, *A Textual and Historical Analysis of the Khuddaka Nikāya.* Colombo 1984
Chizen Akanuma, *The Comparative Catalogue of Chinese Āgamas & Pāli Nikāyas.* Nagoya 1929, Tokyo 1958, Delhi 1990.
Mark Allon, *Style and Function. A study of the dominant stylistic features of the prose portions of Pali canonical sutta texts and their mnemonic function.* Tokyo 1997.
—*Three Gāndhārī Ekottarikāgama-Type Sūtras.* Seattle 2001.
Anālayo, *Satipaṭṭhāna, the Direct Path to Realization.* Birmingham and BPS 2003. A detailed textual study of the Satipaṭṭhāna Sutta including its translation.
—"Some Pali Discourses in the Light of Their Chinese Parallels." 2 parts, *Buddhist Studies Review* 22, 2005, pp.1–14, 93–105.
—"Mindfulness in the Pāli Nikāyas." *Buddhist Thought and Applied Psychological Research,* ed. K. Nauriyal, Abingdon 2006, pp.229–49.
—(with Rod Bucknell) "Correspondence Table for Parallels to the Discourses of the Majjhima Nikāya: Toward a Revision of Akanuma's Comparative Catalogue." *Journal of the Centre for Buddhist Studies* 4, 2006, pp.215–43.
—"Who Said It? Authorship Disagreements between Pāli and Chinese Discourses." *Festschrift für Michael Hahn,* ed. Konrad Klaus and Jens-Uwe Hartmann, Vienna 2007, pp.25–38.
—"The Vekhanassa-sutta and its Madhyama-āgama Parallel—A Case Study in the Transmission of the Pāli Discourses." *Journal of the Centre for Buddhist Studies, Sri Lanka* 5, 2007, pp.89–104.
—"Comparative Notes on the Madhyama-āgama." *Fuyuan Buddhist Studies* 2, 2007, pp.33–56.

—"Oral Dimensions of Pāli Discourses: Pericopes, other Mnemonic Techniques, and the Oral Performance Context." *Canadian Journal of Buddhist Studies* 3, 2007, pp.5–33.
—"The Verses on an Auspicious Night, Explained by Mahākaccāna—A Study and Translation of the Chinese Version" [of the Mahākaccānabhaddekaratta-sutta]. *Ibid.* 4, 2008, pp.5–29.
—"The Vicissitudes of Memory and Early Buddhist Oral Transmission." *Ibid.* 5, 2009.
—"The Chinese Madhyama-āgama and the Pāli Majjhima-nikāya—In the Footsteps of Thich Minh Chau." *The Indian International Journal of Buddhist Studies* 9, 2008, pp.1–21.
—"Reflections on Comparative *Āgama* Studies." *Chung-Hwa Buddhist Journal* 21, 2008, pp. 3–22.
—*From Craving to Liberation—Excursions into the Thought-world of the Pāli Discourses,* Part 1. New York 2009. Collection of revised articles originally published in the *Encyclopaedia of Buddhism.*
—*From Grasping to Emptiness—. . .*, Part 2. *Ibid.* 2010. *Ibid.*
—"Views and the *Tathāgata*—A Comparative Study and Translation of the *Brahmajāla* in the Chinese *Dīrgha-āgama.*" *Buddhist and Pali Studies in Honour of The Venerable Professor Kakkapalliye Anuruddha,* ed. K.L. Dhammajoti and Y. Karunadasa. Hong Kong 2009, pp.183–234.
—"The Development of the Pāli *Udāna* Collection." *Bukkyō Kenkyū* 37, 2009, pp.39–72.
—"Karma and Liberation—The *Karajakāya-sutta* (AN 10.208) in the Light of its Parallels." *Pāsādikadānaṃ. Festschrift für Bhikkhu Pāsādika*, ed. Martin Straube *et al.*, Marburg 2009, pp.1–24.
—"Qualities of a True Recluse (*Samaṇa*)—According to the *Samaṇamaṇḍikā-sutta* and its *Madhyama-āgama* Parallel." *Journal of the Centre for Buddhist Studies* VII, 2009, pp.153–84.
—"The *Āneñjasappāya-sutta* and its Parallels on Imperturbability and on the Contribution of Insight to the Development of Tranquillity." *Buddhist Studies Review* 26, 2009, pp.177–95.
—"The *Bahudhātuka-sutta* and its Parallels on Women's Inabilities." *Journal of Buddhist Ethics* 16, 2009, pp.136–90.
—"The Buddha's Truly Praiseworthy Qualities according to the *Mahāsakuludāya-sutta* and Its Chinese Parallel." JPTS XXX, 2009, pp.137–60.
—"Structural Aspects of the Majjhima-nikāya." *Bukkyō Kenkyū* 38, 2010, pp.35–70.

—"Saccaka's Challenge—A Study of the Saṃyukta-āgama Parallel to the Cūḷasaccaka-sutta in Relation to Notion of Merit Transfer." *Chung-Hwa Buddhist Journal* 23, 2010, pp.39–70.

—"Teachings to Lay-Disciples: The *Saṃyukta-āgama* Parallel to the *Anāthapiṇḍika-sutta*." *Buddhist Studies Review* 27, 2010, pp.3–14.

—"Once again on Bakkula." *The Indian International Journal of Buddhist Studies* 11, 2010, pp.1–28

—"The Mahā cattārīsaka-sutta in the Light of its Parallels – Tracing the Beginnings of Abhidharmic Thought," *Journal of the Centre for Buddhist Studies*, Sri Lanka, 2010, vol. 8 pp. 59–93.

—"Paccekabuddhas in the Isigili-sutta and its Ekottarika-āgama Parallel," *Canadian Journal of Buddhist Studies*, 2010, vol. 6 pp. 5–36.

Masaharu Anesaki, "Traces of Pali Texts in a Mahāyāna Treatise" (Mahāprajñāpāramitāśāstra). *Le Muséon* VII, Louvain 1906, pp.33–45.

—*The Four Buddhist Āgamas in Chinese. A Concordance of their parts and of the corresponding counterparts in the Pāli Nikāyas.* Tokyo 1908.

Naomi Appleton, *Jātaka Stories in Theravāda Buddhism. Narrating the Bodhisatta Path.* Farnham and Burlington (VT) 2010.

B.P. Bapat, "The Different Strata in the Literary Material of the Dīgha Nikāya." *Annals of the Bhandarkar Oriental Research Institute* VIII, 1926, pp.1–16.

D.K. Barua, *An Analytical Study of Four Nikāyas.* Calcutta 1971, New Delhi 2003. An outline of DN, MN, SN and AN.

Marcus Bingenheimer, "The *Suttas* on Sakka in *Āgama* and *Nikāya* Literature—With Some Remarks on the Attribution of the Shorter Chinese *Saṃyukta-āgama*." *Buddhist Studies Review* 25, 2006, pp.149–73.

Kathryn Rennie Blackstone, *Women in the Footsteps of the Buddha.* Richmond (Surrey) 1998. Based on her M.A. thesis (McMaster, Ontario, 1990), "The Struggle for Liberation in the Therīgāthā."

Bodhesako, *Beginnings: The Pali Suttas.* BPS 1984. Reprinted in *Beginnings: Collected Papers of S. Bodhesako.* BPS 2008.

Roderick S. Bucknell, "The Structure of the *Sagātha-Vagga* of the *Saṃyutta-Nikāya*." *Buddhist Studies Review* 24, 2007, pp.7–34.

Grace G. Burford, *Desire, Death and Goodness. The Conflict of Ultimate Values in Theravāda Buddhism.* New York 1991. Based on the Aṭṭhakavagga, Mahāniddesa and Paramatthajotikā II.

Burma Piṭaka Association, *Ten Suttas from Dīgha Nikāya. Three Fundamental Concepts and Comments on Salient Points in each*

Sutta. Rangoon 1985.
Choong Mun-keat, *The Notion of Emptiness in Early Buddhism*. Singapore 1995, Delhi 1999. Based on his M.A. thesis, Univ. of Queensland 1994.
—*The Fundamental Teachings of Early Buddhism. A comparative study based on the Sūtrāṅga portion of the Pāli Saṃyutta-Nikāya and the Chinese Saṃyuktāgama*. Wiesbaden 2000. Based on his doctoral dissertation, Univ. of Queensland 1998.
—*Annotated Translation of Sūtras from the Chinese Saṃyuktāgama relevant to the Early Buddhist Teachings on Emptiness and the Middle Way*. Penang 2004.
—"A comparison of the Pali and Chinese versions of the *Kosala Saṃyutta*, an early Buddhist discourse on King Pasenadi of Kosala." *The Indian International Journal of Buddhist Studies* 7, 2006, pp.21–35.
—"A Comparison of the Pāli and Chinese Versions of the *Bhikkhu Saṃyutta*, a Collection of Early Buddhist Discourses on Monks." *Buddhist Studies Review* 23, 2006, pp.61–70.
—"A Comparison of the Pāli and Chinese Versions of the *Vaṅgīsa-thera Saṃyutta*, a Collection of Early Buddhist Discourses on the Venerable Vaṅgīsa." *Ibid.* 24, 2007, pp.35–45.
—"A Comparison of the Pāli and Chinese Versions of the Brāhmaṇa Saṃyutta, a collection of Early Buddhist Discourses on the priestly Brāhmaṇas." *Journal of the Royal Asiatic Society* 19, 2009, pp.371–82.
Nissim Cohen, "A Note on the Origin of the Pāli Dhammapada Verses." *Buddhist Studies Review* 6, 1989, pp. 130–52.
Sally Mellick Cutler, "The Pāli Apadāna Collection." JPTS XX, 1994, pp. 1–42.
—"A Critical Edition with Selected Portions of the Pāli Apadāna (Yasodharāpadāna)." Ph.D. diss., Oxford 1997.
Gokuldas De, *Significance and Importance of Jātakas with special reference to Bharhut*. University of Calcutta 1951.
Bh. K. Dhammajoti, "The Mahāpadāna Suttanta and the Buddha's Spiritual Lineage." *Sri Lanka Journal of Buddhist Studies* I, 1987, pp.187–96.
—"The Origin and Development of the Dharmapada." *Ibid.* IV, 1994, pp.49–68.
Nalinaksha Dutt, "The Brahmajāla Sutta." *Indian Historical Quarterly* 8, 1932, pp.706–46.
Stephen Evans, "Doubting the *Kālāma Sutta*: Epistemology, Ethics, and the Sacred." *Buddhist Studies Review* 24, 2007, pp.91–107.

—"Epistemology of the *Brahmajāla Sutta*." *Ibid.* 26, 2009, pp.67–84.

Leon Feer, *A Study of the Jātakas, analytical and critical*. Calcutta 1963.

Mavis Fenn, "The *Kūṭadanta Sutta*: Tradition in Tension." *Buddhist Studies from India to America: essays in honor of Charles S. Prebish*, ed. Damien Keown. Abingdon and New York 2005, pp.78–88.

Ernesto Fernandez, *A Guide to the Udāna*. (based on John D. Ireland *The Udāna*, op.cit.). Retrieved on 31.3.2011 from http://www.bps.lk/other library/guide to the udana.pdf

Peter G. Friedlander, "Dhammapada: Translations and Recreations." *One Word, Many Versions*, ed. R. Palapathwala and A.Karickam. Tiruvalla-1 (Kerala) 2007, pp.54–76.

—"Dhammapada Traditions and Translations." *Journal of Religious History* 33, 2009, pp.218–37.

Sean Gaffney, "The Pāli *Nidānakathā* and its Tibetan Translation: Its Textual Precursors and Associated Literature." *The Buddhist Forum* IV, ed. Tadeusz Skorupski, SOAS, London 1996, pp.75–91.

Rupert Gethin, "What's in a Repetition? On Counting the Suttas of the Saṃyutta-nikāya." JPTS XXIX, 2007, pp.365–87.

Andrew Glass, *Four Gāndhārī Saṃyuktāgama Sūtras*. Seattle 2007.

P. Gnanarama, *The Mission Accomplished: A Historical Analysis of the Mahāparinibbāna Sutta of the Dīgha Nikāya of the Pāli Canon*. Singapore 1997.

—*Aspects of Early Buddhist Sociological Thought*. Singapore 1998..

Richard Gombrich, "The Buddha's Book of Genesis?." *Indo-Iranian Journal* 35, 1992, pp.159–78. Repr. in *Buddhism.*

—*Critical Concepts in Religious Studies* I, ed. Paul Williams, Abingdon 2005, pp.129–46.

Ronald M. Green, "Buddhist Economic Ethics: A Theoretical Approach." *Ethics, Wealth and Salvation*, ed. Russell F. Sizemore and Donald K. Swearer, Columbia 1990: "The Aggañña Sutta," pp.227–34.

Devaprasad Guha, "Relative Antiquity of the Khuddakanikāya Texts—A Suggestion." *Journal of the Dept of Pali* 3, Univ. of Calcutta, 1985–86, pp.86–98.

K. Gunaratana, *Maṅgala Sutta Vaṇṇana*. Penang 1952. A commentary on the Maṅgala Sutta.

Hellmuth Hecker, *Similes of the Buddha*. BPS 2009. A description of the similes in the Pali Canon.

I.B. Horner, "Mahā- and Cūḷa-Vaggas and Suttas in the Majjhima-Nikāya." *University of Ceylon Review* XI.3–4, 1953, pp.1–6. Repr. in *Indianisme et Bouddhisme. Mélanges offerts à Mgr Étienne Lamotte*, Louvain-la-Neuve 1980, pp.191–6.

—"Some Notes on the *Buddhavaṃsa* Commentary (*Madhuratthavilāsinī*)." *Buddhist Studies in honour of Walpola Rahula*, ed. S. Balasooriya *et al.*, London 1980, pp.73–83.

John D. Ireland, "The Significance of the Sutta Nipāta in Buddhism." *The Buddhist* [The Sangha Association,London], October 1965, pp.240–47.

—"The Kosambi Suttas." *Pali Buddhist Review* 1, 1976, pp.105–21.

N.A. Jayawickrama, "A Critical Analysis of the Pali Sutta-Nipāta." Serialised in *University of Ceylon Review* VI–IX, 1948–51, and *Pali Buddhist Review* 1–3, London 1976–78. Based on his doctoral dissertation (London 1947), "A critical analysis of the Pali Sutta-Nipāta illustrating its gradual growth."

—"The Exegesis of the Sabbāsavasutta." *The Journal of the Centre for Buddhist Studies [Sri Lanka]* 3, 2005, pp.42–84.

John Garrett Jones, *Tales and Teachings of the Buddha. The Jātaka Stories in relation to the Pali Canon*. London 1979.

David J. Kalupahana, *Causality: The Central Philosophy of Buddhism.* Honolulu 1975. Based on his doctoral dissertation (London 1967), "A critical analysis of the early Buddhist theory of causality as embodied in the Pali Nikāyas and the Chinese Āgamas."

—"A Buddhist tract on empiricism." *Philosophy East and West* XIX.1, 1969, pp.65–67. Texts and translations of SN IV 15 (Sabba Sutta) and its Chinese recension.

Kassapa, *The Simpler Side of the Buddhist Doctrine.* BPS 1960. Extracts from SP with commentary.

Nathan Katz, *Buddhist Images of Human Perfection. The Arahant of the Sutta Piṭaka compared with the Bodhisattva and the Mahāsiddha.* Delhi 1982.

Khantipālo, "Where's that Sutta? A guide to the Discourses in the Numerical Collection (Aṅguttara-nikāya) listing subjects, similes, persons and places." JPTS X, 1985, pp.37–153.

Gisela Krey, "Remarks on the Two Suttas: *Cūḷavedalla-Sutta* and *Khemā (Therī)-Sutta*" (from "On Women as Teachers in Early Buddhism: Dhammadinnā and Khemā"). *Buddhist Studies Review* 27, 2010, pp.23–38.

Tse-fu Kuan, "Annotated Translation of the Chinese Version of the *Kāyagatāsati Sutta.*" *The Indian International Journal of Buddhist Studies* 8, 2007, pp.175–94.

Étienne Lamotte, "Khuddakanikāya and Kṣudrakapiṭaka." *East and West* VII, 1957, pp.341–48.

M.T. Lwin, "A Study of Pali-Burmese *nissaya,* with Special Reference to the Mahāparinibbāna-sutta." M.A. thesis, London 1961.

Larry G. McClury, "The 'Vessantara Jātaka': Paradigm for a Buddhist utopian ideal." Ph.D. diss., Princeton 1975.

Leslie Clifford McTighe, "Mentoring in the 'Majjhima Nikāya': a study of the canonical Buddha's instruction of the laity." Ph.D. diss., Northwestern, Evanston 1988.

Joy Manné, "Categories of Sutta in the Pāli Nikāyas." JPTS XV, 1990, pp. 29–87.

—"The Dīgha Nikāya Debates." *Buddhist Studies Review* 9, 1992, pp. 117–36.

—"On a Departure Formula and its Translation." *Ibid.* 10, 1993, pp. 27–43.

—"Case Histories from the Pāli Canon I: The Sāmaññaphala Sutta Hypothetical Case History." JPTS XXI, 1995, pp. 1–34; II: "*Sotāpanna, Sakadāgāmin, Anāgāmin, Arahat*—The Four Stages Case History." *Ibid.*, pp. 35–128.

—"*Sīhanāda*—The Lion's Roar." *Buddhist Studies Review* 13, 1996, pp. 7–36.

Konrad Meisig, "Chung Têh King. The Chinese Parallel to the Soṇadaṇḍa-Sutta." *Kalyāṇa-Mitta. Professor Hajime Nakamura Felicitation Volume*, ed. V.N. Jha, Delhi 1991, pp.51–62.

—"On the Archetype of the Ambāṣṭasūtra." *Wiener Zeitschrift für Kunde Südasiens—Supplementband*, 1993, pp.229–37.

—"On the Precanonical Shape of the *Kevaddha-sutta* as Compared with the *Kien-ku-King*." *Premier Colloque Étienne Lamotte*, Louvain-la-Neuve 1993, pp.63–70.

—"A Translation of the Chinese Kevaddhasutta Together with the Critical Apparatus of the Pāli Text." *Festschrift Dieter Schlingloff*, ed. Friedrich Wilhelm, Reinbek 1996, pp.187–200.

—"A Stratification of the Śoṇatāṇḍyasūtra." *Studia Tibetica et Mongolica (Festschrift Manfred Taube)*, ed. Helmut Eimer *et al.*, Swisttal-Odendorf 1999, pp.217–24.

Minh Chau, *The Chinese Mādhyama Āgama and Pāli Majjhima Nikāya*. Saigon 1964, Delhi 1991.

Hōjun Nagasaki, "The Khaggavisāṇa-sutta and the Pacceka-buddha." *The Buddhist Seminar* 55, 1993, pp.1–14.

—"The Rhinoceros Sūtra." *Nyāya-Vasiṣṭha. Felicitation Volume of Prof. V.N. Jha*, Kolkata 2006, pp.279–84.

U Ñāṇadicca, *The Thirty-Eight Blessings for World Peace.* A translation of and word-for-word commentary on the Maṅgala Sutta.

N.P. Nimalasuria (tr.) and Mahāgoda Nyāṇissara (rev.), *Dhamma Hadaya Vibhaṅga Sutta* (from the apocryphal Sutta-saṅgaha). Colombo (?) 1910.

K.R. Norman, "Notes on the Sutta-nipāta." *Sri Lanka Journal of Buddhist Studies I*, 1987, pp.100–16; *Collected Papers III*. PTS 1992, pp.137–56.

—"The Dhaniya-Sutta of the Sutta-nipāta." *Journal of the Department of Pali*. University of Calcutta IV, 1987–88, pp.10–18; *Collected Papers IV*. PTS 1993, pp.146–54.

—"On Translating the Dhammapada." *Buddhist Studies Review* 6, 1989, pp. 153–65.

—"The Aṭṭhakavagga and early Buddhism." *Jainism and Early Buddhism. Essays in Honor of Padmanabh S. Jaini*, ed. Olle Qvarnström, Fremont (CA) 2003, pp.511–22; *Collected Papers VIII*. PTS 2007, pp.167–82.

—"The structure of the Sādhu-sutta" [SN I, 20–22]. *Śemuṣi. Padmabhūṣaṇa Professor Baladeva Upādhyāya Birth Centenary Volume*, Varanasi 2004, pp.660–63; *Collected Papers VIII*. PTS 2007, pp.216–23.

—"On Translating the Suttanipāta." *Buddhist Studies Review* 21, 2004, pp. 69–84.

U Nu, *What are Maṅgalas?* Rangoon 1962. A commentary on the Maṅgala Sutta.

Hermann Oldenberg, "The Sutta Nipāta, a Collection of Old Buddhist Poems." *The Buddhist Review II* [The Buddhist Society of Great Britain and Ireland, London], pp.243–68.

P. Oliver, "A critical analysis of the Pali Khuddaka Nikāya in a historical and literary perspective." Ph.D. diss., Lancaster 1972.

W. Pachow, *Comparative Studies in the Mahāparinibbāna Sutta and its Chinese Versions*. Shantiniketan 1946.

Sudharma Pandita, "The Role of Similes in the Pali Nikāyas." *Buddhist Philosophy and Culture. Essays in Honour of N.A. Jayawickrema*, ed. David J. Kalupahana and W.G. Weeraratne, Colombo 1987, pp.279–85.

Bh. M. Paññāsiri, "Sigālovada-Sutta." *Visva-Bharati Annals* III, Shantiniketan 1950, pp.150–228. Annotated translation of the four Chinese recensions of this text

Bh. Pāsādika, "The Madhyamāgama Parallel to the Rathavinīta Sutta of the Majjhimanikāya." *Buddhism for the New Millenium*, London 2000, pp.193–205.

—"The *Ekottarāgama* Parallel to *Aṅguttaranikāya* III, 57–62 (V.50). Translated from the Chinese Version." *Jaina-Itihāsa-Ratna. Festschrift für Gustav Roth zum 90. Geburtstag*, ed. Ute Hüsken *et al.*, Marburg 2006, pp.397–406.

—"The *Ekottarāgama* Parallel to the *Mūlapariyāyasutta*." *The Indian International Journal of Buddhist Studies* 9, 2008, pp.141–49.

W. Pemaratana, "An Introduction to [the] Aggaññasutta." *Essays in Honour of Professor Lily de Silva*. Peradeniya 2001.

L.P.N. Perera, "An Analysis of the Sela Sutta of the Sutta Nipāta." *Pali Buddhist Review* 4, 1979, pp.66–70. Repr. from *University of Ceylon Review* VIII.3, 1950.

Piyasīlo, *Translating Buddhist Sutras* (sic). Petaling Jaya 1989.

Chandra Shekhar Prasad, "Some Reflections on the Relation between the Āgamas and the Nikāyas." *Proceedings and Papers of the Second Conference of the International Association of Buddhist Studies*, Nalanda 1985, pp.131–40.

P.D. Premasiri, *The Philosophy of the Aṭṭhakavagga*. BPS 1972. An elucidation of the themes in Sn 4.

Christopher D.C. Priestley, *A Study of the Pāli and Chinese Versions of the Mahānidānasuttanta*. Toronto 1966.

Vijitha Rajapakse, "Therigāthā: On Feminism, Aestheticism and Religiosity in an early Buddhist verse anthology." *Buddhist Studies Review* 12, 1995, pp. 7–26, 135–55. Offprinted as *The Therīgāthā*. BPS 2000.

Richard Salomon, *A Gāndhārī Version of the Rhinoceros Sūtra*. Seattle 2000.

Jampa Samten, "Notes on the Study of [the] Pali Version and Tibetan Translation of [the] *Mahāparinirvāṇasūtra*." *Mahayana Buddhism. History and Culture*, ed. Darrol and Susan Bryant, New Delhi 2008, pp.101–10.

Sadhanchandra Sarkar, *A Study on the Jātakas and the Avadānas*. Calcutta 1981.

B.C. Sen, *Studies in the Buddhist Jātakas*. Calcutta 1930, 1974.

Eviatar Shulman, "Mindful Wisdom: The Satipaṭṭhāna-sutta on Mindfulness, Memory and Liberation." *History of Religions* 49, 2010, pp.393–420.

Peter Skilling, "Jātaka and Paññāsa-jātaka in Southeast Asia." JPTS XXVIII, 2006, pp.113–73.

R.L. Soni, *Life's Highest Blessing*. Mandalay 1956, BPS 1978. A commentary on the Maṅgala Sutta.

Ajahn Sucitto, *Turning the Wheel of Truth. Commentary on the Buddha's First Teaching*. Boston 2010.

A. Syrkin, "On the First Work in the Sutta-Piṭaka: the Brahmajāla-Sutta." *Buddhist Studies Ancient and Modern*, ed. Philip Denwood and Alexander Piatigorsky, London 1983, pp.153–66.

(Thich) Thiên Thanh, "A comparative study of the Pāli Dīgha-Nikāya and Chinese Dīrghāgama." Ph.D. diss., Magadh Univ., Patna 1976.

Susunaga Weeraperuma, *The First and Best Buddhist Teachings: Sutta Nipāta, Selections and Inspired Essays*. Delhi 2006.

Raymond B. Williams, "Historical Criticism of a Buddhist Scripture: The Mahāparinibbāna Sutta." *Journal of the American Academy of Religion* 38, 1970, pp.156–67.

Alexander Wynne, "How old is the Suttapiṭaka?" (2003). Retrieved on 32.3.2011 from http://www.buddhanet.net/budsas/ebud/ebsut056.htm

D. Abhidhamma Studies

Alka Barua, *Kathāvatthu: A Critical and Philosophical Study*. Delhi 2006.

Amal K. Barua, *Mind and Mental Factors in Early Buddhist Psychology*. New Delhi 1990.

N.K. Bhagwat, *The Buddhistic Philosophy of the Theravada School, as embodied in the Pali Abhidhamma*. Patna University 1929.

Lance Cousins, "The Paṭṭhāna and the Development of the Theravādin Abhidhamma." JPTS IX, 1981, pp.22–46. Repr. in *Buddhism. Critical Concepts in Religious Studies* IV, ed. Paul Williams, Abingdon 2005, pp.52–70.

S.N. Dube, *Cross Currents in Early Buddhism*. Delhi 1980. A critical analysis of the Kathāvatthu.

Erich Frauwallner, "The Abhidharma of the Pali School." *Abhidharma Literature and the Origins of Buddhist Philosophical Systems*, New York 1995, pp.39–95.

Rupert Gethin, "The *Mātikas*: memorization, mindfulness and the list." *In the Mirror of Memory. Reflections on Mindfulness and Rembrance in Tibetan Buddhism*, ed. Janet Gyatso. Albany (NY) 1992, pp.149–72.

—"On the Nature of *dhammas*." *Buddhist Studies Review* 22, 2005, pp.175–94. Review article on Noa Ronkin (see below).

Nina van Gorkom, *Abhidhamma in Daily Life*. Bangkok 1975.

—*Cetasikas*. Bangkok 1977.

—*Conditionality of Life. An Outline of the Twenty-Four Conditions as Taught in the Abhidhamma*. London 2010.

Lama Anāgārika Govinda, *The Psychological Attitude of Early Buddhist Philosophy—and its Systematic Representation according to the Abhidhamma Tradition*. London 1961.

Herbert V. Guenther, *Philosophy and Psychology in the Abhidharma*. Delhi 1974.

David J. Kalupahana, "The Philosophy of Relations in Buddhism" (a study of the Paṭṭhāna). M.A. thesis, Univ. of Ceylon, 1961.

Y. Karunadasa, *Buddhist Analysis of Matter*. Colombo 1967.
—*The Dharma Theory, Philosophical Cornerstone of the Abhidhamma*. BPS 1996.
—*The Theravada Abhidhamma*. Hong Kong, 2010.
Jagdish Kashyap, *The Abhidhamma Philosophy II*. Benares 1943, Patna 1954, Delhi 1982, New Delhi 1996. Comprises an analysis of this Piṭaka.
Ledi Sayadaw, *Paṭṭhānuddesa Dīpanī: Manual of the Philosophy of Relations*. Rangoon 1935. Reprinted as *The Buddhist Philosophy of Relations*. BPS 1986.
U Nārada, *Guide to Conditional Relations I*. PTS 1979, *II* Rangoon 1986.
Nyanaponika, *Abhidhamma Studies*. Dodanduwa 1949, BPS 1965, 2007. Essays mainly based on the Dhammasaṅgaṇī and Atthasālinī.
Nyanatiloka, *Guide through the Abhidhamma Piṭaka*. BSS 1938, BPS 1971, 2008.
Aloysius Pieris, s.j., *Studies in the Philosophy and Literature of Pali Abhidhammika Buddhism*. Colombo 2007.
Karl H. Potter (ed.), *Encyclopedia of Indian Philosophy VII*: Abhidhamma Buddhism to 150 A.D. New Delhi 1996.
Noa Ronkin, *Early Buddhist Metaphysics. The Making of a Philosophical Tradition*. Richmond (Surrey) 2005.
G.D. Sumanapala, *An Introduction to Theravāda Abhidhamma*. Singapore 1998.
—*Reality and Expression, A Study on the Conception of Paññatti in the Theravāda Abhidhamma*. Kadugannawa 1999.
Chandra B. Varma, *A Concise Encyclopaedia of Early Buddhist Philosophy based on the study of the Abhidhammatthasaṅgahasarūpa*. Delhi 1992.
—*Methodology for editing and translating a source material on history of science and the text of the Abhidhammathasaṅgahasarūpa*. Delhi 1995.
Alfonsa Verdu, *Early Buddhist Philosophy in the Light of the Four Noble Truths*. Delhi 1985. Based primarily on the Abhidharmakośa and Vism.
(Paṭṭhān Sayadaw) U Visuddha and Myanaung U Tin, *An Approach to Paṭṭhāna*. Rangoon 1956.
Fumimaro Watanabe, *Philosophy and its Development in the Nikāyas and Abhidhamma*. Delhi 1981.
Alexander Wynne, "The Buddha's 'Skill in Means' and the Genesis of the Five Aggregate Teaching." (Focussing on MN 22.) *Journal of the Royal Asiatic Society* 20, 2010, pp.191–216.

6. Journals

Innumerable popular Buddhist magazines and academic periodicals of the Royal Asiatic Society (JRAS), European, American, Indian, Sri Lankan and Thai University Oriental faculties and learned societies publish translations from the Pāli Canon together with studies of the language and later or related literature in their periodicals. Invaluable studies are recorded in the journals of the Pali Text Society (JPTS 1882–1927, reprinted 1978, and revived in 1981. However, four journals should be singled out for special mention:

The Blessing, ed. Cassius A. Perera (later Kassapa Thera), published by the Servants of the Buddha, Bambalapitiya, Sri Lanka. This appeared in ten issues during 1925 and contained, almost exclusively, translations from the SP (notably MN 51–70) by Nārada and Mahinda.

The Light of the Dhamma, ed. David Maurice for the Union Buddha Sāsana Council, Rangoon 1952–63. Apart from containing (on average) two *suttas* in each issue, this quarterly provided the first popular outlet for the writings of Ledi Sayadaw, Ñāṇamoli, Nyanaponika, Nyanasatta, Nyanatiloka, Francis Story and other leading Theravādins. Many of their translations and essays subsequently appeared in *The Wheel* series of the Buddhist Publication Society, Kandy.

Pali Buddhist Review, ed. Russell Webb for the Pali Buddhist Union, Ilford, Essex (later London) 1976–82. This appeared thrice yearly and included translations and exegeses.

Buddhist Studies Review, the successor of the *Pali Buddhist Review*, ed. Russell Webb and Sara Boin-Webb from 1983 to 2004 (from 1998 on behalf of the UK Association for Buddhist Studies).

7. Encyclopedias

B. Baruah and N.K. Singh, *Encyclopaedic Dictionary of Pali Literature*. 2 vols, Delhi 2003.

Robert E.Buswell (ed.), *Encyclopaedia of Buddhism*. 2 vols, New York 2004.

Ian C. Harris, *Illustrated Encyclopaedia of Buddhism*. London 2009.

Edward A.Irons, *Encyclopaedia of Buddhism*. New York 2008.

Damien Keown *et al.*, *A Dictionary of Buddhism*. Oxford 2003.

Damien Keown and Charles S. Prebish (ed.), *Encyclopaedia of Buddhism*. Abingdon 2007.

T.O. Ling, *A Dictionary of Buddhism*. New York 1972, Calcutta 1996.
Stephan Schuhmacher and Gert Woerner (ed.), *The Rider Encyclopaedia of Eastern Philosophy and Religion*. London 1989, 1999. The sections on Buddhism were offprinted as *The Shambhala Dictionary of Buddhism and Zen*. Boston 1991.
Sridhar Tripathi (ed), *Encyclopaedia of Pali Literature*. 20 vols, Pune 2008.

Encyclopaedia of Buddhism

G.P. Malalasekera et al., *Encyclopaedia of Buddhism*. Colombo 1961–2009. The most informative and relevant entries comprise the following. References to DN, MN and It reflect the *sutta* no. in each collection and Sn according to suttas within each *vagga*. However, as regards SN and AN, the suttas are numbered according to their provenance in the *saṃyuttas* and *nipātas* respectively. In AN I, e.g., the PTS Translation Vol.I (The Book of the Ones) has each of Chapters I–XIII (pp.1–15) including the specific number of suttas for each section followed by Chapter XIV divided into sections (a) to (g). For the purposes of achieving a continuous sequence of suttas, I have calculated that the first thirteen chapters comprise 177 suttas and have counted those sections in Ch.XIV as seven suttas, numbering the succeeding suttas accordingly.

Abhabba Sutta (AN 10:76), Fasc. A–Aca, 1961, p.10
Abhaya S. (SN 46:56; AN 4:184), *ibid.*, 33–34
Abhayarājakumāra S. (MN 58), *ibid.*, 32
Abibhū S. (AN 3:80, 8:65), *ibid.*, 36–37
Abhidhamma, *ibid.*, 37–49
Abhidhammatha-Saṅgaha, *ibid.*, 50–51
Abhidhammāvatāra, *ibid.*, 52–53
Abhidharma Literature, *ibid.*, 64–68, 75–80
Abhijāna S. (SN 22:24), *ibid.*, 90
Abhinandamāna S. (SN 22:64), *ibid.*, 93–94
Abhiññā S. (AN 4:25), *ibid.*, 102–03
Abhisamaya Saṃyutta (SN 13), *ibid.*, 119–20
Abhisambodhi-Alaṅkāra, *ibid.*, 120–21
Abhisanda Sutta (SN 55:31–33, 41–43; AN 4:51–52, 5:51, 8:39), *ibid.*, 121–22
Acchariya-Abbuta-Dhamma S. (MN 123; AN 4:127–30), Fasc. Acala–Ākaṅ, 1963, pp.171–72
Acela S. (SN 12:17, 41:9), *ibid.*, 178
Acelaka Vagga (*Book of the Discipline* II, pp.347–81; AN 3), *ibid.*, 177

Adanta Vagga (AN 1 iv), *ibid.*, 189
Addha Vagga (SN 1:61–70), *ibid.*, 193
Adhamma Sutta (AN 10:113), *ibid.*, 193–95
Adhamma Vagga (AN :140–49), *ibid.*, 195
Adhammika Sutta (AN 4:70), *ibid.*
Adhicitta S. (AN 3:100, vv 11–15), *ibid.*, 196–97
Adhimutti S. (AN 10:21), *ibid.*, 204
Ādhipateyya S. (AN 3:40), *ibid.*, 205
Ādittapariyāya S. (SN 35:28), *ibid.*, 225–26
Āditta S. (SN 1:41, 35:194), *ibid.*, 226
Āditta Vagga (SN 1:41–50), *ibid.*
Ādiya Sutta (AN 3:41), *ibid.*, 227–28
Agārava S. (AN 5:8–10, 21–22), *ibid.*, 254–55
Agati S. (AN 4:17–19), *ibid.*, 255–56
Aggañña S. (DN 27), *ibid.*, 258–60
Aggappas-da S. (It. 90), *ibid.*, 260
Aggavati-Parisā S. (AN 3:93), *ibid.*, 260–61
Aggi S. (SN 46:53; AN 5:219, 7:43–44), *ibid.*, 265–66
Aggika S. (SN 7:9), *ibid.*, 263
Aggikkhandhopama S. (AN 7:68), *ibid.*, 263–64
Aggi-Vacchagotta S. (MN 72), *ibid.*, 266
Āghāta S. (AN 5:161–62, 9:29–30), *ibid.*, 268
Āhara S. (SN 12:11, 46:51), *ibid.*, 283–84
Āhara Vagga (SN 12:11–20), *ibid.*, 284
Ahirikamūlaka S. (SN 14:23ff), *ibid.*, 293
Āhuneyya S. (AN 6:1–7, 8:57–60, 9:10, 10:16), *ibid.*, 296
Ājāniya S. (AN 3:94–96), *ibid.*, 299–300
Ājañña S. (AN 4:256–57, 8:13), *ibid.*, 300
Ajita S. (AN 10:113–16), *ibid.*, 328–29
Ajitamāṇava-Pucchā (Sn V), *ibid.*, 327
Ājīvaka S. (AN 3:72), *ibid.*, 330
Ākaṅkheyya S. (MN 6; AN 10:71), *ibid.*, 336
Ākāsa S. (SN 28:5, 36:12, 40:5, 45:155), Fasc. Ākaṅkheyya S [*sic*]-Anabhirati, 1964, p.348
Akkhaṇa S. (AN 8:29), *ibid.*, 354–55
Akkosa S. (SN 7:2; AN 5:211), *ibid.*, 358
Akkosa Vagga (AN 10:41–50), *ibid.*
Akkosaka Vagga (AN 5:211–20), *ibid.*, 357–58
Akusalamūla Sutta (AN 3:69), *ibid.*, 369
Alagaddūpama S. (MN 22), *ibid.*, 370
Ālavaka S. (AN 3:34; Sn I 10), *ibid.*, 381
Āmagandha S. (Sn II 2), *ibid.*, 401–02

Amata S. (SN 43:12, 47:41; AN 9:54), *ibid.*, 413
Amata Vagga (SN 47:41–50), *ibid.*, 414
Ambalapāli Sutta (SN 47:1, 52:9), *ibid.*, 419
Ambalapāli Vagga (SN 47:1–10), *ibid.*, 419–20
Ambaṭṭha Sutta (DN 3), *ibid.*, 424
Anabhirati S. (SN 46:70), *ibid.*, 504
Anabhisamaya S. (SN 33:1), Fasc.4, 1965, p.505
Anāgāmi S. (AN 6:65), *ibid.*, 509
Anāgata S. (AN 5: 79), *ibid.*, 514
Anāgatavaṃsa, 515
Anālaya Sutta (SN 43:44), *ibid.*, 518
Anamata Saṃyutta (SN 15), *ibid.*, 527–28
Ananaka Sutta (AN 4:62), *ibid.*, 528
Ānañcāyatana S. (AN 3:114), *ibid.*
Ānanda S. (SN 8:4, 9:5, 22:21,37,38,83, 44:10, 51:29,30, 54:13,14, 55:13; AN 3:32, 4:174, 5:106, 6:51, 9:37, 10:5,82), *ibid.*, 543–44
Anaṅgana S. (MN 5), *ibid.*, 545–46
Āneñjasappāya S. (MN 106), *ibid.*, 546
Anantavā S. (SN 24:18), *ibid.*, 556
Ananussuta S. (AN 5:11), *ibid.*, 557
Ānāpāna Saṃyutta (SN 54), *ibid.*, 558
Ānāpāna Sutta (SN 46:66), *ibid.*, 561–62
Ānāpāna Vagga (SN 46:57–66), *ibid.*, 562
Ānāpānasati Sutta (MN 118), *ibid.*, 561
Anāsava S. (SN 43:22), *ibid.*, 562–63
Anāthapiṇḍika S. (SN 56:26–28), *ibid.*, 566
Anāthapiṇḍikakovāda S. (MN 143), *ibid.*, 566–67
Anatta-Lakkhaṇa S. (*Book of the Discipline* IV, pp.20–21; SN 22:59), *ibid.*, 576–77
Anatta S. (SN 22:14,29,33,70, 35:3,6,10–12,32), *ibid.*, 578
Andhakāra S. (SN 56:46; It.87), *ibid.*, 606
Andhakavibda S. (SN 6:13; AN 5:114), *ibid.*, 609
Andhakavinda Vagga (AN 5:111–20), *ibid.*
Aṅga, *ibid.*, 616–17
Aṅgāni Sutta (AN 5:28, 10:12), *ibid.*, 622
Aṅgika S. (AN 5:28), *ibid.*, 625
Aṅguttara-Nava-Ṭīkā, *ibid.*, 629
Aṅguttara Nikāya, *ibid.*, 629–55
Anicca Sutta (SN 22:15,16, 23:13,23–34, 35:1–10,53, 46:76, 48:39; AN 7:16), *ibid.*, 663–64
Aniccatā S. (SN 22:45,46,102), *ibid.*, 664
Ānisaṃsa S. (AN 6:97), *ibid.*, 678

Ānisaṃsa Vagga (AN 6:96–106, 10:1–10), *ibid.*
Āṇī Sutta (SN 20:7), *ibid.*, 678–79
Anna S. (SN 1:42,43, 2:23; AN 4:87), *ibid.*, 702
Añña S. (SN 47:36), *ibid.*
Aññatara-Bhikkhu S. (SN 45:6,7), *ibid.*, 702–03
Aññatara-Brahma S. (SN 1:5), *ibid.*, 703
Aññatara S. (SN 12:46), *ibid.*
Aññatitthiya S. (SN 12:24; AN 3:68), *ibid.*, 703–04
Aññatitthiya Vagga (SN 45:41–48), *ibid.*, 704
Aññatra Sutta (SN 56:102ff), *ibid.*
Anodhi S. (AN 6:102–04), *ibid.*, 712
Anottāpī S. (SN 16:2), *ibid.*, 721
Anottappamūlaka S. (SN 14:23–25), *ibid.*, 722
Anta S. (SN 22:103, 43:14–43), *ibid.*, 737–38
Antavā S. (SN 24:37–44), *ibid.*, 738
Antevāsī S. (SN 35:150), *ibid.*, 740
Anudhamma S. (SN 22:39–42), *ibid.*, 740–41
Anukampaka S. (AN 5:235), *ibid.*, 742–43
Anumāna S. (MN 15), *ibid.*, 746
Anupada S. (MN 111), *ibid.*, 750
Anupada Vagga (MN 111–20), *ibid.*
Anurādha Sutta (SN 22:86, 44:2), *ibid.*, 765–66
Anuruddha Saṃyutta (SN 52), *ibid.*, 772
Anuruddha Sutta (MN 127; SN 9:6; AN 3:128, 8:30,9:46), *ibid.*, 772–74
Anusaya S. (SN 18:21, 35:58,59, 45:42–48, 48:64, 54:20), *ibid.*, 777–78
Anusota S. (AN 6:6), *ibid.*, 778
Anussati S. (AN 6:25), *ibid.*, 779
Anuttariya S. (AN 6:11,12), *ibid.*, 784
Anuttariya Vagga (AN 6:21–30), *ibid.*
Anuvattanā Sutta (AN 5:132), *ibid.*, 784–85
Apadāna, Fasc. II, 1, 1966, pp.2–3
Apaṇṇaka Sutta (MN 60; AN 3:115), *ibid.*, 6
Apaṇṇakatā S. (AN 3:16), *ibid.*, 6–7
Apaṇṇaka Vagga (AN 2:71–80), *ibid.*, 7
Aparihāniya Sutta (AN 6:22,32), *ibid.*, 16
Āpatti S. (AN 4:241), *ibid.*, 23–24
Āpatti Vagga (AN 4:241–50), *ibid.*, 24
Āpāyika Vagga (AN 3:111–20), *ibid.*, 26
Appamāda Sutta ((SN 3:17,18, 12:83ff, 45:63–69; AN 4:116, 6:53, 7:31, 10:15; It.23), *ibid.*, 29–30
Appamāda Vagga (SN 46:89–98), *ibid.*, 30

Appamatta Vagga (AN 1:140–49), *ibid.*, 31
Appasuta Sutta (SN14:14–22), *ibid.*, 32–33
Aputtaka S. (SN 3:19,20), *ibid.*, 39
Ārabbhavatthu S. (AN 8:80), *ibid.*
Ārabhati S. (AN 5:142), *ibid.*
Arahaṃ S. (SN 1:25, 22:110, 48:4,5, 51:8, 56:23; AN 6:66), *ibid.*, 40
Arahanta S. (SN22:76,77), *ibid.*, 55
Arahā S. (SN 23:8, 48:27,28,33), *ibid*
Arahatta S. (SN 38:1; AN 6:76), *ibid.*
Arahatta Vagga (SN 22:63–72; AN 6:75–84), *ibid.*
Araka Sutta (AN 7:70), *ibid.*, 58
Ārammaṇa S. (SN 34:14,15), *ibid.*, 62
Araṇavibhaṅga S. (MN 139), *ibid.*, 62–63
Araṇi S. (SN 48:39), *ibid.*, 63–64
Āraññа S. (SN 1:10; AN 4:259, 5:98,110), *ibid.*, 65–66
Āraññа Vagga (AN 5:181–90), *ibid.*, 66
Arati Sutta (SN 8:2; AN 6:113), *ibid.*, 70
Ariyamagga S. (AN 10: 145), *ibid.*, 82
Ariyamagga Vagga (AN 10: 145–54), *ibid.*
Ariyapariyesana Sutta (MN 26), *ibid.*, 83
Ariyasāvaka S. (SN 12:49,50), *ibid.*, 88
Ariya S. (SN 46:19, 47:17, 51:3), *ibid.*, 88–89
Ariyavāsa S. (AN 10:19,20), *ibid.*, 93
Aruka S. (AN 3:25), *ibid.*, 101
Asaddhamūlaka S. (SN 14:23–27), *ibid.*, 123
Asallakkhaṇā S. (SN 33:26–30), *ibid.*, 125
Asamapekkhaṇā S. (SN 33:41–45), *ibid.*
Asaṅkhata Saṃyutta (SN 43), *ibid.*, 150–51
Āsaṇkhata Sutta (SN 43:12–44), *ibid.*, 151
Asappurisa S. (SN 45:31,32), *ibid.*, 153
Āsavakkhaya S. (SN 45:45, 48:64, 54:20, 56:25; AN 5:69), *ibid.*, 155
Āsava S. (AN 6:58, 10:126; It. 56,57), *ibid.*
Āseva S. (AN 1:51–60), *ibid.*, 169
Āsevitabba S. (AN 3:26), *ibid.*
Āsīvisa S. (SN 35:197; AN 4:110), Fasc. II, 2 (1967), p.177
Āsīvisopama S. (*ibid.*), *ibid.*, 177–78
Assalāyana S. (MN 93), *ibid.*, 219–20
Assutavā S. (SN 12:62), *ibid.*, 228
Assutavata S. (SN 12:61), *ibid.*
Asubha S. (SN 46:67; AN 4:163; It. 85), *ibid.*, 282–83
Asura Vagga (AN 4:91–100), *ibid.*, 291
Āṭānāṭiya S. (DN 32), *ibid.*, 302

Ātappa S. (SN 12:89; AN 3:49), *ibid.*, 303
Ātītānāgatapaccuppana S. (SN 22:9–11), *ibid.*, 315–16
Atītena S. (SN 35:19–36), *ibid.*, 316
Attadaṇḍa S. (Sn 4:15), *ibid.*, 322–23
Attadīpa S. (SN 22:43), *ibid.*, 323
Attakāra S. (AN 6:38), *ibid.*, 324
Attantāpa S. (AN 4:198), *ibid.*, 327
Atta S. (SN 45:64–69), *ibid.*, 328
Aṭṭhakanāgara S. (MN 52; AN 11:17), *ibid.*, 334
Aṭṭhaka Nipāta (AN 8), *ibid.*
Aṭṭhaka Sutta (SN 36:17,18), *ibid.*, 334–35
Aṭṭhakathā, *ibid.*, 335–52
Aṭṭhaka Vagga (Sn 4), *ibid.*, 352; contd. in Fasc. II, 3 (1967), p.353
Aṭṭhaṅgika Sutta (SN 14:28; AN 4:205), Fasc.II, 3, 363–64
Aṭṭhaṅgika-Magga S. (SN 43:11), *ibid.*, 363
Aṭṭhapuggala S. (AN 8:59,60), *ibid.*, 365
Atthasālinī, *ibid.*, 366–68
Atthasata S. (SN 36:22), *ibid.*, 369
Atthavasa Vagga (AN 2:280–84), *ibid.*, 369–70
Atthirāga Sutta (SN 12:65), *ibid.*, 371
Āvaraṇa-Nīvaraṇa S. (SN 46:37), *ibid.*, 428
Āvaraṇa S. (AN 5:51), *ibid.*
Avijjā S. (SN 22:49,50,113, 35:53, 38:9, 45:1, 56:17), *ibid.*, 459–60
Avyākata S. (AN 7:51–60), *ibid.*, 466–67
Āyācana Vagga (AN 2:130–42), *ibid.*, 468
Āyu Sutta (SN 4:9,10), *ibid.*, 483
Āyussa S. (AN 5:125,126), *ibid.*
Bahudhātuka S. (MN 115), Fasc. II, 4 (1968), p.497
Bahukāra S. (AN 3:24), *ibid.*, 497–98
Bahūpakāra S. (AN 5:234; It.107), *ibid.*, 499–500
Bahuvedanīya S. (MN 59), *ibid.*, 505
Baka-Brahmā S. (SN 6:4), *ibid.*, 509
Balām S. (AN 4:151–55), *ibid.*, 519
Bālapaṇḍita S. (MN 129; SN 12:19), *ibid.*, 519–20
Bala Saṃyutta (SN 50), *ibid.*, 520
Bala Sutta (SN 43:12.xxvi–xxx, 45:149; AN 4:58, 5:204, 6:4, 7:3,4, 8:27,28, 10:90), *ibid.*, 520–21
Bala Vagga (SN 50:1–12,55–66; AN 5:11–20), *ibid.*, 521
Bāla Sutta (AN 2:31–40,98–117, 3:1–10), *ibid.*, 521–22
Bandhanā S. (SN 1:65, 3:10, 22:117), *ibid.*, 538
Bhaddāli S. (MN 65), *ibid.*, 625–26
Bhaddekaratta S. (MN 131), *ibid.*, 628–29

Bhaddiya [S.] (AN 4:193), *ibid.*, 630
Bhadra S. (SN 42:11), *ibid.*, 643
Bhaṇḍagāma Vagga (AN 4:1–10), *ibid.*, 690–91
Bhaṇḍana Sutta (AN 3:122, 5:212, 10:50), *ibid.*, 691
Bhāra S. (SN 22:22), *ibid.*, 695
Bhāvanā S. (SN 47:34, 51:20; AN 7:67), Fasc. III, 1 (1971), pp.16–17
Bhava S. (SN 38:13, 45:164; AN 3:76, 6:105), *ibid.*, 21
Bhaya S. (SN 55:29; AN 3:62, 4:119–21, 6:23, 8:56), *ibid.*, 24–25
Bhaya Vagga (AN 4:121–30), *ibid.*, 25
Bhayabherava Sutta (MN 4), *ibid.*, 24
Bhikkhu Saṃyutta (SN 21:1–12), *ibid.*, 48
Bhikkhu Sutta (SN 12:28, 17:30, 19:17, 22:35,36,113,114, 35:81, 36:20,23, 47:3, 51:7,23,29,30, 54:15,16, 55:29,46; AN 7:21), *ibid.*, 48–50
Bhikkhunī Saṃyutta (SN 5:1–10), *ibid.*, 47
Bhikkhunī Sutta (SN 19:18; AN 4:159), *ibid.*
Bhikkhunīvāsaka S. (SN 47:10), *ibid.*
Bhoga S. (AN 5:227), *ibid.*, 63
Bhojana S. (AN 4:59, 5:37), *ibid.*, 67
Bhūmicāla S. (AN 8:70), *ibid.*, 81
Bhūmija S. (MN 126; SN 12:25), *ibid.*, 81–82
Bīja S. (SN 22:54, 45:150, 56:78; AN 1:225–34, 10:104), *ibid.*, 111–12
Bodhirājakumāra S. (MN 85), Fasc. III, 2 (1972), p.220
Bojjhaṅga Saṃyutta (SN 46), *ibid.*, 272
Bojjhaṅga Sutta (SN 43:10, 54:2; AN 4:236), *ibid.*, 272–73
Brahmajāla S. (DN 1), *ibid.*, 310–11
Brāhmaṇadhammika S. (Sn 2:7), *ibid.*, 316
Brāhmaṇa Saṃyutta (SN 6), *ibid.*, 317–18
Brāhmaṇa Sutta (SN 45:4, 47:25, 51:15, 55:12; AN 3:53, 9:38; It.100), *ibid.*, 318–19
Brāhmaṇa Vagga (AN 3:51–60, 5:191–200), *ibid.*, 320–21
Brāhmanimantanika S. (MN 49), *ibid.*, 321
Brahmañña S. (SN 45:37,38, 56:69), *ibid.*, 329
Brahma Saṃyutta (SN 6), *ibid.*, 331
Brahma Sutta (SN 47:18, 48:57), *ibid.*, 332
Brahmāyu S. (MN 91), *ibid.*, 337
Buddhavaṃsa, *ibid.*, 465
Cakkānuvatta S. (AN 5:131,132), Fasc. III, 4 (1977), pp.568–69
Cakka S. (AN 4:31), *ibid.*, 569–70
Cakka Vagga (AN 4:31–40), *ibid.*, 570
Cakkavattisīhanāda S. (DN 26), *ibid.*, 570–72
Cakkavatti S. (SN 46:42; AN 3:14), *ibid.*, 572

Cakkavatti Vagga (SN 46:41–50), *ibid.*
Cakkhu Sutta (SN 18:1, 25:1, 26:1, 27:1; It.51), *ibid.*, 575
Caṅkī S. (MN 95), *ibid.*, 663
Cāpāla Vagga (SN 51:1–10), *ibid.*, 666
Cara Sutta (AN 4:11), *ibid.*, 669
Cara Vagga (AN 4:11–20), *ibid.*
Carita Sutta (AN 4:148,149; It.64,65), *ibid.*, 672
Catukka Nipāta (AN 4), *ibid.*, 705–06
Cātuma Sutta (MN 67), *ibid.*, 706
Dhammacakkappavattana S. (*Book of the Discipline* IV, pp.15–18; SN 56:11), Fasc. IV, 3 (1988), pp.472–78
Dhammapada, Fasc.IV, 4 (1989), pp.488–94
Dhammasaṅgaṇī, *ibid.*, 505–08
Dhātukathā, *ibid.*, 575
Dīgha-Nikāya, *ibid.*, 610–13
Esukāri Sutta (MN 96), Fasc. V, 1 (1990), p.137
Etadagga Vagga (AN 1:168–74), *ibid.*, 137–41
Iṇa Sutta (AN 6:45), Fasc. V, 4 (1993), pp.541–42
Indriya-Bhāvanā S. (MN 152), *ibid.*, 563–64
Itivuttaka, *ibid.*, 604–05
Jātaka, Fasc. VI,1 (1996), pp.2–23
Kakacūpama Sutta (MN 21), *ibid.*, 81
Kālāma S. (AN 3:65), *ibid.*, 84–89
Kandaraka S. (MN 51), *ibid.*, 127–28
Kathāvatthu, Fasc. VI, 2 (1999), pp.155–60
Khuddaka-Nikāya, *ibid.*, 207–11
Khuddakapāṭha, *ibid.*, 211–13
Kīṭāgiri Sutta (MN 70), *ibid.*, 226–27
Kūṭadanta S. (DN 5), *ibid.*, 263–64
Lakkhaṇa S. (DN 30), *ibid.*, 272–74
Madhuratthavilāsinī (Buddhavaṃsa Commentary), Fasc. VI, 3 (2002), pp.362–63
Mahāparinibbāna Sutta (DN 16), *ibid.*, 461–67
Majjhimanikāya, Fasc. VI, 4 (2002), pp.564–77
Maṅgalasutta (Sn 2:4), *ibid.*, 607–08
Manorathapūraṇī (AN Commentary), *ibid.*, 624–26
Milindapañha, *ibid.*, 688–92
Milinda-Ṭīkā, *ibid.*, 693–94
Mūlapariyāyasutta (MN 1), Fasc. VII, 1 (2003), pp.52–55
Nettippakaraṇa, *ibid.*, 156–59
Niddesa, *ibid.*, 168–70
Nikaya, *ibid.*, 173–75
Nissaggiya-Pācittiya, *ibid.*, 179–81

Pāli, Fasc. VII, 2 (2004), pp.265–79
Papañcasūdanī (MN Commentary), *ibid.*, 303–04
Paramatthadīpanī (Khuddakanikāya Commentary), *ibid.*, 307–09
Paramatthajotikā (*ibid.*), *ibid.*, 309–11
Paramatthamañjusā (Visuddhimagga sub-commentary), *ibid.*, 311–12
Pārāyanavagga (Sn 5), *ibid.*, 314–15
Pātimokkha, *ibid.*, 363–65
Pātimokkhuddesa, *ibid.*, 365–67
Paṭisambhidāmagga, *ibid.*, 373–75
Peṭakopadesa, *ibid.*, 395–96
Petavatthu, *ibid.*, 397–403
Puggalapaññatti, Fasc. VII, 3 (2005), pp.451–52
Ratana Sutta (Khuddakapāṭha 6; Sn 2:1), *ibid.*, 513
Rathavinīta S. (MN 24), *ibid.*, 518–20
Sabbāsava S. (MN 2), *ibid.*, 567–70
Saddhammapajjatikā (Niddesa Commentary), *ibid.*, 605–06; Fasc. VII, 4 (2006), p.607
Saddhammappakāsinī (Paṭisambhidāmagga Commentary), *ibid.*, 607–08
Sāmaññaphala Sutta (DN 2), *ibid.*, 665–67
Samantapāsādikā (Vinaya Commentary), *ibid.*, 669–73
Sammohavinodanī (Vibhaṅga Commentary), *ibid.*, 681–82
Saṃyuttanikāya, *ibid.*, 687–90
Sārasaṅgaha (medieval Sinhalese Pāli treatise), *ibid.*, 761–62
Sāratthadīpanī (Samantapāsādikā sub-commentary), *ibid.*, 762–63
Sāratthamañjusā (Manorathapūraṇī sub-commentary), *ibid.*, 763–64
Sāratthasamuccaya (Catubhānavāra [*paritta*] Commentary), *ibid.*, 766
Sāsanavaṃsa, *ibid.*, 791–92
Satipaṭṭhāna Sutta (MN 10), Fasc. VIII, 1 (2007), pp.15–18
Scripture, *ibid.*, 26–29
Sigālovāda Sutta (DN 31), *ibid.*, 86–90
Sumaṅgalavilāsinī (DN Commentary), *ibid.*, 187–91
Suttanipāta, *ibid.*, 205–14
Suttapiṭaka, *ibid.*, 214
Tevijja-Vacchagotta Sutta (MN 71), Fasc. VIII, 2 (2008), pp.302–03
Thera-Therī-Gāthā, *ibid.*, 306–12
Ṭīkā Literature, *ibid.*, 350–58
Tirokuḍḍa Sutta (Khuddakapāṭha 7), *ibid.*, 358–60
Udāna, *ibid.*, 375–84
Uddesavibhaṅga Sutta (MN 138), *ibid.*, 389–90
Upakkilesa S. (MN 128), *ibid.*, 420–22

Upāsakajanālaṅkara, *ibid.*, 435–38
Vammika Sutta (MN 23), Fasc. VIII, 3 (2009), p.494
Vāsettha S. (MN 98; Sn 3:9), *ibid.*, 494–96
Vatthūpama S. (MN 7), *ibid.*, 512–13
Vīmaṃsaka S. (MN 47), *ibid.*, 609–10
Vimānavatthu, *ibid.*, 397–403
Vimativinodanī Ṭīkā, *ibid.*, 610–11
Vimuttimagga, *ibid.*, 622–32
Vinayapiṭaka, *ibid.*, 650–58
Vinayavinicchaya, *ibid.*, 658–59
Visuddhimagga, *ibid.*, 706–12
Vitakkasaṇṭhāna Sutta (MN 20), *ibid.*, 717–18
Yodhājīva S. (SN 42:3), *ibid.*, 798–99
Yuganaddha S. (AN 4:170), *ibid.*, 815–17

8. Pāli Grammars and Dictionaries

Chizen Akanuma, *A Dictionary of Buddhist Proper Names.* Delhi 1994. Translation of *Indo Bukkyō Koyūmeishi Jiten. Genshkihen* ("A Dictionary of Indian Buddhist Proper Names. Primitive Period"), Nagoya 1930–31.

Bhikkhu Ānandajoti, *An Outline of the Metres in the Pāḷi Canon* (3rd rev. ed.), 2006. Retrieved on 31.3.2011 from http://www.ancient-buddhist-texts.net/Textual-Studies/Outline/index.htm

Balangoda Ānanda Maitreya, *Pali Grammar and Composition,* lessons 1–29 out of 34 serialised in *Pali Buddhist Review* 2–6. London 1977–82.

—*Pali Made Easy.* Shizuoka 1993, Dehiwela 1997.

Dines Andersen, *A Pāli Reader.* Copenhagen, London and Leipzig: Part I, 1901, Glossary, 1904–07; Kyoto 1968. Repr. as *A Pāli Reader and Pāli Glossary.* 2 vols, New Delhi 1996.

Kakkapalliye Anuruddha, *A Guide to the Study of Pali: The Language of Theravada Buddhism.* Hong Kong, 2010.

Arayankhura Prayuddha, *Students Thai-Pali-English Dictionary of Buddhist Terms.* Bangkok 1963.

S.C. Banerji, *A Companion to Middle Indo-Aryan Literature.* Calcutta 1977. A dictionary of Buddhist and Jaina texts.

P.V. Bapat and R.D. Vadekar, *A Practical Pali Dictionary for the use of students in High Schools and Colleges.* Poona 1940.

A. Barua, *Introduction to Pali.* Varanasi 1965, Delhi 1977. Pāli terms in Devanāgarī script.

D.L. Barua, *Pali Grammar.* Board of Secondary Education, W. Bengal, Calcutta 1956.

A.P. Buddhadatta, *Tribhasharatnakara*. "A handbook of Pali conversation, with Sinhalese and English versions." Ambalangoda 1928.

—*New Pali Course I*. Colombo 1937, 1962; *II*. 1938, 1974; combined ed., Dehiwela 2006.

—*Concise Pali-English Dictionary*. Colombo 1949, 2000, New York 1992, Delhi 2002 (repr.by another Delhi publisher as *Pāli-English Dictionary*. 1999).

—*Aids to Pali Conversation and Translation*. Colombo 1950.

—*The Higher Pali Course for Advanced Students*. Colombo 1951, repr. as *New Pali Course III*. Dehiwela 2005.

—*English-Pali Dictionary*. Colombo 1955, New York 1992, PTS 1995, Delhi 2007.

—*English to Pali Dictionary*. New Delhi 2008.

—*Palipāthāvalī*. (A supplementary reader to the *New Pali Course*). Dehiwela 2003.

N. Cakravarti and M.K. Ghose, *Pali Grammar*. Repr. Delhi 1983.

K.K. Chandaburinarunath, *Pali-Thai-Sanskrit-English Dictionary*. Bangkok 1969, 1977.

Binayendra Nath Chaudhury, *Dictionary of Buddhist Doctrinal and Technical Terms* (based on Pāli and Sanskrit Buddhist literature). Kolkata (Calcutta) 2005.

R.C. Childers, *A Dictionary of the Pali Language*. London 1872–75, Rangoon 1974, Kyoto 1976, Delhi 2003, New Delhi 2005.

—*A Pali Grammar for Beginners*. (Repr?) New Delhi 1999.

Benjamin Clough (tr. Bālāvatāra), *A Compendious Pali Grammar with a copious vocabulary in the same language*. Colombo 1824, 1832.

Steven Collins, *A Pali Grammar for Students*. Chiang Mai 2006.

Margaret Cone, *A Dictionary of Pāli*. Part I—A–Kh. PTS 2001. Part II—G–N. PTS 2011.

James D'Alwis, *An Introduction to Kachchayana's Grammar of the Pali Language*. Colombo 1863.

H.T. de Silva and K. Upatissa (tr. Bālāvatāra, rev. F.L. Woodward). Pegu 1915.

Lily de Silva, *Pali Primer*. Igatpuri 1995.

W.A. de Silva, *A vocabulary to aid to speak the Hindu and Pali languages*. Colombo 1903.

Harsha V. Dehejia (ed.), *The English-Pali Glossary*. Delhi 1999.

—*A Pali-English Glossary*. *Ibid*.

Mahesh A. Deokar, *Technical Terms and Techniques of the Pali and the Sanskrit Grammars*. Varanasi 2008.

B. Devarakkhita (alias Don Andris de Silva Batuwantudawe, ed. & tr.), *Kaccāyana's Dhātumañjūsā*. Colombo 1872.

Charles Duroiselle, *A Practical Grammar of the Pali Language.* Rangoon 1907, 1921.
—*School Pali Series*—I. Reader, II. Vocabulary. Rangoon 1907–8.
Ernest John Eitel, *Handbook of Chinese Buddhism, being a Sanskrit-Chinese Dictionary with vocabularies of Buddhist terms in Pali, Singhalese, Siamese, Burmese, Tibetan, Mongolian and Japanese.* 2nd rev. & enl. ed., Hong Kong 1888, Delhi 1981.
T.Y. Elizarenkova and V.N. Toporov, *The Pali Language.* Moscow 1976.
K.C. Fernando, *A Student's Pali-English Dictionary.* Colombo 1950. Pāli terms in Sinhala script.
Oscar Frankfurter, *Handbook of Pali.* London-Edinburgh 1883. An elementary grammar.
James W. Gair and W.S. Karunatilaka, *Introduction to Reading Pali.* Cornell University 1975. Repr. as *A New Course in Reading Pali.* New Delhi 1998, Delhi 2001.
Ron Geaves, *Key Words in Buddhism.* Georgetown (WA-DC) 2006. "A basic useful glossary of explanations of important Buddhist terms."
Wilhelm Geiger, *Pāli Literature and Language.* Calcutta 1943, Delhi 1968. Rev. by K.R. Norman as *Pāli Grammar.* PTS 1994.
(Rev.) David C. Gilmore, *A Brief Vocabulary to the Pali Text of Jatakas I–XL for the use of students preparing for the first examination in arts in Calcutta University.* Rangoon 1895.
James Gray, *Pāli Primer.* Adapted for schools in Burma. Moulmein 1879.
—*First Lessons in Pāli.* 3rd ed., Rangoon 1882.
—*Elements of Pāli Grammar.* Rangoon 1883. Pāli terms in Burmese script.
—*Pāli Courses.* 3 parts, including translations of stories 13–31 in D. Andersen, *A Pāli Reader, op.cit.*
—*Pāli Prose.* 2 parts, including translations of portions of D. Andersen, *Pāli Reader, op.cit.*
—*Elementary Pāli Grammar.* 2nd Pāli course. Calcutta 1905.
—*Pāli Poetry.* Calcutta 1909.
—*First Pāli Course.* Calcutta 1913.
—*First Pāli Delectus.* Companion reader to his Pāli course. *Ibid.*
K. Manohar Gupta, *Linguistics in Pāli.* New Delhi 2003.
—*Linguistic Approach to Meaning in Pāli.* New Delhi 2006.
K. Higashimoto, *An Elementary Grammar of the Pali Language.* Tokyo 1965.

P. Holler, *The Student's Manual of Indian Vedic-Sanskrit-Prakrit-Pali Literature*. Rajahmundri 1901.

Peter A. Jackson, *A Topic Index of the Sutta Piṭaka*. Bangkok 1986. Pāli technical terms in Roman and Thai scripts with brief English and Thai translations cross-referred to the books/ sections of SP.

Rune E.A. Johansson, *Pali Buddhist Texts explained to beginners*. Copenhagen 1973, London 1976, Richmond (Surrey) 1998.

C.V. Joshi, *A Manual of Pali*. (Pāli terms in Devanāgari) Poona 1916, 1964, Delhi 2005.

J.R. Joshi, *Introduction to Pali*. Pune 1985.

I.Y. Junghare, *Topics in Pāli Historical Phonology*. Delhi 1979.

D.G. Koparkar, *English Guide to C.V. Joshi's Manual of Pali*. Poona 1942.

D. Kosambi and C.V. Rajwade, *Pali-Reader*. Two parts, Poona 1914–16.

K. Krishna Murthy, *A Dictionary of Buddhist Terms and Terminologies*. Delhi 1991, Calcutta 1999.

B.C. Law, *M.A. Pali Course*. Calcutta 1941.

Lionel Lee (tr.), "The Bālāvatāra, a Pāli Grammar." 4 parts, *The Orientalist II–III*. Kandy 1885–90.

Lim Teong Aik, *A Glossary of Buddhist Terms in Four Languages—English, Chinese, Pāli and Sanskrit*. Penang 1960.

G.P. Malalasekera, *Dictionary of Pāli Proper Names*. 2 volumes, London 1937, 3 volumes, PTS and New Delhi 2007.

Lynn Martineau (ed.), *Pāli Workbook*. Seattle (WA) 1998. Pāli vocabulary from the ten-day courses of S.N. Goenka.

Francis Mason, *Pali Grammar on the Basis of Kachchayano*. Toungoo-London 1866, Delhi 1984.

Ministry of Religious Affairs, *A Dictionary of Buddhist Terms*. Yangon (Rangoon) 1996. Pāli terms in Burmese script.

Madhusudan Mishra, *Comparative and Historical Pali Grammar*. New Delhi 1986.

J. Minayeff (I.P. Minaev), *Pali Grammar, a phonetic and morphological sketch of Pali Language, with introductory essay on its form and character*. Moulmein 1882, New Delhi 1990.

E. Müller, *A Simplified Grammar of the Pali Language*. London 1884, Varanasi 1967, Delhi 1995. Repr. as *Pali Grammar* (Delhi 2003) and *The Pali Language: A Simplified Grammar* (? 2005).

—*A Glossary of Pali Proper Names*. Offprint from JPTS 1888 (repr. 1978), Delhi 1989.

Ñāṇamoli *A Pali-English Glossary of Buddhist Technical Terms*. BPS 1994, 2006.

Medagama Nandawansa, *Abhidhānappadīpikā: A Study of the Text and Its Commentary*. Pune 2001.

Nārada, *An Elementary Pali Course*. Colombo 1941, 1953.

Nyanatiloka, *Buddhist Dictionary*. Dodanduwa 1950, Colombo 1972, New York 1983, Taipei 1987, BPS 1988, 2004.

—*Buddha-Vacanam*. (Texts for *The Word of the Buddha*). BPS 1968.

Thomas Oberlies, *Pāli. A Grammar of the Language of of the Theravāda Tipiṭaka*. Berlin 2001.

Madihe Paññāsīha (ed.), *Pali Dictionary I*. 1: A-Akkhabhañjana. Mahārāgama 1975. Pāli in Sinhala and Roman scripts with Sinhalese and English translations.

Pe Maung Tin, *A Pali Primer*. Rangoon 1914, Delhi 2003.

—*A Pali Reader*. 2nd ed., Rangoon 1920.

—*The Student's Pali-English Dictionary*. Rangoon 1920.

V. Perniola, *A Grammar of the Pali Language*. Colombo 1958. Rev. as *Pāli Grammar*. PTS 1997.

John Powers, *A Concise Encyclopaedia of Buddhism*. Oxford 2000.

Widurupola Piyatissa, *The English-Pali Dictionary*. Colombo 1949. Pāli terms in Sinhala script.

Rajavaramuni, *Pali-English Dictionary of Buddhist Terms*. Bangkok 1963, 1969.

—*Thai-Pali-English Dictionary of Buddhism*. 3rd ed., Bangkok 1970.

—*A Dictionary of Buddhism*. Bangkok 1976, 1985. Pāli terms in Thai script.

T.W. Rhys Davids and W. Stede *Pali-English Dictionary*. PTS 1921–25, 1999; repr. New York 1989, New Delhi 1997, Delhi 2007.

U Sīlananda, *Pāli Roots in the Saddanīti*. Publ. by Centro Mexicano del Buddhismo Theravada, Jilotepec, 2002.

W. Subhūti (ed.), *Abhidhānappadīpikā*. (Dictionary of the Pāli language by Moggallāna.) Colombo 1865, 1938. English and Sinhalese interpretations. Pāli terms in Sinhala script.

S. Sumaṅgala, *A Graduated Pali Course*. Colombo 1913, Dehiwela 1994.

J. Takakusu, *A Pali Chrestomathy*. Tokyo 1900.

Tha Do Oung, *A Grammar of the Pali Language*. 4 volumes, Akyab 1899–1902.

H.H. Tilbe, *Pali First Lessons*. Rangoon 1902.

—*Pali Grammar*. Rangoon 1899.

V. Trenckner, D. Andersen, H. Smith *et al.* (ed.), *Critical Pāli Dictionary*. Copenhagen: I. 1924–48, II.1960.

Tick Twon, *A Short Dictionary of Buddhist Hybrid Pali.* Kalimpong 1969.
Udornganādhikāra (Javinda Sragam), *Pali-Thai-English Dictionary.* 8 vols, Bangkok 1962.
A.C.G. Vidyabhūsan, *Selections from Pali.* Calcutta 1911.
N.C. Vidyabhusan and M.K. Ghose, *A Pali Grammar.* Calcutta 1982.
S.C. Vidyabhūsan, *Kaccāyana's Pali Grammar.* Calcutta 1901.
S.C. Vidyabhūsan and Swami Punnanand (ed. and tr.), *Bālāvatāra: An Elementary Pali Grammar.* Calcutta University 1916, 1935.
J. Wade, *A Dictionary of Boodhism and Burman Literature.* Moulmein 1862, Rangoon 1911.
M.O'C. Walshe, *Pali and the Pali Canon.* English Sangha Trust, London 1968.
A.K. Warder, *Introduction to Pali.* PTS 1963, rev. ed., 1995, 2001. (The PTS also distributes a companion audio recording.)
—*Pali Metre.* PTS 1967.
O.H. de A. Wijesekera, *Syntax of Cases in the Pāli Nikāyas.* Colombo 1993. Doctoral dissertation, London 1951.
U Wimala, *A New Elementary Pali Grammar.* Rangoon n.d.
F.L. Woodward, E.M. Hare, K.R. Norman, A.K. and N. Warder, H. Saddhātissa, I. Fisher (ed.), *Pāli Tipiṭaka Concordance.* PTS, I (A-O) 1955; II (K-N) 1973, 1995; III 1993.

9. Online Texts and Resources

New websites with various materials on Buddhism and other resources, often copied from existing websites, are continuously appearing (and disappearing). The following list is an overview of the most useful ones. If the link is broken, then search for the site's name instead.

Ancient Buddhist Texts. Studies on Pali prosody, etc. www.ancient-buddhist-texts.net/Textual-Studies/TS-index.htm.

Association for Insight Meditation. Includes some books by Ledi Sayadaw as well as Pāli fonts. www.aimwell.org

Beyond the Tipitaka. A Field Guide to Post-canonical Pali Literature (John Bullitt). www.accesstoinsight.org/lib/authors/bullitt/fieldguide.html

Bibliography of Indian Philosophies, by Karl H. Potter (ed.). Part I *Texts Whose Authors Can Be Dated. Authors Listed Chronologically before the Christian Era through 4th century:* faculty.washington.edu/kpotter/xtxt1.htm Part IV *Secondary Literature: Abhidharma, especially Theravāda Buddhism*: faculty.washington.edu/kpotter/xb.htm#[AB]

Bibliography to the Buddhist Religion: A Historical Introduction, by R. H. Robinson, and W. L. Johnson. Extensive bibliography. Section 5.3 deals with Pāli texts, etc. here-and-now.org/buddrel/directory.html.

Buddhanet Ebook Library with Nārada's *Manual of Abhidhamma*, etc. www.buddhanet.net/ebooks_s.htm

Buddhasāsana—English Section. Library http://www.budsas.org/ebud/ebidx.htm.

Buddhism—Buddhist Studies—Academic Info. www.academicinfo.net/buddhism.html

Buddhism in Myanmar. http://www.triplegem.plus.com/# Translations of suttas, articles, etc.

Buddhism Today: Readings in Theravāda and Mahāyāna Buddhism with emphasis on contemporary issues. www.buddhismtoday.com

Buddhist Publication Society Online Library. BPS publications and some Pāli resources. www.bps.lk/onlinelibrary

Buddhist Studies WWW Virtual Library (T. Matthew Ciolek). www.ciolek.com/WWWVL-Buddhism.html —especially "The Internet Guide to Buddhism and Buddhist Studies."

Budsir Thai Tipiṭaka. Online searchable Mahidol Royal Thai edition of the Tipiṭaka. http://www.budsir.org/budsir-main.html

Chattha Sangayana Tipitaka 3 is a searchable exercise with the Sixth Council edition of the Tipiṭaka. Also *Aṭṭhakathās, Ṭīkās*, and other Pāli works. www.vri.dhamma.org/publications/tpmain.html

Chattha Sangayana Tipitaka 4 is the successor of Chattha Sangayana Tipitaka 3. Version 3 has some advantages when searching (as it immediately shows the context in which a word occurs), but version 4 does not crash unlike version 3. www.tipitaka.org/cst.

Dhammaweb. http://www.dhammaweb.net/index.php Translations of suttas, etc.

Dharma Study. http://dharmastudy.com Includes sutta translations and articles on the Pāli Canon and its teachings.

Gretil Elibrary. www.sub.uni-goettingen.de/ebene_1/fiindolo/gretil.htm#Pali Göttingen University Library Register of Electronic Texts in Indian languages and related Indological materials from Central and Southeast Asia.

H-Buddhism (Charles Muller). The Buddhist Scholars Information Network has been created to serve as a medium for the exchange of information regarding resources, events, projects, publications etc. among the worldwide Buddhist scholarly community. www.h-net.org/~buddhism—especially "Resources: Buddhist Studies Links" > "Resources for the Study of Buddhism" (Ron Epstein) and "Tools for Buddhist Studies" (Marcus Bingenheimer)

Journal of Buddhist Ethics: www.buddhistethics.org. Online journal established to promote the study of Buddhist ethics through the publication of research, book reviews, etc. Includes digital Buddha Jayanthi Tipiṭaka and other resources.

[Links] www.greatwesternvehicle.org/pali/index.htm

Metta Lanka. Various books and resources including *Dictionary of Pāli Proper Names* and digital Buddha Jayanti Tipiṭaka. www.mettanet.org/english/index.html (Pāli Canon in Pāli and English) www.mettanet.org/tipitaka/index.html

Pali Text Society. www.palitext.com

Resource Gateways, Individual Web Sites, Online Publications and *Buddhist Publishers*. www.buddhistethics.org/global.html

Sacred Buddhist Texts. Includes some 19th century translations of Buddhist texts such as the Jātaka edited by Cowell. www.sacred-texts.com/bud/index.htm Various individual sutta, etc, translations and articles are at www.sacred-texts.com/bud/etc/index.htm.

Sādhu: The Theravāda Buddhism Web Directory and Portal. Resources and links related to Theravāda Buddhism. www.dhamma.ru/sadhu

SuttaCentral: Online Sutta Correspondence Project. www.suttacentral.net Comparing suttas as transmitted in different schools and languages.

Tipitaka, der Palikanon, die Lehre des Theravada Buddhismus. www.palikanon.com/index.html Includes the *Dictionary of Pali Proper Names* and related texts and resources.

Theravada Online Buddhist Directory. www.thisismyanmar.com/triplegemdotnet and www.buddhistethics.org/global.html (under *Resource Gateways*)

Tipitaka, the Pali Canon of Buddhism. http://oaks.nvg.org/tripitaka.html

Treasures of Pariyatti represents the preservation and dissemination of classical texts related to the teaching of the Buddha. Includes electronic re-publications of issues of the *Light of the Dhamma* and *Light of Buddha*. www.pariyatti.org/treasures

UK Association for Buddhist Studies. www.seacoast.sunderland.ac.uk

Web resources for Pali students. www.accesstoinsight.org/outsources/pali.html

Wikivinaya sites.google.com/site/wikivinaya/Home/goal-and-content-of-wikivinaya Articles and books on Theravāda Vinaya.

Courses, Bulletins and Forums

A Course of the Pali Language www.bodhimonastery.net/bm/programs/pali-class-online/903–audio/55–a-course-in-the-pali-language.html Audio course based on James Gair and W.S. Karunatilleke's, *A New Course in Reading Pali.*

Access to Insight: Theravāda Buddhist website with large sutta translation library and some Pali study resources. www.accesstoinsight.org.

Pāli forum: groups.yahoo.com/group/Pali/

E-sangha, Buddhist Forum and Buddhism Forum www.lioncity.net/buddhism/index.php?showforum=50

Pāli Language Bulletin Board http://emsjuwel.com/palibbs

A Reference Table of Pali Literature

Compiled by

Bhikkhu Ñāṇatusita

INTRODUCTION

This reference table of Pali literature is primarily intended as an aid for Pali scholars and students. It lists all the Pali works found in the catalogues, lists and secondary literature that I had access to, and enables one quickly find out where a particular text is mentioned or described.

The references are not exhaustive; there are more catalogues and other works in which the particular text is listed and described. Providing all references would make the table too large and would require much more research.

The numerical and abbreviation scheme as given in the Abbreviation and Bibliography sections of the *Epilegomena* of the *Critical Pāli Dictionary* (CPD) is followed. This system has its drawbacks: there are not enough text classes in this scheme; a few of the works have been put in the wrong place (e.g. 3.8.6.3 = 3.8.6.2); some works listed are not Pali works, but Sinhalese texts (e.g., *Amāvatura*). (The Epilegomena is online at http://pali.hum.ku.dk/cpd/intro/vol1_epileg_bibliography.html.)

The table is primarily a table of Pali scriptures and, to a lesser degree, of scriptures that contain a large amount of Pali quotations. Many of the Sinhalese word-for-word translations, called *sannaya* or *sannē*, have been included. They can be quite old, sometimes as old as the original Pali works, and can give variant readings, provide quotations from the old *Sīhala-aṭṭhakathā* (Sinh. *Helaṭuvā)* and other lost Pali texts and *sannayas*, and contain historical information, etc. A few important works in Sinhalese and in Sanskrit are listed, especially the ones given in the CPD, which are connected to Pali texts and can provide valuable information about it. The Indochinese Pali traditions have their own word-for-word-translations and commentaries, called *nissaya,* in their own vernaculars. Because there are a great many *nissaya*, only a selection of them is listed.

Individual *suttantas* and *jātakas,* often together with commentaries, translations and verbatim paraphrases (*sannaya*), are commonly found in palm-leaf manuscript collections. They usually are not listed; firstly because they are already part of other collections, and secondly because the table would then become to large. The *Satipaṭṭhānasutta*, *Vessantara-jātaka*, and a few other important suttas are included, though.

The data from the *Lankāve Puskoḷa Pot Nāmāvaliya* has only be partly entered and compared. Only the Vinaya, Sutta, and Anthology sections were completely compared with it. Some data from the Burmese *Piṭaka-samuin* (Piṭ-sm) was entered by a Burmese bhikkhu into a brief list used for the Buddha Jayanti Tipiṭaka digitalisation project, and, unless the Ps has been mentioned as a reference in the CPD *Epilegomena* or Bode's *Pāli Literature of Burma*, I have not been able to confirm these data as I have no access to the Piṭaka-samuin.

When referring to the author Chappaṭa, the Chappaṭa Saddhammajotipāla of the mid 15th century is intended. I follow Godakumbara, who points out in his article "Chapada and Chapada Saddhammajotipāli" that the Chappaṭa who lived in the 12–13th century probably was not an author.

For the Pali works of the Ledi Sayadaw (Leḍī Sayāḍo or Ñāṇadhaja), the *A Directory of the Buddhist Manual written by Ledi Sayadaw* and *Biography of the Venerable Mahathera Ledi Sayadaw* has been followed. Most of the Leḍī Sayāḍo texts mentioned by Bode in *Pāli Literature of Burma*, pp. 97–99, are not in Pali but in Burmese.

There is disagreement whether or not the *Nettipakaraṇa, Peṭakopadesa, Milindapañhā* and *Suttasaṅgaha* are included in the Khuddaka Nikāya in Burma. According to Mabel Bode (*The Pali Literature of Burma*, p. 4) the Burmese tradition includes these four texts in this collection, but Duroiselle (JBRS, I.1. 1911, p. 121,) disagrees with this: "No educated Burman, lay or monk, ever included these four works among the Piṭaka books of the Khuddakanikāya..." Peter Jackson ("The Canonicity of the Netti and Other Works," JPTS XXVIII, 2006, p. 61–62), however, points out that Ñāṇābhivaṃsa Saṅgharāja (19th c.)—in his discussion of the section on the works included in the Khuddakanikāya, (*Sīlakkhandhavagga-abhinavaṭīkā*, intro, section 17)—states that the *Netti, Peṭaka*, etc, come under the Niddesa and Paṭisambhidāmagga. Tha Do Aung ("Buddhistic Literature in Burmah," *The Mahabodhi and the United Buddhist World*, Vol. X, no. 6, Oct. 1901, pp. 56–58) also includes the *Netti* and *Peṭaka* in the Khuddaka Nikāya.

Some spellings are regularised in the table. Although both forms are commonly found in titles of texts, prefix forms with a single *-p-* are consistently listed instead of forms with the double *-pp-*, e.g., *-pakaraṇa* instead of *–ppakaraṇa*, etc. The same applies for *vy-* instead of *by-* (e.g. *vyākaraṇa/byākaraṇa*), and *culla-* instead of *cūḷa-* and *cūla-*.

It is possible that there are some inaccuracies in this work because its scope is very wide. I offer my excuses if there are any mistakes.

I would like to thank all those who have assisted me in various ways with making this table, especially Ven. Ānandajoti for his valuable suggestions regarding the contents and form; Dr. Jacqueline Filliozat for the many suggestions and corrections she made, especially with regards Southeast Asian Pali literature and also for kindly providing her invaluable EFEO Data; Dr. Kieffer-Pülz for her help with sorting out the various texts dealing with boundaries and some other Vinaya texts.

REFERENCES AND ABBREVIATIONS

The system of reference numbers and abbreviations of the *Critical Pāli Dictionary Epilegomena* (CPD) is followed in this table. When there is an abbreviation and reference number before the text listed, then it is listed in the CPD *Epilegomena,* which provides a lot of additional information regarding the texts. Some additions and corrections to the numerical system of the CPD *Epilegomena* are given in Hinüber's *A Handbook of Pāli Literature* pp. 256–57. Texts without a reference number and abbreviation are not listed in CPD. References to other literature that provide information regarding the texts are given after the text-titles.

Abbreviations in bold indicate that the data (page- or paragraph-numbers, etc.) was entered systematically. The data from other works was partly used.

Please note that the table often has shorter abbreviations, than the ones normally used—e.g., H instead of HPL. Although this is not in accordance with the accepted Indological abbreviation standards as given by Bechert, it is necessary in order to cut down on space. For the same reason the abbreviations *f* and *ff* have been used after reference numbers (e.g., LCM 777f), although their use is discouraged by modern style manuals. When there are more than two MSS of a particular text in a collection, the abbreviation *m* is given after the last reference (e.g., LCM 333, 777m).

General abbreviations

beg:	beginning
B:	Burma/Myanmar
CM:	Chiang Mai/Lān^2 Nā
f:	and following
ff:	and following (plural)
I:	India
Ic:	Indochina. (Burma, Cambodia, Laos, Siam, Vietnam)
Kh:	Khmer/Cambodia
La:	Laos
m:	more (More MSS of this text are in this collection.)

MS: manuscript
MSS: manuscripts
S: Siam/Thailand
SI: South-India, Tamil Nadu
C: Ceylon/Sri Lanka
~: identical to the preceding

Abbreviations of catalogues and secondary literature/Bibliography

ABM: "Additions to Burmese Manuscripts in the Library of Congress"; William Pruitt, JPTS XXIV (1998) pp. 171–83.

ANL: "The Apocryphal Narrative Literature of Southeast Asian Buddhism"; Padmanabh S. Jaini, *Buddhism's Contribution to World's Culture and Peace,* pp. 51–56, Ed. N. A. Jayawickrama, Colombo, 1984.

BC: *Book of Chants (a compilation, being the romanized edition of the Royal Thai Chanting Book)*; Bangkok, 1975. First published in Thai script in 1880; see RL 121.

BCL: *Buddhist Commentarial Literature*; L.R. Goonesekere, Kandy 1967. *The Wheel Publication* No. 113. Also published as the article "Aṭṭhakathā"; in pp. 335–352, Vol. II, Fasc. 2 of the *Encyclopedia of Buddhism*, Colombo, 1966.

BMD: *Buddhist Monastic Discipline*; Jotiya Dhirasekera, Colombo, 1996. (2nd digital ed.)

BnF: *Catalogue des Manuscrits Pālis des Collections Françaises;* Jacqueline Filliozat, Jinadasa Liyanaratne, William Pruitt, EFEO DATA Filliozat 101. (MS No.)

BL: *Paritta manuscripts in Pali in the British Library Oriental & India Office Collections.* Jacqueline Filliozat, London, 1994. ED 103.

BLB: "Buddhistic Literature in Burmah," Tha Do Aung, *The Mahabodhi and the United Buddhist World,* Vol. X, no. 6 (Oct. 1901), pp. 56–58.

BLS: *Biography of the Venerable Mahathera Ledi Sayadaw, Aggamahapandita, D.Litt.* In Publications folder in www.ubakhin.com.

BLSL: "Bodhi Literature in Sri Lanka," Kiriwaththuduwe Pragnasara, in H.S.S. Nissanka (ed.) *Maha Bodhi tree in Anuradhapura, Sri Lanka* (New Delhi 1994), pp.169–84.

Bod: *Survey of the Pāli Manuscript Collection in the Bodleian Library.* Jacqueline Filliozat, London, 1994–96. ED 103.

BP: *Bodhi Pūja.* Compiled by K. Seelananda, Penang 2003.

Braun II: *Burmese Manuscripts Part II,* Braun H., Daw Tin Tin Myint, (VOHD XXIII 2), Stuttgart 1985.

BSL: *Buddhism in Sri Lanka in the 17th and 18th Centuries;* A.H. Mirando, Dehiwala, 1985.

CAPC: "The Commentaries to the Anāgatavaṃsa in the Pāli Manuscripts of the Paris Collections"; Jacqueline Filliozat, JPTS XIX (1993), pp. 43–63.

CB: *Catalogue of Cambodian and Burmese Pāli Manuscripts;* C.E. Godakumbara, Royal Library, Copenhagen, 1983.

CCS: "Chapada and Chapada Saddhammajotipāli"; C.E. Godakumbara, JBRS, LII, I, pp. 1–7, June 1969.

CHL: *The Chuang-Hsiung Lu Burmese Manuscript Collection kept in Taipei 1–651,* Jacqueline Filliozat, Taipei, 2002. Also in ED 112. (MS. No.)

CM: *Catalogue of Ceylonese Manuscripts;* C.E. Godakumbara, the Royal Library, Copenhagen, 1980.

CMA: *A Comprehensive Manual of Abhidhamma* (Introduction). U Rewata Dhamma and Bhikkhu Bodhi, Kandy, 1999.

CPD: *Critical Pāli Dictionary, Epilegomena to Vol. I;* Helmer Smith, Copenhagen, 1948. The addenda given in later volumes of CPD and in the *Handbook of Pāli Literature* (H) have also been incorporated. (Online at: http://pali.hum.ku.dk/cpd/intro/).

CS: *Chaṭṭha Saṅgāyana CD-ROM Version 3.0;* Vipassana Research Institute, Dhammagiri, 1999.

CW: *A Bibliotheca Sacra Birmanica in Taipei—The Chung-Hwa Institute of Buddhist Studies Manuscript Collection Summary Catalogue.* Jacqueline Filliozat & Peter Nyunt, Taipei, 2000. ED 112. (MS. No.)

DBM: *A Directory of the Buddhist Manuals—Written by Ledi Sayādaw Aggamahapaṇḍita D.Litt.* Pesala Bhikkhu. http://www.aimwell.org

Dham: *Dhammikarama Buddhist Chanting,* Burmese Temple, Penang, Malaysia. No date.

Dickson: *The Pātimokkha, being the Buddhist Office of the Confession of Priests.* J.F. Dickson; *Journal of the Royal Asiatic Society,* New Series VIII pp. 62–130, 1876.

ED: EFEO DATA Filliozat. Database for Pāli documents, studies and bibliographies of Jacqueline Filliozat. Free CD-ROM available on request at l'École Française d'Extrème-Orient Library, 22 avenue du Président-Wilson 75116, Paris, France.

EP: EFEO Pāli. Manuscript shelfmark number given in: *Catalogue des Manuscrits en Pāli.* Bibliothèque de l'École Française d'Extrème-Orient, Paris. Jacqueline Filliozat, Paris 1986–2003. Published in ED 101. (MS No.)

FEMC: *Appendice Intérêt de la collection, textes inconnus ou rares, nouvelles recensions qui pourraient faire l'objet d'*editio *princeps ou d'éditions critiques.* Jacqueline Filliozat, ED 113. (MS No.)

FPL: Fragile Palm Leaf House Collection, Bankok, Thailand. MS number.

GB: *The Great Book of Protective Blessings.* Compiled by W. Sarada Thero et al., Singapore, 1999.

H: *A Handbook of Pāli Literature.* Oskar von Hinüber; Berlin 1996. (§)

HP: *Handbook of Pāli Literature.* Somapala Jayawardhana; Colombo, 1994.

ICI: *Catalogue des Manuscrits Pālis des l'Institut de Civilisation Indienne Paris,* Jacqueline Filliozat, Paris, 1988, ED 101. (MS No.)

ICP: *Catalogue de Manuscrits Pālis des l'Institute Catholique de Paris, Bibliothèque de Fels, Fonds Grimblot et Feer.* Jacqueline Filliozat, Paris, 1987, ED 101. (MS No.)

IO: *Catalogue of Pāli Manuscripts in the India Office Library.* Jacqueline Filliozat, Paris, 1994, ED 103. (MS No.)

LJ: *La guirlande de Joyaux.* F. Bizot & O. von Hinüber, Paris 1994.

JPSA: "Jātaka and Paññāsa-jātaka in South-East Asia"; Peter Skilling, JPTS XXVIII (2006), pp. 113–173.

JPTS: *Journal of the Pali Text Society.*

L: *Lankāvē Puskoḷa Pot Nāmāvaliya* I and II. K.D. Somadasa; Colombo, 1959 and 1964.

LCM: *Catalogue of Palm Leaf Manuscripts in the Library of the Colombo Museum;* W.A. de Silva; Colombo 1938.

LN: "Lān2 Nā as a Centre of Pāli Literature"; Oskar von Hinüber, JPTS XXVI (2000), pp. 119–37.

LS: "Līnatthapakāsinī and Sāratthamañjūsā"; Primoz Pecenko, JPTS XXVII (2002), pp. 61–113.

LWA: "The literary works of the Abhayagirivihārins"; K.R. Norman, *Collected Papers* IV, pp. 211–17.

MA: *Les Manuscrits Pālis du Musée National des Arts Asiatiques-Guimet Paris.* Jacqueline Filliozat, ED 101, Paris, 1986. (MS No.)

ME: *Séminaire des Missions Étrangeres de Paris, Catalogue Descriptif des Manuscrits du Fonds Pāli.* Jacqueline Filliozat, EFEO DATA 101, Paris, 1988. (MS No.)

MP: *Mahā Paritta*; Rewata Dhamma, Birmingham, 1996.

N: *Catalogue of the Hugh Nevill Collection of Sinhalese Manuscripts in the British Library*, 7 vols.; K.D. Somadasa, London, 1987—95. (MS No.)

NA: National Archives Microfilm Collection. National Archives, Colombo. These are entries from the card-index of the microfilms of manuscripts made by the project sponsored by the Ford Foundation in the 1980s. Most of the microfilms are now badly damaged due to neglect and are unusable. There are no copies of them.

Nāma: *Nāmamālā*; Waskaḍuwe Subhūti, Colombo, 1965.

Par: *Paritta—A Historical and Religious Study of the Buddhist Ceremony for Peace and Prosperity in Sri Lanka*; Lily de Silva, Colombo, 1981.

PD: *Path of Discrimination*, transl. Bhikkhu Ñāṇamoli, introduction A. K. Warder, London 1982.

PCS: *Pāli Literature Transmitted in Central Siam.* Peter Skilling & Santi Pakdeekham; Bangkok 2002. (§)

PGG: "Pali Grammar and Grammarians from Buddhaghosa to Vajirabuddhi—A Survey"; Ole Holten Pind; Bukkyo Kenkyu (Buddhist Studies) Vol. XXVI, 1997.

PI: "A 15th Century Inscription and Library at Pagan, Burma"; G.H. Luce and Tin Htway, in *Malalasekera Commemoration Volume*, Colombo, 1976, pp. 203–56.

PL: *Pāli Literature*; K.R. Norman, Wiesbaden, 1983. (§ and pages.) ("Appendix I" in Norman's *Collected Papers V* , Oxford, 1994, has been consulted.)

PLB: *Pāli Literature of Burma*, Mabel Bode, London, 1909, repr. 1966.

PLC: *The Pali Literature of Ceylon.* G. P. Malalasekera; Colombo, 1958, repr. 1994.

PoI: *Progress of Insight.* Mahāsi Sayadaw, Kandy, 1965.

Ps: *Pitakat samuin* (Burmese History of the Tipiṭaka); Mahasirijeyasū, 19th c.

PS: *Pāḷi Sāhityaya*; A.P. Buddhadatta, Colombo, 1962.

PSA: *Pāli Literature of South-east Asia*; Ven. Dr. Hammalawa Saddhātissa, Singapore, 1992, repr. 2004.

PSC: *Pāli Texts Printed in Sri Lanka in Sinhalese Characters*; Masahiro Kitsumo, Tokyo, 1997. (§)

PV: *Piruvānā Pot Vahansē*. Ariyadasa Seneviratna; Colombo, 1995. (An edition of *Mahā Pirit Pota*. The texts referred to are found in an appendix that is also found in several other printed editons of the *Mahā Pirit Pota*.)

RAS: *Survey of the Pāli Manuscript Collection in the Royal Asiatic Society*. Jacqueline Filliozat, Paris 1996, ED 103. (MS No.)

RB: "Review of Bode 1909"; W.B. Bollée, *Indo-Iranian Journal* 11, 311–18.

RL: "The Rakṣā Literature of the Śrāvakayāna"; Peter Skilling, JPTS XVI (1992), pp. 109–82.

RLL: "Recherches sur la litérature laotienne" L. Finot, BEFEO XIV no. 5, Hanoi, 1914, pp. 42–83.

RPA: "Une recension palie des annales d'Ayuthya; G. Coedès, BEFEO XIV no. 3, Hanoi 1914, pp. 1–31.

SA: *Les manuscrits en pāli de la Société Asiatique de Paris*, Jacqueline Filliozat, Paris 1983, ED 101. (MS No.)

SH: *Singhalesische Handschriften Teil I*; Heinz Bechert and Maria Bidoli, Wiesbaden, 1969. *Singhalesische Handschriften Teil· II*; Heinz Bechert, Stuttgart, 1997. (MS No.)

SL: *Sinhalese Literature*; C.E. Godakumbara, Colombo, 1955.

SLSBT: "A Survey of Literature on the Sacred Bodhi Tree," Somapala Jayawardhana, *Journal of the Royal Asiatic Society of Sri Lanka* XXXV(1990–91), pp. 23–52.

SPB: "Survey of the Pāli manuscript collection in the Bodleian Library"; Jacqueline Filliozat, JPTS XXIV (1998), pp. 1–80.

SR: *Safeguard Recitals*; Ānandajoti Bhikkhu, Kandy, 2004.

SSJ: "A Short Study of the *Jātaka-aṭuvā-gätapadaya*"; D.E. Hettiarachi. *Journal of the Ceylon Branch of the Royal Asiatic Society*, 1944. Vol. xxxvi, Part. I.

STWS: "Sāriputta's Three Works on the Samantapāsādikā"; JPTS XXVIII (2006), pp. 49–59.

SW: "Sāriputta and his works"; Primoz Pecenko, JPTS XXIII (1997), pp. 159–179.

TJM: "Textuality of the Jayamaṅgala Gāthā and its Liturgical Role in Modern Buddhist Marriage Ceremony"; Mahinda Deegala, in *Buddhist Studies in Honour of Professor Lily de Silva*, Peradeniya, 2001, pp. 183–197.

TT: "Theravādin Literature in Tibetan translation"; Peter Skilling, JPTS XIX (1993), pp. 69–201. (§)

TV: "The *Vinayasaṅkhepaṭṭhakathā*: An Unknown Vinaya Handbook"; Petra Kieffer-Pülz and Anne Peters, in *Buddhist and Indian Studies in Honour of Professor Sodo Mori*; Tokyo, 2002, pp. 117–127.

UOR: "Un Outil de Référence pour Déchiffrer les Mantras et Yantras dans les Manuscrits en Pāli de la Péninsule Indochinoise"; Jacqueline Filliozat, Bankok, 2003, In STVDIA ASIATICA IV (2003)—V (2004), p. 489–513.

US: "Uttaravihāraṭṭhakathā and Sārasamāsa"; Sodō Mori, JPTS XII (1988) pp. 1–48.

VH: *Selected Manuscripts in the Library of Vat Hong Ratanaram Rajavaravihan, Thonburi. A Summary Catalogue.* Jacqueline Filliozat & Yohei Shimizu, 2004, ED 115. (MS No.)

VP: *The Pāli Manuscript Collection kept in the Vat Phra Jetuphon Vimol Mangklaram (Vat Po)*, Jacqueline Filliozat, Bangkok, 2002–2003. In ED 108. (MS No.)

Vs: *Vesaturu-dā-sannē*; D.E. Hettiarachi, Colombo, 1950.

W: "Some Problems of the later Pāli Literature"; A.K. Warder, JPTS XI (1987), pp. 198–207.

Wms: "A Survey of the Burmese and Siamese Pāli Manuscript Collection in the Wellcome Institute"; Jaqueline Filliozat, JPTS XIX (1993), pp. 1–41. (MS No.)

Other Literature

Heinz Bechert, "Vimuttimagga & Amatakaravaṇṇanā"; in *Amala Prajñā: Aspects of Buddhist Studies. Prof. P.V. Bapat Felicitation Volume*; ed. N.H. Samtani, Delhi, 1989, pp. 11–14.

Polvatte Buddhadatta (ed.), "'*Paramatthavinicchaya* by Anuruddha"; JPTS X (1985), pp. 155–226.

Eugène Denis (ed.), '*Braḥ Māleyyadevattheravatthuṃ*"; JPTS XVIII (1993), pp. 1–64.

Toshiichi Endo, "The Asgiriya Manuscript of the Pali *Vimuttimagga*: An Inquiry into its Authenticity"; *Kalyāṇī: Journal of Humanities and Social Sciences of the University of Kelaniya*, vol. 1, 1983, pp. 100–108.

Padmanabh S. Jaini (ed.& tr.), "Ākāravattārasutta: An 'Apocryphal' Sutta from Thailand"; *Indo-Iranian Journal* 35 (1992), pp.193–223.

Charles Hallisey (ed.), "Tuṇḍilovāda: An Allegedly Non-Canonical Sutta"; JPTS XV (1990), pp. 170–95.

—'Nibbānasutta: An Allegedly Non-Canonical Sutta on Nibbāna as a Great City," JPTS XVIII (1993), pp. 117–24.

Kanai Lal Hazra, *The Buddhist Annals and Chronicles of South-East Asia;* New Delhi 1986.

P. Jackson, "A Note on Dhammapāla(s)"; JPTS XV (1990), pp. 209–11.

Friedgard Lottermoser, "Minor Pāli Grammar Texts: the *Saddabindu* and its 'New' Subcommentary'"; JPTS XI (1987), pp. 79–109.

Bhikkhu Ñāṇamoli, *Piṭaka Disclosure,* P.T.S., London, 1979.

Aloysius Pieris, "The Colophon to the *Paramatthamañjūsā* and the Discussion on the Date of Ācariya Dhammapala"; in *Buddhism in Ceylon and Studies on Religious Syncretism in Buddhist Countries;* ed. Heinz Bechert, Göttingen, 1978.

Hammalava Saddhātissa (ed.), "*Nāmacāradīpikā* of Chapaṭa"; JPTS XV (1990), pp. 1–28.

VARIANT TITLES OF TEXTS

There is often more than one title in use for a particular text—the *Pāḷimuttaka-vinayavinicchayasaṅgaha* (1.3.5), is the most extreme example—and this can be confusing. Therefore it possible that there are other variations of titles than the ones listed. Sometimes, the same title is given to different works, and therefore, when known, the author and year of a work have been listed for extra clarity. The Pali titles are only given in the normal word order and not in the inverted Siamese way such as given in PLCS, e.g., *Pāḷi-pāḷimuttaka-vinayavinicchayasaṅgaha* (PLCS 1.21).

The name of the text contained in a manuscript is mentioned on the first leaf of South East Asian manuscripts. Sinhalese Pali palm-leaf manuscripts, however, normally do not have a title at the first page of a text or on the cover of the text. Instead of a title there is the "*namo tassa ...*" formula and then the text starts; see LCM p. xxi. There are also no titles given on the wooden covers protecting the manuscripts and this absence can make it difficult to find a manuscript with a specific text in a monastery library if there are no modern tags or stickers with titles and reference-numbers. (On some manuscripts one finds small strips of ola-leaf used as tags bearing the title of the work. The strips are attached by a string to the cover-button. Possibly these tags were more common in the past but were lost or removed.) In this case one has either to be familiar with the text and be able to recognise it by reading the introduction of the text, etc or, if one is not familiar with the text, by reading the conclusion of the text as most texts with "(title) *niṭṭhito*" or something alike. The original titles of works are also often mentioned in the introduction- and/or conclusion-verses made by the author of the work. Commentaries can also be of help in identifying the right title.

Apparently the Sinhalese bhikkhus who used the manuscripts in the past would recognise a manuscript through familiarity with the different wooden covers (painted or plain), the cloth-covers of the texts (still commonly used in Indochina), and the location of the manuscripts in their libraries.

In Sri Lankan manuscript lists and catalogues, the titles of Pali texts are often Sanskritised, e.g., *Prātimokṣaya* instead of *Pātimokkha, artha* instead of *attha, gätapadaya* instead of *gaṇṭhipada, saṅgrahaya* instead of *saṅgaha,* etc. In the table usually the Pali title is given, but while searching in library-indices it is important to check the Sanskrit forms. Sometimes Sinhalese titles are used, e.g. *Dhampiyā* instead of *Dhammapada*.

Classificatory components of texts

Pāḷi (Canonical text) (India)
Aṭṭhakathā (Commentary) (Sri Lanka, South India)
Ṭīkā (Sub-commentary) (Sri Lanka, Burma, Indochina, South India)
Anuṭīkā (New Sub-commentary) (Burma)
Attha-yojanā, Yojanā (Burma, Lān Nā̤)
Gaṇṭhi (-pada), ganthī, gätapada (Sri Lanka, Indochina)
Vivaraṇa (Indochina, Sri Lanka)
Sannaya (Sri Lanka)
Nissaya (Indochina)

TABLE OF PALI LITERATURE

Vinaya-piṭaka: (H II.1, PL 2)

1.1 Pāt Pātimokkha, Pāṭimokkha (S), Mātikā-pāḷi, Pātimokkhuddesa: H 15, PL 2.1, HP 195, CB 4f, BnF, L.

Bhikkhu-bhikkhunī-pātimokkha, Ubhaya-pātimokkha, Ubhaya-mātikā, Dve-mātikā-pāḷī: PLB 6, BnF 8–9, CW, L.

Bhikkhu-pātimokkha: PCS 1.24, L, LCM 56, 1755, EP, BnF 10m, SH 1.

Bhikkhunī-pātimokkha: PCS 1.22, L, LCM 1756, BnF, Bod, CW.

1.1,01 (Bhikkhu-) Pātimokkha-gaṇṭhi-dīpanī (CM, Ñāṇakitti, ± 1493–4.): PCS 1.10, LCM 21, PSA 15f, 61f, BnF 255.3, LN 125f, L.

Pātimokkha-gaṇṭhi, Pātimokkha-gaṇṭhi-padaya: BLB, Ps, L.

Khuddaka-pātimokkha (Gives names of Pm rules.): PCS 1.8.

Pātimokkha-pavāraṇa (B ms): L.

Pātimokkha-nissaya (Pali-Burm.) (Various versions by different authors.): CB 128f, BnF 16m.

Bhikkhu-pātimokkha-padārtha, ~sannaya, ~vistara-sannaya: N 6600(58), SL 19, L.

Pātimokkha-eḷu-sannaya: N 6600(113)iv-v

Prātimokṣaya (Sinhala): N 6600(122), L

Bhikkhu-bhikkhunī-pātimokkha-(pādākhyāna)-sannaya: N 6600(93).

Bhikkhuṇī-pātimokha-pādārtha, ~sannaya: LCM 1693, L.

(1.3.6,1) Pātimokkha-visodhanī (B, Chappaṭa, 15th c.): HP 195, PLB 39, BLB, Ps, L.

Pātimokkha-lekhana, Pātimokkha-lekhanaya (B, Ñāṇavara, 18th c.): PLB 67, PLB, Ps.

Pātimokkha-padattha-anuvaṇṇanā, Pātimokkha-anuṭīkā (B, Vicittālaṅkāra Rājaguru, 17–18th c.): TV 118 n. 9, CB 75, Ps, L.

Pātimokkha-padattha-anuvaṇṇanā-nissaya (B?, Vicittālaṅkāra): CB 79.

Ratanārtha-sūdanī (-sannaya), Namvu-Bhikṣu-bhikṣuṇī- prāti-mokṣa-varṇanāva (C, S. Jinaratana & R. Pragnāśekhara, 1946.)

Pātimokkha-dīpikā (-sannaya) (C, V. Guṇālaṅkāra, 1959)

1.1,1 Kkh Kaṅkhāvitaraṇī, Kaṅkhāvitaraṇī-aṭṭhakathā, Mātikaṭṭhakathā, Pātimokkha- vaṇṇanā, Bhikkhu-bhikkhunī-pātimokkha-aṭṭhakathā (C, Buddhaghosa, 5th c.): H 221, PL 126f, LCM 12, PLC 95, CM 6f, BnF 844m, Bod, CW, L.

Bhikkhu-kaṅkhāvitaraṇī, Bhikkhupātimokkha-vaṇṇanā: BnF 845, BLB.

Bhikkhunī-kaṅkhāvitaraṇī, Bhikkhunīpātimokkha-vaṇṇanā: BnF 15, BLB.

1.1,11 Kkh-pṭ Kaṅkhāvitaraṇī-purāna-ṭīkā, Līnapada-vikāsaka, Kaṅkhā-ṭīkā (C?, later than 1.2,11 Vjb.): H 377, CS, BLB, Ps.

1.1,12 Kkh-ṭ Vinayattha-mañjūsā, Līnattha-pakāsanī, Pātimokkha-navaṭīkā, Kaṅkhāvitaraṇī-[abhi]-navaṭīkā. (C, Buddhanāga, 12th c.): H 378, HP 178, Ps, PCS 1.35, PSC p. 60, PLC 201, LCM 22, CS, CW Burm 90, L.

Līnattha-pakāsanī (Quoted in Sp-ṭ and not identical with 1.1,12.): H 378.

1.1,13 Kkh-y Kaṅkhāvitaraṇi-atthayojanā-mahāṭīkā (Mandalay, B, Shin Paññāsīha/Thit Seint Sayāḍo, 19th c.): H V.1.2/221.

1.1,14 Kkh-gp Kaṅkhāvitaraṇi-piṭapota (= a gaṇṭhipada) (C?, 13th c.): N 6609(12), LCM 13, Vs 74ff, SL 20, L.

Pātimokkha-aṭṭhakathā-gätapadaya: L.

Kaṅkhāvitaraṇi–visturusannaya, Sandehaghātinī (M. Dhammādhāra.): Vs 84.

Sekhiyā (= one section of Pāt): N 6599(2)xx.

Sekhiya-padārtha (Sannaya found together with Sekhiyā)

Meegamana RMV 66.

1,2 Vin Suttavibhaṅga, Ubhaya-vibhaṅga, Ubhato-vinaya, Bhikkhu-bhikkhunī-vibhaṅga: H 22ff, PL 2.1, PCS 1.26, BnF 6, MA, L.

Bhikkhu-vibhaṅga, Mahā-vibhaṅga: H 14, PCS 1.26, BnF 5, CW, L.

Bhikkhunī-vibhaṅga: H 27, PCS 1.23, CW, L.

Pārājika (-pāḷi), Pārājika-khaṇḍa, Ādikamma (~pāḷi, ~sutta): PCS 1.4 & 26, PSA 89, LCM 1f, BnF 1–4m, CB 6, CS, L.

Pācittiya (-pāḷi): PCS 1.19 & 26, BnF 618, LCM 3, EP 99, CS, L.

Bhikkhu-pācittiya-nissaya, Ratanamañjūsā: CB 74.

Khandhaka-pāḷi (= Mahā- & Culla-vagga.): H 28ff, PL 2.2.

Mahāvagga (-pāḷi),: H 28ff, PCS 1.25, CB 69, CM 2ff, BnF 17m, CS, L.

Cullavagga (-pāḷi), (Ubhato-khandhaka): H 28ff, PCS 1.13, EP 98, BnF 20m, CS, L.

Parivāra (-pāḷi), Parivāra-pāṭha: H 40f, N 2.3, HP 115, PCS 1.18, CM 5f, LCM 7, BnF 23, EP 113, VP4.139, CS, L.

Pārājika-(pāḷi)-sannaya: L.

Pārājikā-gaṇṭhi-aṭṭhakathā-yojanā (B): Ps.

Mahāvagga-cullagaṇṭhī-guyhadīpanī: PCS 1.12.

Cullagaṇṭhi-guyhatthadīpanī, Vinaya-samūha, Vinaya-samoha (Cf. Dhammasamūha and Sikkhāpadasamūhana in Unclassified Vinaya below.): ICI Pali 4.

Mahāvagga-sannaya: L.

Mahāvagga-nissaya, Ratanà-mañjūsā (B, Jambudhaja, 1647 or 49.): CB 69f, SPB 33, Bod.

Cullavagga-sannaya.: L.

Cullavagga-nissaya, Ratana-mañjūsā (B, Jambudhaja, 17th c.): CB 71.

1.2,1 Sp Samantapāsādikā, Vinayaṭṭhakathā, Vinaya-saṃvaṇṇanā (C, Buddha-ghosa, 5th c.) (Also MSS on the individual books of the Vinaya: Pārājika, Pācittiya, Mahāvagga, Cullavagga, Parivāra, Bhikkhu- & Bhikkhunī-vibhaṅga, e.g., Parajika-aṭṭhakathā and Pācittiyādi-aṭṭhakathā.): H 208f, PCS 1.44, HP 135, PLC 94f, CB 6, EP 109, BnF 35m, CW, CS, L.

1.2,10 Mahā-gaṇṭhi, Majjhima-gaṇṭhi, Culla-gaṇṭhi (C) (Extinct Sinhala gätapadas.): Ps, PLC 189f, Vs 73f, SL 19.

Samantapāsādika-vinaya-sannaya, Samantapāsādika-mahāsannaya: L.

Samantapāsādika-pūjāpatra, ~pūjāpātraya: L.

Samantapāsādika-nissaya, Ratana-mañjūsā (B, Jambudhaja, 17th c.) (Nissaya on Cullavagga and Pārājika in CB.): CB 70, 72.

(Samantapāsādika-aṭṭhakathā-yojanā) (B?, Siri Sumaṅgala/ Maṅgala, 14th c.): PLB 27.

Mahāvagga-aṭṭhakathā-yojanā: VH 280.12.

1.2,11 Vjb Vajirabuddhi-ṭīkā, Vinayagaṇṭhipada, Vinayagaṇṭhi, Samantapāsādikā- gaṇṭhipada, Samantapāsādikā-purāṇaṭīkā, Samantapāsādika-līnapada, Paṭhama-vinaya-ṭikā. (C/South-India?, Vajirabuddhi, 6th c.): H 367ff, PCS 1.32, HP 172 & 202, PLL 35, PLB 39, BnF 43m, LCM 1, LN 130f, PSC p. 60, VP, CS, CW, Ps, L.

Vinayaganṭhipada (Extant in B, ascribed to C Joti thera and to C Moggallāna, 12th c.): PC 190, PLB 75f, DPPN, Vs 73.

Vinaya-gäṭapadaya (Quoted in 5.3.11 Mogg-p.): SL 19.

Culla-vinayaganṭhipada, Culla-ganṭhipada (C?, 12th c. Moggallāna.): PLB 74ff.

Cullaganṭhi, Cullagaṇḍhi-mahāvagga-vaṇṇanā (B, Nandamāla, 18th c.): ABM 173, BL Or 9238.

Vinayaganṭhipada-vaṇṇanā: L.

Vinayasāra-ganṭhi (Pali-Burm.) (B, Munindasāra, 1801–02.): CB 83.

Vinayārtha-samuccaya, Vinaya-sannaya, Vinayārtha-saṅgrahava (C, Diṁbulāgala Medhaṅkara, 13th c.): PC 202, CM xxix, LCM 31.

Vinaya-sannaya (SL, Sāriputta and Moggallāna, 12th c.): SL 19.

Vinayagāthā-sannaya: SL 19.

1.2,12 Sp-ṭ Sāratthadīpanī, Samantapāsādika-majjhima-ṭīkā, Vinaya-mahā-ṭīkā, Samantapāsādika-dutiya-ṭīkā, Dutiya-vinaya-ṭīkā (C, Sāriputta, 12th c.): H 373, PCS 1.45, HP 142, SW, LCM 14, PLC 192, PSC 60, Vs 73, STWS, BnF, Bod, Ps.

Sāratthadīpanī-saṅkhepa: VP 4/136.

1.2.13 Vmv Vimativinodanī, Vimativinodanī-ṭīkā, Samantapāsādikā-navaṭīkā, Samantapāsādikā-līnatthavaṇṇanā (I, Coḷaraṭṭha Kassapa, 12–13th c.): H 338, PCS 1.42, HP 175, LCM 16, PLC 179/323, BnF 640, PSC 6, CW, STWS, L.

1.2,14 Sp-y Samantapāsādikā-atthayojanā, Vinaya-yojanā, Samantapāsādikā-aṭṭhakathā- yojanā (CM, Ñaṇakitti, 1492 or 1493.): H 379, PSA 15, 61f, PCS 1.29, LN 127f, L.

Pārājika-yojana: BLB.

1.2.14,1 Pāc-y Pācityādi-yojanā, Pācityādi–vaṇṇana-yojanā (B, Jāgara, 1869.): H n. 694, Cs, Ps.

1.2,15 Vin-gp Parivāra-ganṭhipada: PCS 1.11.

Parivāra-līnārtha-gätapadaya, Parivāra-līnatthasannaya: N 6600(126)xiv, L.

Parivāra-ganṭhipada (Pali-Sinh.): N 6601(60)x, 6609(35) SL 352, L.

Parivāra-ṭīkā (Siamese Khom ms.): L.

Parivāra-sannaya: L.

Parivāra-nissaya: CB 74.

1.2,16 Kammav Kammavācā, Nānā-Kammavācā: H 28, PCS 1.16, PLB 6f, 106, CB 4, 62, PL, LCM 1757f, SH 199, 234, BnF 24m, N 6600 (113) ii, ED 205, EP 2.9m.

Kammavācā-sannaya: L.

Vinaya Manuals, Saṅgaha

1.3.1 Khuddas Khuddasikkhā, Khuddasikkhā-pakaraṇa, Khuddakasikkhā (C, Dhammasiri, 4–6th c.?) (The spelling Khuddakasikkhā is only found in the Mil-ṭ on CSCD): H 332 & 368f, PL 169, PCS 1.9, N 6601(5), BnF 371m, PSC 5, PLC 76f, CB 6, CM xxi, CS, BLB, Ps, L.

1.3.1,1 Khuddas-pṭ Khuddasikkhā-purāṇaṭīkā (C, Mahā-yasa or Revata, 13th c. Possibly there are two purāṇaṭīkās. Cf Nevill 6600(126)v.): PC 77f, 109, HP 188f, 192, Ps, L, N 6601(5)ii.

Khuddasikkha-purāṇaṭīkā (C, Revata, 13th c.)

PC 77f, CB 80 & n 3, BLB.

Khuddhasikkhā-aṭṭhakathā (? = 1.3.1,1): PCS 1.1

1.3.1,2 Khuddas-nṭ Sumaṅgala-pasādanī, Khuddasikkhā-navaṭīkā (C, Saṅgharakkhita mahāsāmi, 12–13th c.) (According to the colophon [see CSCD p. 440] the author is Saṅgharakkhita, not Vācissara. It is identical with 1.3.1,3.): PC 204, PCS 1.54, HP 189, L, PSC 5, TV 118 n. 10, BnF 672, VP 1/27, BLB, Ps.

1.3.1,3 Khuddas-ṭ Khuddasikkhā-abhinavaṭīkā (C, Saṅgharakkhita mahāsāmi, 12–13th c.) (Identical with 1.3.1,2.): TV 118 n. 10, PC 77f, 198, 200, CB 79f, HP 189, LCM, 40, Ps, L.

1.3.1,4 Khuddakasikkhā-yojanā, Khuddasikkha-padayojanā (B): PCS 1.28, PSC 5, BLB, Ps, L.

Khuddakasikkhā-vinicchaya, Khuddasikkha-atthavaṇṇanā, Khuddasikkhā-(purāṇa)-ṭīkā: PSC 5, L.

1.3.1,5 Khuddakasikkhā-dīpanī (B, Pan-lhavā Sīlacāra): BnF 372m, CPD, PSC 5.

1.3.1,6 Kudusika-sannaya, (C, Vanaratana Ānanda, 13th c. Cf CPD.) =? Khuddasikkha-purāṇa-sannaya: PC 77, 211, HP 189, PLC 77f, LCM 41, Vs 79, L, PSC 5.

Kudusikha-padārtha, Kudusikha-purāṇa-sannaya, Medhānaṅkara-sanna (C, Udumbaragiri/Diṁbulāgala Medhānaṅkara, 13th c.): N 6600(113)iii, (126) v, L.

Khuddasikkha-atthayojanā, ~vyākhāva ~vivaraṇaya, ~vistaraya, ~nissaya (= Different works in PSC): PSC 5.

1.3.2 Mūla-s Mūla-sikkhā (C?, Mahāsāmi, 4–6th c?): H 332f, PL 169, PCS 1,27, PSC 5, BnF 547m, CM xxi, CS, L, VP, BLB, Ps.

1.3.2,1 Mūla-sikkhā-purāṇaṭīkā (C, Vimalasāra.): Ps, PSC 6, BLB, L?.

1.3.2,2 Mūlasikkhā-ṭīkā (C, Vācissara Mahāsāmi. 12th c.): CPD, L, PSC 6.

1.3.2,3 Mūlasikkhā-(abhi)-navaṭīkā, Vinaya-vimaticchedanī (B, Samantaguṇasāgara): PCS 1.39, Ps, PLC 198, BLB, L.

1.3.2,4 Mūlas-sn Mulusika-sannaya (Maybe this is the Mulsika-sannaya on 1.4.(2). See below.): Vs 80, L, PSC 6.

Mūlasikkha-vyākhāva, Mūlasikkha-padārtha, Mūlasikkha-vistārtha: PSC 6, L.

1.3.3 Vin-vn Vinayavinicchaya, Vinayavinicchaya-saṅgaha, Vanavinisa, Vinayavinicchaya-aṭṭhakathā (C, Uragapura Buddhadatta, 5th c.): H 325, PL 131, HP 177f, PCS 1.38, PLC 108f, EP 63, CS, Ps, L.

1.3.3,1Vin -vn-pṭ Vinayavinicchaya-(purāṇa)-ṭīkā, Vinayasāratthadīpanī, ~sandīpanī, Vinayatthasārasandīpanī-ṭīkā, Vinayavinicchaya-vaṇṇanā, ~saṃvaṇṇanā (C?, Revata, 12th c.): H 325 & 330, PCS 1.36, PSC 4, Ps, L.

1.3.3,2 Vinayavinicchaya-ṭīkā, Yoga-viniccchaya, Vinayattha-sārasandīpanī, Vinayavinicchaya-vaṇṇanā (C, Vācissara Mahāsāmi or Saṅgharakkhita, 12th c.) (In CS both this text and 1.3.4,1 are given under Vinayavinicchaya-ṭīkā.): PC 109, 198, 202, K4, CS, L.

1.3.3,3 Vinayavinicchaya-yojanā (B): Ps, PSC 4.

Vinicchaya-ṭīkā-yojanā: BLB.

1.3.3,4 Vinayavinicchaya-(purāṇa)-sannaya, Vanavinisa-sannaya, Nissandeha (C, Parākramabāhu II, 13th c.) (Extinct?): CC xxix, PSC 4, Vs 84, SL 20, L.

Viniścayārtha-dīpanī, Vinayavinicchaya-sannaya: PSC 4.

1.3.3,5 Vinayavinicchaya-(nava)-sannaya (C, Dhīrananda, 19th c.): CPD.

Other related works: Vinayavinicchaya-atthayojanā, ~nissaya, ~padayojanā, ~vyākhyā, ~vigrahaya.): PSC 4.

1.3.4 Utt-vn Uttaravinicchaya, Uttarasiñjana (in BLB) (C, Uragapura Buddhadatta, 5th c.): H 325, PL 131, Ps, PCS 1.5, HP 167f, EP 63, BLB, CS.

1.3.4,1 Utt-vn-ṭ Uttaravinicchaya-purāṇaṭīkā, Uttaravinicchaya-ṭīkā, Uttaravinicchaya-vaṇṇanā, Uttaravinayavinicchaya-līnatthapakāsinā-ṭīkā, Līnatthapakāsinī (C?, Vācissara, 13th c? Revata is not the author and only had this text and 1.3.3,1 transcribed in Arimaddanapura. See colophon in CS and LCM. In CS both this text and 1.3.3,1 are given under

Vinayavinicchaya-ṭīkā. Ps gives the author as Mahāupatissa; see CPD.): PLC 202, HP 201, PCS 1.31, LCM 28, CS, Ps, L.

1.3.4,2 = 1.3.4,1 Uttara-līnatthapakāsinī , Uttaravinicchaya-navaṭīkā (Disciple of Sāriputta, = Vācissara Mahāsāmi?, 13th c.) (This text is identical with 1.3.4,1. In CS each section of 1.3.4,1 ends with: *Iti uttare līnatthapakāsaniyā.*): H 325, PLL n. 1, PLC 109, LN 131f, PSC 4, BLB, L.

1.3.4,5 Uttaravinicchaya-sannaya, ~navasannaya: LCM 29, L, PSC 4, Ps.

1.3.5 Pāḷim Vinaya-saṅgaha, Mahā-vinayasaṅgaha-pakaraṇa, Vinayasaṅgaha-aṭṭhakathā, Pāḷimuttaka, Pāḷimuttaka-vinaya-vinicchaya, Pāḷimuttaka-vinayavinicchayasaṅgaha, Pāḷimuttaka-vinaya, Vinaya-vinicchaya, Mahāvinaya-saṅgahapakaraṇa, Vinaya-mahāsaṅgaha (C, Sāriputta, 12th c.): H 334, PCS 1.21, CM 52, HP 107, PLC 190f, LCM 23f, N 6601(57), PSC 7, BnF 377m, SW, EP 16, VH, CS, CW, STWS, BLB, Ps, L.

1.3.5,1 Pāḷim-pṭ Vinayasaṅgaha-purāṇaṭīkā, Pāḷimuttaka-ṭīkā, Anuttānatthadīpanī, Anuttānadīpanī, Anuttāna-padavaṇṇanā (C, Sāriputta, 12th c.): H 334+36, LCM 26, HP 194, BnF 255.2, PCS 1.3, PLC 191f L, SW, PSC 7, EP 16, Ps, VP, VH, STWS, BLB.

[1.3.5.12] Pāḷim-nṭ Pāḷimuttakavinayavicchayasaṅgaha-mahāṭīkā, ~navaṭīkā, Vinayālaṅkāra, ~ṭīkā (Ava, B, Munindaghosa Tipiṭikālaṅkāra, early 17th c. Not 1.3.6.2; see H n. 540.): H 334+337, PLB 54, TV 118 n. 11, SH 80, LCM 30, PSC 7, CS, Ps, L, VP, STWS, BLB.

Vinayālaṅkāra-ṭīkā-nissaya: CB 82.

Pāḷimuttaka-nava-mahāṭīkā-sannaya: PSC 7.

Vinayavinicchayasaṅgaha-yojanā (B, Jambudīpa Anantadhaja Mahārājāgarū, 1768.): PLB 72, PCS 1.30.

1.3.5.2 Cullavinaya-saṅgaha: Ps.

(1.3.6.1) (See above in Pātimokkha Section.)

1.3.6.3 Vinayasamuṭṭhāna-dīpanī (B, Chappaṭa, 15th c.): HP 203, PLB 18, .

1.3.6.4 Vinayagūḷhattha-dīpanī, Vinayagūḷhattha (B, Chappaṭa, 15th c.): =? Vinayagūḷhattha-pakāsanīHP 202, PLB 18, BLB, Ps.

1.3.6.5 Vinaya-saṅkhepa-ṭīkā (B): Ps.

Vinaya-saṅkhepa-aṭṭhakathā (? Author unknown, + 12th c.): TV, PCS 1.40, Ps.

Vinaya-saṅkhepa-ṭīkā (B) (Different text than 1.3.6.5.): Ps.

Vinaya-saṅkhepa: BLB.

Vinayasaṅgaha-aṭṭhakathā (-saṅkhepa) (C, Sāriputta, 12th c.): Ps.

Pāḷimuttaka-gätapadaya: PSC 7.

Pāḷimuttaka-sannaya: PSC 7.

Vinaya-lakkhaṇa-rāsī (transliteration from Burmese: *Vinaññḥ mhat cu*) (B, Ñāṇinda, + 17th c. Quotes extensively from some *aṭṭhakathās* and *ṭīkās.*): TV

1.4.(1) Heraṇas Heraṇasikha (In Sinhala. Includes 40 Pāḷi gāthās called *Dasa-sīla.* 11th-12th c.): N 6599(34)xxxvii, 6601(22), LCM 51–8, SL 18f, L.

1.4.(1,1) Heraṇas-vn Heraṇasikha-vinisa (Sinhala. 11th-12th c.): LCM 42, N 6600 (113)ix, SL 18f, L.

Heraṇasikha-gätapadaya, Heraṇasikha-padārtha: L

Heraṇasikha-pävidi–vata (Sinhala): N 6603(208).

1.4.(2) Sikhav Mulsikha-vaḷaňda, Sikhavaḷaňda, Mulsikha, Sarit-varit-sikha. (Before 10th c.) (Sinhalese translation of the Mūla-sikkhā, 1.3.2): N 6600(126)iv & 6601(53), PLC 216, CM xxv, PSC 6, SL 16, L.

Mulsikha-sannaya, Mulsikha-piṭapota, Sikhavaḷaňda-purāṇa-gätapadaya: N 6600(126)iv.

1.4.(2.1) Sikhav-vn Sikhavaḷaňda-vinisa (Sinhalese commentary on 1.4.[2] and a companion volume to it in manuscripts. Before 10th c.): N 6600(126)iii & 6601(53), PLC 216, LCM 32f, PSC 6, CM xxv, SL 16, L.

Sikhavaḷaňda-vinisa-piṭapota: N 6600(126)xv, L.

1.4.3 Sikkhāpada-valañjanī, ~valañjana (C, Pañcamūla-vihārādhipati, 13th c.) (Pāḷi translation of Sikhavaḷaňda-vinisa with additional material from Sikha-vaḷaňda; see N 6600(126)iii): HP 147f, PCS 1.47, PSC 9, PLC 216, LCM 34, BLB, Ps.

Sikkhāpadavalañjanī-arthadīpanī: PSC 8.

Sikkhāpadavalañjanī-gätapadaya: PSC 8.

Sikkhāpadavalañjanī-sannaya: PSC 8.

1.4.4 Pārupana-pāḷi (C, Ñāṇaloka, 1934): PSC 14, H n. 693.

Pārupana-vādaya, ~vata, ~vādaya-gänalipi, ~vidhiya, ~vinisa, ~viniścaya, ~vistaraya, ~saṅgrahaya (C. Different works about the parūpana dispute.): PSC 14, L.

Sīmā-manuals

1.5.1 Sīmāl Sīmālaṅkāra (-pāḷi, -pāṭha, -gāthā, -aṭṭhakathā) (C, Vācissara, 13th c. Maybe identical with 1.5.2.): H 339, PL 171, HP 200, PLC 202, L, Ps, VP, PSC 8, BLB, L.

1.5.1,1 Sīmālaṅkāra-ṭīkā, Sīmālaṅkāra-vaṇṇanā (B or C, Chappaṭa, 15th c.) (Maybe identical with 1.5.2.1. Sīmalaṅkāra-vaṇṇana is given on the title page in the NA though in the text it clearly is called Sīmālaṅkāra-saṃgaha-vaṇṇanā.): PL 171, PLB 18, PLC 202, PSC 8, CCS, Ps, L, NA (RN 1, EN 230–233), BLB.

Sīmālaṅkāra-saṅgaha-vaṇṇanā, Sīmālaṅkārasaṅgaha-ṭīkā, ~aṭṭhakathā, Vinayattha-padīpanī (B or C, Chappaṭa, 15th c.) (Maybe an autocommentary or 2nd ṭīkā on the Sīmālaṅkāra-saṅgaha, or identical with 1.5.1.1.): PCS 1,14, CCS, L.

Sīmālaṅkāra-gaṇṭhipada, Sīmālaṅkāragaṇṭhi (In the Sīmālaṅkāra-saṅgaha- vaṇṇanā the Sīmālaṅkāraka mentioned in the Sīmālaṅkārasaṅgaha as a source (vs. 2) is identified with a Sīmālaṅkāragaṇṭhi.): PSC 8, BMD p. 76 fn. 2, L.

Sīmā-gaṇthipada: NA (RN 140, EN 103), L.

Sīmālaṅkāra-purāṇasannaya (Sinhalese glossary on Vācissara's Sīmālaṅkāra.): PSC 8, L.

1.5.2 Sīmāl-s Sīmālaṅkāra-saṅgaha (= abbridged version of 1.5.1, C, Vācissara, 13th c.) (A versified and abridged version of a text called Sīmālaṅkāraka (vs. 2), identified by Chappaṭa's commentary with a Sīmālaṅkāragaṇṭhi. Whether it is an abbreviated version of (1.5.1) or is identical, is not certain. Probably 1.5.1 and 1.5.2. are identical with only varying titles.): H 339, PL 171, HP 148, PSC 8, PCS 1.51, PLL, L, Ps.

Sīmā-saṅgaha (-ṭīkā): Ps, L

1.5.3 Sīmā-saṅkara-chedanī, (C, T. Rāhula Vācissara, 15th c.): PL 172, PLC 251, PSC 8, RN 27, L, NA (RN 27, EN 240–5.)

Sīmā-saṅkara-vinodanī: L, NA (RN 10, EN 292–293.)

Sīmā-saṅkhā-vinodanīya: L, NA (RN 77, EN 128–131.)

Sīma-saṃkara-chedanī, Sīmāsaṅkara-vinodani, ~vinodaniya, Sīmā-saṅgaham- uttama, Sīmā-saṅgraha (Sinh.–Pāḷi. C, Pupphārāma mahāthera, 1826.): N 6603(216 & 232), LCM 47, L.

Sīmā-saṅgrahaya, Sīmasaṅgaha: NA (RN 16, EN 225–32.), L

Sīmāsaṅkaravinodanī-sannaya: PSC 8, L.

1.5.4 Sīmāv Sīmā-vivāda-vinicchaya-kathā, Sīmā-vinicchaya (B, Ñeyyadhamma Saṅgharāja, 1858.) (Letter to Amarapura Nikāya in C.): H 339, PL 172, CB 86, PSC 8, BMD p. 175, L.

Sīmā-vinicchaya-sannaya (A sannaya on 1.5.4?): L, PSC 8.

Sīmāvinicchaya, Sīmāvinicchaya-gaṇṭha (Mahādhamma-pālathera, Siamese Khom MS.): ICI 2.

Sīmā-saṅkara-vinicchaya (CM, Ñāṇakitti, 15th c.): PSA 62, PCS 1.53, L.

Sīmā-visodhanī, Sīmā-visodhanī-ṭīkā (B, Sāgarabuddhi, 16th c.): PCS 1.50, PSC 8, CS, BLB, L.

1.5.5 Sīmā-nayadappana (C, Dhammalaṅkāra, 1882. Describes one side of the case judged in 1.5.4.): PCS 1.48, PSC 13, BMD p. 176 and n. 880.

1.5.6 Sīmā-lakkhaṇadīpanī (C, Vimalasāra, 1881. Describes the other side of the case judged in 1.5.4.): PL 172, PLC 311, PSC 11, BMD p. 176 and n. 880, L.

Sīmā-bandhanī, Sīmā-bandhana (Vācissara, 13th c.) (Identical with 1.5.1?): Ps 275, L.

Sīmābandhanī-ṭīkā, (15th c) (Identical with 1.5.1,1?): PLB 39, fn. 1.

Sīmābandhana-kathā (B, Ñāṇābhivaṃsa Saṅgharāja, 19th c.): De Zoysa 13.

Sīmābandhanaya (Sinhalese version of aforementioned?): L.

Vinayalakkhaṇa-vinicchaya-dīpaka, Vinayalakkhaṇa-dīpaka, Sīmā-vicāraṇa (= Thai title). (S, letter (*sandesa*) from Siam to L. Dhīrananda in C by Rāma IV as bhikkhu, 1844.): PCS 1.49, BLB, L, (cf. BMD 175.)

Sīmā-vivāda (Message sent to Siam.): L.

Sīmāsaṅkara-vādaya (C, L. Dhīrānanda, 19th c.): N 6603(216), PSC 8, 11, L.

Saṅkara-vinicchaya (Ganegodäla-vihāra, C, 1855): LCM 48.

Sīmā-vivaraṇaya: PSC 8.

Sīmā-kammavāca: N 6600(126)ii, L.

Visuṃgāmasīmā-vinicchaya (B, Visuddhācāra, 1899.): PLB 97.

Udakukkhepa-sīmāvinicchaya (Colombo, C, K. Indagutta, 1949) (Pāḷi with Sinhalese, 12 p.):

Unclassified Vinaya texts

Adhikamāsa-vinicchaya (CM, 15th c.): LN 121.

Anāpatti-dīpanī (C, Pañcapabbata-vihāra thera, 14th or 15th c.): PC 247, PCS 1.2, PSC 10, LCM 49.

Āpatti–vinicchaya (B, Paññasāmi, mid 19th c.): PLB 93.

Cātu-pārisuddha-sīla (S?): PSA 89f.

Catu-sāmaṇera-vatthu (Amarapura, B, Ñāṇa/Ñāṇabhivaṃsa, 18–19th c.): PLB 78.

Culla-kaṭhina-mahā-kaṭhina-kathā: PCS 2.96.2, VP 4/151, (VH 234.20).

Daḷhīkamma-upasampadā-kathā (C, A. Devānanda, 1930): PSC 14.

Daḷhīkamma-vinicchayo (C, A. Devānanda, 1930): PSC 14.

Daḷhīkammma-dīpanī (B. Leḍī Sayadāw, 19–20th c.): DBM 14.

Dasa-sikkhā-[pada]-vivaraṇa-pañhā-gāthā (S?): VP 1/38.

Dasa-sīla-gāthā, Bāla-sikkhā, Sāmaṇera-sikkhā (C) (Pāḷi, 48 gāthās.): N 6603(205).

Dhammagārava-dīpanī (C, M. Medhānanda, 1909): PC 312f, PSC 14.

Dhammasamūha, Dhammaguṇa, Dhammaguṇasaṃvaṇṇanā (Ic?): PCS 1.15, VP 1/38m, EP 75.31, VH.

Dhūtaṅgavinicchaya (B?): CW Burm 80.

Dinacariyā, Dinacāritta-saṅgaha: LCM 984f, N 6599(37) viii, 6601(22)v.

Gāravagārava-vinicchaya (B, Leḍī Sayāḍo, 19–20th c.): PSC 14, DBM 10.

Kammākamma-vinicchaya (-kathā).: PCS 1.7, L.

Kaṭhina-dīpanī (B, Vimalācāra, 1820.): CB 85f.

Kaṭhinatthāra-aṭṭhamātikā-pañcānisaṃsa-sannaya, Kaṭhina-vibhāgaya: N 6600(133).

Kaṭhina-vinicchaya (B. Nissaya): CW 104.

Katikāvata, Parākramabāhu-katikāvata (Sinh.) (C, 12th c.): SH 321, PLC 213f, LCM 1298.

Khalitakhalita: BLB

Mahā-vipāka (Ic. Thai-Pāli): PSA 90, 121, BnF 405, VH 243ṃ.

Nipuṇa-saṅgaha, Nipuṇṇa-saṅgaha, Nipuṇa-pada-saṅgaha: PCS 1.17, VP, BLB, Ps.

Ovādānusāsana (S, requested by Vanaratana Saṅgharāja, ± 1720.) (Instructions for novices and new monks. = Thai-Pāli Nissaya.): PSA 90, BnF 403.

Pārisuddhi–vinaya: PCS 1.20.

Pasvisi-avahāraya: LCM 44–45.

Pratyavekṣa-Kāndaya: LCM 59.

Sādhujanapasādanī (C, A. Devānanda, 1909): PSC 14.

Saṃsaya-vibhedanī (B?, Sāsanavaraghosa thera.): CW Burm 80.

Sāmaṇera-sikkhā (S.): BC 22–23.

Sammohanāsiṇī (C, K. Upasena, 1911): PC 313, PSC 14.

Satarapratyavekṣā: LCM 43.

Sikha-karanīya: LCM 62, L.
Sikkhāpada-samūhana: L.
Sikkhāpada-uddānaya (-pāḷi, -gāthā): L.
Sīlāvaha-aṭṭhakathā, Sīlāvaha: Ps, BLB.
Sīluddesapāṭha (Recited after pātimokkha.): BC 120.
Suddhanta-parivāsa (Saṅghādisesā procedures): PSA 90, LCM 1506f
Sugata-vidattha-vidhānaya (C, A. Sīlakkhandha, 1894): PSC 14.
Surāvinicchaya (B, Ñāṇavara, 18th c.): PLB 67.
Surāvinicchaya (Taungu, B, Mahāparakkama, 16th c.): PLB 46.
Terasakhandha-ṭīkā, Terasakan-ṭīkā (C, Sāriputta.): Ps, BLB.
Uposatha-vinicchaya (B, Paññasāmi, mid 19th c.): PLB 44, 93.
Vatta-vinicchaya: PCS 1.33, VP.
Vinaya-dhara-sikkhāpada: PCS 1.37, VP.
Vinaya-kkhandhaka-niddesa: PCS 1.34, VP.
Vivāda-vinicchaya (B, Paññasāmi thera, mid 19th c. Nissaya?): PLB 93, CW Burm 26.
Vohāratthabheda (B, Paññasāmi thera, mid 19th c.): PLB 93.

Sutta-piṭaka: H II.2, PL 3.

Dīgha-nikāya

2.1 D Dīgha-nikāya, Dīrghāgama: H 52ff, PL 3.1, PCS 2.81, HP 51f, CM 7f, LCM 68, BnF 46m, CS.

2.1.1 Sv (D-a) Sumaṅgalavilāsinī, Dīgha-nikāya-aṭṭhakathā (C, Buddhaghosa, 5th c.): H 226–44, PCS 2.248, HP 151f, CM 9ff, LCM 88, EP 12, BnF 52m, CS.

2.1.11 Sv-pṭ (D-pṭ) Līnattha-pakāsinī (-purāṇaṭīkā) I, Digha-nikāya-ṭīkā (C, Dhammapāla, 6th c.): H 358, PL 149, PCS 2.186, HP 52, PSC p. 60, CS.

2.1.12 Sv-ṭ (D-ṭ) Sāratthamañjūsā I (C, Sāriputta, 12th c. Although H and HP state that this work is extinct, it is extant see LS.): LS 105, H 376, PLC 192f/ 324.

2.1.13 Sv-nṭ (D-nṭ) Sādhujanavilāsinī (-navaṭīkā), Sīlakkhandhavagga-abhinava- ṭīkā. (Amarapura, B, Ñāṇa/ Ñāṇābhivaṃsa, 18–19th c.): H 382, PLB 78, PCS 2.229, LS 70ff, Ps.

Majjhima-nikāya

2.2 M Majjhima-nikāya: H 63f, PL 3.2, PCS 2.150, HP 83f, CM 12f, LCM 69, BnF 60m, CS.

2.2.1 Ps (M-a) Papañcasūdanī, Majjhimanikāya-aṭṭhakathā. (C, Buddhaghosa, 5th c.): H 226ff, LCM 89, PCS 2.109, HP 110f, CM 16f, EP 17, BnF 67m, CS.

2.2.11 Ps-pṭ (M-pṭ) Majjhimanikāya-ṭīkā, Līnatthapakāsinī II, Līnatthavaṇṇanā (SI, Dhammapāla, 6th c.): H 358, PCS 2.187, HP 192, LCM 108f, CB 88f, CS, Ps.

2.2.12 Ps-ṭ (M-ṭ) Sāratthamañjūsā II (C, Sāriputta, 12th c. Although H and HP state that this work is extinct, it is extant; see LS.): LS 105, H 376, PLC 192–3/324, HP 199, LCM 108.

Saṃyutta-nikāya

2.3 S Saṃyutta-nikāya: H 69ff, PL 3.3, LCM 70f, CM 17ff, N 6599(40), PCS 2.253, BnF 71m, CS.

2.3.1 Spk (S-a) Sāratthapakāsinī, Saṃyutta-nikāya-aṭṭhakathā (C, Buddhaghosa, 5th c.): H 226–241, PCS 2.230, HP 143, EP 149, LCM 90, BnF 73m, CS.

Sāratthapakāsinī-saṅkhepa: PCS 2.230.

2.3.11 Spk-pṭ (S-pṭ) Līnatthapakāsinī III, Saṃyutta-ṭīkā (SI, Dhammapāla, 6th c.): H 358, PCS 2.188, HP 198, LCM 110, CS, Ps.

2.3.12 Spk-ṭ (S-ṭ) Sāratthamañjūsā III (C, Sāriputta, 12th c. Although H and HP state that this work is extinct, it is extant; see LS.): LS 105, H 376, PLC 192–3/324, LCM 111, CPD.

Aṅguttara-nikāya

2.4 A Aṅguttara-nikāya, Aṅguttara-saṅgiya, Aṅguttarāgama: H 76ff, PL 3.4, PCS 2.1, HP 11f, CB 7, CM 22f, LCM 73, BnF 77f, CS, L.

2.4.1 Mp (A-a) Manorathapūraṇī, Aṅguttara-nikāya-aṭṭhakathā (C, Buddhaghosa, 5th c.): H 226ff, PCS 2.155, HP 89, CM 24ff, LCM 92, BnF 87f, CS, L.

2.4.11 Mp-pṭ (A-pṭ) Purāṇaṭīkā I, II, III. (SI, Dhammapāla, 6th c. Although HP states in PLC 324 that this work is extinct, it is extant; see LS.): LS 105, Ps, PLC 324.

2.4.12 Mp-ṭ (A-ṭ) Sāratthamañjūsā (IV), Aṅguttara-nikāya-ṭīkā (C, Sāriputta, 12th c.): H 376, HP 199, PLC 192f/324, LCM 111, SW, PSC p. 60, CS.

Aṅguttara-anuttānadīpanā-gaṇṭhi: PCS 2.3, VH 244.

Khuddaka-nikāya

Khuddaka-pāṭha

2.5.1 Khp Khuddakapāṭha: H 86f, PL 3.5.1, PCS 2.35, HP 73f, LCM 74, 1697, BnF 91f, CS.

2.5.1.1 Pj I Paramatthajotikā I, Khuddakapāṭhaṭṭhakathā, Khuddakapāṭha-vaṇṇanā (C, Buddhaghosa, 5th c.): H 252–4, PL 129, PCS 2.110, HP 74, LCM 93, 1698, BnF 92m.

2.5.1.12 Khp-ṭ Paramatthasūdanī, Khuddakapātha-ṭīkā (Ādicca-vaṃsa?): Ps.

Dhammapada

2.5.2 Dhp Dhammapada (-pāḷi, -gāthā), Dampiyā: H 88ff, PL 3.5.2, PCS 2.89, LCM 75f, 389, 1698, CB 76, CM 27f, N 6599(34 & 38), BnF 91, CS, L.

2.5.2.01 Dhp-sn Dhammapada-purāṇasannaya (13th c.?): Vs 86, SL 26, L.

Dampiyā-sannaya, Dhammapada-sannaya, Dhampiyā-gāthārtha (C, 10th c.): N 6600(49)f, LCM 396, SH 51, Vs 72.

Dhammapada-sannē 2: N6600(52).

Dampiyā-gāthā-sannaya, Dampiyāva: D 394.

2.5.2.1 Dhp-a Dhammapada-aṭṭhakathā, Dhammapada-tthavaṇṇanā (C, Buddhaghosa?, 5th c.): H 261, PL 127f, PCS 2.90, HP 47f, LCM 94, SH 52, CM 28f, EP, BnF, ME, CS, L.

2.5.2.12 Dhp-ṭ Dhammapadattha-dīpanī (B): Ps, CPD.

2.5.2.13 Dhp-nṭ Dhammapadattha-navaṭīkā (B, Varasambodhi, 1866.): H 261, RB, Ps.

2.5.2.14 Dhp-a-gp Dampiyā-atuvā-gätapadaya, Dampiyā-atuvā-sannaya (C, Kassapa Rāja, 10th c.): LCM 395, HP 47, H 261.

2.5.2.15 Rt Saddharma-ratnāvaliya (C, Dhammasena, 13th c. = Sinh. Based on Dhp-a.): N 6603(78), PLC 97f, H 269, HP 47, SL 81f, SH 98.

2.5.2.16 Dhp-a-y Dhammapada-aṭṭhakathā-gāthā-yojanā (S?, Siri Sumaṅgala): H 262.

Dhammapada-gāthā-vivaraṇa, Dhammapada-vivaraṇa (Beg: *Namatthu mahāmohatamonadde loke*...): PCS 2.199, BnF 121.

Dhammapada-gaṇṭhi (Before 1442.): PCS 2.38, PLB 106.

Dhammapadaṭṭhakathā-nissaya (B.): CB 92, CW.

Udāna

2.5.3 Ud Udāna (-pāḷi): H 91, PL 3.5.3, PCS 2,26, HP 165f, LCM 1700, BnF 91, CS.

2.5.3.1 Ud-a Paramatthadīpanī I, Udāna-aṭṭhakathā, Vimalavilāsinī (C,·Dhammapāla, 6th c.): H 273, 277, PL 134, PCS 2.112, HP 166, PLC 114 (+ n 4), LCM 95, CS.

2.5.3.12 Ud-ṭ Udāna-ṭīkā (Extinct text?): Ps.

Itivuttaka

2.5.4 It Itivuttaka (-pāḷi): H 92f, PL 3.5.4, PCS 2.24, HP 56f, LCM 78, 1700, BnF 91m, CS.

2.5.4.1 It-a Paramatthadīpanī II, Itivuttaka-aṭṭhakathā, Vimalavilāsinī (C, Dhammapāla, 6th c.): H 273, 277, PL 134, PCS 2,112, HP 58, PLC 114 (+ n 4), LCM 96, BnF 122, CS.

2.5.4.12 It-ṭ Itivuttaka-ṭīkā (Extinct text?): Ps.

Suttanipāta

2.5.5 Sn Suttanipāta (-pāḷi): H 94f, PL 3.5.5, PCS 2.245, HP 152f, LCM 78, 1701, BnF 123m, CS.

2.5.5.1 Pj II Paramatthajotikā II, Suttanipāta-aṭṭhakathā (C, Buddhaghosa, 5th c.): H 255f, PL 129, PCS 2.111, HP 156, N 6601(56), LCM 97, BnF 126m, CS.

2.5.5.12 Sn-ṭ Paramatthajotikā-dīpanī, Suttanipāta-ṭīkā (C): H 255, Ps.

Sūtranipāta-purāṇa-vyākhyā, ~sannaya, ~padārtha, Sūtrasannaya (C, 12–13th c. Partly published old *sannē* of a part of Sn and Pj.): N 6600(140), Vs 86, SL 25f, L.

Vimānavatthu

2.5.6 Vv Vimānavatthu, (-pāḷi, -gāthā, -pakaraṇa): H 100f, PL 3.5.6, PCS 2.198, HP 174, LCM 81, 1702, BnF 123.2, CS, L.

2.5.6.1 Vv-a Paramatthadīpanī III, Vimānavatthu-aṭṭhakathā, ~vaṇṇanā, Vimala-vilāsinī (SI, Dhammapāla, 6th c.): H 273, 280, PCS 2.118, HP 174, PLC 114 (+ n. 4), LCM 98, BnF 128, Bod, CS, L.

2.5.6.12 Vv-ṭ Vimānavatthu-ṭīkā: Ps, L2.

2.5.6.15 Vv-pk?? Eḷu-Vimānavastu-prakaraṇaya (Sinhala & Pāḷi) (C, G. Ratanapāla, 1770.): SH 55, BC 105, BnF 127, L.

Vimānavatthu-sannaya: L.

Petavatthu

2.5.7 Pv Petavatthu (-pāḷi, -gāthā): H 100f, PL 3.5.7, PCS 2,132, HP 118, LCM 82, BnF 123m, CS, L.

2 .5.7 Pv-a Paramatthadīpanī IV, Petavatthu-aṭṭhakathā, Petavatthu-vaṇṇanā, Vimala-vilāsinī (SI, Dhammapāla, 6th c.): H 273, 280f, PL 134f, CB 42, PCS 2.117, HP 119, PLC 114, BnF 130m, LCM 99, CS.

Petavatthu-[saṅkhepa]-vaṇṇanā (C? Abridged version of 2.5.7.): BnF 129.

Petavatthu-saṅkhepa-pakaraṇa, Petavatthu (Ic. Apocryphal story?): PCS 2.93, BnF 256, VP 4/152, EP 75.37.

2.5.7 Pv-ṭ Petavatthu-ṭīkā (Extinct text?): Ps.

Petavatthu-sannaya: L.

Thera-gāthā

2.5.8 Th Thera-gāthā (-pāḷi): H 103–7, PL 3.5.8, PCS 2.74, HP 160f, LCM 1704, BnF 91, CS, L.

2.5.8.1 Th-a Paramatthadīpanī V, Theragātha-aṭṭhakathā (SI, Dhammapāla, 6th c.): H 273, 283f, PL 134f, HP 161, PCS 2.115, LCM 100, CM 31f, N 6601(80), BnF 290ff, VH, CS.

2.5.8.12 Th-ṭ Theragāthā ṭīkā (Extinct text?): Ps.

Therigāthā

2.5.9 Thī Theri-gāthā, Theri-pāḷi: H 103f, PL 3.5.9, PCS 2.75, HP 162, LCM 1705, BnF 91, VH, CS, L.

2.5.9.1 Thī-a Paramatthadīpanī VI, Therīgātha-aṭṭhakathā (SI, Dhammapāla, 6th c.): H 273, 283f, PL 134f, PCS 2.116, HP 162f, CS, L.

2.5.9.12 Thī-ṭ Theri-gāthā-ṭīkā (Extinct text?): Ps.

Jātaka

2.5.10 J Jātaka-pāḷi, Jātaka-gāthā: HP 59, LCM 83, BnF 135f, CS, L.

2.5.10.01 J-sn Jātaka-gāthā-sannaya (On first 448 verses.) (C, Rājamurāri, 13th c.?): SSJ, Vs 101, L.

2.5.10.1 Ja Jātaka-aṭṭhakathā, Jātakatthavaṇṇanā, Jātaka-vaṇṇanā (C, Buddhaghosa?, 5th c.?): H 260f, PL 3.5.10 & p. 128f, PCS 2.53, HP 59f, PLC 117ff, CB 8m, BnF, CM 33f, LCM 83m, N 6603 (75), Vs 97ff, CS, JPTS XXVIII (2006), 113–73.

2.5.10.11 Ja-pṭ Līnatthappakāsinī, Jātaka-ṭīkā, Jātakaṭṭhakathā-purāṇa-ṭīkā (C, Dhammapāla, 6th c.?): H 260f, 359, PL 150, PLC 114, PCS 2.189, Vs 109f, ME 30, FPL 2248, ED 403, Ps.

2.5.10.12 Ja-ṭ Asammoha-vilāsinī: CPD.

Jātaka-visodhana (Ava, B, Ariyavaṃsa, 15th c.): PLB 43.

2.5.10.14 Ja-gp Jātaka-aṭuvā-gäṭapadaya, Jātakaṭṭhakathā-gaṇṭhi-padatthavaṇṇanā, Jātaka-gaṇṭhi-padaya (C, 13th c?): H 260, HP 62, SSJ, N 6609(11), PLC 124, 126f, LCM 456, Vs 101, L.

Jātaka-aṭṭhakathā-sannaya: L.

Jātaka-gaṇṭhi (Before 1442): PLB 106.

2.5.10.15 Ja-pot Pansiyapanas Jātaka-pota, Jātaka-pot-vahanse, Sinhala Jātaka Atuvāva (Sinhalese trans. of Ja by Parākramabāhu IV, 14th c.): N 6603(75), PLC 127, 233, HP 63, LCM 457, Vs 100, L.

Jātaka-pūjapotraya: L.

Aṭṭha-jātaka: N 6603(75)

Aṭa-dā-sannē, Aṭṭha-jātaka-sannaya (C, 12th c.?) (Old sannē on the Aṭṭha-jātaka.): SSJ, Vs 101f, N 6603(75), D 419, L.

Dasa-jātaka (S. Compilation of ten jātakas found in Thailand and Laos.): PSA 30, N 6603(5).

Dasa-jātaka (Sinhala translation.): Vs 101.

Jātaka-paṭuna (Index-list of titles in Ja.) (C, early 14th c.): N 6603(100).

Demaḷa-jātaka-gätapadaya (Extinct Tamil sannaya quoted in the 15th c. Pañcikā-pradīpaya.): Vs 72, 103.

(Jtn) Nidāna-kathā, Jātatthakī-nidāna, Jātattagī~ (Introduction to Jātaka, consisting of 3 [or 4] sections: [Sumedhakathā], Dūre-nidāna, Avidūre-nidāna, Santike-nidāna.) (2.5.10,5 Jtn is identical with this text.): H 111, PCS 2.87, PL 78f, HP 63, BnF 648, VP 4/141, ED 403, BLB, L.

Sumedha-kathā (-gāthā) (Ava, B, Sīlavaṃsa, 15th c.) (Poetical version of Sumedha-kathā of the Dūre-nidāna.): PLB 43.

Samoha-nidāna (S. Compilation of Jātakas.): BnF 627.

Vesantara-jātaka

Ves-ja Vesantara-jātaka (-pāḷi), Vessantara~, Mahāvessantara~ (= HP 550.): Vs 98, PL 3.5.10, BnF 203m, VP, ME, L.

Vessantara-jātaka-gāthā, Mahāvessantara-gāthā: CB 14, SPB 32, BnF 204f, VH 253, ME.

Vesantarā-gīti (B?): CS.

Vesantara-jātakaya (Sinhalese translation.): Cf N 6599(24)I, 6603(194), LCM 596–623, SH 66, 227.

Vessantara-jātaka-kāvyaya (Sinhalese verse.): SL 173, N 6603(192), SH 228f, LCM 593f.

Ves-a Vesantara-jātaka-aṭṭhakathā, Mahā-vessantara-jātaka (S?, 1351): PCS 2.9, PSA 99, BnF 206, 418f.

Ves-sn Vesataru-dā-gäṭapadaya, Vesaturu-dā-sannē, Vesantara-jātaka-gāthā-sannē, Vesaturu-gāthā-padārthaya, Vesantara-jātaka-atthavaṇṇanā (C, 12th c?): SSJ & Vs, N 6600(112.), LCM 625, 627–8.

Līnatthappakāsinī-mahāvessantara-jātaka-ṭīkā, Vessantara-jātaka-ṭīkā, Vesantara-jātaka-līnattha- ppakāsanī. (Part of 2.5.10.11 Ja-pṭ.): Vs 109f, LCM 626, N 6599(28–9), VP.

Gantha-sāra-cintā: PCS 2.36.

2.5.10.13 Vess-dīp Vessantara-jātaka-dīpanī, Vessantara-dīpanī, Mahā-vessantara-dīpanī (CM, Siri Maṅgala, 1517): H 390, PSA 21, 62f, PCS 2.84, CB 15f, VP, VH, EP 48, 56.

Vessantara-jātaka-vivaraṇa, Mahājātaka-vivaraṇa: PCS 2.200, BnF 813, VP, Gv.

Sakkābhimata: PCS 2.206, Gv.

Vessantara-jātaka-nissaya (Pali-Burm, Pali-Thai.): SPB 36, 65, BnF 205m.

Ummagga-jātaka

Ummagga-jātaka, Mahā-ummagga~, Mahosatha~, Mahāsatha~ (Ja 446.): BnF 173m, ME 31.14, L.

Mahosadha-jātaka-vivaraṇa, Ummagga-jātaka-vivaraṇa (Ic.): CB 13.

Umaṃ-dā-gäṭapadaya, Ummagga-jātaka-gäṭapadaya (Before 15th c.) (C. Extinct.): Vs 72, 104.

Ummagga-jātakaya, ~purāṇa-piṭapata: Vs 101, LCM 578ff, L.

Ummagga-jātaka-sannaya: L.

Ummagga-jātakaya (Siṃhala), Umaṃdāva & Umandā Kavi (Sinh. verse versions.): SL 173f, LCM 577ff, L.

Ummaggajātaka-nissaya (Pali-Burm, Pali-Thai.): SPB 53, BnF 414f, Bod.

Pāḷi commentaries on other individual Jātakas

Nārada-jātaka-vivaraṇa, Mahānāradakassapa-gāthā- vaṇṇanā (Ic.) (On Ja 544.): CB 13.

Apocryphal Jātaka Texts

2.5.10 Sj-ja Sivijaya-jātaka, Sīvijaya-jātaka (Ic.): H 431, PSA 99, PCS 2.238, BnF 328, ED 403, EP 18, VP 4/154, BnF 328m, VH.

Sivirājānāmavatthu: ME 31.6.

2.5.10,4 Smn Sotatthakī-mahānidāna(-nidāna, -pakaraṇa, -ṭīkā), Sotattha-kiṃ~, Sodattakī, Sotattagī, Sodattakī, So (C, Culla-Buddhaghosa, pre 1442 see PI and SL 91.): PCS 2.252, PSA 123PLB 104, VP4/122, FPL 2248, ED 403, PI, Gv.

Sampiṇḍita-mahānidāna, Sampiṇḍi-mahānidānaya, Mahā-sampiṇḍita-nidāna,: H 432f, PSA 86f, PCS 2.223, LCM 1452, VP4/122, PSC 75, BnF 623f.

2.5.10,5 Jtn Jātatthakī-nidāna = Nidānakathā (See Jātaka section above.): H 434, FPL 2248, PLB 104, EP 403, PI.

Paññāsa-ja Paññāsa-jātaka, Zimmè/Chiengmai Paṇṇāsa, Lokipaṇṇāsa-jātaka (CM, Sāmaṇera?, 15–16th c.) (3 recensions: B, C, S.): PL 177f, PSA 30, 98f, 109ff, PCS 2.102, BnF 324m, EP 54, 60 m, VP, ANL, ED 509, JPSA.

Cakkhānavutti-jātaka, Cakkhānavuttipāpa-sutta (La?): PSA 118f, ED 403.

Gandhaghāṭaka-jātaka (La?): PSA 117, ED 403.

Nandakumāra-jātaka, Candakumāra~ (= Khaṇḍahāla-jātaka, J 542.): PSA 109f, BnF 189f.

Pācittakumāra-jātaka, Arabhimba-jātaka: EP 31, VP 4/154.

Supinakumāra-jātaka: ME 31.13.

Bālasaṅkhyā-jātaka, Varavaṃsa~ (S or La): PSA 114, ED 403.

Mahākappinarāja-jātaka, Mahākappina-vaṇṇanā, Mahākappina-therā (S?): = Mahākappina-dhaja-sūṭra (S?) EP 75.30, VP 4/141.

PCS 2.159.: Mūlakitti-jātaka (La?)

PSA 118, ED 403.: Lokaneyya, Dhanañjaya-jātaka, Lokavinaya

See: 2.10.5 Loka-n: Lohagoṇa-jātaka (La?)

PSA 117, ED 403.: Vijādhāra-jātaka, Vijjñadhamma~ (Kh.)

PSA 99, BnF 211, ED 403.: Sīla-jātaka, Sīlavimaṃsaka~, Sīlavanāga~ (Kh.): PSA 99, BnF 212f, VP 4/150.

Sirisāra-jātaka (S?): ME 42.3, VP 4/151.5.

Sīso-jātaka (S?)VP 4/154.

Sudattayaññakamma-nidānānisaṃsa (S? Part of Paramattamaṅgala.): VP 4/150.

Suddhakamma-jātaka, ~vaṇṇanā, Sudukamma~ (Kh.): PSA 99, BnF 412.

Suvaṇṇa-jīvha-jātaka (La.): PSA 115.

Suvaṇṇa-megha-jātaka (La.): PSA 115, ED 403.

Suvaṇṇa-haṃsa-jātaka (La.): PSA 116, ED 403.

Sūkara-jātaka (S?): PCS p. 165, VP 4/147.

Niddesa

Sutta-niddesa, Niddesa: H 116, PL 3.5.11, LCM 1707, BnF 837.

2.5.111 Nidd I Mahā-niddesa (-pāḷi): H 116f, PL 3.5.11, PCS 2.162, LCM 84, BnF 214, CS.

2.5.112 Nidd II Culla-niddesa (-pāḷi): H 116f, PL 3.5.11, PCS 2.49, LCM 85, CS.

2.5.11.1 Nidd-a I–II Saddhamma-pajotikā, Saddhamma-jotikā, Niddesa-aṭṭhakathā, Mahā-niddesa-aṭṭhakathā, Culla-niddesa-aṭṭhakathā, Saddhamma-ṭṭhitikā (C, Upasena, 6th or 9th c.?): H 287f, PL 133, PCS 2.216, HP 128, 132, PLC 117, 322, LCM 102, BnF 781, CS, VP, L.

2.5.11.12 Nidd-ṭ Mahā-niddesa-ṭīkā (Extinct text?): Ps.

Paṭisambhidāmagga

2.5.12 Paṭis Paṭisambhidāmagga, Paṭisambhidā-pakararaṇa: H 119f, PL 3.5.12, PCS 2,104, HP 115f, LCM 1708, BnF 215, CS.

2.5.12.1 Paṭis-a Saddhamma-pakāsinī, Paṭisambhidāmagga-aṭṭhakathā (C, Mahānāma, 499 or 559.): H 291ff, PL 132, PCS 2.217, HP 128f, LCM 103f, CS.

2.5.12.13 Paṭis-gp Paṭisambhidāmagga-gaṇṭhipadatthavaṇṇanā, Paṭisambhidāmaggagaṇṭhipada, Paṭisambhidāmagga-pakaraṇaṭṭhakathāvaṇṇanā- gaṇṭhipadatthavinicchaya, Paṭisambhidāmaggaṭṭhakathā-gaṇṭhi, Līnatthadīpana (C, Mahābhidhāna Thera?, 9th–10th c?): PLB 104, PD xliii, li–lx, CS 2.39, BLB, Ps, L, Gv.

Līnattha-dīpaṇī, Saddhamma-pakāsinī-ṭīkā (C, Vācissara. Extinct text or identical with the previous?): HP 189, PLC 217, VP 3/93.

Apadāna

2.5.13 Ap Apadāna, Thera-therī-apadāna (-pāḷī): H 121f, PL 3.5.13, PCS 2.13, HP 13ff, L, SH 69, LCM 1709, EP 46, BnF 216, CS.

2.5.13.1 Ap-a Visuddhajana-vilāsinī, Apadāna-aṭṭhakathā (SE-Asia?, late.): H 302, PL 146f, PCS 2.201, HP 179f, SH 70, CB 8, EP 47, CS, CW, VP, VH, BLB, L.

2.5.13.12 Th-Ap-ṭ Thera-apadāna-ṭīkā: CPD.

Therī-apadāna-dīpanī (B, Kumārābhivaṃsa, late 1980s or 1990s) Private correspondence.

Buddhavaṃsa

2.5.14 Bv Buddhavaṃsa (-pāḷi): H 124f, PL 3.5.14, PCS 2.142, HP 34, LCM 86, BnF 123m, CS.

2.5.14.1 Bv-a Madhurattha-vilāsinī, Madhurattha-pakāsinī, Buddhavaṃsa-aṭṭhakathā (Buddhadatta, 5th c.): H 298ff, PL 145f, PCS 2.152, HP 76, PLC 109, N 6601(96), LCM 650m, BnF 131m, VH, CS, L.

2.5.14.12 Bv-ṭ Buddhavaṃsa-ṭīkā (C): CPD.

Buddhavaṃsa-jātakaya, Buddhavaṃsa-gāthā, Buddhavaṃsa-sannaya: L.

Cariyāpiṭaka

2.5.14 Cp Cariyāpiṭaka (-pāḷi), Buddhāpadāna: H 126f, PL 3.5.15, PCS 2.46, HP 36, LCM 87, 1711, BnF 124, PSA 107, CS, L.

2.5.14.1 Cp-a Paramatthadīpanī VII, Cariyāpiṭaka-aṭṭhakathā, Vimala-vilāsinī (SI, Dhammapāla, 6th c.): H 273, 285, PL 134ff, PCS 2.113, HP 36, PLC 114 (+ n. 4), LCM 105, CS, L.

2.5.14.12 Cp-ṭ Cariyāpiṭaka-ṭīkā: Ps.

Semi-canonical Texts (See H III, PL III.)

2.6 Mil Milindapañhā, Milindapaṇhā (Title is plural: see Mil 419: ... *milindapañhā samattā* ... *tisatapañhā honti, sabbāva milindapañhā ti saṅkhaṃ gacchanti.*): H 172ff, PL 110ff, PCS. 2.176, HP 93f, BnF 359f, LCM 1154, SH 237, CM 49, PLB 4, ME, CS.

Milindapañha-saṅkhepa: PCS 2.175, VP 4/126.

Milindapañha-gaṇṭhipada: N 6609(19), SH 237.

2.6.1 Mil-ṭ Madhurattha-pakāsinī, Milindapañha-ṭīkā, Milinda-pañha-vivaraṇa (CM?, Mahātipiṭaka Cūḷābhaya or Cullavimalabuddhi, 1474): H 172m, PL 150, PSA 100f, HP 75, PCS 2.151, SH 237, VP 4/126, CB 49, EP 58, CS.

Milindapañha-aṭṭhakathā (B, Thatōn Mingun Zetawun Sayāḍo/Ū Nārada Jetavana, 1949.): RB, EP 58.

2.6.0(1) Hīnaṭ Sri Saddharmādāsaya, Dharmādāsaya, Milindapraśnaya, Hīnaṭiku (Pāḷi–Sinh.) (C, Sumaṅgala, 1777–8.): PC 284, LCM 1155f, N 6603(79), BSL 104f.

2.7.1 Peṭ Peṭakopadesa (I, Kaccāyana, B.C.?): H 167ff, PL 108f, PCS 2.131,LCM 1802, HP 117, PLB 5, N 6601(38), BnF 357, VP 4/131, CS.

Peṭakopadesa-ṭīkā (Ñāṇamoli—*Piṭaka Disclosure* p. xxxiv—suggests that this text does not exist.) (Gv (JPTS 1886, p. 65).

Peṭakopadesa-aṭṭhakathā (Mandalay, B, 1926): *Piṭaka Disclosure* p. xxxiv

2.7.2 Nett Netti, Neti, Nettipakaraṇa (-pāḷi). (I, Kaccāyana, B.C.?): H 158ff, PL 108f, PCS 4.75, LCM 1801, PLB 5, BnF 357m, CS, L.

2.7.2.01 Nettipakaraṇa-gaṇṭhi: CPD.

2.7.2.1 Nett-a Netti-aṭṭhakathā, Nettipakaraṇa-aṭṭhakathā, Nettipakaraṇatthasaṃvaṇṇanā (SI?, Dhammapāla?, 6th or 10th c.?): H 362, PL 133ff, 149, PCS 4.3, HP 100, N 6608(37), LCM 1231, BnF 720m, BLB, L.

2.7.2.11 Nett-pṭ Netti-purāṇaṭīkā, Nettipakaraṇa-ṭīkā, Līnatthavaṇṇanā, Līnatthappakāsinī (Badaratittha Dhammapāla or Culla-dhammapāla, 6th or 8–9th c?): H 363, W, PSC p. 60, BLB, Ps.

2.7.2.12 Net-ṭ Netti–vibhāvanī (-ṭīkā), Netti–vibhāvanā (B, Saddhammapāla Rājaguru, 1564. Cf author of Saddavutti [5.4.4]: Saddhammapāla/ Saddhammaguru.): H 381, HP 194, PCS 4.76, VP, BLB, Ps.

Ratana-vaḷī, Nettipakaraṇa-ṭīkā: PCS 4.102 (? BLB).

2.7.2.13 Net-mhṭ Netti-ṭīkā, Netti-mahāṭīkā, ~navaṭīkā, Peṭakālaṅkāra,: =? Saṇhatthasūdanī (Amarapura, B, Ñāṇābhivaṃsa, 18–19th c.): H 382, PLB 78, PCS 4.45, LS 70ff, PSC p. 60, BLB, L, Ps.

Netti-ratanākaro (C, Kōdāgoda Upasena, 1924): Printed edition.

Netti-atthayojana (Pali-Burmese) (Ava, B, Sīlavaṃsa, 15th c.): PLB 43.

Netti–vavatthaṃ: BLB.

Netti-hāranaya: BLB.

Netti-anusandhi: BLB.

Vimutti- and Visuddhimagga

2.8.0 Vim Vimuttimagga (Extinct in Pāḷi.) (I?, Upatissa,—5th c.): H 245ff, PL 113f, HP 175f, PLC 86, TT 2.1. (Modern Sri Lankan re-translation from English into Pāḷi, 1963: SH II p. 52–4.)

2.8.1 Vism Visuddhimagga (C, Buddhaghosa, 5th c.): H 245ff, PL 120f, PCS 2.202, PLC 84ff, HP 179f, LCM 1614f, SH 83, PSC 9, EP, VH, CS, L.

2.8.1.01 Vism-gp Visuddhimagga-gaṇṭhi (-pada) (B, Saddhammajotipāla, 15th c.): H 245, PCS 2,41, PSC 59, BnF 356, VP, Ps.

Visuddhimagga-gaṇṭhipadattha (Ava, B, Sāradassī, 17th c.): PLB 56.

2.8.1.1 Vism-mhṭ Paramatthamañjūsā (-ṭīkā), Visuddhi-magga-mahā-ṭīkā, Visuddhi-magga-ṭīkā (C, Dhammapāla, 6th of 9th c.): H 245, 361, PCS 2.121, LCM 1300, HP 11f, CS, VP.

Paramatthasāra-mañjūsā (C, [? Culla-] Dhammapāla, 6th or 9th c?): PC 113 (+ n.2), W, PSC 59, L.

2.8.1.2 Vism-ṭ[1] Visuddhimagga-saṃkhepa-ṭīkā (C): H 245, HP 180, Ps.

2.8.1.2 Vism-ṭ[2] Visuddhimagga-culla-ṭīkā, Saṅkhepattha-jotanī (S?): PCS 2.211, PSA 25, 97f, VP, VH 244.

Visuddhimagga-saṅkhepa: PSC 59.

2.8.1.3 Vism-dī Visuddhimagga-dīpanī (CM, Uttarārāma thera, 16th c.): PSA 23, 62, PLB 97.

2.8.1.4 Vism-sn Visuddhimagga-mahā-sannaya, ~vistara-padārtha- vyākhyānaya, Parākramabāhu-sannaya (C, Parākramabāhu II of Dambadeniya, 13th c.): N 6601(58), LCM 1616f, HP 180, Vs 80–4, L.

2.8.1.5 Vism-bh Visuddhimārga-(abhinava)-saṃksepa-bhāva-sannaya (C, M. Dharmaratna): CPD.

Visuddhimagga-pūja-pāthaya: L.

Attha-pakāsana (C, Vācissara, 12–13th c.): PC 217.

Visuddhi-magga-gaṇṭhi: PCS 1.43, VP 4/110.

Visuddhimagga-nidānakathā (B, Chaṭṭha-saṅgīti-bhāra-nitthāraka-saṅgha- samitiya, 1950s.): CS.

Anthologies, Paritta, Cosmology, Medicine, and Lexicography

2.9.1 Parit Catubhāṇavāra, Mahā-pirit-pota, Piruvānā-potvahanse. (Current in an older recension of 22 texts and a newer of 29 texts. Sinhalese printed editions often also contain an appendix with various other paritta texts and mantras and yantras. The PVV contains 48 of these.): PL 174, RL 118f, N 6599(36), H 87, HP 37f, PSC 1, PLC 75, CM 25f, L, LCM 283, 1712, SH 128, PSA 101, BC 129–69, EP 2, BnF 217. Paritta, Mahā-paritta (Burmese collection of 11 texts; see MP.)

PL 173f, RL 119, PLB 3, MA: Pirit-nava-sūtra, Nava-sutta-paritta, Äṇavum-piritpota (Sri Lankan collection of 9 texts.)PL 174, RL 118f.

Paritta-saṅkhepa, Parittasaṅkhepa-gaṇṭhi, ~vaṇṇanā (S, 17–18th c.) (Commentary on 9 parittas which are the same as in the Pirit-nava-sūtra.): BL OR 1246 A, RL 121. Pirit-navasūtra-padārtha, Äṇavum-padārtha: N 6599(2)xix, (36)iv. Dasasutta-paritta, Pirit dasa sūtraya (C, 10 texts.): N 6600(113) vi. Dasa-paritta (Siam or Khmer. Not identical with the above one.): CB 34, EP 2.11.Vata-paritta, Vat Pirit Potha, Pirit Potha (3): N 6601(73), BC 14f. Aṭavisi-pirit, Aṭṭhavisa-paritta (C.) (28 texts.): CC 25f. 'Khmer' Paritta collection

PSA 101.: 'Arakan' Paritta collection (Arakan area in Burma/ Bangladesh) BL Add 12258/B.

Paritta (Unidentified) (S): EP 39.7. Satta-paritta, Culla-rājaparitta, Jet Tamnan (Ic) (7 texts. Abridged version of Mahārājaparitta.): RL 120, BC 67–80, EP 2.E, BnF 771f. Dvādasa-paritta, Mahārāja-paritta, Sipsong Tamnan (Ic) (12 texts.): RL 120, 124, BC 83ff, CB 35f, EP 2.15, ED 401. Sīrimaṅgala-paritta (B, 20th c.) (31 texts, incl. the 11 of the Paritta.): RL 120f.

2.9.1.1 Parit-a Sāratthasamuccaya, Catubhāṇavāra-aṭṭhakathā, Parittaṭṭhakathā. (C, Anomadassī, 13th c.): H n. 152, HP 143f, PCS 2.233, PSC 1, LCM 883, CB 38f, BnF 217m, L.

Saṅkhepa-vivaraṇa, Pirit-purāṇasannaya: N 6600(48).

Catubhāṇavāra-aṭṭhakathā-sannaya: L.

Catubhāṇavāra-ṭīkā, Paritta-ṭīkā, Paritta-vaṇṇanā: L.

Sārārtha-dīpanī, Satarabaṇavara-sannaya, Catubhāṇavāra-sannaya, Pirit-sannaya. (C, V. Saranaṅkara, 18th c.): HP 143f, 199, SH 314, N 6600(151), BSL 100f, Vs 88, PSC 1, LCM 1465, PLC 282, SL 353, L.

2.9.1.11 Parit-ṭ Parittā-ṭīkā, Paritta-vaṇṇanā (B, Tejodīpa thera, 1672.): PLB 57, PCS 2.122, PSC 1, Ps.

Paritta-gaṇṭhi: PCS 2.40, ED 401.

2.9.2 Suttas Sutta-saṅgaha (C?, Ariyavaṃsa?, before 12th c.): H 157, PL 172f, HP 156f, BnF 791, N 6599(19), PCS 2.246, PLB 5, PSC 2, EP 66, 146, L.

2.9.2.1 Suttas-a Suttasaṅgaha-aṭṭhakathā, Suttasaṅgaha-vaṇṇanā: H 157, HP 158f, N 6599(27), BnF 626m, PCS 2.10, LCM 656, PSC 2, EP 24, 67, L.

Suttasaṅgaha-sannaya: PSC 2, L.

Sūtrasaṅgraha-padārthavyākhyānaya: PSC 2.

Suttasaṅgaha-nissaya: PSC 2.

(Laotian) Sutta-saṅgaha (La.): PSA 106.

2.9.3 Ss Sārasaṅgaha (Sometimes mistakenly called Sāratthasaṅgaha; see next entry.) (Siddhattha the pupil of

Dakkhinārāmadhipatti Buddhappiya, 13–14th c.) (Encyclopedia.): H 384f, PL 173, HP 141, CB 50f, CM 60, LCM 1459, N 6601 (78), PSC 3, PLC 228, PLB 107, BnF 296m, EP 14, ED 302, L.

Sārasaṅgaha-sannaya: L.

Sāratthasaṅgaha (Sometimes mistakenly called Sāra-saṅgaha; see previous entry.) (CM, Nandācāriya / Ānandācāriya, 13 th c.) (= Encyclopedia.): PCS 2.232, PLB 108, H n. 620, EP 59, PSA 63.

Sāra-piṇḍa (Before 1442.): PLB 107.

Sārārtha-saṃgrahaya, Śrī Saddharmasārārtha- saṃgrahaya (Sinh. with Pāḷī quotations. C, V. Saraṇankara, 18th c.): HP 140, SL 66f, PLC 282, BSL 93ff.

Saddharma-ratnākaraya (Sinh. C, Dhammadinna Vimalakitti, 1417): N 6603(36), SL 94f, SH 261, HP 42, H 385.

2.9.3.1 Ss-gṭ-dī Citragaṇṭhidīpanī, Sārasaṅgaha-aṭṭhakathā: PCS 2.48, PSC 3, RLL 71, VP 4/133.

2.9.41 Upās Upasakālaṅkāra, Upasakālaṅkāraṇā, Upāsakajanālaṅkāra (C, Sīhalācariya Ānanda, 12th c.): H 386f, PL 170, HP 168, L, Ps, PCS 2.27, LCM 1568f, PSC 71, BnF 255, LWA, N 6601(61m), CM 54, Bod, VP.

Upāsakajanālaṅkāraya-vaṇṇanā: PSC 71.

Upāsakajanālaṅkāraya-vyākhyāva: PSC 71.

Upāsakajanālaṅkāraya-sannaya: PSC 71.

2.9.42 Upāsakavinicchaya (B, 1882): PLB 95, BnF 380f, 555f.

2.9.43 Paṭip-s Paṭipatti-saṅgaha, Pratipatti-saṅgraha, Gihi–vinaya (Before 1442): H 386, LCM 60, PLB 107, PCS 2.103, N 6600(60), PSC 68, L.

2.9.5 Amāv Amāvatura, Purisa-damma-sārathi-pada-varṇanāva (Eḷu Sinh.) (C, Guruḷugomī, 12th c.): H 6603(41), LCM 713, PLC 158, SL 56f, L.

2.9.6 Dharmapr See 4.1.3,2.

2.9.7 Buts Butsaraṇa, Amṛtāvaha I (Sinh.) (C, Vidyācakravarti, 12th c.): SH 259, LCM 875–78, L.

2.9.8 Dhms Daham-saraṇa, Amṛtāvaha II (Sinh.) (C, Vidyācakravarti, 12th c.): N 6603(72), LCM 903, L.

2.9.9 Saṅgs Saṅga-saraṇa, Amṛtāvaha III (Sinh.) (C, Vidyācakravarti, 12th c.): N 6603(52), L.

2.9.10 Maṅg-d Maṅgalatthadīpanī, Maṅgala-dīpanī, Maṅgaladīpanī-maṅgalasutta-aṭṭhakathā (CM, Siri Maṅgala,

1524): H 389, PSA 22, 62f, PCS 2.149, LCM 248, 1786, LN 122, PSC 62, BnF 631, 755, ME, ED 323, EP 13m, VH, Ps.

Maṅgalasutta-aṭṭhakathā, ~vaṇṇanā, ~padatthavaṇṇanā.: VP 4/ 140, L.

Maṅgalasutta-ṭīkā (C, Sāriputta, 12th c.): HP 191, SW.

Maṅgalasutta-vistara-sannaya. ~sannaya. ~mātikā, ~pada-änuma. (= different texts): N 6600(87–8), L.

2.9.111 Paṭham Paṭhamasambodhi (S, 15th c.): H 391, PSA 24, 84, 124f, BnF 300m, ED 212, EP 9 m.

(2.9.112) Ext Paṭham Paṭhamasambodhi–vitthāra (S, Suvaṇṇaraṃsi, 1845): H 391, PCS 2.106, ED 212.

Paṭhamasambodhi-saṅkhepa (S, Suvaṇṇaraṃsi, 19th c.): PCS 2.107, ED 212.

Vivāha-maṅgala, Vivādha~, Vivāca~, Maṅgala-vivāha (S?) (= First chapter of Paṭham as a separate work.): PSA 86, BnF 389f, EP 143.

2.9.12 Pañca-g Pañcagati-dīpanī, Pañcagati-dīpana, Pañcagati-pāḷi (Ic, 11–12th c.): H 393, PL 160, PCS 2.99, PSA 96, BnF 346f.

2.9.12.1 Pañcagatidīpanī-aṭṭhakathā, Pañcagati-ṭīkā (Ic): PCS 2.64, PSA 96, BnF 347, EP 53, ME 44.

2.9.13 Cha-g Chagati-dīpanī (Thatōn, B, Saddhammaghosa/ Asamaghosa, 12–13th c.?): H 394, PLB 104, Ps, (cf PCS 2.99).

2.9.13.1 Cha-g-ṭ Chagati-dīpanī-ṭīkā (B): H 394.

2.9.14 Loka-p Lokapaññatti (Thatōn, B, Saddhammaghosa, 11–13th c.?): H 395, PL 174, PLB 104, PCS 2.194, EP 112, Ps.

2.9.15 Okāsa-d Okāsa-dīpanī, Okāsa-lokadīpanī: H 398, PCS 2.28, CB 53, EP 51.3, VP 4/144, ICI 10, Ps.

2.9.16 Loka-dīpanī (CM, Saṅgharāja?): PSA 22, PCS 2.190, FPL 3058, Ps.

2.9.17 Loka-d (Lok-s) Loka-padīpika-sāra-pakaraṇa, Loka-dīpaka-sāra, Lokadīpasāra (Martaban, B, Medhaṅkara Saṅgharāja, mid 14th c.): H 397f, PLB 36, HP 190f, PCS 2.191, LCM 1096, PSC 49, CM xxix n. 4, EP 49, 77, 112, VP 4/143, Ps.

2.9.18 Lokuppatti-pakāsinī (B, Aggapaṇḍita): Ps.

Lokuppatti: PCS 2.195.

2.9.19 Candasuriyagati-dīpanī (Asamaghosa): H 401, Ps.

2.9.20 Saṅkh-p Saṅkhyā-pakāsaka (CM, Ñāṇavilāsa thera, 15–16th c.): H 390, PSA 23, 68, PCS 2.210, PLB 47, FPL 634, Ps.

2.9.20,1 Saṅkh-p-ṭ Saṅkhyāpakāsaka-ṭīkā, Saṅkyāpakāsaka-dīpanī (CM, Siri Maṅgala/Sumaṅgala, 1520.): H 390, PSA 23, 62, 68, PCS 2.70, PLB 47, EP 74, Ps.

2.9.21 Vajirasārattha-saṅgaha (-pakaraṇa), Vajirasāra-saṅgaha, Vajirakhandāna-pakaraṇa (CM, Ratanapañña, 1535.): PSA 20, 64, PCS 4.108, LCM 1588, ICI 2, L, Ps.

2.9.21.1 Vajirasārasaṅgaha-ṭīkā, ~vaṇṇanā, Vajirasāratthasaṅgaha-ṭīkā (According to Ps, quoted in PSA and CPD, by Ratanapañña in Ratanupura, see above.): PCS 4.48, PSA 64, PSC 74, L, Ps.

2.9.22 Bhesajjamañjūsā (C, Pañcapariveṇa-adhipati/Atthadassi thera, 1261 or 1267): PL 163, HP 24f, PCS 2.148, PLC 215, PSC 125, L.

2.9.22.1 Bhesajjamañjūsā-ṭīkā (C, Pañca-pariveṇa-adhipati, 13th c.): PC 216.

2.9.22.2 Bhesajjamañjūsā-sannaya (C, Pañca-pariveṇa-adhipati in 13th c. [18 sections] & Välanvitta Saraṇankara [who added 42 sections in] 1734.): HP 23f, 140, N 6612(2), BnF 560, PLC 215, Vs 87, PSC 125, BSL 94f, L.

Yogapiṭakaya (Bhesajja-mañjūsā-parivartanaya) (C, D. Dhammajoti, 18th c.): HP 25, PCS 2.181, L.

2.9.112 Jina-m Jinamahānidāna (S): H 392, PCS 2.58, VP 4/124.

2.9.172 Cakkav-d Cakkavāḷa-dīpanī, Cakkavāḷatthadīpanī (CM, Siri Maṅgala, 1520): H 400, PL 175, EP 50, 61, 76, PSA 21, 68, HP 185, PCS 2.43, LCM 79f, PSC 76, LN, VP 4/142, VH, L.

Unclassified anthologies, etc.

Abhisambodhi-kathā: L.

Ācariyavaṃsa: PCS 2.21.

Aggasāvaka-pāṃben-pāramī (Maybe identical with Sāvaka-nibbāna.): PCS 2.17, VP 4/140, VH 250.

Anattavibhāvana (B. Leḍī Sayāḍo, 19th–20th c.): DBM 82, BSL.

Arahattamagga-vaṇṇanā (B): Ps.

Ariyasaccāvatāra (B?, before 1442.): PLB 107.

Upāyakathā (B, Paññāsāmi Saṅgharāja, mid 19th c.): PLB 93.

Kāya-nagara, Kāyanagara-sutta (S or Kh?): PSA 95, BnF 566.

Kusaladhamma-vinicchaya-kathā (La?) (Based on Dhammasaṅganī mātikā.): PSA 124.

Gaṇṭhi-sāra, Gandhisāra, Gaṇḍhisāra (B, Chappaṭa, 15th c.): PLB 18f.

Cakāṅka-nicchaya (B?) (Pāḷi & Burm.): CB 121.

Catusacca-bhayavināsaka-dīpanī (B. Leḍī Sayāḍo, 19th–20th c.): DBM 69.

Culla-sīla-vimaṃsa: LCM 887.

Jālīkaṇhābhiseka: PCS 2.54.

Tam Wat Chow, Tam Wat Yen (S, King Mongkut, 19th c.) (Morning and evening service chants in Pāḷi.): BC 2ff.

Tiṃsa-pāramī: PSA 124.

Tilakkhaṇa-suttasaṅgaha, Dhammapada-suttasaṅgaha-tilakkhaṇa- vinicchaya-kathā (La.): PSA 108f.

Tiloka-dīpanī, Lokadvīpa, Lokadīpaka: PSA 125, EP 49, 77.

Tilokavinicchaya (S, ordered by Rāma I, 1790.) (Extinct? Pāḷi original of Trailokavinicchaya-kathā.): PSA 97.

Trai-lokavinicchaya-kathā (S?) (Pali-Siamese.): PSA 97, BnF 395m, VH.

Tepiṭaka-gaṇṭhi (C?): PCS 2.72, VP 4/138, Wms Thai 11.

Dasa-bodhisatta-vidhiya: N 6601(21).

Devadhitapañhā (La?): PSA 121.

Dhammacakka-aṭṭhakathā, Saddhammavilāsinī, Dhammacakka-pavattana- suttatthasaṃvaṇṇanā: PCS 2.118, VP 4/114.

Dhammacakka-gaṇṭhi: PCS 2.38.

Dhammacakka-saṅkhepa-aṭṭhakathā: PCS 2.6.

Dhammacakka-sutta, Dhammacakkappavattana-sutta: LCM 194ff, N 6599(2 & 9), SH 6ff, PLB 105, CB 35, BnF, Bod, ME 45, ED 401.

Dhammacakkasutta-pada-änuma.: LCM 171f, 217ff, N 6600(47)ii.

Dhammacakka-sutta-sannaya, Dhammacakka-purāṇa- sannaya, ~sūtrārtha-vyākhyāna, ~padārtha.: LCM 180f., 198ff, N 6600(47)ii, SH 6, BnF 874.

Dhammacakka-ṭīkā: PCS 2.62, PLB 105.

Dhamma-samūha: PCS 2.91.

Nandopanandadamanaya (Sinh. C. Extracted from another treatise that included Navaguṇasannaya.): LCM 1207, SL 354.

Nandopananda-vatthu, Nandopanandanāgarāja (Buddhasiri?) (Part of Bāhuṃ-ṭīkā.): BnF 320f.

Namo-ṭīkā: PCS 2.63.

Nirayakathā-dīpaka (B, Paññasāmi thera, mid 19th c.): PLB 93.

Niraya-varṇanāva (2) (Pāḷi gāthas and Sinhala description): N 6601(71)

Niyama-dīpanī (Leḍī Sayāḍo, 19th–20th c.): DBM 16, BLS.

Pabbājaniya-kammavācā (B, Leḍī Sayāḍo, 19–20th c. A paritta for dispelling danger.): PLB 98, DBM 50a, 59a.

Pañca-dussīla: N 6599(39).

Pañcakkhara-saṃkhepa: PCS 2.98.

Pañca-nīvaraṇaya: N 6599(17).

Pasādanīya-kathā: PCS 2.123, BnF Ic 487(3), VP 4/137.

Pituguṇakathā, Pituguṇa-sutta (S?): PCS 2.128 VP 4/157.

Porāṇa-saṅgaha (La.): PSA 106

Buddhānuparivatta: PCS 2.143, VP 4/118.

Buddhānusati–vaṇṇanā: ME 31.4.

Buddhapāda-maṅgala (Cf Poetry: Aṭorāśiyak Magul-lakuṇu.): PCS 2.140, VP 4/115.: Buddhavassa-ācikkhaṇa, Buddhavarṣaya-kīma (Announcing the Buddhist year at Vata-paritta): N 6601(75)vi. Buddhavipāka: PCS 2.141, VH 249.

Buddhavipāka-aṭṭhakathā: PCS 2.7.

Bojjhaṅgapāṭha-bhāvanā (S or Kh?): BnF 74–5, PSA 91f.

Bhikkhu-dussīla: N 6601(39).

Bhumma-saṅgaha (Dhammaraṃsī thera): PCS 2.147, Gv.

Bhumma-niddesa: Gv.

Mahā-buddhaguṇa, Buddhaguṇā, Namaskāra-gāthā (S?) (Beg: *Iti pi so...* or *Buddhaṃ jīvitaṃ yāva nibbānaṃ...*): PSA 95, PCS 2.163, LCM 1175, BnF 385m, ED 401, EP 2.2m, BnF 385, MA.

Mahā-buddhaguṇa-aṭṭhakathā, ~vaṇṇanā: PCS 2.8, 2.164, BnF 877, EP 132, VH.

Mahā-buddhaguṇa-ṭīkā: PCS 2.68.

Mahākappa-lokasaṇṭhāna-paññatti, Mahākappa-lokasaṇṭhāna (S?): PCS 2.158, CB 54, BnF 717, EP 51.2.

Mahā-nekkhamma-campū (Gāthā & prose. C, Widurapola Piyatissa, 1935): PSC 80, printed edition.

Maṅgala-aṭṭhatthasāra-aṭṭhakathā, Maṅgala-aṭṭharasā-aṭṭhakathā (Kh or S?, Buddhapādamaṅgala-mahādevarāja) (On auspicious signs on Buddha's feet.) (Cf Buddha-pāda-maṅgala above.): PSA 96, BnF 391.

Mātuguṇa-kathā, ~sutta (S?): PCS 2.173, BnF 561, VP 4/157.

Mo Paritta, Ngayanmin Paritta, Ñāyanmin Paritta (B. Leḍī Sayādaw, 20th c. Against drought): DBM 50a, 59b.

Moggallānabimba-pañhā (S?): PCS 2.179, VP 4/150.

(Mongkut-rāja-saṅgaha), Prachum Phra Rachaniphon Bhasa Bali nai Phra Bat Somdet Phra Chom Klao Chao Yu Hua (S, Bangkok, 2004. Collection of letters, chants, edicts, and the like in Pali King Mongkut/Rāma IV, from 1830s-1862.): Private correspondence.

Yasasassattha (Ic. Beg: *Paṭhamaṃ dānapāramī...*): PSA 97, BnF 411.

Yasavaḍḍhana-vatthu (Ava, B, Tipiṭakālaṅkāra, early 17th c.): PLB 53.

Rāhu-damana-sannaya (C): LCM 1243, 1371.

Rājasevaka-dīpanī (B, Paññasāmi thera, mid 19th c.): PLB 93.

Loka-saṇṭhāna-jota-ratana-gaṇṭhi, Loka-jotika, Jotaratana-satthavaṇṇanā (S?): PCS 2.193, VP 4/144, EP 51, FEMC A5.

London Pāḷi Devī Puccha-vissajanā (B. Leḍī Sayāḍo, 20th c. Mrs C.A.F. Rhys Davids' Questions and Sayāḍo's Answers): DBM 33, 44, BSL.

Veda-vinicchaya (B? Royal Burmese astrological handbook): PCS 2.204.

Visuddhakūṭadīpanī (B? Might not belong to this section.): CW Burm 80.

Saddhammavilāsinī-Dhammacakka-aṭṭhakathā: PCS 2.218.

Saddhammamālinī: Gv.

Sambhāra-vipāka, Sambhāravipāka-sutta (S?): PCS 2.224, VP 4/121, VH 145m.

Sammādiṭṭhi-dīpanī (B. Leḍī Sayāḍo, 19th–20th c.): DBM 22, BSL.

Sammoha-nidāna: PCS 2.225, VP 4/125.

Sampasādanī (C, Sāriputta, 12th c.) (Maybe extinct.): SW.

Saṅkhyā-pakaraṇa, Tepiṭaka-saṅkhyā (Ic?) (Ennumeration of contents of Pāli canon & commentaries.): EP 121, VP 4/157.

Sārasaṃvaṇṇanā: L.

Sāsanasampatti-dīpanī, Sāsanavisodhanī (B, Leḍī Sayāḍo, 19th–20th c.): BSL, DBM 3.

Sāsanavipatti-dīpanī, Sāsanavisodhanī (B, Leḍī Sayāḍo, 19th–20th c.): BSL, DBM 3.

Satta-vipāka: PCS 2.213.

Satyakkriyāva (= Saccakiriyā): LCM 1471

Sīla-kathā (B, Paññāsāmi Saṅgharāja, mid 19th c.): PLB 93.

Siri-mahāmaya-vatthu: Ps.

Siri–vicittālaṅkāra (Mahāsvāmi Dhammakitti): PCS 2.237.

Sotabbamālini (S or C, 14th c. or earlier): N 6601(54), PSA 25, HP 148f, PCS 2.251, PLB 106, PSC 64, BnF 342, VP 4/145, EP 42, ED 518, L.

Sotabbamālini-aṭuvāva: PSC 64.

Surājamagga-dīpanī (B, Ñeyya-dhamma Saṅgharāja, mid 19th c.): PLB 93.

Suvaṇṇamālā, ~gaṇṭha, ~sutta (S?): PCS 2.250, VP 4/150.

Ānisaṃsa: Benefits

See PL 178, ED 203.

Aṭa-pirikāra-ānisamsaya (C. Sinh. prose & Pāḷi verses.): SH 244f, L.

Ādhārakapattadāna-ānisaṃsakathā (S?): PCS 2.22, VP 4/151, VH 227.

Āvāsa-dānānisaṃsa-vaṇṇanā, Pasāda-jananī (C, V. Dharmaratana, 1932): PSC 14.

Āvāsa-dānānisaṃsa-prakaraṇaya (Dharmaratana): PSC 14.

Uddesa-dakkhiṇānumodanā-jhāpanakiccakathā (S?): VH 234.4.

Kaṭhina-ānisaṃsa-kathā, Tiṇṇaka-vatthu, Tiṇṇapālakavatthu (S?): PCS 2.96.3, PSA 97, BnF 404.

Kaṭhina-dānānisaṃsa (Sannaya & Nissaya): VH 234, SH 246, LCM 1071, SL 80.

Caṇḍāgāra-ānisaṃsakathā (S?): PCS 2.44, VP 4/151, ME 45.

Jhāpanakiccānānisaṃsa (S?): VH 234.

Tepiṭaka-ānisaṃsakathā, Tepiṭakalekhānisaṃa, Piṭakattayakārakānisaṃsa (S?): PCS 2.73, VP 4/151, VH 234, H n. 671, PL 178.

Dāna-ānisaṃsa-kathā, Dānānisaṃsaya: PCS 2.80, VP 4/151, VH, N 6600(60)7, SL 355.

Dīpa-dānānisaṃsakathā: LCM 82, VP 4/151, VH 227.

Dhajadānā-thomanānisaṃsa (S?): VP 4/151.

Dhammānisaṃsaya (C?): N 6599(3), LCM 949ff, VH 227, SH 92.

Dhammasavanānisaṃsaya (S?): PCS 2.92, VP 4/151, VH 227.

Dhūtaṅgānisaṃsaya (Sinh. with Pāḷi quotations.): LCM 57.

Paṭisaṃkharaṇa-ānisaṃsakathā (S?): PCS 2.105.

Pañca-sīla-ānisaṃsakathā (S?): PCS 2.101, VP 4/151.

Paṃsukūla-dānānisaṃsakathā (Kh?) (An apocryphal jātaka.): H n. 671, PSA 104 (n. 5).

Paṃsukūla-ānisaṃsa (-kathā), Paṃsukūlikavattha-ānisaṃsa: H n. 671, PL 178, PCS 2.212,6, EP 75.39, VP 4/141, VH 244.6.

Parittānisaṃsa, Ānisaṃsa (S or Kh?): PSA 95.

Pabbajjānisaṃsa (-sutta) (Ic. Apocryphal sutta. Cf Paramatthamaṅgala.): PSA 121, VH 234, VP 4/150, ED 203.

Piṭakattayānisaṃsakathā (S?): VH 234.11.

Pupphaggi-dāna-ānisaṃsakathā (S?): PCS 2.130.

Bhūmi-dānānisaṃsa (C?): N 6600(138)iii.

Mettānisaṃsaya (C?): LCM 1149.

Maitri-bhāvanānisaṃsaya (-sannaya) (C): LCM 1138.

Yāna-ānisaṃsakathā (S?): PCS 2.180, VP 4/151, VH 227.

Likkhitakamma-ānisaṃsa, Akkharalikkhitānisaṃsa (S?): EP 75.27, VH 265.

Vattha-kaṭṭha-ānisaṃsakathā (S?): PCS 2.196.

Vatthadāna-ānisaṃsakathā (S?): PCS 2.197, VP 4/151, VH 227.

Vihāra-dānānisaṃsaya, Vihāradānānisaṃsakathā: PCS 2.203, VP 4/151, VH, LCM 1606.

Vesantara-jātaka-ānisaṃsa (= 4.1.4: Mth-v??): PCS 2.23.

Saṅgha-bhatta-ānisaṃsakathā (S?): PCS 2.212.3.

Sāradavatthuvaṇṇanā-ānisaṃsa (S?): VH 282.

Sīmā-ānisaṃsakathā (S?): PCS 2.240, VP 4/151.

Sīlānisaṃsa (C?): N 6599(37)vii.

Sutta-jātaka-nidāna-ānisaṃsakathā, Suttajātakanidānānisaṃsa (S or Kh?): PCS 2.244, PSA 94, EP 1, 35m, ED404

Suvaṇṇa-thambha-ānisaṃsakathā (S?): PCS 2.250, VP 4/151.

Setuka-ānisaṃsa-kathā, Setukānisaṃsa (S?): PCS 2.212.3, VP 4/147.

Bhāvanā, Meditation

Asaṅkhatadhammapakāsinī-kyan (B, U Pyin-nya-thika, 1899.): PLB 97.

Atīta-paccavekkhaṇa (-pāṭho): N 6601(45), BC 29, L.

Aīta-pasvikum-sannaya, Pratyavekṣā-gāthā-sannaya: LCM 1306, 1361.

Parikkhāra-paccavekkhaṇa, Taṅkhaṇika-paccavekkhaṇa-pāṭho: N 6600(115), SH 210, BC 28, SR 37f.

Dhātupaṭikūla-paccavekkhaṇa-pāṭho: BC 27.

Anityāsmṛutiya (Pali-Sinh.): LCM 742–3.

Abhidharma-kamaṭahan (Pali-Sinh.): N 6599(37)iii, LCM 685f.

Āhāra-viharaṇaya (Pali-Sinh.): LCM 705.

Bhūta-kammaṭṭhāna, Yathābhūta~, Uyyojanadīpanī~: CW.

Kāyagatā-satiya (Pali-Sinh.): LCM 690.

Paṭicca-samuppāda (Vin I 1–2 & Dhp 153–4.): N 6599(2)ii, SH 203, MP 102f, SR 5f.

Paṭiccasamuppāda-sannaya: N 6599 (34)xi.

Pilikul Bhāvanāva (Pali-Sinh.): LCM 1317–32.

Bālacittapabodha-gaṇṭha, Bālacittapabodhana: PCS 2.136, VP 4/157, Gv.

Bhāvanā Kāṇḍayak (Pali-Sinh.): LCM 1240.

Maitribhāvanā (-gāthā), Metta-bhāvanā, Brahmavihāra-pharaṇā, Brahmavihārā-bhāvanā (Different versions. Beg. *Ahaṃ avero homi...*): LCM 1135, 1147f, N 6559 (2)x, BC 32–3, MP 107f, Dham 25.

Maitri-bhāvanā (-sannaya): LCM 1136.

Mettānusmṛutiya (Pali-Sinh.): LCM 1150.

Satipaṭṭhāna-sutta (MN 10): LCM 317–334, VP 4/113, L.

Satipaṭṭhānasutta-padārtha: LCM 337–44, L.

~pada-änuma: LCM 311–6m, L.

~sannaya: DC 335–6, 339, L.

~aṭṭhakathā, ~vaṇṇanā, ~bhāvanā-sastaraya, ~pujāpota, ~purāṇa-sannaya, ~vistara-sannaya, ~vistara-deshanāwa (Different works.): L.

Satipaṭṭhānasutta-sannē (C, D. Dhammarakkhita, 18th c.): PC 285.

Mahāsatipaṭṭhāna-sutta (DN 22): N 6599(1), SH 19, CM 8, BnF, Bod, VP.

Mahāsatipaṭṭhānasuttaṃ vitthāra-mukhena: N 6599(3)

Mahāsatipaṭṭhānasutta-sannaya (C, T. S. Buddharakkhita?, 1760.): SH 19, Vs 88, CM xxxix.

Mahāsatipaṭṭhānasutta-pada-änuma: SH 21, BNF 725, Bod.

Vipassanā-dīpanī (B. Leḍī Sayāḍo, 19th–20th c.): DBM 32, BSL.

Saggāvatāra, Sattāvitarā (S?): PCS 2.208, VP 4/157.

Visuddhiñāṇakathā (B, Mahāsi Sayāḍo, 1950): PoI.

Vipassanā-naya-ppakaraṇa (B, Mahāsi Sayāḍo. Translation from Burmese *Vipassanā Shu Ney Kyan* by Ven. Kumārābhivaṃsa, published in Burmese script in 1999.): Private correspondence.

Sārīrika-vinicchaya: PCS 3.85, VP 5/56.

Yogāvacara manuals, Esoteric Meditation

Vidarśanā pota, Vidarśanā bhāvanā pota, Dhyāna pota, Samasatalis karmasthāna-dhyāna-bhāvanā, Bambaragalē Pota,

Vipassanā Niddesa (Pali-Sinh. C. Compiled by Rambukavällē Ratanajoti on advice of Siamese theras, 18th c. Different versions? Beg: *Okāsa vandāmi bhante...* Eng. trans.: *Manual of a Mystic.* The material of this and the below entries is similar.): N 6601(6; 7; 23; 43 i & ii, 50; 76), LCM 699–702, SH 236.

Parikamma-bhāvana (C? Pāḷi. Beg: *Upāda uppajjantu...*): N 6601(23iii)

Kasina-bhāvanā-pota, Cattālisa-kammaṭṭhāna (Pali-Sinh. Beg: *Ahaṃ yācāmi uggahanimmitaṃ...*): N 6601(6 & 64).

Kasina-bhāvanā-pota, Cattālisa-kammaṭṭhāna (Pali-Sinh. Beg. *Okāsa accayo no bhante accagamā...*): N 6601(51).

Ratana-amatākara-vaṇṇanā, Amatākaravaṇṇanā, Yogijanakanta-vimuttimagga (Pāli verse. 18th c? Beg: *Niccaṃ kilesamalavajjitadehadhāriṃ.* The title *Vimuttimagga-uddāna* is arbitrary according to Somadasa in N.): N 6601(85i), SH 236, LCM 687, L.

Samatha-vipassana-bhāvana-vākkapprakaraṇaṃ, Dvidhā-vutta-kammaṭṭhāna (Pāḷi prose. Beg. *Vanditvā sirasā buddhaṃ ... Okāsa okāsa bho sabbaññu Gotama sitthakadīpa...* The 13 chapter titles are same as in Amatākaravaṇṇanā with which it is found in the same MS bundle. Maybe *dvidhā* refers to the verse text followed by the prose text. Cf prec. and next entries.: N 6601(85ii).

Duvidha-kammaṭṭhāna, (C? In same entry as Kammaṭṭhānasaṅgaha in L. Beg: *Vanditvā... Okāsa sabbaññu Gotama sitthakadīpa...* 4 chapters.): N 6601(23ii), SW, L.

Kammaṭṭhāna-saṅgaha (C, Sāriputta, 12th c. Maybe identical with the preceding entry.): SW, Ps, HP 144.

Kammaṭṭhāna-dīpanī (Sāriputta. Maybe identical with the preceding entry.): Ps, SW.

Kammaṭṭhāna-vibhāga (C?): L.

Kammaṭṭhāna-gahananiddesa-sannaya,: L.

Kammaṭṭhāna, Kammaṭṭhāna-bhāvanā, Karmaṣthāna, Kamaṭahan, Kamaṭahan-sannaya (C. Different works?): LCM 1067, N 6600 (145), L.

Vimutti-saṅgaha (Pāḷi.) (C?): L.

Vimutti-saṅgaha-sannaya (C): L.

Vimukti-saṃgrahaya ((Pāḷi verse + sanna + Sinh. prose.C, Laṅkāsenavirat pirivena adhipatti, late 14th c. Often together with the Skhandhādingē- vibhāgaya and Nava-arahādībuddhaguṇa- vibhāgaya. Beg: *Natvā buddhañca...*): N 6601(55), CM xxxii, SL 53, L.

Vimukti-margaya (C?): L.

Mūla-kammaṭṭhāna, Mahā-mūlakammaṭṭhāna (Ic.): PCS 2.165, PSA 108, VP 4/120.

Yokappako Ācāriya (La?): PSA 121.

Law

2.9.23.1 Manu-dhammasattha, Dhammasattha, Dhammavilāsa Dhammathat (Dala, B, Dhammavilāsa, 1174.): PLB 32f, 85, Ps.

(Dhammasattha-vaṇṇana) (B, 1656): PLB 33.

2.9.23.2 Wagaru Dhamma-sattha, ~that (Tailang, B, Wagaru Rāja, 13th c.) (In Tailang language.): PLB 33, 85f, CPD.

2.9.23.3 Manusāra (B, Buddhaghosa, 16th c.) (Pāḷi translation of Wagaru Dhammathat): PLB 86, BnF 551f, FPL 2630.

2.9.23.4 Nava-Dhamma-sattha: CPD.

(Nava-) Manu-dhamma-sattha (B, Dhammavilāsa II, 1650.): PLB 87.

2.9.23.5 Manu-vaṇṇanā (Vanna-kyaw-din, between 1776 and 1774.): PLB 87f, CPD.

Vinicchaya-pakāsinī (Vanna-kyaw-din, between 1776 and 1774.): PLB 88.

Mohavicchedanī (B, Rājabala-kyaw-din, 1832.): PLB 88.

Mahārāja-satta-vinicchaya (Paḷi-Burm.): BnF 550.

Nīti Texts

2.10.1 Dhn Dhamma-nīti (B, 14–15th c.? Transl. of Sanskrit Cāṇakya *subhāṣitas* with a few additional stanzas from Canonical Pāḷi texts as well as Burmese proverbs.): H 420f, PL 176, PLB 51, FPL, CHL, CS.

2.10.3 Mhn Mahāraha-nīti (B, + 15th c.): H 420f, PL 176, CS.

2.10.4 Rn Rāja-nīti (B, Anantañāṇa & Gaṇāmissa, 16th c. Mostly a transl. of stanzas of the Sanskrit *Yogayātrā* of Varāhamihira.): H 420f, PL 176, PLB 51, BnF 711, CHL, FPL.

2.10.5 Loka-n Lokaneyya-pakaraṇa, Lokanaya-jātaka, Dhanañjaya-paṇḍita-jātaka, Dhanañjaya-jātaka, Mahāpurisa-jātaka, Lokavinaya, Lokaneyya-dhanañjaya, Lokaneyya, Dhanañjaya (Kh?): H 423, PCS 2.192, ANL, BnF 330m, PSA 99, PSA 112f, BnF 330m, EP 33, VP 4/153, VH, ME, ED 403.

Lokaneyya-gāthā (S. Pali-Siamese): BnF 338.

2.10.6 Manus Manussa-vineyya: H 424.

2.10.21 Ln Loka-nīti (B. Before early 19th c. Transl. of Sanskrit Cāṇakya *subhāṣitas* with some additional stanzas from Canonical Pali texts.): H 420f, PL 176, PLB 51, 95, CB 129, CHL, FPL.

Loka-nīti (B, Visuddhācāra) (See colophon in CS.): CS.

2.10.22 Ln Loka-nīti (S): H 422, NLBSL.

Sutavaḍḍhanta-nīti, Paṇḍitālaṅkāra-nīti (B, 18th c.): PL 176.

Cāṇakya-nīti (-pāḷi), Cāṇakya-sāra-saṅgaha (B, late 19th c.) (Pāḷi trans. of Skt Cāṇakyanītiśāstra.): PL 176, CS.

Gihiviniya-saṅgaha-nīti (B, 1830): PL 176.

Suttanta-nīti (B.): CS.

Sūrassatī-nīti (B.): CS.

Kavidappaṇa-nīti & mātikā (B.): CS.

Nīti-mañjari (B.): CS.

Naradakkha-dīpanī (B?): CS.

Apocryphal Suttantas (See PL 183 in App. I.)

2.11.1 Tuṇḍ-s Tuṇḍilovāda-sutta (C): H 436, PL 183 in App. I, N 6599(21), JPTS XV 170–95.

2.11.2 Nibbāna-s Nibbāna-sutta, Mahānagaranibbānasutta, Mahānagaranibbānasutta-vaṇṇanā (Ic): H 436, PCS 2.96.1, PL 183 in App. I, PSA 116, VP 4/152, EP 30, JPTS XVIII, 117–24.

2.11.3 Ākārav-s Ākāravattāra-sutta, Ākaravatta-sutta (Kh or Ic): H 436, PSA 120, PL 183 in App. I, RL 122, BnF 602, ED 401, EP 2.8 & 119.

Aruṇavatī-sutta, Aruṇavatī (Ic.): PCS 2.18, PSA 122f, VP 4/140.

Aruṇavatī-sutta-aṭṭhakathā: PCS 2.4, FEMC C54, VP 4/140.

Ādhārana-paritta, Ādhārina~ (Apocryphal sutta) (End: ...*phalāni paññāyissantīti*...): EP 2.12, 75.17.

Jambupatti-sutta, Jambūpati-sūtra, Mahā-jambupatisarājā (S?): PSA 31, 101, PCS 2.52, BnF 401m, VP 4/140, VH, ED 403.

Jarā-sutta (Ic?): EP 30, VP 4/152.

Kusala-sūtraya, Kosamāvata, Kosabāvata (C? Pāḷi intro, rest Sinhala): N 6599(33)vi, SH 779f.

Kosalabimba-vaṇṇanā, Bimba-vaṇṇanā (C?): PL 179, SH 110f, N 6599(33), LCM 2336ff, PSC 77, SL 80, L.

Kosalabimba-pañhā: PCS 2.33.

Kosalapañhā, Sakkarājānisaṃsavaṇṇanā (Cf Saṃkrājasaṃvacchara-kosalapañhā = ME 31.6) (S?): PCS 2.93, VP 4/151.6, VH 242.10, ME 31.6.

Cakka-paritta (-sutta) (Contains gāthās & apocryphal sutta.) (Beg: *Dasa saññojanajito buddho…*): N 6599(4)i, LCM 1243, PV 11, RL 123.

Cakka-paritta aparaṃ (Beg: *Uddhaṃ yāva bhavaggā…*): N 6599(4)ii.

(Mahā-) Cakkavāḷa-paritta (S?): PSA 101.

Catuvekka (C?, 12th c. Parakramabāhu is mentioned.) (Beg: *Mayā saddhiṃ imasmiṃ…*): BnF 662

Cuttimaraṇa-sutta (S?): EP 75.25, VP 4/136.

Cundasūkarika-sutta, Dhammikapaṇḍita-jātaka (La?): PSA 119.

Cetanābheda (-sutta), Cetanābheda-vaṇṇanā, (Anuruddha-sutta) (La?): PSA 121.

Cha-kesa-dhātu-vaṃsa (B): See 4.1.71 Cha-k

Chadisapāla-sutta (B): RL 123.

Chadisabhāga-sutta (B?): Braun II p. 50 no. 223.

Disapāla-paritta, Mahāmegha-paritta (S? Apocryphal sutta. End: … *indā ca brahmānayassuti.*): EP 2.13, EP 2.13, 75.20, ED 401.

Mahādisapāla-paritta (Apocryphal sutta. S? End: … *sabbe te vinassantuti.*): EP 75.21, ED 401

Sabbadisabuddhamaṅgala-paritta (Beg: *Padumuttaro purabbāyaṃ…*): EP 75.13, ME 49.3, ED 401.

Culla-sabbadisabuddhamaṅgala-paritta (Beg: *Buddho ca majjhimo…*): EP 75.14, ED 401.

Maṅgala-paritta (S? Contains Catuvekka, see above BnF 662.) (Beg: *Na hi sīlavataṃ…*): EP 75.15.

Culla-maṅgalaparitta (S? Beg: *Imassa ratanattaya tejasānubhāvena…*): EP 75.16.

Sabbadisa-paritta (S? Beg: *Puratthimasmiṃ disābhāge santi devā…* Cf Āṭānātiya-paritta.): EP 75.23, ED 401

Sabbadisa-paritta (S? Beg: *Sabbe puratthimāya…* End: … *attānaṃ pariharantu.*): EP 75.22.

Mahāvīra-paritta (S? Beg: *Sabbe puratthimāya…* End: … *cutti cutti dhāraṇīti.*): BnF 600.6

Dhāraṇīya-paritta (S? End: … *cutticutti dhāraṇidhāraṇīti …*): EP 75.4, ED 401.

Dhāraṇa-paritta (B): RL 123, ED 401.

Nagaraṭṭhāna-paritta (Apocryphal sutta.) (End: … *saṅghajālaparikkhite rakkhantu…*): EP 75.19.

Nandabrāhmaṇa-sutta (S?): PCS 2.93,2, VP 4/152, EP 75.36.

Pabbajjānisaṃsa (-sutta) (Apocryphal sutta.) (La?): PSA 121, VH 234, VP 4/150.

Paramatthadhamma-sutta (S?): PCS 2.119.

Paramatthamaṅgala (S? A compilation starting with a sutta on the 3 *paramattha- maṅgala*, followed by 4 apocryphal jātakas and the Uṇhissavijaya-vaṇṇanā.): PCS 2.121, VP 4/150.

Parimittajāla-sutta (B): RL 123.

Parivāsadāna-sutta (S?): EP 75.32.

Puṇṇovāda-sūtra (S?): PCS 2.129, EP 35, VP 4/152.

Puṇṇovādasuttavaṇṇanāsaṅkhepakathā (Pali-Siamese Nissaya.): BnF 400.

Bimbābhilāya-sutta, Bimbābhilya-gaṇṭhi (S?) (Bimbādevī's Story. Also in Suttajātakanidānānisaṃsa.): PSA 87, BnF 397, ED 404.

Bimbābhilābha-vaṇṇanā (S?) (Pāli-Siamese Nissaya.): PSA 87, BnF 398f, ED 404.

Brāhmaṇa-sutta (S?): EP 75.29, VP 4/151.

Bhūmi-paritta (? Arakan, Burma): BL Add 12258/B.23.

Manussavinaya, Upāsakamanussavinaya-vaṇṇanā (Verses & prose. Beg. *Saṃsāre saṃsarantaṃ*... The text at VP is listed as Sirisāra-jātaka, but the colophon has Manussavinaya.): N 6599(21)ii m, VP 4/151.5.

Maraṇasati-sutta, Maraṇañāṇa-sutta (See N 6600(91)ii.) (Sinh. transl. of AN sutta.): N 6600(90), BSL 108, L.

Maraṇañāṇa-sutta-padārthaya: N 6600((91)ii.

Maraṇañāṇa-ṭīkā, Maraṇañāṇa-dīpanā: N 6599(12).

Mahākappinadhaja-sūṭra (S?) = Mahākappinarāja-jātaka (S?): PCS 2.159.: EP 75.30.

Mahāvijayaseṭṭhi-sutta, Vijeyyaseṭṭhisutta (S?): PCS 2.169, EP 75.26, VP 4/136m, ME.

Cuddasamātāpitu-kata-puñña-sutta (S?): EP 75.24.

Mahākaṃsānaphalaparitta: BnF 600.3

Mātrasūtra, Mata-sutta, Sucira-vatthu-vaṇṇanā (S?): PCS 2.93.4, VP 4/151.

Metta-paritta (S?. Beg: *Atthāya hitāya sukhāya*...): EP 75.18.

Metteyya-sutta (Cf. Sinhalese Metteyya-vastu, Metteyya-kathāva in LCM and L.): PSA 107, TT 1.5, 1.14.

(Rakkha-sutta?): EP 2.14.

Rāhula-paritta (C?. Apocryphal Pāḷi sutta/paritta.): SH 132, EP 75.7, BnF 662.

Sappurisa-sutta, Sappurisa-dāna (La?): PSA 107–8.

Salākarivijjasutta (La?): PSA 122.

Saraṇagamana-sutta: N 6599(3), BnF 743, ICP 5, 81, 82.

Saraṇagamana-sutta-sannaya: N 6600/127.

Sāsanāyu-pakaraṇa (B.) (Apocryphal Vinaya story.): PSA 91, BnF 374.

Sāra-sutta: N 6599(3).

Sārasutta-padānuma: N 6599(3).

Sārasutta-sannaya: N 6599(3).

Sīvali-paritta, Sīvali-thera~ (Arakan, Burma? Not identical with Sīvali-pirit): BL Add 12258/B.5.

Sunandarajā-sutta, Nanda-sutta (La?) = Nandarāja-jātaka, Sunandarāja-jātaka, Dhammasunda-rāja?: PSA 118.: VP 4/155, Vh 255.4, 282.

Subhūta-sutta (S?) (based on Th-a I 25, J I 332) (Cf Väsa-pirita.): EP 75.35, ME 45.7.

Soḷasa-maṅgala-paritta (Kh) (Beg: *Solasamaṅgalañce...*): PSA 101, BnF 600, 611, FEMC D112.

Abhidhamma-piṭaka (See H II.3, PL 4, CMA 11f.)

The subcommentaries by Ānanda are collectively called Līnatthapada-vaṇṇanā, Mūla-ṭīkā or Satta-ppakaraṇa. Separated in three sections, they are Dhs-mṭ, Vibh-mṭ and Pañca-ppakaraṇa.: PLC 210.

3.1 Dhs Dhammasaṅgaṇī, Dhammasaṅgaṇi-pakaraṇa, Dhamma-saṅgaha, Saṅgaṇī, Saṅgiṇī, Abhidhamma-saṅgaṇī: H 131ff, PL 4.1, HP 49f, PCS 3.18, LCM 657, SH 31f, CB 104, CM 43, BnF, CS.

Dhammasaṅgaṇī-mātikā: LCM 658f, N 6599(2 & 35), BC 301ff, CB 46, BnF 239.

Dhammasaṅgaṇī-mātikattha-sarūpa (CM, Ratanapañña, 16th c.): PSA 63, PCS 3.44, VP 5/1.

Dhammasaṅgaṇī-guyhadīpanī-gaṇṭhi (? [Ratanapura], Sāradassī): PCS 3.12.

(Dhamma-saṅgaṇī-) Paccaya-dīpanī: PCS 3.26.

3.1.1 As Atthasālinī, Sālinī, Dhammasaṅgani-aṭṭhakathā (C or SI, Buddhaghosa, 5th c.): H 308 & 315, PL 122f, HP 20, PCS 3.1, CM 43f, EP 5, 80, BnF 220m, CS.

3.1.11 As-mṭ Atthasālinī-mūlaṭīkā, Dhammasaṅgaṇī-mūlaṭīkā, Paramatthapakāsanī I, Līnattha-jotikā I, ~jotanā I, ~padavaṇṇanā I, Abhidhamma-mūlaṭīkā I (C, Ānanda, 6th or 8–9th c.): H 356, HP 74f, W, PCS 3.63, Ps, PLC 210f, PSC p. 61, LCM 671f, BnF 264m, CS, CW.

3.1.12 As-anuṭ Dhammasaṅgaṇi-anuṭīkā, Abhi-dhamma-anuṭīkā I, Līnatthavaṇṇanā I, Līnattha-pakāsinī I (C, Culla-Dhammapāla?, 6th or 8–9th c.): H 360, HP 74f, 189f, W, BnF 804, 882 PCS 3.70, PLC 211, CS, Ps.

3.1.13 Maṇi-dīpa Maṇi-dīpa (-ṭīkā), Maṇi-padīpa (B, Ariyavaṃsa [-Dhammasenāpati], 15th c.): PLB 42f, PCS 3.41, H n. 513, RB, VPJ 5/34–37, BLB, Ps.

3.1.14 Madhu-ṭ Madhu-sārattha-dīpanī, Madhu-ṭīkā (Haṃsāvati/Pegu, B, Ānanda [not Mahānāma], 15–16th c.?): PCS 3.42, H n. 513, PLB 47f, PLL , RB, Ps.

Madusāradīpanī-anuṭīkā: BLB.

3.1.151 As-y1 Atthasālinī-aṭṭhakathā-yojanā (B?, Sumaṅgala, 14th c.): PSA 17, PLB 27, Ps.

3.1.152 As-y2 Atthasālinī-atthayojanā (CM, Ñāṇakitti, 1495) (This is not to be confused with the Atthasālinī-aṭṭhakathā-yojanā; see PSA and the previous entry.): H 379, PCS 3.49, PSA 16, 62, LN 125f, PSC p. 61 (? VP 5/3), BLB.

3.1.161 Abhidhamma-gaṇṭhipada (Mahākassapa): Ps.

3.1.162 Atthasālinī-gaṇṭhipada (B, Ñāṇavara, 18th c.): PLB 67, CPD.

Atthasālinī-gaṇṭhi, Atthasālinī-nava-gaṇṭhi (-thit) (B, 1900.): PLB 96.

Atthasālinī-nissaya (Pali-Burm.) (Different versions.): CB 105ff.

3.1.17 Vīsati–vaṇṇanā (on As) (Ava, B, Tipiṭakālaṅkāra, early 17th c.): PLB 53, Ps.

(Saṅgiṇi-saṅkhepa) (S?, Pra Aphithaṃ): EP 21.1.

Dhammasaṅganī (lee) aṭṭhakathā (S. Abridged commentary on Dhammasaṅganī-mātikā.): BnF 266ff, EP 5m, ME 10M.

3.2 Vibh Vibhaṅga (-pakaraṇa): H 138f, PL 4.2, HP 173, PCS 3.77, LCM 661, SH 74, BnF 218m, CS.

3.2.1 Vibh-a Sammohavinodanī, Vibhaṅgaṭṭhakathā (C, Buddhaghosa, 5th c.): H 308f, 318f, PL 122ff, HP 136, PCS 3.81, CM 44, VP 5/6f, BnF 223m, CS.

3.2.152 Vibh-a-y2 Sammohavinodanī-atthayojanā, Sammohavinodanī-yojanā (This is probably not the Vibhaṅgaṭṭhakathā-atthayojanā; see PSA and the next entry) (CM, Ñāṇakitti, 1495.): H 379, PSA 17, 62, PCS 3.57, LN 127, PSC p. 61, VP 5/10, BLB, Ps.

Vibhaṅgaṭṭhakathā-atthayojanā (B?, Sumaṅgala, 14th c.): PSA 17, PLB 27, Ps.

3.2.11 Vibh-mṭ Vibhaṅga-mūlaṭīkā, Paramatthapakāsanī II, Līnattha-jotikā II, ~jotanā II, ~padavaṇṇanā II, Sammohavinodanī-mūla-ṭīkā (C?, Kalasapura Ānanda, 6th or 8–9th c.): H 356, PCS 3.68, PLC 210f, CB 48, CM xxvi, 44, VP 5/8, CW, CS.

3.2.12 Vibh-anuṭ Vibhaṅga-anuṭīkā, Abhidhamma-anuṭīkā II, Līnattha-vaṇṇana II, Līnattha-pakāsinī II (C, Culla-Dhammapāla?, 6th or 8–9th c.): H 360, PCS 3.75, PLC 211, BnF 882, CS.

Vipassanā-bhūmi-pāṭha (S.) (= First part of the mātikā of the Vibhaṅga.): BC 302f.

(Vibhaṅga-aṭṭhakathā-saṅkhepa) (S?, Pra Aphithaṃ): EP 21.2.

Vibhaṅga (lee) aṭṭhakathā (S. Abridged commentary on Vibhaṅga-mātikā.): BnF 266ff, EP 5m, ME 10M.

3.3 Dhātuk Dhātu-kathā (-pakaraṇa): H 140, PL 4.3, HP 50, PCS 3.19, LCM 662, SH 75, BnF, CS.

3.3.1 Dhātuk-a Dhātukathaṭṭhakathā, Pañca-pakaraṇa-aṭṭhakathā I, Paramattha-dīpanī I (C, Buddhaghosa, 5th c.): H 308–9, HP 109, PCS 3.30, BnF 265m, CS.

3.3.11 Dhātuk-mṭ Dhātukatha-mūlaṭīkā, Pañca-pakaraṇa-mūlaṭīka I, Paramatthapakāsanī III, Līnattha-jotikā III, ~jotanā III, ~padavaṇṇanā III (C?, Ānanda, 6th or 8–9th c.): H 356, PCS 3.64, VP 5/11, CS, CW.

3.3.12 Dhātuk- anuṭ Dhātukathanuṭīkā, Pañca-pakaraṇa-anuṭīkā I, Līnatthavaṇṇaṇā III, Līnattha-pakāsinī III, Abhidhamma-anuṭīkā III (C, Culla-Dhammapāla?, 6th or 8–9th c.): H 360, VP 5/11ff, CS.

3.3.15 Dhātuk-a-y Dhātukathā-atthayojanā, Dhātukathā-yojanā (CM, Ñāṇakitti, 1493–4 c.): H 380, PSA 62, PCS 3.52, LN 125f, Ps.

Dhātukathā-yojanā (B, Sāradassi, 18th c.) (? Pāḷi or Burmese): PLB 67.

3.3.18 Dhātukathā-ṭīkā-vaṇṇanā (Sagaing, B, Tilokaguru, early 17th c.): PLB 54, CPD, Ps.

3.3.19 Dhātukathā-anuṭīkā-vaṇṇanā (Sagaing, B, Tilokaguru, early 17th c.): PLB 54, CPD, Ps.

Dhātukathā-vaṇṇanā: BLB.

Dhātukathā-gaṇṭhi: PCS 3.10.

(Dhātukathā-) Paccaya-dīpanī: PCS 3.27.

Dhātukathā lee aṭṭhakathā (S. Abridged commentary on Dhātukathā-mātikā.): BnF 266ff, 654f, EP 5.2, ME 10M.

3.4 Pp Puggala-paññatti (-pakaraṇa): H 140f, PL 4.5, HP 120, PCS 3.38, LCM 663f, SH 76, BnF, ME, CS.

3.4.1 Pp-a Puggalapaññatti-aṭṭhakathā, Pañca-pakaraṇa-aṭṭhakathā II, Paramatthadīpanī II, (C, Buddhaghosa, 5th c.): H 308f, HP 109, PCS 3.32, LCM 666, BnF 265m, CS.

3.4.11 Pp-mṭ Puggalapaññatti-mūlaṭīkā, Pañca-pakaraṇa-mūlaṭīka II, Paramatthapakāsanī IV, Līnattha-jotikā IV, ~jotanā IV, ~padavaṇṇanā IV (C, Ānanda, 6th or 8–9th c.): H 356, PCS 3.66, CS.

3.4.12 Pp-a-anuṭ Puggalapaññatti-anuṭīkā, Pañca-pakaraṇa-anuṭīkā II, Līnattha-vaṇṇaṇā IV, Līnattha-pakāsinī IV, Abhidhamma-anuṭīkā IV (C, Culla-Dhammapāla?, 6th or 8–9th c.): H 360, PCS 3.73, BnF 882, CS.

3.4.15 Pp-a-y Puggala-paññatti-yojanā, Puggala-paññatti-atthayojanā (CM, Ñāṇakitti, 15th c.): PCS 3.55, PSA 62, LN 127.

Puggalapaññatti-gaṇṭhi: PCS 3.11.

Puggalapaññatti lee aṭṭhakathā (S. Abridged commentary on Puggalapaññatti-mātikā.): BnF 266ff, EP 5.3m, ME 10M.

3.5 Kv Kathāvatthu (-pakaraṇa/-pāḷi): H 144f, PL 4.5, HP 70f, PCS 3.8, LCM 667, SH 77, BnF, CS.

3.5.1 Kv-a Kathāvatthu-aṭṭhakathā, Pañca-pakaraṇa-aṭṭhakathā III, Paramatthadīpanī III, (C, Buddhaghosa, 5th c.): H 308f, 322, PL 125, PCS 3.29, BnF 229m, CS.

3.5.11 Kv-mṭ Kathāvatthu-mūlaṭīkā, Pañca-pakaraṇa-mūlaṭīka III, Paramatthapakāsanī IV, Līnattha-jotikā IV, ~jotanā IV, ~padavaṇṇanā IV, (C, Ānanda, 6th or 8–9th c.): H 356, PCS 3.62, H 355, CS, CW.

3.5.12 Kv-a-anuṭ Kathāvatthu-anuṭīkā, Pañca-pakaraṇa-anuṭīkā III, Līnattha- vaṇṇaṇā V, ~pakāsinī-anuṭīkā V (C, Culla-Dhammapāla?, 6th or 8–9th c.): H 360, PCS 3.69, BnF 410, BnF 882, CS.

3.5.15 Kv-a-y Kathāvatthu-yojanā, Kathāvatthu-atthayojanā (CM, Ñāṇakitti, 15th c.): PCS 3.50, PSA 62, LN 127.

Kathāvatthu lee aṭṭhakathā (S. Abridged commentary on Kathāvatthu-mātikā.): BnF 266ff, EP 5.4, ME 10M.

3.6 Yam Yamaka, Mūla-yamaka (-pakaraṇa, -pāḷi): H 152f, PL 4.6, HP 182f, PCS 3.48, LCM 668, CB 107f, SH 78, BnF, CS.

3.6.1 Yam-a Yamaka-aṭṭhakathā, Pañca-pakaraṇa-aṭṭhakathā IV, Paramatthadīpanī IV (C, Buddhaghosa, 5th c.): HP 109, PCS 3.33, BnF 266m, CS.

3.6.11 Yam-mṭ Yamaka-mūlaṭīkā, Pañca-pakaraṇa-mūlaṭika IV, Paramatthapakāsanī V, Līnattha-jotikā V, ~jotanā V, ~padavaṇṇanā V (C, Ānanda, 6th or 8–9th c.): H 356, PCS 3.67, PLC 210f, CS.

3.6.12 Yam-a-anuṭ Yamaka-anuṭīkā, Pañca-pakaraṇa-anuṭīkā IV, Līnattha-vaṇṇaṇā VI, ~pakāsinī-anuṭīkā VI, Abhidhamma-anuṭīkā VI (C, Culla-Dhammapāla?, 6th or 8–9th c.): PCS 3.74, PLC 211, BnF 882, CS.

3.6.12 Yam-v-ṭ Yamaka-vaṇṇanā-ṭīkā, Yamaka-vaṇṇanā (Sagaing, B, Tilokaguru, early 17th c.): PLB 54, BLB, Ps.

3.6.15 Yam-a-y Yamaka-yojanā, Yamaka-atthayojanā (CM, Ñāṇakitti, 15th c.): PCS 3.56, PSA 62, LN 127.

Yamaka lee aṭṭhakathā (S. Abridged commentary on Yamaka-mātikā.): BnF 266ff, EP 5.5, 21.5f, ME 10M.

Yamaka-puccha-visajjana (B. Leḍī Sayāḍo, 19th–20th c.): BSL.

3.7 Paṭṭh Paṭṭhāna (-pakaraṇa), Mahāpaṭṭhāna, Mahāpakaraṇa (Often sections such as the Dukapaṭṭhāna are transmitted as separate MSS.): H 154f, PL 4.7, PCS 3.28, LCM 669f, CMA 12, SH 79, CB 111f, BnF, CS.

3.7.1 Paṭṭh-a Paṭṭhānaṭṭhakathā, Pañcapakaraṇaṭṭhakathā V, Paramatthadīpanī V (C, Buddhaghosa, 5th c.): HP 109, PCS 3.31, CM 44f, BnF 265m, CS.

3.7.11 Paṭṭh-mṭ Paṭṭhāṇa-mūlaṭīkā, Pañca-pakaraṇa-mūlaṭika V, Paramatthapakāsanī VII, Līnattha-jotikā VII, ~jotanā VII, ~padavaṇṇanā VII, (C, Ānanda, 6th or 8–9th c.): H 356, PCS 3.65, (CB 110), CS, CW.

3.7.12 Paṭṭh-a-anuṭ Paṭṭhānānuṭīkā, Pañca-pakaraṇa-anuṭīkā V, Līnatthavaṇṇaṇā VII, Līnattha-pakāsinī-anuṭīkā VII, Abhidhamma-anuṭīkā VII (C, Culla-Dhammapāla, 6th or 8–9th c.): H 360, PCS 3.72, BnF 882, CS.

3.7.15 Paṭṭh-a-y Paṭṭhāna-atthayojanā, Paṭṭhāna-yojanā (CM, Ñāṇakitti, 15th c.): PCS 3.54, PSA 62, LN 127.

3.7.18 Paṭṭh-v-ṭ Paṭṭhāna-vaṇṇanā-ṭīkā (Sagaing, B, Tilokaguru, early 17th c.): PLB 54, Ps.

3.7.19 Paṭṭh-ṭ Paṭṭhāna-sāra-dīpanī (-ṭīkā) (Haṃsāvatī/Pegu, B, Saddhammālaṅkāra, 1551.): PLB 47, PSC 31, BLB, Ps.

Paṭṭhāna-gaṇa-nāyana (B, Chappaṭa, 15th c.): HP 195, PLB 19, PSC 31.

Paṭṭhāna-paccaya-dīpanī (C, Dhammabodhisiri): PCS 3.25, VP 5/31.

Paṭṭhāna-paccaya-sarūpa: PCS 3.84.

Paṭṭhāna-mātika-pāṭha, Paṭṭhāna-paccayuddesa: BC 304, MP 106.

Mahā-paṭṭhāna lee aṭṭhakathā (S. = commentary on Paṭṭhāna-mātikā?): EP 5.6, 21.7.

Paramatthakathā (Title used in Gandavaṃsa for all 7 Abhidhamma aṭṭhakathā.): PL 123.

Paṭṭhānuddesa-dīpanī (-pāṭha), Paccayuddesa-dīpanī (B, Leḍī Sayāḍo, 19–20th c.): CS, DBM 51 & 58, BLS.

Paṭṭhāna lee aṭṭhakathā (S. Abridged commentary on Paṭṭhāna-mātikā.): BnF 266ff, EP 5m, ME 10M.

Pañca-pakaraṇa-aṭṭhakathā (Coms. on Dhātuk, Pp, Kv, Yam, Paṭṭh bundled.): BnF 726, BLB.

Mūla-ṭika (Mūlaṭīkas on Dhātuk, Pp, Kv, Yam, Paṭṭh bundled.): BLB.

Anuṭīkā (Anuṭīkas bundled.): BLB.

(Abhidhamma-aṭṭhakathā?) (S. A common MS with a compilation of abridged versions of the Abhidhamma commentaries. First title: *braḥ vibhaṅga lee [braḥ] aṭṭhakathā tmā prasaṅgaparipuṇṇa.*): BnF 266–82m, EP 5m, ME 10M.

Abhidhamma Manuals

3.8.1 Abhidh-s Abhidhammattha-saṅgaha (-pakaraṇa), ~saṅgiṇī, Abhidhammattha-gāthā (C, Anuruddha, 12th c.): H 344, PL 151, HP 2, CMA 15, PCS 3.5, PLB 61, PSC 19, PLC 167, N 6601(19), BnF 350f, LCM 680, EP 7m, CB 47, ME, Ps

3.8.1.1 Abhidh-s-pṭ Abhidhammatthasaṅgaha-ṭīkā, ~porāṇaṭīkā (C, 12th c.) (PLC, N: by Sāriputta Mahāsāmi [? called Nava-vimalabuddhi in B, cf CPD 3.8.1.1], but HP: Udumbagiri Kassapa.): HP 3, CMA 17, N 6601(1), PLC 173, 178, 204, LCM 681, PSC 20, Ps.

3.8.1.2 Abhidh-s-mhṭ Abhidhammatthavibhāvinī, Vibhāvinī-ṭīkā, Abhidhammatthasaṅgaha- mahāṭīkā, ~ṭīkā, ~vaṇṇanā, Ṭīkā-gyaw (C, Dambadeni Sumaṅgala , 12th c. Sumaṅgala was a pupil of Sāriputta Mahāsāmi): H 345f, HP 3f, PCS 3.4, PLB 61, PSC 21, PLC 173, LCM 681f, N 6601(19), EP 20.2m, BnF 379m, CMA 17, Ps.

Abhidhammatthavibhāvinī-sannaya, Paramārthasuddhanidhi: PSC 21.

3.8.1.21 Maṇis Maṇisāramañjūsā, Paramattha-maṇisāramañjūsā, Abhidhammatthasaṅgaha-navaṭīkā, ~anuṭīkā (B, Ariyavaṃsa, 15th c.) (Ṭīkā on Abhidhammatthavibhāvinī.): H 345f, PLB 42, PLC 201, PCS 3.40, PSC 22, LCM 691, N 6601(19), Bod, BLB, Ps, RB.

3.8.1.22 Abhidh-s-mhṭ-y Abhidhammatthavibhāvinī-atthayojanā, Pañcikā, Abhidhammatthasaṅgaha- ṭīkā-yojanā (CM, Ñāṇakitti, 1502–03): H 380, PCS 3.51, 3.53, PSA 17, 62, LN 125f.

3.8.1.3 Abhidh-s-sv Saṅkhepa-vaṇṇanā (-ṭīkā), Abhidhammatthasaṅgaha-saṅkhepa-ṭīkā, ~saṅkhepavaṇṇanā (C, Saddhammajotipāla/Chappaṭa, 15th c.): H n. 559, PLB 18, PLC 197, 201, CCS, HP 199, PCS 3.86, PSC 23, CW Burm 44m, Ps, N 6601(19), CMA 17, BLB.

3.8.1.31 Apheggusāra-dīpanī (-ṭīkā), Apheggu-sāratthadīpanī, Apheggu-pāṭha, Apheggusāra, Abhidhammatthasaṅgaha-culla-ṭīkā, Culla-ṭīkā-vaṇṇanā (Haṃsāvatī/Pegu, B, Mahāsuvaṇṇapadīpa, 14th c.): PLB 36, PCS 3.2, N 6601(19), BnF 645, MA, IO, BLB, Ps.

3.8.1.4 Abhidh-s- abhinava-ṭ Abhidhammattha-saṅgahạ-dīpanī (B, Sīlācāra, 1801): H 348, CW Burm 42, RB, Ps.

3.8.1.5 Paramatthadīpanī, Abhidhammattha-saṅgaha-mahāṭīkā (B, Leḍī Sayāḍo, 19–20th c. A criticism of the Abhidh-s-mhṭ.): PSC 24, CS, CMA 17, DBM 31, BLS.

Aṇudīpanī (-pāṭha), Paramatthadīpanī-aṇudīpanī (B, Leḍī Sayāḍo, 19–20th c.): CS, DBM 21, BLS.

Paramatthasaṃkhitta (B, Leḍī Sayāḍo, 19–20th c.): DBM 74.

Aṅkura-ṭīkā (B, Vimala thera, 20th c. A defense of the Abhidh-s-mhṭ): CMA 18.

3.8.1.6 Abhidh- s-sn Abhidharmārtha-saṅgraha-sannaya, ~purāṇasannaya, ~vistarasannaya, Abhidhammatthasaṅgaha-sīhala-atthavaṇṇanā (C, Sāriputta, 12th c.): HP 4, LCM 1743, PLC 173, 204f, Vs 78f, PSC 19, SW.

Abhidharmārthasaṅgraha-praśnottarasannaya: PSC 19.

Abhidhammatthasaṅgaha-nissaya: PCS 3.24, BnF 265.

Paramatthamañjūsā, Paramatthasāramañjūsā-anuṭīkā, Abhidhammatthasaṅgaha-anuṭīkā, (B, Vepullabuddhi, 14th c.): PLB 28, PCS 3.35, N 6601(19), VH 255.3.

Dasagaṇṭhi–vaṇṇanā (B, Vepullabuddhi, 14th c.): PLB 28, Gv.

Abhidhammattha-līnattha-saṅgaha: PCS 3.62.

Abhidhammatthasaṅgaha-sarūpaka (Requested by Bh. Siribandha.): PCS 3.82, BnF 353.

Sarūpattha-dīpanī (B, U Tin, 1883): PLB 95.

Abhidhammatthasaṅgaha-gaṇṭhi-padattha (B, Ñāṇavara, 18th c.): PLB 67.

Abhidhammatthasaṅgaha-paritta (B, Maung Tun Aung, 1897.): PLB 95.

Abhidhammatthasaṅgaha-nava-gaṇṭhi (-thit) (B, U Tissa & Janinda, 1898.): PLB 95.

Navanīta-ṭīkā (I, Kosambi Dhammānanda, 1933): CMA 18.

Paramatthajotikā, Mahā-abhidhammatthasaṅgaha-ṭīkā (S, Saddhammajotika, 1963): Printed edition.

3.8.2 Pm-vn Paramatthavinicchaya (C, Anuruddha, 12th c.): H 348, PL 152, HP 113f, PSC 27, PCS 3.36, PLC 173f, CS, JPTS X 155–226, Ps.

3.8.2.1 Mukhamatta-kathā, Mukha-mattakā, Mukhamaṭṭhakathā Paramatthavinicchaya-porāṇaṭīkā (S?, Devoyaraṭṭha Mahābodhi): PSA 28, PLC 174, 205, PCS 3.46, PSC 27, PS 324, BLB, Ps, L.

3.8.2.2 Paramatthavinicchaya-abhinavaṭīkā: BLB, Ps.

Paramatthavinicchaya-ṭīkā (P-ṭ or abhinava-ṭ?): PCS 3.15, VP 5/51.

Paramatthavinicchaya-vibhāvinī: PSC 27.

3.8.3 Nāmar-p Nāmarūpa-pariccheda (C, Anuruddha, 12th c.): H 348f, PL 151, HP 99, PCS 3.20, PLC 173, PSC 25, CS, Ps.

(Saṅkhepa-) Nāmarūpa-pariccheda-pāḷī: PCS 3.21.

3.8.3.1 Nāmarūpa-pariccheda-purāṇaṭīkā, Līnatthapakāsinī (C, Vācissara, 13th c.): HP 193, PCS 3.76, PLC 174, 202–4, PSC 25, Ps.

Nāmarūpa-pariccheda-ṭīkā, Nāma-rūpa-pari-ccheda-vibhāvinī (-ṭīkā) (C, Sumaṅgala, 13th c.): HP 193, PLC 174, PSC 26.

3.8.3.2 Nāmarūpa-pariccheda-(abhi)-navaṭīkā: PLB 104, Ps.

Nāmarūpa-pariccheda-nissaya: PSC 26.

3.8.4 Abhi-av Abhidhammāvatāra (-pāḷi, -aṭṭhakathā) (C, Buddhadatta, 5th c.): H 340f, PL 131, HP 5f, PCS 3.7, LCM 684, PSC 15, PLC 107f, PLB 61, RAS, CS, BLB, Ps.

3.8.4.1 Abhi-av-pṭ Abhidhammāvatāra-purāṇaṭīkā (C, Vācissara Mahāsāmi or Sāriputta, 12th c.): H 340–2, PCS 3.39, PSC 15, PLC 108, CS, BLB, Ps

3.8.4.2 Abhi-av-nṭ Abhidhammāvatāra-abhinavaṭīkā, Abhidhammattha-vikasīnī (C, Sumaṅgala, 13th c.): H 340, 343, HP 4–5, PCS 3.3, PLC 108, 200f, PSC 15, CS, Ps.

Abhidhammāvatāra-līnattha: PCS 3.60.

Hattha-sāra: PCS 3.87, VP 4/41f, Gv.

Abhidhammāvatāra-sannaya, Vijamāvatāra-sannaya: Vs 80, PSC 15.

Abhidhammāvatāra-saṅgaha (purāṇa and nava): BLB.

3.8.5 Rūpār Rūpārūpa-vibhāga (C, U. Buddhadatta, 5th c.): H 340f, PL 131, HP 98, PCS 3.59, PLC 108, 202, PSC 16, BLB, Ps.

Rūpa-vibhāga: PCS 3.58, PSC 29, BLB.

3.8.5.1 Rūpārūpa-vibhāga-ṭīkā: Ps. (Cf PLC 202.)

3.8.6 Sacc Sacca-saṅkhepa (-pāḷi) (C, Culla-Dhammapāla [Maṇis & Gv], or his teacher Ānanda [Saddh-s], or Dhammapāla thera [Sās], 8–9th c.?): H 351, PL 152, W, PCS 2.207, HP 125, PSC 17, PLC 202f, PLB 61, CS, BLB, Ps, L.

3.8.6.1 Sacc-pṭ Nissayatthakathā, Sacca-saṅkhepa-vaṇṇanā (C, Mahābodhi, 12–13th c.): PC 205, PSC 17.

Sacca-saṇkhepa-ṭīkā (=? Attha-dīpana [PC 217]) (C, Vācissara, 12–13th c.): HP 196, PLC 202–4, 217, PCS 2.71, BLB, Ps.

Sacca-saṅkhepa-yojanā (?, Dhammapāla): PCS 2.182.

3.8.6.2 Sacc-nṭ Saccasaṇkhepa-(abhi)-navaṭīkā, Sāratthasālinī (C, Sumaṅgala, 12–13th c.): HP 196, 199, PLC 200, 204, PSC 17, BLB, Ps.

3.8.6.3 = 3.8.6.2 (CPD lists the Sāratthasālinī as a different work, but see J, PLL and PC.):

Sacca-saṅkhepa-sannaya: PSC 17.

Sacca-saṅkhepa-nidhāna-paññatti-dīpikā: PSC 17.

3.8.7 Moh Mohavicchedanī (-aṭṭhakathā), Abhidhamma-mātikatthavaṇṇanā, Mohacchedanī (SI, Coḷaraṭṭha Kassapa, 12–13th c.): H 354, PL 147f, HP 97f, PSC 28, PCS 3.47, PLC 178f, 323, CS, VP, BLB, Ps, L.

3.8.7.1 Moh-ṭ Mohavicchedanī-ṭīkā (SI, Coḷaraṭṭha Kassapa, 12–13th c.): PC 179, BLB, Ps.

Abhidhamma-mātikā (-pāḷi) (The mātikās of all 7 Canonical Abhidhamma texts on which 3.8.7 comments. In CS the mātikā precede Moh.): PCS 3.6, N 6600(130), LCM 673ff, EP 2, 39m, VP

4/139, BnF, MA, ME, CS, L.

Abhidhammamātikā-vitthāra (Expanded version of the above.): N 6601(75)ix.

Aṭṭha-abhidhammamātikā, Sahassaneyya, Sahassanaya, Sahassanaya-gaṇḍa (S?): CB 47, EP 39f, 70.4.

Mātikā-dīpanī, Mātikatthadīpanī (B, Chappaṭa, 15th c.): HP 192, PLB 19, PCS 3.43, VP 5/56.

Mātikā-sarūpa-vibhāvinī: PCS 3.45, VP 5/50.

Chāyārāma-pakaraṇa (= Mātikaṭṭhakathā): PCS 3.13.

Ṭīkā-lvaṅ (= aṭṭhakathā on the Mātikā): PCS 3.16, VP 5/52.

3.8.8 Nāmar-s Khema-pakaraṇa, Khema, Nāmarūpa-samāsa, Paramatthadīpa (C, Khema, 12th c.): H 352, PL 152, HP 73, PCS 3.9, 3.22, PSC 18, PLC 155f, BLB, Ps.

3.8.8.1 Nāmar-s-ṭ Khemapakaraṇa-ṭīkā (C, Vācissara, 12–13th c.): HP 188, PCS 3.14, PLC 202, PSC 18, Ps.

(3.8.8.13.8.9 Nāmac)? Khemapakaraṇa-ṭīkā (C, Mahābodhi, 12–13th c.): PC 205.

Nāmacāra-dīpakā, ~dīpikā, Cāradīpika (B, Chappaṭa?, 15th c.): H 353, PL 153, PLB 18, HP 193, PCS 3.23, PSC 30, JPTS XV 1–28, BLB, Ps.

3.8.9.1 Nāmac-ṭ Nāmacāradīpaka-ṭīkā (B, Chappaṭa, 15th c.): Ps.

Khemapakaraṇa-vivaraṇa-naya: PCS 3.78.

Nāmarūpa-samāsa-vyākhyāva: PSC 18.

Nāmarūpasamāsa-(purāṇa)-sannaya, Sili piṭapota (15th c.?): N 6601(72), Vs 76f, PSC 18.

Supplementary Abhidhamma Treatises

3.9.1 Sucittālaṅkāra (C?, Kalyāṇasāra thera, 1656 or 1717): PCS 2.243, LCM 698, PSC 31, VP 4/131, BLB, Ps.

3.9.2 Paramatthabindu, Paramatthabindu-sāko (B, King Kyacvā/ Kya-swa, 13th c.): PLB 23, PSA 18 n. 3, BLB, Ps.

3.9.2.1 Paramatthabindu-ṭīkā (Pagan, B, Arimaddanapura Mahākassapa): PLB 25, Ps.

3.9.3 Abhidhamma-gūḷhatthadīpanī, Abhidhamma-gūḷhatthadīpanī –vinicchaya, Gūḷhatthavinicchaya (B): H n. 516, BLB, CPD.

Unclassified Abhidhamma

Abhidhamma-kathā (C, Bandāra): LCM 688.

Abhidhamma-gaṇṭhi: Ps.

Abhidhamma-gūḷhattha-dīpanī (Ava, B, Sāradassī, 17th c.): PLB 56.

Abhidhammapaṇṇarasaṭṭhāna (B, [Nava-/Culla-] Vimalabuddhi, 13th c.): PLB 28.

Dhammavibhūsanī: PCS 3.17.

Paramatthadhamma-sāra: PCS 3.34, VP 5/52.

Paramatthasāra: PCS 3.37, VP 5/52.

Vīsati–vaṇṇanā: Ps.

Sattappakaraṇābhidhamma-tām-prasaṅga: PCS 3.79, VP 5/55.

Sabhāva-ganthā: PCS 3.80, VP 5/53.

Skhandhādingē-vibhāgaya, Vijam Piṭapota (Pāḷi verse + *sannaya* + Sinh. prose. Often with Vimuktimargaya, but also independent. C. Beg. *Yo sabbalokamahito*...): N 6600 (145, 6601(59)5.

Non-Canonical Works
Chronicles

4.1.00 Sīhaḷaṭṭhakathā (? = Mahā-aṭṭhakathā) (Extinct): CPD, CM xxii.

4.1.1 Dīp Dīpavaṃsa (C, 4–5th c.): H 182f, PL 115f, HP 53f, PCS 2.85, LCM 1849f, BnF 365m, PSC 32, PLC 131ff, CM xx, VP 6/ ta.4, Ps.

4.1.1.1 Dīp-ṭ Dīpavaṃsa-ṭīkā (B, ± 1850): Ps, CPD.

4.1.2 Mhv Mahāvaṃsa, Padyapadoru-vaṃsa (-gāthā), Sīhala-rājavaṃsāvatāra (C, Dīghasandaparivena Mahānāma, etc., 5th c.): H 182, 185f, PL 117f, HP 81f PLC 139f, N 6605(1), LCM 1908f, CM xxv, 64, PSC 33, CS.

Ext Mhv Mahāvaṃsa-vitthāra, Kambujja-Mahāvaṃsa (also called, "Extended Mhv" or "Cambodian Mhv") (SE-Asia, Moggallāna, 9–10th c.?): H 189, PL 140, PSA 73f, VP 6 ta. 5 & 12, EP 34, BnF 632m, VH 183m.

Sīhala-rājavaṅśāvatāra, Māhavaṃsa-sīhalarājavaṃsāvatāra (PCS says it is an adaptation of Mhv, but it seems to be identical judging from the VP MS.): PCS 2.2.42, VP 6/ta. 7 & 8.

Mahāvaṃsa-nissaya (S): BnF 798.

4.1.2 Cullavaṃsa (= Continuation of Mahāvaṃsa) (C, Dhammakitti, etc., 13th—19th c.): H 187, PL 140, CM 64, SL 9, Ps.

4.1.2.1 Mhv-ṭ Vaṃsattha-pakāsinī, Vaṃsattha-dīpanī, Mahāvaṃsa-ṭīkā, Mahāvaṃsa-gāthā-anutthānatthavaṇṇanā, Pajjapadoru-vaṃsa-vaṇṇanā, Padyapadānuvaṃsa (C, pupil of author Mahāvaṃsa, + 7th c.): H 182, 188, PL 138f, HP 172f, PSC 34,N 6605(2), PCS 2.108, PLC 142f, VP 6ta.6, LCM 1913f, BnF 367, CM xxv, 66, BnF.

4.1.2.2 Mhv-ṭ Vaṃsamālinī-vilāsinī, Vaṃsamālinī, Mahāvaṃsa-mālinī (-pakaraṇa): H 190, PCS 2.205, CB 54–56, VP 6/ta.9, EP 44.

Vaṃṣamālinī-ṭīkā, Padyapadorupa-saṃvaṇṇanā (in VP colophon, but not same text as 4.1.2.1 Mhv-ṭ.): PCS 2.69, VP 6/ta.10.

Bāhira-nidāna, Vinaya-nidāna (Introduction to Samantapāsādika) (C, Buddhaghosa, 5th c.): PL 116, L I.

4.1.3 Mhbv Bodhi–vaṃsa, Mahā-bodhi–vaṃsa (-pāḷi) (C, Upatissa, 10th c.) (Based on Mahābodhivaṃsakathā of the Vaṃsatthappakāsinī: 4.1.2.1.): H 191, PL 141, 156, HP 77f, CM xxv, PLC 157f, PCS 2.145, N 6605(3), LCM 1823f, PSC 36, VP 6/ta.4, Ps, SLSBT, BLSL.

Culla-bodhivaṃśaya: SL 121, PSC 36, HP 78.

Bodhivaṃśaya, Siṃhala Bodhivaṃśaya (Sinh.) (C, Vilgammula Saṅgharāja, 14th c.): SL 118f, LCM 1825f.

4.1.3.1 Sahassa-raṃsi-ṭīkā, (Mahā)-Bodhivaṃsa-ṭīkā (Pagan B, A. Mahākassapa, 12th c.): HP 78, PLB 104, PSC 36, Ps, L.

Sahassaraṃsi-mālinī: PLB 104.

Bodhi-kathā, Bodhi–vaṃsa-kathā: HP 78, PSC 36.

Bodhi–vaṃsa-aṭṭhakathā: HP 78, PSC 36.

4.1.3.2 Dharmapr (Mahā-) Bodhi–vaṃsa-parikathā, Dharma-pradīpikāva (Sinh. & Pāḷi & Sanskrit.) (C, Guruḷugomi, 12th c.): H n. 626, CM xxvi, N 6603(27), LCM 960f, 1659, Vs 87, L, PSC 36.

4.1.3.3 Bodhi–vaṃsa-gaṇṭhipada, ~gätapada, Mahā-bodhivaṃsa- granthi-pada-vivaraṇaya, (C, 12th c.): HP 77f, N 6609(13), PSC 36, CM xxvi, Vs 72.

4.1.3.4 Mhbv-sn Madhurārtha-prakāśanī, Mahā-bodhivaṃsa-sannaya, ~arthavyākhānaya (C, V. Saranaṅkara, 18th c.) (1725? See N 6601[47]): HP 77f, N 6605(4),PC 282, LCM 1902, Vs 88, PSC 36, BSL 94.

4.1.41 Thūp Thūpa-vaṃsa (-vitthāra), Mahāthūpa-vaṃsa, Mahācetiyavaṃsa (C, Vācissara Devapāda, second half 13th c.): H 192, PL 142, HP 163f, SH 124, SL 107, N 6600(141), PCS 2.214, PLC 216ff, LCM 2007f, PSC 37, BnF 368, EP 25, CS, Ps.

4.1.42 Culla-thūpa-vaṃsa, Thūpavaṃsa-saṅkhepa (C): PCS 2.215, Ps.

Thūpavaṃsaya, Ratnamālīcetiyakathā (Sinh. Parākrama Paṇḍita, 13–14th c.): SL 107f.

4.1.5.1 Sādhujanānanda-vikāsinī, Dāṭhavaṃsa-ṭīkā (C, Mahāsāmi, before 1442): PSC 38, L, Ps.

Dāṭhā-vaṃsa, Danta-dhātu-vaṇṇanā, Dāṭhā-dhātu-vaṃsa, Jinadantadhātu-vaṃsa (C, Dhammakitti I, shortly after 1211.): H 193, PL 142, PLC 65f, 207f, PLB 105, PSC 38, VP 6/ta.3, PLB 105, CS, Ps.

Dāṭhādhātuvaṃsa-ṭīkā: PLB 105 (Pagan Inscr.)

Dantadhātu-pakaraṇa-ṭīkā: Gv.

Dantadhātu-nidāna: PCS 2.76, VP 6/ta.3.

Jinaguyhadhātu: RLL 70.

Dāṭhāvaṃsa-sannaya (C, Dhammakitti, 13th c.): PC 209, N 6605(7), PSC 38, LCM 1846–8.

Dāṭhavaṃsa-vyākhyāva: PSC 38.

Daḷadāsirita (Eḷu-Sinh.) (C, Devradadampasiṅginävan, 1325?): SL 112, PC 232, PSC 38, LCM 1836f, (N 6601[63]).

Daḷadāsirita II (Sinh.) (C, Kitsirimevan Rājasundara, 16th c.?): N 6603(101).

Daḷadā-pūjāvaliya (Sinh.) (C, Parākrama-bāhu IV?, 14th c.): PSC 38, LCM 913, 1833f, N 6601(63), CM xxxii, SL 114.

Eḷu-Daḷadāvaṃsaya (Sinh. 17th c.): SL 115, PSC 38, LCM 1840.

Eḷu-Daḷadāvaṃsaya (Lost poem. Dāṭhavaṃsa is said to be based on this. 311 CE.): PLC 65.

4.1.6 Dhātuvaṃsa, Nalāṭa-dhātuvaṃsa, Nalāṭadhātuvaṃsa-vaṇṇanā, Nalāṭadhātu-saṃvaṇṇanā, Lalāṭa-dhātuvaṃsa, Dhātuvaṃsa-pakāsaka, Dhātuvaṃsa-pakāsana (C, 13th c.?): H 194, HP 50f, PCS 2.79, PLC 255f, PSC 40, EP 73, ED 507, BnF 369, LCM 1891, VP 6/ta.3, ME, L, CS, Ps.

4.1.6.1 Nalāṭadhātuvaṃsa-ṭīkā: PCS 2.94, PLC 255, PSC 40.

Dhātuvaṃsaya, Seruvāvila-vistaraya, Tissamaha-vehera Dhātu-pilivela-kathāva (Sinh.) (C, Kakusandha Thera, 14th c.?): SL 116, N 6603(81), HP 51, 255f, CM xxxii, L.

4.1.71 Cha-k Chakesadhātuvaṃsa (B, 19th c.?) (Apocryphal Suttanta): H 195, PL 143, N 6605(6), PSC 39, Ps.

4.1.72 Kesadhātuvaṃsa (C, 13th c.?): PC 227, LCM 1879f, PSC 39.

Aṭṭhakesadhātu, Aṭṭhakesadhātu-vaṃsa (S? Part of Suttajātakanidānānisaṃsa.): ED 501, BnF 787, VH, VP, EP 35m.

Aṭṭhakesadhātu-nidāna: PCS 2.11.

4.1.8 Att Attanagalluvihāravaṃsa, Hatthavanagallavihāravaṃsa (C, pupil of Anomadassī, 13th c.): H 196f, PL 143, HP 55f, PCS 2.254, PSC 41, PLC 218f, LCM 1815m, BnF 885, SL 121, CS.

Attanagaluvaṃsasannaya , Eḷu-Attanagaḷuvaṃśaya (C, pupil of Maitrī Mahāsāmi, 1392): SH 125, PC 219, 253, PSC 41, BnF 885.2, CM xxxii.

4.1.9 Samantak Samantakūṭavaṇṇanā, Sumanaddisu-vaṇṇanā, Sumanakūṭa-vaṇṇanā (C, Vanavāsi Vedeha, 13th c. Vedeha is called Deva in the Gv.): H 198, PL 159, PCS 2.221, HP 133f, LCM 1442, PLC 223f, PSC 57, CS.

Samantakūṭavaṇṇanā-gätapadaya, Samankuluvana-gätapada: N 6609(17).

Samantakūṭavaṇṇanā-sannaya (C, Dhammānanda & Ñāṇissara, 1890): PC 224.

4.1.10 Ras Rasavāhinī, Madhu-rasavāhinī, Madhurasavāhinī-laṅkādīpa, Madhuravāhinī (C, Vanavāsi Vedeha, 13th c. (Cf N 6603[38].): H 413f, PL 155, HP 121f, N 6601(87f.), PCS 131, PLC 223f, LCM 1643f, PSC 48, SH 99m, CM 56, BnF, MA,VP4.149.

Jambudīpa-Rasavāhinī, Rasavāhinī-Jambudīpuppatti-kathā, Madhurasa-jambu: PCS 2.154, BnF 340f, CS.

4.1.10.1 Ras-ṭ Rasavāhinī-ṭīkā, ~gaṇṭhi, Sāratthadīpikā, Madhurasavāhini-ṭīkā (C, Siddhattha, 13th c.): H 413f, HP 142, PCS 2.67, PLC 230, N 6601(90), LCM 1648, BnF 716, PSC 48, VP 4/149.

Rasavāhinī-arthavivaraṇaya (= Sannaya): N 6601(89).

Rasavāhinī-gätapadaya (Older than the above.): N 6609(4).

Rasavāhinī-gāthā-purāna-sannaya: N 6609(4, 44).

4.1.10,(1) Saddharmālaṃkāraya (= Sinh. & Pāḷi quotations. Gaḍalādeṇiya, C, Devarakṣita Jayabāhu Dhammakīrti II, late 14th c.): HP 21f, 42f, SL 89f, PSC 48, LCM 1395, 1649f, PLC 226, N 6603(38), L, SH 100f.

Saddharmālaṃkāra-gāthā-sannaya: LCM 1655, PSC 48.

Rasavāhinī-vyakhyāva: PSC 48.

Rasavāhinī-gaṇṭhipada: LCM 1647.

4.1.11 Sīh Sīhalavatthu (-pakaraṇa), Sīhaladīpa-vatthu, Laṅkādīpa-Rasavāhinī (I, Dhammanandi or Dhammadinna, before 1442.): H 416f, PL 154, HP 146f, ED 513, PLB 104f,PCS 2.153, PLC 226, N 6601(87f), PSC 46, CW, Ps.

4.1.12 Sah Sahassavatthu (-pakaraṇa) (C, Raṭṭhapāla, late Anuradhapura period, before 1442.): H 409f, PL 154f, HP 130f, ED 512, N 6601(49), PLC 226, PCS 2.226, LCM 1409f, PLB 104f, PSC 47, VP 4/146, CM xxi, Ps.

4.1.12.1 Sah-a Sahassavatthu-aṭṭhakathā (Probably the extinct model and forerunner of Sah.): H 410f, PL 155f.

4.1.13 Dasav Dasavatthu-pakaraṇa, Dasavatthu, Dasadānavatthu-pakaraṇa (Ic?, before 1442.): H 409, PL 153, PCS 2.77–8, PSA 93, PLB 104, BnF 343ff, VP 4/145, EP 81, ED 503, Ps.

Dasapuññakiriyavatthu, Dasapuññakiriyāvatthu-kathā, ~vaṇṇanā: BnF 345, VP 4/147, FEMC A7.

4.1.14 Mth-v Māleyyatthera-vatthu, Māleyyathera-sutta, Māleyya-sutta, Māleyyadeva-nidāna, Māleyyadeva-thera-vaṇṇanā (CM/S, 15th c.): H 435, PSA 18, 122, PL 162 in App. I, PCS 2.174, BnF 326f, 658f, EP 140, JPTS XVIII 1–64.

Māleyyasūtra-dīpanī, Māleyya-dīpanī (S?): PCS 2.83.

Māleyyadevathera-ṭīkā, Māleyya-ṭīkā, Dutiya-māleyyadīpanī-ṭīkā (Buddhavilāsa?): VH 253.3.

Extra History and legend

4.2.01 Rājavaṃsa (B, Sīlavaṃsa): CPD.

(Nava-) Rājavaṃsa (B, 1830): PLB 90.

Rājindarāja-nāmābhidheyya-dīpanī, Rājinda-rājābhidheyya-dīpanī (B, Ratanakāra, 17th c.): PLB 52, Ps.

Rājindarāja-nāmābhidheyya-visodanī (B): Ps.

Rājādhirājanāmattha-pakāsanī (B, Ñāṇavara, 18th c.): PLB 67, Ps.

Rājādhirājavilāsinī, Mahādhammarājapavattivibhāvinī (Amarapura, B, Ñāṇabhivaṃsa, 1782.): PLB 78f, 92, PSC 50, PCS 2.184, LCM 1376, 1941.

Rājiṇdarāja-sudhammacara-dīpanī (B): Ps.

Rājinda-rāja-puñña-dīpanī (B): Ps.

(Rājavaṃsaya) [= Sinhalese Prose]: (LCM 1960f.)

Rājovāda (Amarapura, B, Ñāṇa/Ñāṇabhivaṃsa, 18–19th c.): PLB 78, PSC 71.

Rāja-ratnākaraya (Sinh. & Pāḷi) (C, Abhayarāja-pirivena-adhipatti, 16th c.): SL 127, SH 144, CM xxxv.

Rājāvaliya, Rājāvalī (Sinh. 18th c.): SL 127f, PLC 319f.

Rājābhisekagandha (B): PLB 74.

Chaddantanāgarājuppatti-kathā: PLB 78.

Nāgarājuppatti-kathā (B, Paññāsāmi Saṅgharāja, 1857.): PLB 92.

Pokkārāma-mahārāja-vaṃsa-pāṭh, Pokkaṃ Mahārājavaṃsa (Pagan, B): EP 111.

4.2.1 Jinak Jinakāla-mālinī (CM, Ratanapañña, 1516–17, enlarged in 1527): H 428, PL 143f, PSA 19 m, HP 65f, PCS 2.55, LN 122, VP 6/ta.11.

4.2.2 Sgv Saṅgīti–vaṃsa (S, Rājaguru Vanaratana Vimaladhamma, 1789): H 199, PL 144, PSA 26, 66.

4.2.31 Rb-v Ratanabimba-vaṃsa, Mahā-ratanabimbavaṃsa, Ratanabimbavaṃsa-pakaraṇa- vaṇṇākathā (Sukhodaya, S, Brahmarājapañña, 14–15th c.): H 427, PSA 15, 65, 88, PCS 2.183, EP 127, VP 6/ta.4, BnF 407, FEMC D164.

4.2.32 Amarakaṭa-buddharūpa-nidāna, Amarakaṭa-nidāna (B, Ariyavaṃsa, 15th c.): PSA 15, 66, EP 122.

4.2.33 Aḍḍhabhāga-buddharūpa-nidāna (B, Ariyavaṃsa): PSA 66, PCS 2.2, EP 128, 137, ME 30, VP 4/140.

4.2.4 Bu-up Buddhaghosuppatti, Buddhaghosavaṇṇanā, Buddhaghosālaṅkāra (B, Mahāmaṅgala, 15th c.): H 207, PL 145, HP 32, PSC 43, PLC 79, BnF 392, SA Khmer E 10, VH.

Buddhaghosācariya-nidāna, Buddha-ghosa-nidāna, Buddhaghosa-jātaka: PCS 2.139, PSA 17, BnF 393.

4.2.5 (See Sandesa-section below):

4.2.7 Cdv Cāmadevī-vaṃsa (CM, Bodhiraṃsi, 15th c.): H 426, PSA 14, 65, PCS 2.47, EP 124, 129, VP 6/ta.4, ICI 6.

4.2.8 Sbn Sihiṅga-nidāna, Sihiṅga-buddharūpa-nidāna (CM, Bodhiraṃsi, 15th c.): H 427, PSA 14, 65, PCS 2.239, EP 27, 126, VP 4/141, ICI 7.

4.2.12 Pbv Pacceka-buddha-vyākaraṇa: H 429.

Unclassified History and Legend

Amarapura-vaṃsa (C.): RAS Sinh 14.

Kalyāṇi-pakaraṇa, Kaḷyāṇi-śilā-lipi, Kaḷyāṇi-lekhā, Rāmañña-samaṇa-vaṃsa (Pegu, B, Dhammaceti Rāja, 1478): H 339, 445, , ED 214, PLB 38f, PSA 28, PCS 2.29, PLC 257f, N 6605(14), LCM 1877f, PSC 45.

Kalyaṇi-pakaraṇa-vinicchaya-kathā, Rāmaññadesa-sāsana-patiṭṭhāpanaṃ (B): N 6605(14), PSC 50.

Kaḷyāṇi–vaṃsa-Guṇaratanatissa-Sāsanavaṃsa: PSC 53.

Cullayuddha-kāla, Cullayuddhakāra-vaṃsa (S, Somdet Paramānujit making use of Phra Vanarat's work, mid 19th c.): PSA 27, PCS 2.50.

Jananandа (-sannaya) (? = sannaya of 4.1.5.1 Sādhu-janānanda-vikāsinī?): SPB 52, Bod.

Jambudīpasaṅgīti-niddesa: RPA 4.

Tathāgatuppatti (B, Ñāṇagambhīra, 11th c.?): PLB 16, 105, Ps.

Duṅyanti-nidāna (S): PCS 2.26.

Dhammakāya, Dhammakāyādi, Dhammakāyatthavaṇṇanā: PCS 2.88, EP 2.6, VP 4/150.8.

Ñāṇodaya-pakaraṇa, Gambhīra-ñāṇodaya (S, 11–13th c.) (Many quotations from Mhv, Dīp and *porāṇas*. There are Thai printed editions.): VP 4/150.6.

Pūjāvaliya (Sinh. with Pāḷi quotations. Account of offerings to the Buddha.) (C, Mayūrapāda thera (using the epithet *Buddhaputra*, 13th c.): N 6606(2), LCM 161ff, SL 61f, SH 104, PLC 109, CM xixf.

Buddhacarita: LCM 840–41.

Buddha-lakkhaṇa (On the characteristics of Buddha-images.) (S): PSA 28.

Braṭ-Rājabaṅsāvatāra-Kruṅ-Śri-Ayudyā: PCS 2.134.: Mahāyuddha-kāla, Mahāyuddhakāra-vaṃsa (S, Paramānujit making use of Phra Vanarat's work, mid 19th c.): PSA 27, PCS 2.166.

Mahā-vihāraparamparā-kathā: LCM 1917.

Laṅkā kaṭhava: LCM 1896.

Vāmadantadhātu-sutta: PSA 107.

Saṅgāyana-nāya, Saṅgīti-nidāna (S. Various nissaya works dealing with the first 4 councils and those involved.): VH 239.

Saṅkhepa (S, Phra Narai, 1680.) (History of Ayodha.): PSA 24.

Sāsanasuddhi-dīpikā (B, Nandamāla, around 1776.): PLB 73.

Sāsana-dīpanī (S, Banyen Limsavati under the auspices of Sangharaja Somdet Phra Ñāṇasaṃvara, 2004): Private correspondence.

Siyāmopasampadā-vata, Siyāmūpasampadā (C, Tibbaṭuvāvē Siddhattha Buddharakkhita, ± 1760.): PC 284, CM xxxviii, SL 9, CPD.

Sāvaka-nibbāna literature

Siam, Laos, Cambodia. See ED 404, 504.

Sāvaka-nibbāna (Ic.) *(Dr. Skilling: A collection [+ 40] of texts on the nibbāna of arahants and others. Some are transmitted as separate texts, but the relation between the collection and separate texts, far less than 40, is unclear. EP 64 contains: Koṅdañña-nibbāna, Sāriputta~, Bakula~, Moggallana~, Kassapa~, Dabbamallaputta~, Bāhiya~, Asokarāja~, Devānampiyatissa~, Maṅgalavāsikuṭatissa,*

Vyaghathera~, Suddhodana, Sānusāmaṇera~, Pajāpati~.): PCS 2.235, EP 64, VP 6/ta.3, ED 404, 504.

Asoka-parinibbāna (-kathā), Asoka-dhammarāja-nibbāna: PCS 2.20, PSA 126, EP 29, VP 6/ta.3.

Ānanda-nibbāna: RLL 66

Koṇḍaññathera-nibbāna: PCS 2.32.

Bakulathera-nibbāna: PCS 2.135.

Bāhiyathera-nibbāna: PCS 2.137.

Bimbābhikkhunī-nibbāna, Bimbāyasodharā-bhikkhunī-parinibbāna: PCS 2.138, EP 65, ED 404.

Mahākaccāyanathera-nibbāna, Mahākaccāyana-nibbāna, Gavampati-sutta, Gavampati-nibbāna-sutta: ED 504, PCS 2.156, BnF 298, 409, EP 64, VP 4/152, ME 25.3.

Mahākassapathera-parinibbāna-kathā, Mahākassapanibbāna, Kassapanibbāna: PSA 125, BnF 298m, VH.

Moggallānathera-nibbāna, Mahāmoggallānaparinibbāna-dhātu-kathā, ~vatthu: PCS 2.178, PSA 125, BnF 298–99.

Sāriputta-nibbāna, Mahāsāriputta-parinibbāna-sutta, Sāriputtanibbāna-vaṇṇanā: PSA 125, BnF 298f.

Bibliographies

4.3.1 Saddh-s Saddhamma-saṅgaha (Ayodhyā, S, Dhammakitti Mahāsāmi, 14th c. [N: 1371] or: CM, Ñāṇakitti, 15th c. [PCS]): H 4, PL 179f, PCS 2.219, LS 63f, PSA 13m, N 6601(44), PLC 10m, PSC 42, HP 129f, LCM 1402, VP 4/135, ME.

Culla-saddhamma-saṅgaha: PSA 67, PCS 2.51, VP 4/135, ME 25.8.

4.3.2 Nikāya-s Nikāya-saṃgrahaya, Śāsanāvatāraya (Sinh. & Pāḷi quotations. Gaḍalādeṇiya, C, Devarakṣita Jayābahu Dhammakīrti II, late 14th c.): SL 122f, PC 11, 243, LCM 1929–31, SL 93.

4.3.3 Gv Gandhavaṃsa, Ganthavaṃsa, Culla-gandhavaṃsa, Culla-ganthavaṃsa (B, Nandapañña, 17th c?): H 4, PL 180f, PLB x, LS 68, PSC 51, CS.

4.3.4 Sās Sāsanavaṃsa, Sāsanavaṃsa-padīpikā (B, Paññasāmi, 1861): H 4, PL 181, HP 144f, PLB xi, PCS 2.236, LS 69, PSC 50, CS.

4.3.5 Sās-dīp Sāsanavaṃsa-dīpa (C, Vimalasāratissa, 1880): PL 182, PLC 10, 311, LS 71, PSC 51.

4.3.6 Piṭ-sm Piṭakat samuin, Piṭakat thamain (B, Mahāsirijeyasū, 1888) (Different texts.): H 4, LS 72, PSA 17, FPL.

Piṭaka-saṅkhyā (S): PCS 2.127.

Piṭaka-mālā (S): H n. 10.

Caturāsīti-dhammakkhandha-sahassa-saṃvaṇṇanā, Dhammakkhandha (La?): PSA 126, RLL 76.

Pagan Inscription (Pagan, B, 1442.) (List of 299 texts donated to a monastery.): H 205, LS 67, PLB 101–09, PI.

Saṅgāyana-puccha-vissajjanā (B, Chaṭṭha-saṅgāyana, 1950s.): CS.

Buddha-sāsana: VP 4/140.

Future Buddhas: See ED 202.

4.4.1 Anāg Anāgatavaṃsa (-pāḷi), Anāgatabuddhavaṃsa, Anāgatadasabuddhavaṃsa, Dasa-anāgatabuddhavaṃsa (SI, Coḷa-raṭṭha Kassapa, 12–13th c.): H 200, PL 161, PSA 87, 126, W, PCS 2.14, Ps, HP 9, PLC 160f, LCM 714f, N 6603 (52), PSC n. 29, ED 202.

4.4.1.1 Anāg-a Samantabhaddikā, Samantasaddikā, Anāgatavaṃsa-aṭṭhakathā (C, Paññālaṅkāra [LCM]. Colophon in EP and LCM: Requested by Mahābodhi, made in the Kāḷavāpivihāra (built by Dhātusena). EP colophon: written in 2120 BE = 1577.): PL 162, HP 132, PCS 2.222, PLC 160/323, LCM 736f, N 6603(52), CAPC, EP 84, ED 202, Ps.

4.4.1. Anāg-ṭ Amatarasa-hārā, Anāgatavaṃṣa-ṭīkā, Amata-hārā, Amatarasadhāra-ṭīkā, Amatadhāranāgatavaṃsa-aṭṭhakathā, Anāgatavaṃsa-aṭṭhakathā, Amatarasadhārānāgata-buddhavaṃsa-vaṇṇanā (C?, Upatissa, 10th c.): PSA 87, PCS 2.16, PLC 160/ 323, BnF 322m, N 6603(52), CAPC, EP 26, 82f, VH, ED 202.

Amatadhārā-ṭīkā: PCS 2.60, ED 202.

Dasa-buddhavaṃsa (SI, Coḷaraṭṭha Kassapa, 12–13th c.): Gandhavaṃsa, PLC 160.

4.4.1(3) Mete-budu-sirita, Anāgatavaṃsaya (Sinh.) (Vilgammuḷa thera, ± 1250.): N 6603(52), CPD.

4.4.2 Dasab Dasa-bodhisatta-uddesa, Anāgata-buddha-vaṃsa (Kh?): H 201, PL 162, N 6603(52), PSC 69, BnF 629m, EP 41, CAPC.

4.4.31 Dbv Dasa-bodhisatta-vidhi (Dasabo-dhisatta-anāgata-vaṃsaya, ~caritaya PSC 69.): H 202, PL 162, PSC 69.

4.4.3 Dbk Dasabodhisatta-uppatti-kathā, Dasabodhisatta-kathā (C, 14th c?): H 202, PL 161, N 6601(21), 6603(52), LCM 922, PSC 69, ED 202.

Pañcabuddha-vyākaraṇa (S?): PCS 2.100, PSA 104, VP 4/141, EP 75.38, 123.

Poetry

4.5.1 Narasīha-gāthā, Rāhulakumāravandana-gāthā (From Pujāvāliya. Based on Skt original (Cambridge MS Add. 1614). One verse in Ja I 89. Beg: *Lokanisañcita- dhammasudhoghaṃ...* or *Cakkavaraṃkhita-ratta-supādo...*): SL 64, N 6559(2)xxxi, 6600(59), LCM 1211, GB 176, PV 20.

4.5.2 Mahājayamaṅgala-gāthā, Jayamaṅgala-gāthā (Different versions, 16–40 verses. Beg: *mahākāruṇiko nāṭho.*): N 6599(2)xv, LCM 1033, SR 26f, 260f, RL 123, ED 401, GB 139.

Jayamaṅgala-gāthā, Dvitīya-jayamaṅgala-gāthā (45 or 46 gāthās. Beg: *mahākaruniko* or *phalanibbāṇajaṃ.*): LCM 1025, N 6599(2)xv, ED 401.

Jayaparitta, Jayamaṅgalaparitta (Short version of prec. Beg: *mahākaruniko* or *jayanto.*): BC 97, EP 102.25.

Pubbaṇhasutta (B.) (19 verses, incl. Jaya-paritta. Beg: *Yaṃ dunnimittaṃ.*): MP 94ff, EP 89.L.

Jayamaṅgala-aṭṭha-gāthā, Jayamaṅgala-aṭṭhaka, Jayamaṅgala-gāthā, Buddhajayamaṅgala, Buddhamaṅgala, Mahā-aṭṭhajeyyamaṅgala (Beg: *Bāhuṃ sahassamabhinimitta...*): PSA 102, CB 12, CM 62, BC 314f, LCM 1029, N 6599(2)xv, SR 9f, RL 123, ED 303, EP 2.3, BnF 865, PV 3, GB 137.

Jayamaṅgala-aṭṭhagāthā-sannaya: N 6602(7)iv, LCM 1036, ED 401.

Bāhuṃ-ṭīkā, Ṭīkā-bahūni, Bāhuṃsa, Bāhuṃsa-cintāmaṇi-ratana, Jayamaṅgalagāthā-parikathā (S?): PSA 102, PCS 2.65, CB 43f, CM 62, BnF 320m, EP 2m, VP 4/136.

Aṭṭha-maṅgala-gāthā: RL 123.

Jayamaṅgala-gāthā (SL, Väliviṭa Sorata, 1964. Reconstructed version of the Jayamaṅgala-aṭṭha-gāthā.): TJM.

4.5.3 Kāyaviratigāthā, Jātidukkhavibhāga (C. 18th c. Beg: *Sambuddhamabhivanditvā...*): PLC 285f, PCS 2.31, N 6601(83), PLB 44, PSC 63.

4.5.3.1 Kāyaviratigāthā-ṭīkā (Pakudhanagara [Pegu?].): PLB 44, CPD.

Dasavatthu-kāyavirati-ṭīkā: Gv.

4.5.3.2 Kāyaviratigāthā-sannaya, ~padārtha (Laṅkātilaka-vihāra?, C, author of Vimukti-saṃgraha?, 14th c.): N 6601(83), PLC 285, LCM 1075, PSC 63.

4.5.4 Pajj Pajjamadhu (I, Buddhappiya/Dīpaṅkara, 13th c.): H 403, PL 158f, HP 106, PCS 2.97, PLC 220f, PSC 65, CS.

4.5.4.1 Pajj-sn Pajjamadhu-sannaya: N 6601(31), LCM 1271f, PLC 222, PSC 65.

Pajjamadhu-sāraya: PSC 65.

4.5.5 Tel Telakaṭāha-gāthā, Telakaṭāra-gāthā (C, 10–11th c.) (Beg: *Laṃkissaro jayatu*...): H 404f, PL 156, HP 159, PLC 162f, LCM 1534, PSC 60, CS.

4.5.5.1 Tel-sn Telakaṭāha-gāthā sannaya, Dharma-gāthā sannaya: N 6599 (35)v, LCM 1535, PSC 60.

Telakaṭāha-gāthā-viggaha: PSC 60.

4.5.5.A Pāramīsataka, Pāramī-mahāsataka (C, Sīlavaṃsa Dhammakitti Saṅgharāja, 1347. Beg: *Lokodayācalatale paṭijambhamānaṃ*...): HP 114f, PLC 242, N 6599(3)xiv, PCS 2.126, PSC 66, CM xxxi.

4.5.6 Jina-c Jinacarita (C, Vanaratana Medhaṅkara, 13th c.): H 406, PL 158, HP 64, PLC 230f, PCS 56, PSC 56, CS, L.

Jinacarita-sannaya (13–14th c?): LCM 1041, PSC 56, N 6601(3), Vs 86, L.

4.5.6.1 Jina-c-vy Śiṣyaprabodhinī, Jinacarita-vyākhyā (C, K. Ñāṇuttara): CPD, PSC 56.

4.5.7 Saddh Saddhammopāyana (C, Abhayagiri Kavicakravarti Ānanda [-Upatissa], before early 12th c.): PL 159f, LCM 1389, N 6601(8), PSC 61, PCS 2.220, VP 4/139, PLB 197, A, L.

4.5.7.1 Saddh-sn Saddhammopāyana-sannaya (C, monastic brother of the above Ānanda, 12th c.?): N 6601(8), PLC 212, LCM 1390f, L, PSC 61.

Saddhammopāyana-atthapadīpikā, Atthapadīpikā, Saddhammopāyana-ṭīkā, ~vaṇṇanā: PCS 2.12, VP 4/139.

Saddhammopāyana-viggaha (-ṭīkā): PSC 61, PL 160, PLC 212.

Saddhammopāyana-viggaha-sannaya: LCM 1392f, L, PSC 61.

Saddhammopāyana-cintā: PSC 61.

Saddhammopāyana-nirutti-sannaya: PSC 61.

Saddhammopāyana-vyākhyāva: PSC 61.

4.5.8 Vuttamālā, ~sandesa, ~sataka (C, Satarāparivena Upatapassi, 15th c.) (Trans. of Vṛtamālākhyāva. Used for training proper pronunciation, also examples of metres + panegyric.): HP 180f, PLC 253f, LCM 1619, 2333, SH 127, PSC 127, Bod.

Vuttamālā-ṭīkā: PSC 127.

Vuttamālā-viggaha: PSC 127.

Vuttamālā-vyākhyāva: PSC 127.

Vuttamālā-sannaya, Vuttamāla-sandesa-sataka-(sanna)ya: PC 254, PSC 127, SH 127, LCM 1619.

Vṛttamālākhyāva (Skt. source of 4.5.8) (Gauḍadeśiya Bhūsura Ācāryya): SH 126.

Vṛttamālākhyā (Skt.) (C, Rāmacandra Kavibhārati, 15th c.): SH xxxiii.

Vṛttamālākhyā-sannaya: SH 126.

4.5.9 Sādhu-c Sādhu-caritodaya (C, Cūtaggāma Sumedha, 14th c.): H 408, HP 130, PLC 247, LCM 1406, PSC 72.

Sādhucaritodaya-ṭīkā: PSC 72, L Pt I.

4.5.101–2 Buddhālaṅkāra, etc. (Presumably the 'etc.' in CPD stands for the below entry.) (Ava, B, Sīlavaṃsa, 15th c.): PLB 43, CPD.

Pabbatabbhantara (Ava, B, Sīlavaṃsa, 15th c.): PLB 43.

4.5.111–3 Bhūridatta-jātaka (-gāthā), etc. (Presumably the 'etc.' in CPD stands for the below entries.) (Ava, B, Raṭṭhasāra, 15th c.) (= HP 543.): PLB 44, CPD.

Hatthipālajātaka (-gāthā) (Ava, B, Raṭṭhasāra, 15th c.) (= HP 509.): PLB 44.

Saṃvarajātaka (-gāthā) (Ava, B, Raṭṭhasāra, 15th c.) (= HP 462.): PLB 44.4

4.5.12 (See Sandesa-section.):

4.5.13 Jināl Jinālaṅkāra, ~pāṭha (C, Rohaṇa Buddharakkhita [Gv: Buddhadatta], 1156–7. First verse: *Sukhañca dukkhaṃ samathāyupekkhaṃ...*): H 407, PL 157f, HP 66f, PCS 2.59, PLC PSC 55, EP 45.2, VP 4/119, CS, L.

4.5.13,1 Jināl-pṭ Jinālaṅkāra-purāṇaṭīkā, Jinālaṅkāra-vaṇṇanā (C, Rohaṇa Buddharakkhita, 1156–7) (The close relation between this and the Jināl is confusing.): H 407, PL 157, HP 67, PCS 2.61, PLC 110m, CM 50, PSC 55, BnF 354m, LCM 1042f, EP 45m, VP 4/119, FPL, Ps, L.

4.5.13,2 Jināl-gul Jinālaṅkāra-gūḷhatthadīpanī: PL 157, CPD, FPL 495.

Jinālaṅkāra-gaṇṭhi: FPL 3077.

Jinālaṅkāra-dīpanī (B): Ps.

Jinālaṅkāra-sarko: Ps.

Jinālaṅkāra-nissaya: CPD 4.5.13, FPL.

Jinālaṅkāra-sannaya: L.

5.5.14 Jina-b Jinabodhāvali, Abhinīhāra-dīpanī (C, Devarakkhita Jayabāhu Dhammakitti, 14th c.): H 408a, HP 63f, BEFEO 72 (1983).

Unclassified Poetry

Accaya-vivaraṇa, Khamāyācana (Beg. *Kāyena vācā cittena, pamādena mayā kataṃ...*): GB 181, BP 45.

Aṭavisi-sugatavandanā, Aṭavisi-muni–vandanā (Beg: *Vande Taṇhaṅkaraṃ buddhaṃ...*): SH 315, N 6559(2)vii, GB 172, L.

Aṭavisi-bodhivandanā-gāthā (Beg: *Taṇhaṃmedhaṃkarānamhi...*): SH 315, N 6559 (2)viii, L.

Aṭṭhavīsati-paritta, Aṭavisi-pirita, (Before 11th c.) (Different versions.) (Beg: *Taṇhaṅkaro mahāvīro...*): SH 315, LCM 779, 1656f, SCC 254ff, N 6559 (2)vi & 36, RL 123, GB 147, PV 7, L.

Aṭṭhavīsatibuddha-vaṇṇanā (Beg: *Namo me sabbabuddhānaṃ uppannānaṃ...*): EP 2.5, 75.12, ME 49.

Aṭavisi Budunge da Mātrapītru hā bodhīnge da nām (Aṭṭhavisati-buddha- buddhamātupitu-mahābodhi-nāma-gāthā) (Beg: *Taṇhaṃkarodayo buddhā...*): N 6559(2)xxvii.

Aṭorāśiyak Maṅgul-lakuṇu (gāthā), (Aṭṭhādhikasata-maṅgala-lakkhaṇa-gāthā) (Beg: *Pādesu yassa jātāni...*): LCM 781, N 6559(2)xxviii.

Aṭuvā-prārthanā-gāthā (Asīti-adhiṭṭhāna-gāthā) (Aspiration verses from the end of the aṭṭhakathās.) (Beg: *Puññaṇena pappomi buddhataṃ...*): LCM 782, 784, N 6559(2) xxv, SH 232.

Aṭuvā-prārthanā-gāthā-padārtha: LCM 783f, N 6559(2)xxvi.

Aṅgulimālaparitta (Beg: *Yatohaṃ bhagini...*): N 6600(138), BnF 600, GB 148, PV 8, L.

Aṅgulimālaparitta-padārtha: L.

Anumodanagāthā (saṅgaha): N 6599(25)7.

Anumodanāvidhī (S. Beg: *Yathā vārivahā pūrā...*): BC 173.

Aśīti Mahā-śrāvakaya, Asūmahasavuvanvahansēgē nam (Beg: *Kondañño bhaddiyo vappo...*): LCM 755, 760, N 6559(2).

Asītyānubyañjana-gāthā, Buddharūpabhiseka-gāthā (S?) (Beg: *Eso no satthā...*): PCS 2.19, VP 4/147.

Aṣṭaka-potha (C. Collections of different *aṣṭaka* poems.): LCM 757, N 6601(11–18, 94, 98, 101–2)

Aṣṭaka-sannaya (C, Veheragoda Medhaṅkara): LCM 758.

Abhayaparitta, Yandunnimittaṃ (Beg: *Yandunnimittaṃ...*) (Different versions): BC 96, SCC 26, BnF 544, 609, EP 102.23, 138, Dham 40, PV 3.

Abhisambodhi-alaṅkāra (C, Välanvitta Saraṇankara, 18th c. 100 verses. Beg: *Buddhaṃ buddhaguṇākaraṃ dasabalaṃ...*): HP 9, N6601(47), PLC 281f, PCS 2.15, PSC 79, PL 160 App. I, L.

Ārakkha-gāthā (8 verses. Beg: *Buddhaṃ suddhaguṇākaraṃ dasabalaṃ...*): PV 41.

Abhisambodhi-alaṅkāra-sannaya (C, Välanvitta Saraṇankara, 18th c.): PC 282, PSC 79, L.

Abhisambodhi-alaṅkāra-varṇanāva, Abhisambodhi-alaṅkāra-vyākhyāva: PSC 79.

Āṭānāṭiya-paritta (Different versions. Some gāthā of DN 32 & Aṭṭhavīsati-paritta. Beg: *Vipasissa namatthu...*): BC 78f, 90f, BnF 600.8, 743, MP 73f, PV 40, RL 123.

Ānanda-aṣṭaka-sannaya (C, Vikramasinghapura Buddhaghosa): LCM 738.

Āsiravādaparitta (S? Beg: *Itipi so...* End: ... *sabbesaggaparāyanā.*): EP 75.8.

Āhārapūja-gāthā (C? Verses from different sources.): LCM 704.

Äṇuvum-pirita (Beg: *Ye santā santacittā...* Cf Devatārādhana-gāthā): GB 142, PV 5, cf BC 68.

Indasāva (S or Kh?) (A *dhāraṇi*) (Beg: *Indasāvaṃ devasāvaṃ...* End: ...*hulū hulū svāhāya.*): PSA 95, BnF 383, 600, EP 39.7j, 75.5–6, ED 401.

Uppātasanti (CM, Sīlavaṃsa, 16th c.) (271 Paritta verses. End: ... *ārogyañca jayaṃ sadā.* Or: ... *sadā sotthiṃ karontu me.*): PSA 23, 68, PLB 47, RL 123, RAS Burm 17, FPL.

Mahā-Uppātasanti-gāthā: VP 4/139.

Uddisanādhiṭṭhāna-gāthā (S) (Beg: *Iminā puññakammena upajjhāya...*): BC 36.

Kamalāñjalī (B): CS.

(CPD 2.9.1) Khandha-paritta (Verse part of A II 72) (Beg: *Virūpakkhehi me mettaṃ...*): BC 74f, MP 50.

Gini-paritta, Aggi-paritta (Starts with *Jalo mahājalo...* Influenced by *dhāraṇīs* in the Saddharmapuṇḍarīka; see Par 10. Cf Jaya-pirita, Culla- & Mahāmaṅgalacakkavāḷa.): LCM 1012, RL 124, Par 10, GB 148, PV 12.

Gini-pirita pesāmālāva, Gini-pirita II (Hybrid Pāḷi gāthas with Sinhala translation.): N 6600(132), LCM 1011.

Candasukaragiri-sutta (Kh. Beg: *Namo me sabbabuddhānaṃ dvatiṃsavarakhaṇo...*): ED 401

Caturārakkhā, Catu-kammaṭṭhāna, Satara-kamaṭahan (C?) (Beg: *Buddhānussati mettā ca...* End: *... mataṃ sukhena cāti.*): PCS 2.45, PSA 92, 121, ED 401, LCM 689m, N 6599 (34)xiii, BnF 348, GB 168, PV 16.

Caturārakkhā-aṭṭhakathā (S?, Ñāṇamaṅgala. Beg: *Catusaccadasso nātho...*): PCS 2.5, PSA 93, BnF 349, VH, ED 401.

Caturārakkha-dīpanī (Ranakuna, B, Aggadhamma): CS.

Satara-kamaṭahan-padārtha, Satara-kamaṭahan-sannaya: LCM 693ff.

Catuvīsatidesanā (S? Beg: *Buddhasāvaṃ guṇaṃ vijjaṃ...*): EP 39.7.

Chalaṅkāra-paritta (Apocryphal sutta. End: *... bahupuñño bhavatu sabbadāti...*): EP 75.3.

Janānurāga-carita (Extinct.) (C, Sīlavaṃsa Dhammakitti Saṅgharāja, 14th c.): HP 58.

Jaya-pirita (Beg: *Siridhitimatitejo,* combines parts of the Culla- and Mahāmaṅgalacakkavāḷa and Giniparitta.): N 6601(75), GB 150, PV 9.

Jalanandana-partita (Beg: *Catūvīsati buddhoti, yo bhavissati uttamaṃ ...*): GB 177, PV 15, EP 145.

Javara-pirita, Jvara Paritta (28 verses. Against fever. Starts with *Taṇhaṃkaro nāma jino...* Ends: *... pajjaro te vinassatu.*): GB 157, PV 39.

Jinapañjara (-gāthā), Māha-jinapañjara (Various different versions. One by Buḍḍhācariya, S, mid 19th c, but original must be older than that.) (Beg: *Jayāsanāgatā vīrā...*): SH 316, PCS 2.57, SR 256f, LCM 1044f, RL 123, N 6559(2), Par 9, GB 144, PV 6, L.

Khuddaka-jinapañjara-paritta, Culla-jinapañjara-paritta (Beg: *Dīsāsu dasabhāvesu...*): N 6559(4)iii, PV 36.

Jinapañjara-mātikā: L.

Jinacarita-prārthanā-gāthā (C. Beg: *Iminā puññakammena ito'haṃ bhavato cuto...*): N 6600(59)viii.

Jinavaṃsa-dīpanī, Jinavaṃsa-dīpa, Pabandha-siromaṇi (C, M. Medhānanda, 1917): PC 11, 313f, PSC 58, CS.

Taṇhaṅkara-buddhavaṇṇanā (S?) (Beg: *Suṇantu bhonto ye devā...*): EP 75.10.

Tiloka-vijaya-rāja-pattidāna-gāthā (S. *Yaṅkiñci kusalaṃ kammaṃ...*): BC 36.

Tividha-ratana-namakāra, Trividharatna-namaskāraya (C. Beg: *Satatavitatakittiṃ...*): LCM 1546.

Tiratana-namakāra-gāthā (S? *Yo sannissino varabodhimūle*...): BC 109f (Cf ME 49.3)

Tiratana-paṇāma-gāthā (S, King Mongkut, 19th c. Beg: *Buddhaṃ name ratana*...): BC 110f.

Tirokuḍḍha-sutta (+ sannaya) (From Pv, Khp. Beg: *Tirokuḍḍesu tiṭṭhanti*...): N 6600(6), SH 215, BC 182f, EP 2, GB 178.

Tekālikā-buddha-dhamma-saṅgha-vandanā (Beg. *Ye ca buddhā atītā ca, ye ca buddhā anāgatā*...): Dham 19f, Dickson.

Dantadhātu-vandanā-gāthā (Beg. *Ekādāthānidasapure*...): LCM 1175.

Dāṭhadhātu-vandanā-gāthā (C. Beg: *Buddhaṃ lokaguruṃ vande*...): N 6601(12)i.

Daḷadā-aṣṭakaya, Danta-dhātu-aṭṭhaka (C. Different poems.): LCM 907, 1244, N 6601(12–18).

Dasa-māra-pirita (Beg: *Iti tadubhaya senā*...): PV 38.

Ducaritādinava-gātha-sannaya: N 6599(3).

Detis-mahāpuruṣa-lakṣaṇa-gāthā, Dvatiṃsa-mahāpurisa-lakkhaṇā (Beg: *Satthuppasattacaraṇaṃ*...): LCM 929, N 6559(2)xxix.

Devatārādhana-gāthā, Devārādhanā (Beg: *Samantā cakkavāḷesu*... Cf Äṇavum Pirita.): SH 319, BC 67, 83, MP 21f, SR 4.

Devatā-uyyojana-gāthā (Beg: *Dukkhappattā ca niddukkhā*...): BC 95.

Dhātu-vandanā (-gāthā, -aṣṭaka) (C. Different poems.): LCM 978–80, N 6559(2 & 35)xi, 6601 (11–18), BnF 581.

Dharmarāja-aṣṭaka, Jinarāja-aṭṭhaka (Pāḷi) (C. Different poems): N 6601(11–18), BnF 564.

Namaskāra-gāthā (Pāḷi. *Namāmi buddhaṃ guṇasāgarantaṃ*...): LCM 1174, 1176, PLB 95.

Namaskāra-gāthā-sannaya: LCM 1177.

Namakkāra-pāḷi, Mahānamakāra-pāḷi (B): CS, CW Burm 123, PLB 95.

Namakkāra-ṭīkā, Buddhaguṇa-padīpikā (B, 1945): CS.

Namaskāra-aṣṭaka-sannaya: LCM 1173.

Namaskāra-sannaya, Namaskāra-pāṭhāya (Different works.): LCM 1172, 1177, 1179–85.

Namaskāra-padārthaya, Pañcapatiṭṭhitā-namaskāra-sannaya (Beg: *Tavadā mē*...): N 6599(2 & 31)

Namakārasiddhi-gāthā (S, Vajirāñāṇavarorasa, 20th c. Beg: *Yo cakkhumā mohamalā*...): BC 111f.

Namokāraṭṭhaka (S, Mongkut, 19th c. Beg: *Namo arahato sammāsambuddhassa mahesino.*): BC 113.

Nava-guṇa-gāthā (Beg: *Arahaṃ arahoti nāmena…*): GB 173, N 6599(35)ix.

Nava-arahādi-gāthā-pādārtha-sannaya, Nava-arahādī-buduguṇa-vibhāgaya (C. Beg: *Ārakattā hatattā ca…* Often with Vimuktisaṃgraha. Pāḷi verse + sanna + Sinh. prose.): N 6601(59)vi.

Nava-arahādi-budu-guṇa (Beg: *Puphēnivāsānam…*): LCM 1212.

Navaguṇa-sannaya (Different versions. Maybe originally together with Nandopanandadamanaya. Ends: *…Bhagavā nam vana sēka.*): LCM 1213–24, N 6599(31).

Navaguṇa-sannaya (Different works.): SH 310, N 6599 (31)ii.

Trividha-ratna-guṇa-padārtha: LCM 1221.

Nava-arahaguṇa-gāthā (S, Saṅgharāja Sā. Beg: *Arakkattā kilesehi…*): BC 119.

Pañcamāra-vijaya-paritta (Beg: *Jeyyā santigatā buddhā…*): EP 75.2.

Pattānumodanā (Beg. *Ettāvatāca amhehi sambhataṃ… iminā puññakammena mā me…*): Dham 48.

Pattidāna (Beg. *Dukkhapattā ca niddukkhā … Ettāvatāca amhehi…* End: … *rājā bhavantu dhammiko.* Or: *Idaṃ me ñātinaṃ hotu…*): GB 180, BP 45.

Pattidāna-gāthā (S, King Mongkut, 19th c. Beg: *Ye devatā santi vihāravāsinī…*): BC 34f.

Padalañchana-aṣṭakaya (C, *Sattuttamo dasabalo karuṇādhivāso …*): LCM 1268–9.

Parittārambha-gāthā (C? Beg: *Bhikkhūnaṃ guṇasaṃyuttaṃ …*): PV 34.

Paritta-ārādhana (Beg: *Vipattipaṭibāhāya …*): BC 322, PV 1.

(Dasa- & Pañca-) Pāramitā-aṣṭakaya: LCM 1289, 1299.

Pāramī-sārasa-mālā (C, Disciple of V. Saraṇankara. Beg: *Ādhāro tvaṃ nutiṇamiha…*): N 6599(2)xxiv.

Patthanā-gāthā, Prāthanā-gāthā (Beg. *iminā puññakammena mā me…*): LCM 1350f, CB 35, BP 45.

Puññānumodanā, Anumodanā (SL, Beg. *Ākāsaṭṭhā ca bhummaṭṭhā, devā nāgā …*): GB 141, BP 43.

Bodhi–vandanā-gāthā (Beg: *Sonuttareniddhimatena nītā…*): N 6599(2)xxiii, LCM 834.

Bodhi–vandanā (Beg. *Yassa mūle nisinno va…*): BP 36.

Bojjhaṅga-paritta (Beg: *Saṃsāre saṃsarattānaṃ...* or *Bojjhaṅgo satisaṅkhāto...*): BC 90, MP 87f, RL 124, BnF 596, EP 75.9, GB 162, PV 10, LCM 835.

Buddhaguṇa-gāthā-valī (I, S.N. Goenka, 1999): CS.

Buddhamaṅgala-gāthā (Cf Jinapañjara) (Beg: *Sambuddho dipadaṃ...*): BC 107–8.

Buddha-vandanā (C. Beg: *Namo namo buddhadivākarāya...*): LCM 833f.

Buddhavandanā-gāthā, Tiratana-vandanā-gāthā (Beg: *Mahākaruṇikā buddhā dhammañca...*): N 6599(34)xxv, (35)xxv, 6601(75), LCM 865f.

Buddha-sahassa-gāthā-nāmavalī (I, S.N. Goenka, 1998): CS.

Buddhābhiseka-pakaraṇa (S?): PCS 2.144, VP 1/1.

Buddhābhiseka-gāthā (S? Beg: *Buddhādicco mahātejo...*): EP 75.40.

Buddhalakkhaṇa-bhāvanā (-gāthā), Lakuṇu-bhāvanā-gāthā (Beg: *Battiṃsā yassa...*): N 6559(2)xxx

Dasavarañāṇa-buddhābhiseka, Buddhābhiseka (La?): PSA 120.

Bhava-virati-gāthā (C. Beg: *Bhavesu sabbesu sadā asesato...*): PCS 2.146, LCM 819f, PSC 63, N 6599(2)xviii.

Bhava-virati-gāthā-sannaya: LCM 822.

Maitri-bhāvanā-gāthā, Metta-bhāvanā (37–38 verses. Beg: *Puññenānena me yāvajīvaṃ...*): LCM 1137, N 6600(120)xvi, PV 18.

Matsya-rāja-pirita (From Cp 99. Beg: *Punāparaṃ yadā homi maccharāja...*): PV 37.

Maraṇānusmṛuti bhāvanā (C. Beg: *Yameka rattiṃ paṭhamaṃ...*): LCM 1128.

Mahākassapa-carita (C, V. Piyatissa, 1924): PC 314, PSC 54.

Mdm Mahā-dibba-manta, Dibbamanta (S, 15th c.? A paritta/mantra containing the Mahājayaparitta and the Sabbadisa-paritta, etc.): PSA 102f., RL 122–24, H n. 152, ED 401, PCS 2.161, EP 39, 75, BnF 600, 662.

Mahājaya, Mahājaya-paritta (S?) (Beg: *Jaya jaya pathavī...* or *Jeyya jeyya paṭhavī...*): PCS 2.160, EP 75.1, BnF 662.3, BN Vient in ED 401, VP 4/139.6–7.

Mahā-paṇāma-pāṭha, Vāsamālinī, Buddhavandanā (B): CS.

Mahā-maṅgala-cakkavāḷa (Beg: *Siridhitimatitejo...*) (Cf Jayapirita & Giniparitta): BC 99–100, EP 39.7h, Bnf 600.4.

Culla-maṅgalacakkavāḷa, Sabbabuddhā (Beg: *Sabbabuddhānubhāvena...* Cf Jayapirita.): BC 177, EP 102.27, 138.8,

VP 4/146.11.

Mahāsaraṇagunto (B, Leḍī Sayāḍo, 19–20th c.): DBM 5, 65.

Mahā-sāra (S? Beg: ... *Aṭṭhavīsatime buddhā mahātejā* ...): EP 39.7E, BL or. 13703

Muni-guṇālaṅkāraya (C, Välanvitta Saraṇankara, 1728. Beg: *Mama sirasi munindaṃ*...): PCS 2.177, PLC 282, LCM 1166, N 6601(128), PSC 78.

Muninda-vandanā-gāthā, Sugatāṣṭaka (C. Beg: *Sakalāgama samayākula*...): LCM 1508, 1594.

Muni-rāja-aṣṭakaya (C, Disciple of Saraṇankara. Beg: *Sakyākulambara indusamāmaṃ*...): LCM 1167–8.

Mettānisaṃsa-gāthā (Beg: *Disvā nānappakārena kodho*...): N 6599(2)xxii.

Mettā-bhāvanā (37 verses. Beg. *Puññenānena me yāva, jīvaṃ sabbattha sabbadā*...): GB 163.

Mettā-karuṇā-bhāvanā (Beg. *Uddhaṃ yāva bhavaggāca*...): Dham 33.

Mokkhupāya-gāthā (S, King Mongkut, 19th c. *Sabbavatthuttamaṃ ñatvā*...): BC 113f.

Yot braṭkaṇḍatraipiṭaka (S): RL 124.

Loka-vaḍḍhi-saṅgaha (C, M. Premaratana, 1964? Translation of the Sinhala poem *Lōvädasaṅgarāva*?): PSC p. 60.

Randenē-gāthā, Randeṇē~ (C. Beg: *Sabbasaṅkhatadhammesu*... or *Namo te karuṇāhāra*...): LCM 1377f, GB 175, PV 19.

Tri-ratna-aṣṭakaya, Ti-ratna-stotra-gāthā, Ti-ratna-namaskāra-gāthā, Ratna-traya-vandanā-gāthā (Different poems in Sanskritised & Sinhalised Pāḷi.): N 6600(22), (41)iv, (66)ii), 6601(11), (37), LCM 1382f

Ratanattaya-pabhāvābhiyācanagāthā (S, King Mongkut, 19th c.): BC 121f.

Ratanattaya-pabhāvasiddhi-gāthā (S, Phra Sāsanasophon.): BC 123.

Ratana-vikāra-pākāra-paritta, Rakkaṅgu-pirita (C or B? Beg: *Taṇhaṃkaro metaṃkaro munindo*...): N 6559(4)iv.

Ratana-pañjara (B): PLB 95, EP 89.4, BnF 548.

Ratana-māla (S or Ic., 19th c.? *Iṭṭho sabbaññutañāṇaṃ*...): LJ

Ratanamālā-bandhana-gāthā (Beg: *Saṃsāra-sārogha-vinītaṇīsaṃ*...): PV 42.

Lakkhaṇāto: Buddhathomanā-gāthā, Buddha-vandanā, Uṇṇālomika-nātha-vandanā (B): CS.

Vaṭṭaka-paritta (Beg: *Purentaṃ bodhisambhāre...*): CB 89, GB 149, PV 14.

Väsa-pirita (Vassa-paritta) (Beg: *Subhūto ca mahāthero...*): PV 13, Par 9

Vināyaka-aṣṭaka (C. 18th c. Pāḷi with sannaya. Beg: *Punnindu-sannibha...*): N6601(11)iii.

Saṃvegavatthu (Beg: *Bhāvetvā caturārakkhā...* or *Jāti jarā vyāyi...* Part of *Caturārakkhā.*): PV 17, VH 253.7.

Saṃvegavatthu-dīpanī (Nissaya. Pāli-Burm. Jāgarābhidhaja): CW.

Satta-maṅgala-sutta, Sotthi-gāthā, Sotthi-maṅgala-gāthā (Buddhaghosa. Beg: *Buddho varaṭṭhamaṅgalasattamaṅgala...*): PCS 2.212.1, VP 4/147.

Sambuddhe aṭṭhavīsañcādi-gāthā (S? Beg: *Sambuddhe aṭṭhavīsañca dvādasañca...*): BC 112f.

Sarabhañña-gāthā-visākha-gāthā (S. Beg: *Visākhapuṇṇamāyaṃ yo...*): BC 57f.

Sīvali-pirita, Sīvali-paritta (Different versions. Beg: *Nāsāsīme camosīsaṃ...* or *Pūrentā pāramī sabbe, sabbe pacceka nāyakaṃ ...*): GB 152, PV 26, Bod.

Sukhābhiyācana-gāthā (S, Phra Buddhaghosāchārn. Beg: *Yaṃ yaṃ devamanussānaṃ...*): BC 122.

Sutta-vandanā (B.): CS.

Sumaṅgala-gāthā (Beg. *Bhavatu sabbamaṅgalaṃ rakkhantu ...* Part of Mahājayamaṅgala-gāthā.): Dham 43.

Sūvisivivaraṇa (-gāthā) (C, Sīlavaṃsa Dhammakitti. 14th c. Beg: *Taṇhaṃkaro sakirino.*): HP 159, PSC 67, LCM 1518, 1525f.

Sūvisi–vivaraṇaya-sannaya: LCM 1524.

So atthaladdho (Beg: *So atthaladdho...*) 1 verse. (S?): BC 97

Solasa-pūja-gāthā (C. Beg: *Ye dhammā hetuppabhavā...* & *Vaṇṇagandhaguṇopetaṃ...*): N 6599(2)xiv, LCM 1489ff.

Solasa-mahāṭṭhāna-vandanā-gāthā, Soḷos mahāsthāna-vandanā-gāthā, Solasa-pūja-gāthā (C. Beg: *Laṃkāya yattha paḷhumaṃ...*): N 6599(2)xiii, LCM 1486, 1496.

Śṛṅgāra-rasa-ratna-mālā (Pāḷi gāthā & Sinh. trans. On 8 dancing forms. C, 18th c?): PC 285f.

Mantras & Yantras

See UOR and LJ for more mantras & yantras.

Uṇhissa-vijaya, Uṇhīsa-vijaya, Uṇhassa-vijaya, Uṇhassa-vijaya-jātaka (-gāthā) (Ic. Different versions. Beg: *Vanditvā sirasā buddhaṃ...*): ED 401, PCS 2.25, PSA 121, EP 39f, 138.7, VP 4/139m.

Uṇhissavijaya-vaṇṇanā (Ic. Apocryphal narrative jātaka? Cf PCS 2.25): VP 4/150.4.

Mahāsānti, ~pakaraṇa-gāthā (S? Beg: *Vanditvā sugataṃ nāthaṃ.*): PCS 2.172, VP 4/139.

Sīvalī-dähäna (C. Beg: *Namo siddha sīvalī rāja...* Cf Sīvalī-pirita. *Dähäna = jhāna.*): GB 155, PV 27, 29

Sīvalī-yantraya (Start of table: *Iti pi* | *arahaṃ* | *sammā* | *vijjā* | ...): PV 28.

Ratana-yantra (Start of table: *yā a sa sa* | *nī nna kka bbe* | ...): PV 30.

Navaguṇa-yantraya (Start of table: *i* | *ti* | *ti* | *vā* | *pi* | *ga* | *so* |...): PV 31, cf UOR.

Abhisambhidāne mantra hā yantra (Beg: *Namo abhisambhidāne yutte yutte...*): PV 33.

Grammar

Kaccāyana

5.0.1 Nir-p Nirutti-piṭaka, Nirutti (Mahākaccāyana): PLB 29, 108, CPD.

5.0.2 C-nir Cullanirutti (Yamaka mahāthera) (Cf Cullanirutti at 5.4.17.): HP 185, PSC 89, PLB 105.

Cullanirutti-mañjūsā, Cullanirutti–vaṇṇanā: PLB 107.

5.0.3 Nir Mahānirutti: CPD, Kacc-Nidd/PGG 3.

Mahānirutti-saṅkhepa: PCS 4.91.

Mahānirutti-ṭīkā: PCS 4.46.

Mahānirutti-yojanā: PCS 4.97.

Nirutti-nidāna: PCS 4.68.

Nirutti–vyākyāna (~byākhyan), Bījākhyāna, Bījākhyā: PLB 108, Kacc-nidd/PGG 3, Pagan Inscription.

Nirutti-saṅgaha (B, Jambudhaja, 1651.): HP 194, PLB 55, PSC 110.

Nirutti-dīpanī, Moggallāna-dīpanī, Vuttimoggalāna-ṭīkā (B, Leḍī Sayāḍo, 1905.): PLB 97, CS, DBM 20, BLS.

Nirutti-jotaka (Nirutti-jotanā in Gv): Kacc-nidd/PGG 3.

Nirutti-jotaka-vaṇṇanā: Kacc-nidd/PGG 3.

5.0.4 Nir-m Nirutti-mañjūsā (Not Nirutti-sāra-mañjūsā [PLB] which is 5.1.111.) (Pagan, B, Saddhammaguru, maybe identical with the one who wrote Saddavutti [5.4.4]): PLB 29, PSC 89.

5.1 Kacc Kaccāyana-pakaraṇa, ~vyākaraṇa, ~gandha, ~pāṭha, Mūlakaccāyana-sutta, Mahākaccāyana, Mūlasutta (Mahā-Kaccāyana) (Sections like *Sandhikappa, Nāmakappa, Samāsa~, Dhātu~, Uṇādi~* are often independent MSS.): PL 163, PLC 179ff, HP 68f, PSC 81, CB 122f, PCS 4.15, CM xxiv, BnF 425f, ME, CW, CS.

5.1.1 Kacc-v Kaccāyana-vutti (C?, Saṅghānandi): PC 180, PSC 81, CW Burm 54?

Kasayin-piṭapota (Old extinct Sinh. transl. cited in 5.3.11(2) Mogg-pd): SL 317.

Kaccāyana-aṭṭhakathā (Saṅghanandi Sāmaṇera): PCS 4.13.

Kaccāyana-atthavinicchaya (Rājaputta mahāthera): PCS 4.21.

Pabheda-pakaraṇa: PCS 4.84.

Kaccāyana-sutta-pāṭha (First section of Kacc.): CB 100.

Suttāvāli (Kaccāyana-sutta) (? -1442): PLB 106.

Mūlakaccāyana (= Thai compilation based on Kaccāyana's grammar): PLB 28, PCS 4.96, BnF 430m.

Mūlakaccāyana-nissaya (S): BnF 826m.

(Mūlakaccāyana-) Atthavyākhyāna (B?, [Culla] Vimalabuddhi or Culla Vajirabuddhi, or C Culla-buddhi.): PLB 28, 107, PCS 4.6.

Mūlakaccāyana-atthaviggaha: PCS 4.7.

Mūlakaccāyana-gaṇṭhi (S, Mahādebakāvī): PCS 4.32.

Mūlakaccāyana-nissaya: PCS 4.70.

Kaccāyana-nissaya, ~pakaraṇa (B? Before 13th c.): Kacc-nidd/PGG3, Gv, PI.

Padamālā: PCS 4.81.

Māgadhī-vyākaraṇa (Buddhadatta): PCS 4.93, VP 4/157.

Kaccāyana-vaṇṇanā-cakka-kyan (B, Visuddhicāra, 1896.): PLB 97.

5.1.11 Mmd Mukhamatta-dīpanī, ~dīpaniya, Nyāsa, Ñāsa, Kaccāyana-(purāṇa)-ṭīkā (Pagan, B or C, Vimalabuddhi, 11–12th c.): PL 164, HP 98f, PLB 21, PLC 179, PCS 4.94, PSC 82, LCM 2103, BnF 444m, MA, RB, Ps, IO, L.

Ñāsapadīpa, Nyāsapadīpa, Nyāsapadīpa-ṭīkā, Nyāsapadīpa-hāraṇa, ~pakaraṇa (Thanbyin, B, ordered by king Narapatisithu, 12th c?): PL 164, HP 194, PLB 21, PSC 83, SPB 26, Bod, Nāma, Kacc-nidd/PGG 3.

5.1.111 Nirutti-sāra-mañjūsā (Sagaing, B, Dāṭhānāga-rājaguru, mid 17th c.) (ṭīkā on Ñāsa): PLB 55, HP 194, LCM 2112, PSC 84, Ps.

5.1.112 Mmd-pṭ Mukhamattadīpanī-purāṇaṭīkā, Saṃ-pyaṅ-ṭīkā: Ps.

Mukhamattasāra-ṭīkā, Saṃ-pyaṅ-ṭīkā (B, Mre tuiṅ saṃpyaṅ, 12th c.): PCS 4.126.

5.1.113 Mukhamattasāra (B, Arimaddana Guṇasāgara/Sāgara, 13th c.): PLB 25, 105, PCS 4.95, Ps, PGG 3, Gv, Pagan Inscription.

5.1.114 Mukhamattasāra-ṭīkā (B, Arimaddana Guṇasāgara/ Sāgara, 13th c.): PLB 25, 105, Ps.

5.1.2 Kacc-nidd Kaccāyanasutta-niddesa, Sutta-niddesa (C, Chappaṭa, 15th c.): PL 164, HP 200f, CCS, PGG 3, PLB 17f, PCS 4.129, LCM 2091, BnF 675f, PSC 85.

5.1.3 Kacc-vaṇṇ Kaccāyana-vaṇṇanā, Sandhikappa-ṭīkā: (B, Mahā Vijitāvi/Vijjāgāvī, 1626 or 1627.): HP 67f, PLB 46, PCS 4.17, PLC 180, LCM 2092, BnF 442m, PSC 86.

Kaccāyana-sandhi–visodhanī-ṭīkā: L.

Sandhi–visodhanī: PCS 4.124.

Kaccāyana-vivaraṇa: Gv.

Culla-sandhi–visodhana: PLB 105.

Sandhikappa-pakaraṇa, Sandhikappa, Sandhikaccāyanattha, Mūlakaccāyana-sandhi, Dhamma Mūn (C, Kaccāyana thera): CB 124, LCM 2089f, BnF 436m.

Kaccāyana-sandhikappa-padavigraha-sannaya (Pali-Sinh.): N 6608(41).

Kaccāyana-viggaha-ṭīkā, Galumpyan-pāḷi: PSC 86, L.

Kaccāyana-pada-vigrahava: LCM 2088f.

Kaccāyana-sūtra-bhāva-sannaya (Pali-Sinh.): 6608(50).

Bālasikkhaka (Kaccāyana-attha-gaṇṭhi?) (Ācariya Sumedha): PCS 4.88, VP 4/150.5.

5.1.4 Rūp Rūpasiddhi, Mahārūpasiddhī, Padarūpasiddhi (I, Buddhapiya thera/Damiḷavasu Dīpaṅkara, 13th c. [or 11th c.; see N.]): PL 164, PLC 220f, HP 123f, PLC 220f, PSC 87, LCM 2135f, SH 159, BnF 496m, N 6608(25), PLB 105, CS, Ps.

Mūlakaccāyana-rūpasiddhi: PCS 4.103.

Rūpasiddhi-sutta-pāṭha (Part, i.e., suttas, of Rūpasiddhi): N 6608(25), PSC 87.

5.1.41 Rūp-ṭ (Mahā-) Rūpasiddhi-ṭīkā (I, Buddhapiya, 13th c.) (= Rūpasiddhi-atthavaṇṇanā, Rūpasiddhi-aṭṭhakathā?): HP 124, PCS 4.47, PLC 221, LCM 2139, PSC 87, PLB 105, Ps.

5.1.42 Kaccāyana-rūpa-dīpanī, Sandhi-rūpadīpanī, Mūlakaccāyana-sandhi-yojanā Mūlakaccāyana-yojanā (CM, Ñaṇakitti, 15th c.): PSA 64, PCS 4.99, LN 123, 128, BnF 502f, 850.

5.1.4(3) Rūp-sn (Mahā-) Rūpasiddhi-sannaya, Rūpasiddhi-gätapada (12–13th c.): N 6608(24), SL 317, PSA 16, PLC 221f, LCM 2137, Vs 73, 86, PSC 87.

5.1.4(4) Sandeha-vighātinī, Rūpasiddhi–vistara-sannaya, ~vyākhyāva (Later than Rūp-sn): HP 198, SL 317, Vs 86, PSC 87.

Culla-rūpasiddhi: LCM 2068.

Rūpasiddhi-nāmika-saddamālā, ~varanägilla.: PSC 87

5.1.5 Bālāv Bālāvatāra, Bālāvatāra-gaṇṭhipada, Bālāvatāra-gaṇṭhipadatthavinicchayasāra (C, Dhammakitti Saṅgharāja [Gv: Vācissara], 14th c.): PL 164, HP 20f, PLC 243/325, PCS 4.89, LCM 2060, PSC 88, SH 160, BnF 534f m, CM 69, CS, Ps.

5.1.51 Bālāv-(p)-ṭ Bālāvatāra-(purāṇa)-ṭīkā (B, Uttama): PSC 88, PLB 22, Ps.

5.1.52 Subodhikā-ṭīkā, Bālāvatāra-ṭīkā (C, H. Sumaṅgala, 1892): PSC 88.

5.1.5(3) Gaḍalādeṇi-sannaya, Bālāvatāra-purāṇa-vyākhyānaya, Bālāvatāra-saṅkṣepa-sannaya, Bālāvatāra-saññaka. (Gaḍalādeṇiya, C, Devarakṣita Jayabāhu Dhammakīrti II, late 14th c.): HP 54f, N 6608(30, 32), PLC 244/325, Vs 86, SL 318, SH 335, CM xxxii, PSC 88.

5.1.5(4)1–2 Okaṅdapola-sannaya, Bālāvatāra-liyana-sannē, Liyana-sannaya, Padasiddhi-sannaya (C, Diyahunnata Dhammajoti, 18th c.): HP 101f, N 6608(35), PLC 244, LCM 2064f, Vs 86, PSC 88.

Bālāvatāra-saṅgraha, Bālāvatāra-sūtra-saṅgrahava (C, Siṭināmaluvē Dhammajoti, 18th c.): HP 22–3, N 6608(5), PLC 284, Vs 87, PSC 88, SL 318, BSL 110.

Bālāvatāra-vyākhyānayasannaya, Bālāvatāra-balana-sannaya, Balana-sannaya (C, Dhammadāsa, 18th c.): N 6608(31, 33), BSL 110, Vs 87.

Sāratthasaṅgaha (=Bālāvatāra-ṭīkā) (Tipiṭaka thera) (Cf Sāratthasaṅgaha /? = Saddatthabhedacintā-navaṭīkā by Tipiṭakadhara Abhaya thera below 5.4.1,3.): PCS 4.127.

Bālāvatāra-gaṇṭhi-sāraya, Sugaṇṭhi-sāra (-sannaya) (C, G. Saṅgharakkhita, before 1756.): N 6608(16), LCM 206f, SH 163, Vs 87, PSC 88, BSL 110.

Bālāvatāra-vaṇṇanā: PSC 88.

Bālāvatāra-gāthā-sannaya: SH 332.

Bālāvatāra-sūtra-nirdeśaya, Bālāvatāra-kiyana-sannaya (C, 18th c.): N 6608(2), SH 336, CM 118.

Saddanīti

5.2 Sadd Saddanīti, ~vyākaraṇa, ~pakaraṇa (B, Aggavaṃsa, 1154.): PL 164, PLB 16f, HP 126, LCM 2146, PSC 103, PLC 185, CB 57, BnF 537m, Ps.

Mahāsaddanīti & Cullasaddanīti (B, Aggavaṃsa) (Subdivison of Sadd into 2 parts.): PCS 4.34, 4.92, LCM 2069, 2099.

5.2 Saddanīti-padamālā & Sadda-nīti-dhātu-mālā & Saddanīti-suttamālā (B, Aggavaṃsa) (Subdivison of Sadd into 3 parts.): PLB 16, BnF 693, CPD, CS, Ps.

5.2.1 Sadd-ṭ Saddanīti-ṭīkā, -saṃvaṇṇanā (B, Paññāsāmī, mid 19th c.): PLB 93, PSC 103, Ps.

5.2.2 Sadd-ns Saddanīti-nissaya: CPD.

Saddanīti-sutta-vaṇṇanā: PSC 103.

Saddanīti-samāsa-pakaraṇa: BnF 692.

Moggallāna

5.3 Mogg Moggallāna, ~sutta, ~vyākaraṇa, Mūla-moggallāna, Sadda-lakkhaṇa (-pāḷi), Māgadha-saddalakkhaṇa (= original author's title of the *sutta* & *vutti* combined), Sadda-sattha, Moggallāna-sadda (C, Moggallāna, late 12th c.): PL 165, HP 95f, PSC 104, PLC 179, 186f, SL 315, PCS 4.119, CS, Ps.

5.3.1 Mogg-v Moggallāna-vutti, Vutti-moggallāna, Moggallāna-sutta-vutti, Vipulatthapakāsinī (C, Moggallāna, 12th c.): N 6608(28), BnF 515m, LCM 2100f, PLC 187, BnF 515m, PLB 105, PSC 105, CS, Ps.

5.3.11 Mogg-p Moggallāna-pañcikā, Vutti–vaṇṇanā-pañcikā (Extinct. C, Moggallāna, 12th c.): PL 165, PLC 187, PSC 105, PLB 106, SL 316, CS.

5.3.111 Sāratthavilāsinī, Pañcikā-ṭīkā (=? Susaddhasiddhi, 5.3.4, see PLC 200.) (C, Saṅgharakkhita, 12–13th c.): PSC 104f, PLC 200.

5.3.11(2) Mogg-pd Moggallāna-pañcikāpradīpaya, Pañcikāpradīpaya (C, Toṭagamuva Rāhula, 1460) (In Sinhala, has many quotations from Pāḷi works.): HP 96, 109f, SL 316, LCM 2125, N 6608(46), PLC 187f, 251, CM xxxiii, PSC 104f, Vs 87, 102f, PLB 105.

5.3.12 Moggallāna-(vyākaraṇa)-tīkā (C, Vācissara, 12–13th c.): HP 192, PLC 204, Ps.

5.3.1(3) Mogg-sn Virita-sannē, Moggalānā-virita-sannaya, Moggallāna-vutti-sannaya: Vs 87, SL 316, PSC 104, LCM 2102.

Saddalakkhaṇa-virita-saṅkhepa-sannaya: N 6608(49).

Nāma-varanāgillak, Moggallāna-varanāgillak (Pali-Sinh.): N 66008(55).

5.3.2 Pds Padasādhana, Padasādhaka, Moggallāna-saddattha-ratnākara (-padattha), Moggallāna-padasādhana (C, Piyadassi, 12–13th c.): HP 103f, N 6608(11), PCS 83, PLC 187, 205, PSC 107, BnF 516m, CS.

5.3.21 Pds-ṭ Buddhipasādanī, Padasādhana-ṭīkā (C, T. Rāhula Vācissara, 15th c.): HP 34–5, 96, PLC 205, 252f, LCM 2115, PSC 107, CM xxxiii.

5.3.2(2) Pds-sn Padasādhana-sannaya (C, Vanaratana Ānanda, 13th c.): HP 104f, LCM 2114, N 6608(10), PLC 205, SL 316, Vs 87, CM xxix, PSC 107.

Padasādhana-liyana-sannaya, ~kiyana-sannaya: LCM 2113, N 6608(11 ii).

Padasādhana-padasiddhi-sannaya (Before 16th c?): N 6608(26).

Padasādhana-sūtra (Only the sūtras of the Padasādhana.): N 6608(27).

Padasādhana-sūtra-sannaya: N 6608(27).

5.3.3. Padāvatāra (SI?, Coḷiyācariya Sāriputta, 12th c.?) (Extinct?): PC 190, SW.

5.3.4 Susaddasiddhi (See 5.3.111) (C, Saṅgharakkhita, 12–13 c.) (Extinct?): HP 200, PLC 198, 200, PSC 109, Nāma xxxiv, PLC 284f.

5.3.5 Pay Payogasiddhi (-pāṭha) (C, Vanaratana Medhaṅkara, first half 13th c.): PL 165, HP 96, 117, N 6608(9), PSC 108, PLC 231f, LCM 2128f, CS.

Payogasiddhi-sannaya: PSC 108.

5.3I Mogg-VII (Moggallāna-) ṇvādi: PSC 106, Ps.

5.3I.1 Mogg- v VII (Moggallāna-) ṇvādi–vutti (C, Saṅgharakkhita Mahāsāmi, 12–13th c.): PSC 106, PLB 106, Ps.

Saddatthabhedacintā

5.4.1 Saddatthabhedacintā (Pagan, B, Saddhammasiri thera, 12–14th c.): PLB 20, 22f, PSA 63, PCS 4.117, PSC 101, BnF 510m, RB, Ps.

5.4.1,1 Saddatthabhedacintā-porāṇaṭīkā, Saddatthabhedacintā-dīpanī, Mahā-ṭīkā (Pagan, B, Abhaya, 12–14th c.): PLB 22, PCS 4.86, BnF 510, HP 196f, Ps.

5.4.1,2 Saddatthabhedacintā-majjhima-ṭīkā: CPD.

5.4.1,3 Saddatthabhedacintā-navaṭīkā, Saddatthabhedacintā-abhinava-mahā-ṭīkā (B, Vimalavaṃsālaṅkāra): RB, Ps.

Sāratthasaṅgaha (? = Saddatthabhedacintā-navaṭīkā) (Tipiṭakadhara Abhaya thera) (Cf. Sāratthasaṅgaha/ Bālāvatāra-ṭīkā by Tipiṭaka thera under 5.1.5(4)1–2.): PCS 4.128.

Saddatthabhedacintā-ṭīkā I (Tipiṭaka Dharāphaya): Ps.

Saddatthabhedacintā-ṭīkā II: Ps.

Saddatthabhedacintā-dīpanī-culla-ṭīkā: PCS 4.59.

Saddatthabhedacintā-dīpanī (B, Suvaṇṇaguhā, 14th c.): PSC 101.

Saddatthabhedacintā-padakamma-yojanā, Padakkama, Saddatthabhedacintā-yojanā (CM, Dhammasenāpati, 15th c.): PSA 63, PCS 4.79.

Gūḷhasāra-saddatthabheda, Saddatthabhedacintā-ṭīkā: BnF 510.

14 Minor Texts

5.4.2 Kaccāyanasāra (Thatōn, B, Mahāyasa [J] or Dhammānanda [Gv], 14–15th c.): PL 164, HP 67, 124, 192, PLB 36f, CM 68, PSC 90, EP 78, BnF 500m, Bod, Ps.

5.4.2.1 Kaccayānasāra-ṭīkā (Thatōn, B, Mahāyasa, 14–15th c.): PL 164, PLB 36f, BnF 500.

5.4.2.2 Kaccāyanasāra-purāṇaṭīkā, Kaccāyanasāra-atthayojanā (Pagan, B, Siri Saddhammavilāsa, 13th c.): Ps, Nāma.

5.4.2.3 Kaccāyanasāra-navaṭīkā, ~abhinavaṭīkā, Sammoha-vināsini, Saddhammanāsinī (Pagan, B, Siri Saddhammavilāsa, 13th c.): PLB 26, 37, HP 198, PSC 90, Ps, Nāma lxxxvi.

Sammoha-vighātani (Commentary on Sandhikappa.): BnF 443, 528, 736f.

5.4.2.4 Kaccayānasāra-yojanā (Kaḷyāṇasāra): CCM 68, BnF 500, Ps.

Kaccayānasāra-atthayojanā: BnF 533.

Kaccāyanasāra-vaṇṇanā: PCS 4.20.

Kaccāyanasāravaṇṇanā-ṭīkā: PCS 4.39.

Kaccāyanasāravaṇṇanā, Kaccāyanasāra-navaṭīkā (Rataññū bhikkhu): PCS 4.64. EP 78.2.

Kaccāyanasāra-sannaya (Before 1457): HP 124.

5.4.4 Sadda-vutti, Saddavutti-pakāsaka (Pagan, B, Saddhammapāla/Saddhamma- guru, HP: before 17th c. PLB: 14th c. If S. is the author of the Nett-ṭ [2.7.2,12] then maybe 16th

c. Cf PLB 46 where S. lives at Taungu.): PLB 29, 46, HP 197, PCS 4.122, BnF 704, PSC 98, Ps.

5.4.4,1 Saddavutti-abhinavaṭīkā (B, Jāgarācariya, 18th c.?): PSC 98, PLB 29, Nāma xcii.

5.4.4,2 Saddavutti-purāṇaṭīkā, Saddavutti–vitthāraṭīkā (Pagan, B, Sāriputta[ra]): PCS 4.55, PSC 98, L, Ps.

Saddavutti-saṅkhepaṭīkā (Pagan, B, Sāriputta): PCS 4.56.

5.4.4,3 Saddavutti-navaṭīkā: PLB 29, Ps.

5.4.4,4 Saddavutti–vivaraṇa: PLB 29, CPD.

5.4.5 Saddabindu (-pakaraṇa) (B, Rājaguru Nārada thera [not by King Kyacvā/Kya-swa in 1234], 1481.): HP 196, N 6608(15), PSA 18, PLB 23, PCS 4.118, LCM 2143, PSC 99, CS, PL164 in App. I, Ps, JPTS XI 79–109.

5.4.5,1 Līnattha-sūdanī (-purāṇaṭīkā), Līnattha-visodhanī, Sadda-bindu-(saṅkhepa)-ṭīkā, Saddabindu-vaṇṇanā (Pagan, B, Arimaddana Ñāṇavilāsa, 16th c.): HP 189 & 196, PCS 4.52, N 6608(15), PSC 99, LCM 2144, Ps.

Saddabindu-līnatthavaṇṇanā: L I & II.

5.4.5,2 Ganthasāra, Ganthasāra-abhinavaṭīkā, Saddabindu-abhinava- ṭīkā, Saddabindu-vinicchaya (Haripuñjaya, B, Saddhammakitti Mahāphussadeva 15–16th c.): PSA 18, 65, PLB 25, PSC 99, PL 164 in App. I, JPTS XI 79–109.

Saddabindu-ṭīkā (-vitthāra) (Ñāṇamaṅgala thera): PCS 4.53.

Saddabindu-khuddaka-ṭīkā: PCS 4.28.

5.4.6 Saddasāratthajālinī, Sāratthajālinī, Jālinī (B, Kaṇṭakakhīpa Nāgita, 1357.): HP 126f, PLB 27, PCS 4.123, PSC 102, LCM 2147, BnF 511m, Bod, Ps, L.

5.4.6,1 Saddasāratthajālinī-ṭīkā, Jālinī-ṭīkā, Sāra-mañjūsā (B?, Vepullabuddhi, 14th c. See PLB 28.): HP 127, PLB 28, PCS 4.57, BnF 531, PSC 102, VH 244, Nāma lxii, Ps.

5.4.7 Sambandhacintā (C, Saṅgharakkhita Mahāsāmi, 12–13th c.): HP 135, N 6608(40), PCS 4.125, PSC 100, PLC 199, BnF 518m, Ps.

5.4.7,1 Sambandhacintā-ṭīkā (C, 12–13th c., Vācissara): HP 199, PSC 100, PLC 204, BnF 520, Nāma lvii.

5.4.7,2 Sambandhacintā-ṭīkā (Pagan, B, Abhaya, 13–14th c.): HP 136, PLB 22, PSC 100, PLC 199, Ps.

Sambandhacintā-ṭīkā (C, Tipiṭaka Dharāphaya): Ps, Nāma lvii.

Canda-sārattha-ṭīkā, Sambandhacinta-ṭīkā (B, Saddhammañāṇa, 14th c. *Canda-* is prob. a Pāḷization of Skt *Candra*, i.e., the Skt grammarian Candragomin.): HP 185, PLC 198.

5.4.7,(3) Sambandha-cintā-sannaya (C, Vanavāsi Gotama, 13th c.): HP 136, N 6608(52), PLC 199, 220, PSC 100, SL 316.

5.4.8 Vibhattyattha (-pakaraṇa) (Pagan, B, PLB 25: daughter of king Kyacvā, 13th c; CPD & PLB 26: Saddhammañāṇa, 14th c.): PLB 25f, LCM 2170, PSC 93, Ps. (Cf. PCS 4.112).

5.4.8,1 Vibhattyattha-dīpanī, Vibhattyattha-ṭīkā, -vaṇṇanā (B.): PSC 93, Nāma lxxiii, Ps.

5.4.8,2 Vibhattyattha-ṭīkā (Sutabuddhi?, 19th c.): PSC 93.

Vibhattyattha-ṭīkā (B. Leḍī Sayāḍo, 19th–20th c.): BLS.

Vibhattyattha-jotanī (B, Vimalābhidhaja Rājaguru): PSC 93, PI.

Vibhatti-kathā: PCS 4.112, ME 2, LCM 2168, Gv.

Vibhattikathā-vaṇṇanā: LCM 2169.

Vibhattikathā-ṭīkā: PCS 4.50.

Vibhattipabheda-vivaraṇa: PCS 4.113.

Coda-vibhatti, Coda-sandhi–vibhatti, Vibhatti-ākhyāta (S? Nissaya only?): BnF 523f.

5.4.9 Vācavācaka, Vaccavācaka (Pagan, B, Dhammadassī, 14th c.): HP 201f, PCS 4.104, BnF 704, PLB 22, PSC 95, Ps.

5.4.9,1 Vācavācaka-ṭīkā, Vācavācaka-vaṇṇanā (B, Saddhammananda/-nandi, 1769 c.): HP 202, PCS 4.105, PLB 22, PSC 95, Nāma xc, Ps.

5.4.9,2 Vācavācaka-dīpanī (B): PLB 22, Ps.

(5.4.9,3 Vācavācaka-ṭīkā (B): PLB 22, Ps.

Vācavācaka-ṭīkā (B. Leḍī Sayāḍo, 19th–20th c.): BLS.

Vācavācaka-vaṇṇanā (B): PLB 22.

Vācavācaka-nissaya (B): PSC 94.

(Vacca-) Vācakopadesa (Panyā, B, Mahāvijitāvī, 16th c.): PLB 46, PCS 4.106, PSC 94.

Vācakopadesa-ṭīkā (Sagaing, B, Vijitāvī, 1606.): PLB 46, PSC 94.

5.4.10 Gandhābhāraṇa-sāra, Ganthābhāraṇa, Gaṇṭhābharaṇa, Gandhābhāraṇa, Gaṇḍābhāraṇa, Nipātattha-vibhāviṇi (Khema, B, Ariyavaṃsa Dhammasenāpati, 1436–7 c.): HP 187, PLB 43, CB 57, PCS 4.31, PSA 23, PSC 97, BnF 499m, ME, Ps.

5.4.10,1 Ganthābhāraṇa-(abhinava)-ṭīkā (B, Jāgarācariya, 18th c.?): PSC 97, BnF 696 (nissaya), L, Ps.

5.4.10,2 Ganthābhāraṇa-(purāṇa)-ṭīkā (-vitthāra), Gandhābhāraṇatthadīpaṇī (CM or Vientiane, Suvaṇṇaraṃsi

Saṅgharāja, 1584 or 85): HP 187, CB 58f, PSA 23, 64, PCS 4.43, PSC 97, BnF 505, EP 72, ME 2, Ps, Nāma lxxviif.

Ganthābhāraṇa-saṅkhepa-ṭīkā: PSA 65, PCS 4.44, VP 6/20.

5.4.10,3 Ganthābhāraṇa-yojana: Ps.

5.4.10,4 (Ganthābhāraṇa-sāra)?= 5.4.10?: CPD.

Ganthābhāraṇa-dīpanī-ṭīkā: L.

Ganthābhāraṇa-nissaya: PSC 97.

Ganthābhāraṇa-dhātupāṭhaya: PSC 97.

Gandhābhāraṇasāra-atthavyākkhyāna (S?): CB 58, ME 4.

Atthavyākhāyana (B?, Cullavajira, before Kacc-nidd): Kacc-nid/ PGG 3–4, Gv, PI.

Gandhābhāraṇa-sannaya, Ganthābhāraṇa-sāraya: PSC 97, CB 57.

5.4.11 Ganthaṭṭhi-pakaraṇa, Gandhatthi, Gandhaṭṭhi ((HP: I. PLB: Pagan, B, Maṅgala, 14th c. In PCS the author is Sirivipullabuddha of Parampura): HP 187, PLB 26, PCS 4.30, BnF 504m, 701, PSC 96, Ps.

Ganthaṭṭhi-ṭīkā (Tikapaññā thera): PCS 4.43.

5.4.13 Kaccāyanabheda, Kaccāyanabheda-dīpikā, ~dīpanī (B, Mahāyasa [or Dhammānanda], 14th c.): HP 187, PLB 36, PCS 4.16, LCM 2081, PSC 91, BnF 498m, VH 244, Ps.

5.4.13,1 Kaccāyanabheda-purāṇaṭīkā, Sāratthavikāsinī, Kaccāyanabhedadīpanī- vaṇṇanā (Sagaing, B, Ariyālaṅkāra II, 1606): HP 188, 199, PLB 55, PSC 91, BnF 498, Nāma lxvi, Ps.

5.4.13,2 Kaccāyanabheda-ṭīkā, ~navaṭīkā, ~mahāṭīkā, Kaccāyanabheda-vaṇṇanā (B, Uttamasikkha, 1669.): HP 188, PSC 91, LCM 2082, BnF 532f, Ps.

5.4.13,(3) Kaccāyanabheda-sannaya (C, Jinavaṃsa Paññāsāra, 19th c.): N 6608(39), PSC 91.

Kaccāyanabheda-vyākhāva: PSC 91.

5.4.14 Kārika (-pāḷi) (Pagan, B, Dhammasenādhipati, 11th c.): PLB 15f, 105, PCS 4.27, PSC 92, Ps.

5.4.14,1 Kārika-ṭīkā (B?, Dhammasenāpati, 11th c.): PLB 16 n. 1, 105, S 4.41, PSC 92, Ps.

Kārika-(attha)-vaṇṇanā: PSC 92.

Kārikāva sanna sahita (C, Ñāṇatilaka, 1897): Printed edition.

5.4.15 Etimāsami-dīpikā, Etamāsami-dīpanī (B, Dhammasenāpati, 11th c.): PLB 16, CPD.

5.4.15,1 Etimāsami-dīpikā-ṭīkā: CPD.

5.4.16 **Sambandha-mālinī** (Pagan, B, Saddhammalaṅkāra, before 1442.): PLB 29, 106, Ps.

5.4.17 **(Abhinava-)** Culla-nirutti (-pakaraṇa) (Saddhammābhilaṅkāra thera) (Cf 5.0.2): HP 185f, LCM 2067, BnF 495.

Mañjūsā-ṭīkā-vyākhyāna: PLB 107.

5.4.18 **Nirutti-bheda,** Niruttibheda-saṅgaha (pāṭha) (Ava, Ū Budha, first half 19th c.): BnF 703, RB, CPD.

5.4.19 **Bālappabodhana,** Bālappabodhanī, Bālappabodhi (B?, before 1442.): HP 185, PCS 4.87, PLB 107, N 6608 (1), LCM 2055f, CM 72, PSC 111, BnF 507, VH, Ps.

5.4.19,1 **Bālappabodhana-ṭīkā,** Vicitra-sāra (Ñāṇa thera): HP 185, PCS 4.109, LCM 2058, BnF 507m, PSC 111, IO 149.

Varasāra, Bālappabodhana-suganṭhisāra,? Bālappabodhana-ṭīkā II (Dhammapāla) (A ṭīkā on 5.4.19,1 acc. to N, but might be another ṭīkā on 5.4.19.): N 6608(1).

Bālappabodhana-sannaya: PSC 111, N 6608(1).

5.4.20 **Padavibhāga** (B, Ñāṇa/Ñāṇālaṅkāra, 18th c.): PLB 71, CPD.

5.4.21 Padacintā: Ps.

5.4.22 Cādyattha-dīpanī: Ps.

5.4.23 Akkhara-kosalla: Ps.

5.4.23,1 Akkhara-kosalla-ṭīkā: Ps.

5.4.24 Akkhara-sammoha-cchedanī: PLB 106, Ps.

5.4.25 Akkhara-bheda: Ps.

5.4.26 **Akkhara-visodhanī** (B, Paññasāmi thera, mid 19th c.): PLB 93.

Unclassified Grammars

Akhyāta-pada, Akhyāta-pada-mālā, Akhyāta-varanänagilla (Pāḷi–Sinh.) (C, by Vagägoḍa thera on request of Moraṭota Dhammakkhandha thera [N] or by Vaggatthala/Vagegoda Dhammakkhandha [D], 18th c.): N 6608(13,19, 42), LCM 2044f, PSC 112, BSL 110.

Akhyāta-pada-sannaya: N 6608(19), PSC 112.

Attha-dīpa-nāma-pakaraṇa (Dhammapāla): PCS 4.5.

Ākhyāta-varanägilla, Akhyāta-mālā (-pāḷi) (C, Attaragama Baṇḍāra, 18th c.): N 6608(13), PSC 112.

Ākhyāta-Varanägili-sannaya: N 6608(42), LCM 2050.

Ākhyāta-padayojanā-sannaya: N 6608(44).

Upasarga-nipāta-sannaya: LCM 2163.

Kalāpa (Pāḷi translation of Skt Kātantra) (Pagan, B, Saddhammañāṇa, 14th c.): PLB 26, 106 (BnF 685f = Burm. lang.)

Kāraka-puppha-mañjarī (C, Attaragama Baṇḍāra, 18th c.): HP 72f, PCS 4.25, N 6608(38), PLC 283, PSC 100m, LCM 2093, CM xxxix, SL.

Kāraka-puṣpa-mañjarī-sannē (C, Attaragama Baṇḍāra, 18th c.): PSC 100, 113, HP 73, SL 316.

Kāraka-puṣpa-mañjarī-vyākhyāva: PSC 113.

Kāraka-saṅkhepa: PCS 4.26.

Gati-pakaraṇa-pāḷī (Saddhammacula thera): PCS 4.29.

Nāma-mālā (C, Waskaduwe Subhūti, 1876): PCS 252, 310.

Nava-niyama-dīpanī (B, Jagarabhidhaja, late 19th c.): PLB 96.

Nipāta-dīpanī: PCS 4.67.

Nepātika-vaṇṇanā (Pali-Sinh): LCM 2111.

Pāli–vaiyākaraṇa (S, Somdet Mahāsamaṇa Chao): PCS 4.77.

Paṭicchanna-pakaraṇa: PCS 4.78.

Pūraṇa-padasandhi, Padapūraṇa-sandhi: PCS 4.80.

Padamañjarī: CS.

Padamālā-kita-viggaha-sandhi: PCS 4.82.

Padasiddhi-kramayak: LCM 2116.

Padabhedaya (C, Saddhammajotipāla-Ñāṇanandatissa, 1890): Printed edition.

Pañcikālaṅkāra (12 c.): PC 190.

Pāḷi–vacana: LCM 2117.

Pāḷi–vyākaraṇa: LCM 2120–4.

Mahānaya-sāra-vilāsinī (C, Saddhammacakka Mahāsāmī, mid 18th c.): PCS 4.90.

Manohāra (B, Dhammasenāpati, 11th c.): PLB 16.

Rūpamālā, Rūpamālā-vaṇṇanā, Pāli-nāma-varanāgilla, Varanāgilla, Vibhattyattha-pakāsinī (C, Sumaṅgala? (see BnF and N 12). Beg: *Buddhādiccaṃ namassāmi...* or *Buddho buddhā he buddha...* There are different versions and titles of this and the next 3 entries appear mixed up.): BnF 517, CC 70, LCM 2105, 2133f, N 6609(12, 28; 31), PSC 112.

Ākhyāta-rūpamālā, Rūpamālā (C, Välanvitta Saraṇankara, 1760. Pali-Sinh. Beg. *Jinendrasīhaṃ abhivanditvā...*): HP 195, PLC 281, LCM 2046–9, 2133f, PSC 112.

Tunliṅguyehi Rūpamālā (Pāḷi gāthās & sannaya. Beg. *Evaṃ surāsuranaro...*): N 6609(28).

Gāthā-rūpamālāva, Nāmavaranägili-gāthā-sannaya (C.): LCM 2077f, 2108.

Rūpabheda-pakāsanī (B, Jambudhaja/Jambudīpadhaja, 17th c.): PLB 56, CW Burm 123.

Liṅgatthavivaraṇa (Pagan, B, Subhūtacanda, before 1442): PLB 22, 105.

Liṅgatthavivaraṇa-pakāsaka (Pagan, B, Ñāṇasāgara): PLB 22.

Liṅgatthavivaraṇa-ṭīkā (Pagan, B, Uttama, before 1442): PLB 22, 105.

Liṅgatthavivaraṇa-vinicchaya (B): PLB 22.

Saṃvaṇṇanā-nāya-dīpanī (B, Jambudhaja, mid 17th c.): PLB 55, HP 198.

Saṭkāraka-vibhāgaya: LCM 2149.

Saddakārika: PLB 107.

Saddavācakalakkhaṇa: PCS 4.120.

Saddavidhāna-lakkhaṇa: PCS 4.121.

Saddavidhānalakkhaṇa-ṭīkā: PCS 4.54.

Saddamālā, Śabdamālā (C, A. Baṇḍāra, 1779): HP 125f, N 6608(51), PLC 283, PSC 112, CM xxxix.

Saddamālā-sannaya, Śabdamālāva (A. Baṇḍāra, 1779): N 6608(17), PLC 283, LCM 2142.

Saddākaṅkhāvitaraṇī (B?): BnF 844.

Sandhidīpanī: PSC 114.

Sandhivigraha: LCM 2148.

Sudhīra-mukhamaṇḍana, Samāsa-cakka, Sīhala-mukhamaṇḍana (C, Attaragama Baṇḍāra, 18th c.): HP 150, N 6608(14), PLC 283, SH 164, PCS 4.132, LCM 2160, PSC 114, CM xxxix, VP 6/41.1.

Samāsa-rūpa-dīpanī, Samāsa-yojanā, Yojanā-samāsa (Ic): PSA 98, BnF 635.

Samāsa-taddhita-dīpanī (B?, before 1442.): PLB 106.

Mūla-viggaha-samāsa (S?): BnF 513.

Soḍi-sannaya, Mūlakkhara-vikāsani (-padārtha), Akṣara-mālāva (C, Nāgasena, 18th c.?): SH 165, LCM 2155f, N 6608(56).

Orthoepy

Akkharajāta-saṅkhyā: PCS 4.1.

Uccāraṇadīpanī (-gaṇṭhi) (Dhammarakkhita thera) (= Uccāraṇa-vidhi-dīpanī?): PCS 4.11.

Uccāraṇadīpanī-ṭīkā: PCS 4.37.

Verbal Roots

5.5.1 Dhātup Dhātu-pāṭha: PL 166, LCM 2070, HP 186, PSC 112, BnF 487.

Dhātupāṭha-vilāsiniyā (C.): CS.

Dhātupāṭha-sannaya: M 6609(38), PSC 122.

5.5.2 Dhātum Dhātumañjūsā, Kaccāyanadhātumañjūsā, Kaccāyanamañjūsā (C, Yakkhaḍḍileṇa Sīlavaṃsa, 14th c.): PL 166, HP 186, N 6609(3–4), PLC 237, PCS 4.14, SH 166, CM 71, BnF 487m, LCM 2083f, PSC 118, Bod, CS.

Dhātumañjūsā-artha-vyākhyāva: PSC 118.

Kaccāyanadhātumañjūsā-sannaya: N 6609(3).

Dhātvattha-dīpika (B?, Aggadhamma/Aggadhammālaṅkāra, 19th c.): BnF 489, PSC 119.

Dhātvattha-dīpanī, Dhātuvattha-dīpanī, Dhātvatthavaṇṇanā: PSC 120, PCS 4.60.

Dhātvattha-saṅgaha (B, Visuddhicāra, late 19th c.): PLB 97.

Dhātu-akkhara: PCS 4.61.

Dhātu-samuccaya (Ñāṇasāgara thera): PCS 4.62.

Nayalakkhaṇa-dīpanī (B, Vicittācāra, latter half of 18th c.): HP 193, Nāma lxxiv f.

Nayalakkhaṇa-vibhāvanī (Vicittācāra thera. Sinhalese Ms. Probably identical with preceding title.): PCS 4.63.

Nūtanadhātumālā (B, Kalyāṇābhivaṃsa, 1907): PSC 121.

Dictionaries, Lexicons

5.6.1 Abh Abhidhāna-padīpikā (-pāṭha), Pāḷi-nighaṇḍu (C, Sarogāma Moggallāna, 12th c.): PL 166f, HP 7f, PCS 4.9, SH 168, PLC 187ff, LCM 2040f, CB 77, CM 73, PSC 115, N 6609(2), PLB 105, BnF, CS, Ps.

5.6.1,1 Abh-pṭ Abhidhānappadīpikā-purāṇaṭīkā (C, Vācissara, 12–13th c.): PL 167, HP 184, PLC 188f, PLB 105.

5.6.1,1 Abh-nṭ Abhidhānappadīpikā-(nava)-ṭīkā, Abhidhānappadīpikā-saṃvaṇṇanā, Abhidhānappadīpikā-atthavaṇṇanā (B, Paññasāmi, 14th c.) (Prob. same as 5.6.1,2, but revised by Paññasāmi according to colophon; see PL 167: App. I .): HP 184, PL 167 in App. I, PSC 116, Ps, LCM 2043, CS.

5.6.1,2 Abhidhānappadīpikā-saṃvaṇṇanā, ~vaṇṇanā, ~ṭīkā, Caturaṅga-dhāriṇī (-ṭīkā) (Vijayapura, B, Caturaṅgabalāmacca,

1313): PL 167, PCS 4.33, PLC 189, PSC 116, RB, PL 172 App. I, BnF 493m, Ps.

5.6.1,(3) Abh-sn Abhidhānappadīpikā-sannaya, Nighaṇḍu-sannē (12th c.): HP 184, N 6609 (26), Vs 87, PLC 187f, LCM 2042, SL 321, BnF 540.

Abhidhānappadīpikā-sūci, Nigha-ṇḍusūciya (C, W. Subhūti, 19th c.): PCS 4.10, PLB 105, PSC 116.

Abhidhānappadīpikā-padārtha, Abhidhānappadīpikā-vyākhyānaya: PSC 116, L.

Abhidhānappadīpikā-nissaya: PSC 116.

5.6.2 Ekakkh Ekakkhara-kosa, Akkharakosa-nava-pāḷi (Taungu, B, Saddhammakitti, PLB: around 1525. HP & PL: 1465 c.): PL 167, HP 186, 197, PLB 45, PCS 4.12, LCM 2074, PSC 117, BnF 494m.

5.6.2,1 Ekakkh-ṭ Ekakkharakosa-ṭīkā, Sāra-saṃvaṇṇanā (B, 15th c.): HP 186, PCS 4.38, PSC 117, BnF 494.

Akkharakosa-purāṇa, Akkharakosa-pāḷi: BnF 494.

Akkharakosa-nava, Ekakkharakosa: BnF 494.

Ekakkharakosa-sannaya: PSC 117.

Akkhara-mālā (C, Nāgasena, 18th c.): PC 285.

Akkhara-mālā-sannē (C, Nāgasena, 18th c.): PC 285.

Akkhara-gaṇṭhi (Part of Caturāsītidhammakkhandha-sahassa-saṃvaṇṇanā) (La?): PSA 126.

Akkhara-pada-mañjūsā: Kacc-nidd/PGG 3.

Aṭṭhakathā-sūci (C, Kosgoda Sirisumedha, 1961–62. Only entries *a* to *e*?): Printed edition.

Sabbadhamma-vaṇṇanā, Sabbadhammādikāra (S?): PCS 2. 30, VP 4/130.

Gamanakāra-vaṇṇanā (S?): VP 4/130.

Paribhāvaggakāra (S?): VP 4/130.

Khandasantānakāra (S?): VP 4/130.

Adhigamakāra (S?): VP 4/130.

Saccābhisambodhanakāra (S?): VP 4/130.

Sabbaññukāra (S?): VP 4/130.

Ratanamālābhidhāna: PCS 4.101.

Vidagdhamukhamaṇḍana (Skt & Pkt verses. On riddles & words with multiple meanings.) (I?, Dhammadāsa, before 11th c.): PCS 4.111, DPPN 879.

Vidaggamukhamaṇḍana, Vidagdha~, Vidadhi~, Vidattha~ (Pāḷi translation of the above Skt work. B, Vepullabuddhi, 14th c.): PCS 4.111, PLB 28, VP 6/40.1, DPPN 879.

Vidaggamukhamaṇḍana-ṭīkā (B, Nava-vimalabuddhi): Gv.

Vidagdhamukhamaṇḍanadīpanī-ṭīkā (Vajirapañña.): PCS 4.49, VP 6/40.2

Vidagdhamukhamaṇḍana-yojanā (B, Dhammakitti Lokarājamolī.): PCS 4.99, VP 6/40.3, PCS 4.99.

Vidagdhamukhamaṇḍana-upadesa (S?, Sumaṅgalācāra or Buddhamaṅgala): PCS 4.110, VP 6/40.4.

Vidagdhamukhamaṇḍana-nissaya: PCS 4.72, VP 6/41.2.

Metrics

5.7.1 Vuttodaya (-pāṭha) (C, Saṅgharakkhita, 12–13th c. Beg. *Namatthu janasantāna*...): PL 168, HP 181f, CB 77f, PLC 198f, N 6610(7), PSC 123, PCS 4.115, LCM 2171, BnF 514.1, 707, IO, CS, Ps.

5.7.1,1 Vutt-pṭ Vuttodaya-(porāṇa)-ṭīkā (Pagan or Panyā, B, [Nava-/Culla-] Vimalabuddhi, 13th c.): PLB 27f, (108), PSC 123, BnF 514.2, 698, Ps.

Vuttodaya-ṭīkā (Saṅgharakkhita, 12–13th c.): HP 203,? PCS 4.51,? IO 514.2, L.

Vuttodaya-aṭṭhakathā: PCS 4.4.

Vuttodaya-yojanā: PCS 4.100.

Vuttodaya-mālinī (-pāḷi): PCS 4.116.

Kavikaṇṭhābharaṇa (= Vuttodaya-ṭīkā): PCS 4.22, RLL 63.

Vuttodaya-vyākhyāva (C, Labugama Laṅkānanda, 1936.): CB 77, PSC 123.

5.7.1,2 Chandosārattha-vikāsinī, Chandosārattha-dīpanī (BnF colophon), Vuttodaya-pañcikā (B, Saddhammañāṇa, 14th c.): PLB 26, PLC 199, PSC 123, BnF 699, L, Ps.

5.7.1,21 Chandosāratthavikāsinī-ṭīkā (B, Saddhammañāṇa, 14th c.): IO 510.4, CPD.

5.7.1.3 Vutt-nṭ Vacanatthajotikā, Vacanatthajoti, Vuttodaya-(nava)-ṭīkā, Chandasī-ṭīkā (B, Vepulla/Vepullabuddhi, 14th c. Beg. *Ñatvā buddhādiccaṃ*...): PL 168, PLB 28, PLC 199, PCS 4.107, PSC 123, CB 77, BnF 514, IO 510, L, Ps.

5.7.1.31 Vācanatthajotikā-ṭīkā, Chappaccayavaṇṇanā (B, Vepulla?) (Colophon in BnF 699.2: *Vācanattha-jotikāya nāma*

Vuttodayaṭīkāya Chappaccayavaṇṇanā. No author mentioned): BnF 699.2, CPD.

5.7.1,4 Kavisāra-pakaraṇa, Kavisāra-ṭīkā, Kavisāra-porāṇaṭīkā (Dhammananda at Haṃsāvatī): BnF 514, 708, IO 510.5, PSC 123, L, Ps.

Kavisāra-ṭīkā-nissaya (B): BnF 709

5.7.1,41 Kavisāra-ṭīkā (Buddhadhāta): PSC 123.

5.7.1,5 Sududdasa-vikāsinī (Paṭhama-Chit-phrū): IO 510.6, Ps, L.

5.7.1,6 Chappaccaya-dīpakā (-ṭīkā), Chappaccaya-dīpanī, Vuttodaya-paṇṇarasā-ṭīkā (B, K: Paññāsīha Mahāsaddhammasāmi, PLB: Saddhammañāṇa, 14th c.): PLB 26, CB 77, PSC 123, IO 510.7, L, Ps.

Chappaccaya-sīka (B?): BnF 698.

Paccayarāsī kyaṃ (B?): CW Burm 80.

5.7.1,7 Vuttodaya-vivaraṇa (-ṭīkā) (C, Vācissara, 12–13th c.): N 6610(10)vi, PLC 204, PSC 123, Gv, L.

5.7.1,(8) Vuttodaya-sannaya, ~sannē (Saṅgharakkhita?): PC 199, N 6610(7), LCM 2171, PSC 123.

5.7.1,(9) Vuttodaya-nissaya, Chanda-nissaya, Chando-nissaya (B, Cakkindābhisiri Vimalabuddhi): PCS 4.73, CB 77, IO 508.2, BnF 697, 707.2.

Vuttodaya-pada-gatārtha-sannaya: PSC 123.

Vṛttaratnākara (Skt source of Vuttodaya.) (I, Kedāra Bhaṭṭa): N 6610(10)iv-v, LCM 1620.

Vṛttaratnākara-pañcikā (C, Rāmacandra Kavibhārati, 15th c.): CC xxxiii.

Vṛttaratnākara-sannaya: N 6610(10)v.

Vṛuta-chandasa: LCM 1618.

Unclassified Metrics

Anuvutti–vyākhyāna: PCS 4.8.

Kāvyagantha, Kābyagantha: PCS 4.23.

Kāvyagantha -ṭīkā: PCS 4.40.

Kāvyasāra-vilāsinī: PCS 4.24, RLL 63.

Kāvyasāraviḷāsinī-aṭṭhakathā (Sārabuddhima thera): PCS 4.2.

Kāvyasāratthasaṅgaha (B, Cakkindā-bhisiri/Chakkinābhisiri, 1872): PLB 95

Chandanidāna: PCS 4.35, VH 255.13.

Chandomañjari (B, Visuddhācāra, late 19th c.): PLB 97.

Chandavutti-padīpa (Ñānamaṅgala thera): PCS 4.36.

Chandavutti–vilāsinī: RLL 63.

Paribhāsajjhāsaya: PCS 4.85.

Vutti–vyākhyāna: PCS 4.114.

Vṛttāvatāra (Skt?) (C, A. Bandāra, 18th c.): CC xxxix.

Rhetoric

5.8.1 Subodh Subodhālaṅkāra (C, Saṅgharakkhita Mahāsāmi, 12–13th c.): PL 167f, HP 149f, PCS 4.130, CB 76, PLC 199, PSC 124, LCM 2158, PLB 107, BnF 701, IO, CS, Ps.

5.8.1,1 Subodh-pṭ Subodhālaṅkāra-(purānā)-ṭīkā (C, Vācissara Mahāsāmi, 12–13 c.): PL 168, PLC 204, EP 68, PCS 4.58, HP 150 & 200, PLB 107, CB 76, PSC 124, RB, CS, Ps.

5.8.1,2 Subodh-nṭ Subodhālaṅkāra-navaṭīkā & Subodhālaṅkāra-nissaya/Alaṅkara-nissaya (B, Yaw-mya-sā Atwin-wun, 1880): PLB 95, CB 76, PSC 124, PLC 199f, Ps.

Subodhālaṅkāra-abhinavaṭīkā (B, Dhammakitti Ratanapajota): RB.

5.8.1,3 Subodh-sn Subodhālaṅkāra-(*purāṇa*)-*sannaya*: HP 150, SL 330, N 6610(19), LCM 2159, CB 76, PSC 124.

Subodhālaṅkāra-vyākhyāva: PSC 124.

Lokopakāra (C, S. Dhammānanda, 1893): PC 311.

Sandesa: Messages & Letters

4.2.5 Sand-k Sandesa-kathā, Saṅgharāja-sandesa-kathā (B, letter/historical text by Ñāṇābhivaṃsa to C, 1801.): PL 144, HP 442, PSC 129, 131.

4.2.6 Mānāv-s Mahānāgakula-sandesa, Mānāvulu-sandesa, Rāmañña-sandesa (C, Nāgasena to Kassapa, 12th c.): H 441, LCM 1124, HP 88f, PSC 126.

4.5.12 Rāma-sandesa, Garuḷa-sandesa (C, K. Sumaṅgala, 18–19th c.): PC 288f, PSC 128.

Mahā-nāga-kula-sandesa-sannaya: PSC 126.

Jina-danta-dhātu-sandesaya (C, Kirti Sri Rāja Sinha to King of Siam, 1746.): LCM 1864, PSC 131.

Siyam-(rāja)-sandesaya I (C, letter to King of Siam, 1756.): LCM 2000, PSC 131, EP 144, (? CPD 4.2.5.).

Siyam-sandesaya I (S, letter from Siamese army-commander to his Sinhalese counterpart, 1756 or 57.): N 6605(9).

Laṅkāsāsana-suddhi-kathā (B, Sirisaddhammavaṃsapāḷajāgara, 1880): PCS 2.185, PSC 12, (cf. BMD p. 175).

Upasampadā-dīpanī (B, Rājaguru Medhānanda to K. Guṇaratana, 1809.): PSC 130.

Pāḷi Sandesa (S to C, Pavaranivesa-vihāra-Sirisumana to L. Dhīrānanda, 1816): N 6605(10)

Pāḷi Sandesa (C to S, Paramānanda-vihāra-Sirisumanatissa to Ñeyyadhamma Saṅgharāja in Siam.): N 6605(10)

Pāḷi-sandesāvalī (C, P. Buddhadatta, 1962) (Collection of *sandesa* including the following five:): PSC 131.

Vanaratana-sandesa (C, B. Atthadassī to Vanaratana Saṅgharāja, 1844.): PSC 131.

Vajirañāṇa-saṅgharāja-sandesa (C, Vajirañāṇa Saṅgharāja?, 1846.): PSC 131.

Kesarathera-sandesa (C, P. Paññānanda): PSC 131.

Ñeyyadhamma-saṅgharāja-sandesa (C, L. Dhīrānanda to Ñeyyadhamma- saṅgharāja, 1861.): N 6605(5), PSC 131 (cf. BMD p. 175.)

Pāḷi Sandesa (Thailand to Sri Lanka, Paramanivesārāma monks at Bangkok, 1842): N 6605(8).

Pāḷi-gāthā-sandesa (Sri Lanka to Thailand by the 5 Paramanivesārāma monks who visited C, 1842. Not in Pāḷisandesāvālī.): N 6605(13).

(Pāḷi-sandesāvalī) Correspondence with the Sinhalese Saṅgha (Published in 1925. Pāḷi title not given in SA) (S, Rāma IV/ Mongkut, mid 19th c.): PSA 28.

Bible Translations

Mativu-maṅgala-vuttanta [C & B, (partial) translations of the Gospel according to Matthew, 19th c.]: ED 110, BnF 613.

Extinct Commentaries, the Sīhalaṭṭhakathā, Porāṇaṭṭhakathā

All data from BCL p. 15 ff, PLC 91f, 133f, and US.

Mahā-aṭṭhakathā, Mūla-aṭṭhakathā, Aṭṭhakathā. Probably identical with: Porāṇaṭṭhakathā, Pubbopadesaṭṭhakathā, Pubbaṭṭhakathā (Originally Indian sources, but translated into Sinhala and used by the Mahāvihāra. Commenting on Tipiṭaka.)

Uttaravihāra-aṭṭhakathā (Ditto, but used by Uttaravihāra/ Abhayagiri.): US

Vinayaṭṭhakathā, Suttantaṭṭhakathā, Abhidhammaṭṭhakathā, Sīhalamātika-ṭṭhakathā, Dīghaṭṭhakathā, Majjhimaṭṭhakathā,

Saṃyuttaṭṭhakathā, Aṅguttaraṭṭhakathā, Jātakaṭṭhakathā, Vibhaṅgappakaraṇassa Sīhalaṭṭha-kathā (Prob. part of Mahā-aṭṭhakathā.)

Vinayaṭṭhakathā (In Vism. Prob. abbreviation for various Vinaya com-mentaries such as Mahāpaccāri, etc.)

Mahā-paccariya-aṭṭhakathā, Mahāpaccarī (C. On Vinaya.)

Cullapaccarī (Mentioned in Vjb. Prob. abridgement of Mahāpaccarī.)

Kurundī-aṭṭhakathā, Kurundī (C. On Vinaya. On Vinaya.)

Andhakaṭṭhakathā (Andhra Pradesh, SI. On Vinaya.)

Saṅkhepaṭṭhakathā (SI. On Vinaya)

Āgamaṭṭhakathā (Only mentioned in Atthasālinī and Puggalapaññatti-aṭṭhakathā)

Sīhala-aṭṭhakathā-mahāvaṃsa (C)

Uttaravihāra-mahāvaṃsa

Dīpavaṃsaṭṭhakathā

Mahā-cetiya-vaṃsa-aṭṭhakathā, Cetiya-vaṃsa-aṭṭhakathā

Mahābodhivaṃsakathā

Mahāgaṇṭhi, Majjhimagaṇṭhi, Culla-gaṇṭhi (C) (Extinct Sinhala gätapadas.): PLC 189f, Vs 73f, SL 19.

Sīmā-kathā

Sahassavatthu-aṭṭhakathā

Ñāṇodaya, Ñāṇodaya-gantha (I, Buddhaghosa. Mentioned in Mv and Vism.): Cf. PLC 81ff.

Parittaṭṭhakathā (I, Buddhaghosa. Mentioned in Mv and Vism.)

Sārasamāsa (Commentary on the Nikāyas by the Dakkhiṇāgirivihāra): US

THE BUDDHIST PUBLICATION SOCIETY

The BPS is an approved charity dedicated to making known the Teaching of the Buddha, which has a vital message for all people.

Founded in 1958, the BPS has published a wide variety of books and booklets covering a great range of topics. Its publications include accurate annotated translations of the Buddha's discourses, standard reference works, as well as original contemporary expositions of Buddhist thought and practice. These works present Buddhism as it truly is—a dynamic force which has influenced receptive minds for the past 2500 years and is still as relevant today as it was when it first arose.

You can support the BPS by becoming a member. All members receive the biannual membership book and are entitled to discounts on BPS books.

For more information about the BPS and our publications, please visit our website, or write an e-mail, or a letter to the:

Administrative Secretary
Buddhist Publication Society
P.O. Box 61
54 Sangharaja Mawatha
Kandy • Sri Lanka

E-mail: bps@bps.lk
web site: http://www.bps.lk
Tel: 0094 81 223 7283 • Fax: 0094 81 222 3679